# Vonnegut and Hemingway

# Vonnegut and Hemingway

## Writers at War

*Lawrence R. Broer*

The University of South Carolina Press

© 2011 University of South Carolina

Published by the University of South Carolina Press
Columbia, South Carolina 29208

www.sc.edu/uscpress

Manufactured in the United States of America

20  19  18  17  16  15  14  13  12  11
10  9  8  7  6  5  4  3  2  1

*Library of Congress Cataloging-in-Publication Data*
Broer, Lawrence R.
  Vonnegut and Hemingway : writers at war / Lawrence R. Broer.
     p. cm.
  Includes bibliographical references and index.
  ISBN 978-1-61117-035-1 (cloth : alk. paper)
  1. Vonnegut, Kurt—Criticism and interpretation. 2. Hemingway,
Ernest, 1899–1961—Criticism and interpretation. 3. War and
literature—United States—History—20th century. 4. American
fiction—20th century—History and criticism. I. Title.
  PS3572.O5Z555 2011
  813'.54—dc22

                                         2011012508


Portions of Lawrence R. Broer, "Duty Dance with Death: *A Farewell
to Arms* and *Slaughterhouse-Five*," in *New Critical Essays on Kurt Vonnegut*, edited by David Simmons, 2009, Palgrave Macmillan, are
reproduced with permission of Palgrave Macmillan.

This book was printed on Glatfelter Natures, a recycled paper with
30 percent postconsumer waste content.

In Memory of Verlinda and Wallace Wolfrum

# Contents

# Acknowledgments

I am foremost thankful for the encouragement and editorial assistance of Jerome Klinkowitz, Linda Wagner-Martin, and Christian Moraru, who read *Vonnegut and Hemingway* in manuscript. I am grateful as well to those scholars whose work informs this study: Frank McConnell, Carl Eby, Ann Putnam, Susan Beegel, Linda Miller, Mark Spilka, Michael Reynolds, Debra Moddelmog, Gail Sinclair, Loree Rackstraw, Kathryn Hume, James Meredith, Marc Baldwin, Kathleen K. Robinson, and J'aimé Sanders. I wish also to thank my research assistants, Scott Neumeister and Gloria Holland, as well as the many students whose enthusiasm for Hemingway and Vonnegut and thoughtful insights proved invaluable. I would especially like to thank Kevin Boon, whose book *At Milennium's End* was a major stimulus for *Vonnegut and Hemingway: Writers at War.* My thanks go to David Simmons for allowing me to reprint parts of my essay from *New Critical Essays on Kurt Vonnegut.* I am especially grateful for research grants from the John F. Kennedy Library Foundation and the Office of Research and Scholarship at the University of South Florida and specifically for the kindness of Sandra Justice, Denise Burgan, and Susan Wrynn. Special thanks go to Lee Davidson and Karen Rood for their editorial acumen and careful preparation of this manuscript, and finally love and thanks to Beatrice Froute de Domec and my new friends Tom and Pam Purol, whose steady encouragement and support I could not have done without.

# Introduction

## Vonnegut's Secret Sharer

■

The world breaks everyone and afterward many are
stronger at the broken places.
                    Ernest Hemingway, *A Farewell to Arms*

We are healthy only in so far as our ideas are humane.
                    Kurt Vonnegut, *Bluebeard*

When Kurt Vonnegut described "the soul's condition in a man at war" as hideously deformed,[1] he indicated the plight of his and Ernest Hemingway's protagonists alike. The horrors of war and the idiocies of battle permeate the works of both writers. However, while Frank McConnell accurately views Vonnegut as the most recognizably Hemingwayesque of the new generation of writers to emerge after World War II,[2] my subtitle, *Writers at War*, refers also to Kurt Vonnegut's near-unceasing hostility toward Hemingway, his tormenting alter ego and his career-long nemesis. As this book explores each writer's embattled psyche, my subtitle assumes a third meaning as well: that of writers at war with themselves in the ceaseless combat of anima and animus for control of the writer's creative imagination. When I first wrote of Vonnegut's antagonisms toward Hemingway in an article titled "Vonnegut's Goodbye: Kurt Senior, Hemingway, and Kilgore Trout,"[3] I said that it would take a book to explain properly why the writer whose life and work so strikingly resembles Hemingway's should speak so disdainfully of Hemingway's humanity. This is that book.

Hemingway was as important and certainly as unsettling a force in Vonnegut's fiction as Dresden, or as the science fiction writer Kilgore Trout, or as the gun-loving nut of a father, who in *Timequake* is described as looking like Trout himself. Certainly Vonnegut recognized Hemingway as an artist of the highest order, a "first-rate musician,"[4] and a superb craftsman with an "admirable soul" the size of Kilimanjaro.[5] In *Fates Worse than Death* he praised Hemingway's "brushwork,"

1

his simple language, and his power of omission and repetition, and he applauded Hemingway's "much deserved Nobel Prize."[6] Yet here as elsewhere—in *Happy Birthday, Wanda June; Palm Sunday; Deadeye Dick; Bluebeard;* and *Timequake*—it was to separate himself from Hemingway, to damn not praise, that Vonnegut usually spoke of his fellow artist-warrior. While admiring Hemingway's best stories, Vonnegut scorned the Hemingway mystique, his idealization of valor and physical prowess. If Hemingway's soul was large, it is also in Vonnegut's critique a soul corrupted by a primitive delight in the killing of animals and so-called arts of war. It is probably with Hemingway in mind that Vonnegut quipped in *Timequake*, "I can't stand primitive people. They're so stupid."[7]

In *Timequake* (1997)—but especially in his prolonged treatment of Hemingway in *Happy Birthday, Wanda June* (1970) and *Fates Worse than Death* (1991)— Vonnegut decried Hemingway's passion for blood sports, so alien to Vonnegut's own conservationist sympathies. Viewing the shooting of big animals for pleasure as inhumane and outdated, Vonnegut asked us to imagine nowadays boasting of killing three lions and reporting delight at the prospect of killing a fourth one. As to the glamour of big-game hunting, Vonnegut explained that "it is predicted that the last East African elephant will die of starvation or be killed for its ivory in about eight years."[8] Vonnegut also looked askance at what he called "the greatest reward" for a character in a Hemingway story, the "celebration of male bonding," the feeling one man has for another in the neighborhood of danger.[9] Vonnegut wrote to me: "In a nutshell: The anthropologist Margaret Meade was asked when men were happiest, most satisfied with their lives, and she said it was when they were on a war or hunting party, leaving the women and children behind. It was that sort of happiness Hemingway not only wrote about but managed to experience almost incessantly."[10] Vonnegut contrarily shared the view of a female friend who found it ridiculous that men had to get outdoors and drink and kill before they could express something as simple and natural as love.[11]

In *Happy Birthday, Wanda June*, which Vonnegut described as "a simpleminded play about men who enjoy killing and those who don't," he delivered his most impassioned assault on what he called "the part of Hemingway which I detest—the slayer of nearly extinct animals which meant him no harm."[12] The bully ghost of Hemingway permeates the character of Harold Ryan from first to last—from such surface resemblances as their favorite pastime of twitting weaklings, their sexual attitudes about male and female roles, and their open joking about death to more revealing spiritual parallels in their attitudes toward death and killing and toward a defiant, chin-protruding brand of heroism. Like Vonnegut's Harold Ryan, Hemingway held honor, pride, and the demonstration of worth through physical strength as ultimate priorities and killing as noble behavior. Harold Ryan boasts that, as a professional soldier, he has killed perhaps two hundred men and thousands of animals as well.[13] He relishes matador-like displays of manhood—choices between fighting and fleeing—and as a soldier in the Abraham Lincoln Brigade during the Spanish civil war, glories in his nickname: "La Picadura—the sting."

Though the critique in *Happy Birthday, Wanda June* is directed at Hemingway's work as a whole, Vonnegut might well have had in mind Philip Rawlings, the protagonist of Hemingway's play *The Fifth Column*, as a likely candidate for what Norbert Woodly, the Vonnegut persona in *Happy Birthday, Wanda June*, derides as Harold Ryan's macho posturing, "heroic balderdash." Both Ryan and Rawlings represent that "unwelcome image of himself" that Vonnegut attributed to Hemingway late in life, "a Shakespearean buffoon of hyperventilating manliness." Vonnegut wrote after Hemingway's death, "I would in fact make such a man, modeled as much after Odysseus as 'Papa,' a buffoon in my play *Happy Birthday, Wanda June*. The play is about the decline of the ancient system of patriarchy, in which women are the property of men."[14]

By contrast Norbert Woodly, whose age difference from Rawlings and Harold Ryan matches that between Vonnegut and Hemingway, ridicules Ryan as a living fossil, as obsolete as cockroaches or horseshoe crabs.[15] Finding it disgusting and frightening that a killer should still be a respected member of society, Woodly articulates Vonnegut's moral outcry from *Player Piano* to *Timequake*: "Gentleness must replace violence everywhere, or we are doomed."[16] Unlike Harold Ryan, who associates manhood with toughness and physical challenge, Woodly says he wants to cry whenever he comes into a room containing animal heads, "a monument to a man who thinks that what the world needs most is rhinoceros meat." "Any one of these poor dead animals," he tells Harold, "was a thousand times the athlete you could ever hope to be. Their magic was in their muscles—your magic is in your brains."[17] Woodly plays a violin in a doctors' quartet, was a stretcher bearer in the Korean War, does not play sports, always takes the path of least resistance, uses his brains instead of his muscles, and attempts to change people with the weapons of compassion, unselfishness, and maudlin concern.[18]

Vonnegut continued in *Timequake* to challenge what he saw as Hemingway's relatively romantic treatment of war and death, his hard-boiled pose that mixes heroism with physical valor and killing with honor. Contrasting his own Purple Heart for frostbite—this country's second lowest decoration—with Hemingway's War Cross and Silver Medal of Honor for being shot, Vonnegut accused Frederic Henry of *A Farewell to Arms* of getting Catherine Barkley pregnant to prove his manhood, declaring that the novel really proclaims Hemingway's detestation of civilian life, of marriage.[19] The tears Henry sheds are those of relief for having been saved from an unglamorous life of civilian responsibilities—getting a regular job, a house, and life insurance. Despite Hemingway's vivid depiction of the horrors of war, Vonnegut suggested that Frederic and Catherine have too many wonderful experiences, thus representing the most popular story a writer can tell about a good-looking couple having a really good time copulating outside wedlock and having to quit for one reason or another in the full blush of romantic feeling.[20]

Vonnegut portrayed his own more sardonic version of war through several stories attributed to by Kilgore Trout, a soldier-artist who shares Vonnegut and Hemingway's military background. In Trout's account of Albert Hardy, Vonnegut's World War I soldier not only has his penis shot off like Jake Barnes in *The Sun Also Rises*, but his body is atomized, and his penis, his "ding-dong," is blown into oblivion.[21] In a Trout story that appears to parody the ending of *A Farewell to Arms*, reflecting what McConnell calls the "stylized brutality" of Hemingway's depiction of war and bullfighting, the knights of the Round Table are equipped with Thompson submachine guns. Probably with Frederic Henry in mind as Lancelot and Catherine as Guinevere, Lancelot, the "purest in heart and mind," puts a slug through the Holy Grail and makes "a Swiss cheese of Queen Guinevere."[22] Vonnegut shares with Trout a real-life antiheroic tale about his friend David Craig. Craig shoots a German tank with a bazooka, but no Germans pop out of the turret; no one celebrates. As if again parodying Frederic Henry's convenient exit from humdrum domesticity, Kilgore Trout concludes that at least the tank's occupants died in glory, that David Craig's true heroism was in sparing his victims years of disappointment and tedium in civilian life.[23]

We might explain Vonnegut's satire by supposing he drew apart from Hemingway, just as Hemingway did from his mentor Sherwood Anderson, to better define his own stylistic identity. Or we might wax Freudian, citing the fact that, as McConnell explains, every artist must kill or castrate his artistic father before he can function on his own, especially the symbolic father who liked to be called "Papa."[24] Vonnegut himself suggested in *Fates Worse than Death* that differences in their respective cultures and war experiences made Hemingway his natural adversary. Explaining that they were divided by booms and busts and wars radically different in mood and purpose and technology, which separated not only himself from Hemingway but the first half from the last half of the twentieth century,[25] Vonnegut declared that, while he and Hemingway were only twenty-three years apart in age, the difference might have been a thousand years.[26] In particular Vonnegut attributed their differences in temper to the differences between World War I and World War II and between both of these wars to the war in Vietnam. The nature of true battle stories by Americans was utterly debased by World War II, he explained, "when millions of us fought overseas and came home no longer needing a Hemingway to say what war was like."[27] Vonnegut declared that, while neither he nor Hemingway ever killed anyone, he himself "almost killed his first German" when he got home and his Uncle Dan clapped him on the back and bellowed, "You're a man now."[28]

Vonnegut suggested that the nightmare of hydrogen bombs and the atrocities of the Nazi death camps necessarily created a new historicist sensibility, one that no longer believed that "death before dishonor" was a fate worse than death, since the military death of one man might easily mean the death of everything.[29] What made the Vietnam soldier particularly "spooky," Vonnegut explained, is that he never had illusions about war, never had Hemingway's need to return from war with the shocking news that war was repulsive, stupid, and dehumanizing.[30] Rather, the Vietnam veteran was the first American soldier to know from childhood that war was a meaningless butchery of ordinary people like himself and that death was plain old death, the absence of life. This sentiment is precisely what Harold Ryan's wife, Penelope, reminds Harold of in *Happy Birthday, Wanda June* when she accuses him of confusing heroism and honor with killing and death. "It is not honor to be killed," she chides, "it is still just death, the absence of life—no honor at all."[31]

Vonnegut's explanation of his differences from Hemingway—the thousand years he said divided them—is important to our exploration of variances both in style and sensibility: Hemingway as modernist and Vonnegut as postmodernist. But such disparities obscure more significant artistic affinities, which are the focus of this study. Vonnegut's summary of their common origins and experiences exposes but the tip of the iceberg: "We were both born in the Middle West, we set out to be reporters, our fathers were gun-nuts, we felt profoundly indebted to Mark Twain, and we were the children of suicides."[32] Though Vonnegut acknowledged that Hemingway was one of the best reporters of war the world has ever known but not technically a soldier,[33] their war experiences and resultant wounds—Hemingway's physical one at Fossalta, Italy, in World War I, and Vonnegut's psychological one in Dresden, Germany, in World War II—were remarkably similar. At the age of eighteen, Hemingway was literally blown up by an Austrian trench mortar while serving as a civilian ambulance driver on the Italian front. As a lowly twenty-year-old private first class, albeit an intelligence and reconnaissance scout, Vonnegut first was captured "intact" during the Battle of the Bulge while looking for enemies and then witnessed the hideous firebombing of Dresden.

In his move east from Indianapolis to Barnstable, Massachusetts, Vonnegut was not a literal expatriate like Hemingway but was certainly a spiritual disaffiliate. Vonnegut could have been speaking for a disenchanted Hemingway when he asked in *Timequake*, "Why did so many of us bug out of a city built by our ancestors, where our family names were respected, whose streets and speech were so familiar, where there was the best and worst of Western civilization?"[34] Parallels extend even to the fact that both writers experienced serious writer's blocks that prevented them from completing works in progress. Vonnegut explained that it was only after a ten-year silence that Hemingway produced *Across the River and into the Trees* (1950) and *The Old Man and the Sea* (1952), the first of which was widely panned and the second of which Vonnegut debunked in *Timequake*. When Vonnegut asked a commercial fisherman what he thought of *The Old Man and the Sea*, the fisherman called Santiago "an idiot," insisting that Santiago should have "hacked off the best chunks of meat and put them in the bottom of the boat, leaving the carcass for the sharks."[35]

In the winter of 1996 Vonnegut—just as Hemingway failed to complete his famous "Land, Sea, and Air" novel—found himself the creator of a novel that refused to be written.[36] But, as if to undercut the heroism of Santiago's adventure at sea, Vonnegut set about to filet, "improvise, and reinvent[37] his own unwieldy fish, producing "Timequake II," a "stew" made from the best parts of "Timequake I." Perhaps it was this capacity for reinvention that Vonnegut had in mind when he said that "the suicide Ernest Hemingway"[38] almost made it to sixty-two, while he himself had lasted to the age of seventy-three.[39] Hemingway was not an old man when he wrote *The Old Man and the Sea*, but "he obviously felt like one,"[40] felt that his work—and thus his life—was done.[41] Wondering what he would have missed if his own thoughts of suicide had been as successful as Hemingway's, Vonnegut rejoiced not only in the writing of at least four more books and some "swell" essays,[42] but in the accomplishments of his children and in the births of three more grandchildren.[43] However strong his gloom, however much he was disappointed in the economic and physical violence of his society, Vonnegut was not about to give up life for death, to stop trying to protect nature, or to end his attempts to slow down, at least a little bit, crimes against "those Jesus Christ said should inherit the Earth someday."[44]

Hemingway wrote in *A Farewell to Arms* that people who survive terrible wounds are sometimes stronger in the broken places. In view of Vonnegut's portrait of himself and Hemingway at the ends of their respective careers—Vonnegut's evolution to his salubrious role as "canary bird"[45] and years of renewed creativity versus Hemingway's devolution to the blocked and despairing consciousness of the years following his Nobel Prize, which culminated in his self-inflicted death at age sixty-one—Hemingway's remark seems to describe Vonnegut better than Hemingway. Some years ago I sent Vonnegut Ray Bradbury's story about Hemingway's death, "The Kilimanjaro Device," which Vonnegut subsequently discussed in *Fates Worse than Death*. It was a "made up" story, Vonnegut explained, about a person with a "magic" jeep who encounters a grizzled, terminally depressed Ernest Hemingway along a "wilderness" road near Ketchum, Idaho, and who offers Hemingway a lift to a better death than the one he was headed for.[46] Afterward Vonnegut wrote to me: "The Bradbury story brought a lump to my throat—I realize now that I see Hemingway as a good man who blundered into a forest, and never got out again."[47] In Vonnegut's view the jeep might represent the liberating force of imagination and—as I argue in *Sanity*

*Plea: Schizophrenia in the Novels of Kurt Vonnegut* (1989)—an acceptance of the feminine creative principle within himself by which he saved himself from depression to create a new, more humane, and artistically vital career. Conversely the "forest" is Hemingway's self-created machismo, the rigid and aggressively male persona represented by Harold Ryan in *Happy Birthday, Wanda June*, whose militant code of ethics Vonnegut saw as undermining Hemingway's personal and artistic growth and contributing to his tragic death.[48] "We all see our lives as stories," Vonnegut wrote in *Deadeye Dick*, "and the ends of those lives as epilogue." Hemingway, Vonnegut concluded, found his epilogue so uncongenial that he committed suicide,[49] a form of "typography, a period," the only consistent conclusion to the "story" he carried in his head.[50] "I place as much value on a period," Vonnegut wrote, "as on the painting careers of my father or my sister."[51]

While these surface comparisons do as much to dispute as to support McConnell's view of Vonnegut as the most "Hemingwayesque" of post–World War II writers, in fact Vonnegut's life and work exist as a veritable palimpsest of Hemingway's. The two intersect and illuminate one another in myriad surprising ways. Vonnegut might have described his critical reinscription of Hemingway as a "timequake," a freak of nature that compels people to repeat earlier phases of their lives. In this case Vonnegut recrafted Hemingway's own tale of trauma and despair but challenged the artistic integrity of Hemingway's original story. Yet, to understand Vonnegut's unabating hostility fully, one must examine Hemingway as the "secret sharer"[52] of Vonnegut's literary imagination, a relationship more intimate and ominous than Vonnegut's simple account explains. Rather than Hemingway's adversary, the author who ironically reflects Vonnegut's own rent soul bears the same deterministic wounds, a legacy of childhood trauma, family insanity, deforming war experience, and depression, which nearly drove Vonnegut to suicide.

In their respective psychodramas, Hemingway and Vonnegut each invites us to follow the mythic journey of essentially one individual, the same person under different names, whose wounds, sins, and hopes for redemption carry over from one protagonist to the next and are nearly always those of their creator.[53] The experiences that shape the young manhood of Nick Adams shape as well the character of Frederic Henry and Jake Barnes. The childhood traumas that plague Rudy Waltz haunt as well his adult incarnations as Billy Pilgrim or Howard Campbell. And nearly always these fictional self-creations have their author's history behind them—the wound, the psychic fragmentation, and the quest of the wounded soldier for positive values and for ways of ordering his life in a hostile, naturalistic world.

Nothing better explains the authors' common story of psychic pain and the therapeutic manner of its telling than Earl Rovit's observation that Hemingway was addicted to scraping at apparently unhealed wounds.[54] When Vonnegut wrote in *Timequake* of Kilgore Trout's "ghostly childhood" and of nightmarish episodes of war and carnage, he evoked the central crisis of every Vonnegut and Hemingway protagonist, the literary purging of which McConnell says allowed both writers to come to terms with their experience of "apocalypse."[55] "These were memories," Kilgore Trout says, "he could only exorcise by telling what they were."[56] Trout's remark has major interpretive implications for the psychoanalytic direction of this study. For a long while what is not told, what the Hemingway/Vonnegut hero cannot bear to tell is what the story is mainly about, a story the author-protagonist must hide because it is too dangerous, forbidden, and fraught with sorrow.[57]

One thinks of Michael Reynolds's observation that there were things the young Hemingway did not know and did not want to know[58] and of Vonnegut's remark to me that the collective weight of traumatic family history in his novels was so personal that for a long time it made him "thick of speech."[59] Yet descending into the shadowy world of the unconscious to expose and exorcise unspoken terrors and bringing the untold story out of the tangled dark and into the light is precisely the challenge of the Vonnegut/Hemingway hero, the prelude to psychic healing and wholeness. How each author-hero manages these secret depths has much to do with the relative success each makes in healing his respective wounds.

Ann Putnam has explained that Hemingway's psychically maimed hero is like Lot's wife, the one who must turn back to see what must not be seen, "remembering what ought to be forgotten, hearing what ought not to be heard, seeing what ought not to be seen."[60] Vonnegut described the therapeutic value of his return to Dresden in precisely these terms. The humanity of Lot's wife, he said, was in her willingness to look back where all those people and homes had been. Like the author of *Slaughterhouse-Five*, "she was turned to a pillar of salt." But he loved her for that, "because it was so human."[61] Simultaneously understanding and interpreting the buried portion of the writer-hero's story—his resistance to the story's mysterious silences and its guarded memories—is the task of the discerning reader. As that hopefully more willing and attuned reader, I borrow a page from Vonnegut's description of himself in *Palm Sunday* (1981) as a worker in the field of mental health, an "eclectic" psychoanalyst probing his own subconscious, "a little Jungian, a bit Freudian, a little Rankian."[62]

To comprehend the hero's most personal and potentially disabling psychological wounds, including the mystery of Hemingway as Vonnegut's bête noire, we must accompany the hero on his descent into the murky depths of Hemingway's "iceberg," the immersed part of the story where its secret, most complex meanings reside. As Hemingway explains in *Death in the Afternoon*, "If a writer of prose knows enough about what he is writing about he may omit things that he knows and the reader, if the writer is writing truly enough, will have a feeling of those things as strongly as though the writer had stated them. The dignity of movement of an iceberg is due to only one-eighth of it being above water."[63] Hemingway does not say the writer must know "everything" about the underwater portion of the iceberg, just "enough." In this study we will investigate the iceberg's intriguing problematic—that is, when and where the author and/or his hero's underwater knowledge of self are conscious, unconscious, or incompletely understood.[64] I suggest that how we view both writers' management of these secret depths over the course of their careers has major consequences both morally and aesthetically, that only by understanding why meanings omitted early on become increasingly conscious and overt over time can we appreciate the nature of the spiritual quest and its progression at the heart of their work, a struggle for healing and psychic balance I call "creative advance."[65]

The irony of Vonnegut's critique is that his protagonist's quest for understanding and wholeness—for psychic balance—is exactly the same as that of his supposed adversary. In this study we first come to understand the similar wounds suffered by Vonnegut and Hemingway's maimed protagonist—feelings of vulnerability, impotence, and what Jung called a "mechanism of deprecation and denial,"[66] the flight from women and the female within, Jung's "anima," which the hero equates with a fear of loss and death. To deflect pain and suffering, the protagonist splits himself into separate warring beings, the masculine-feminine division of soul Jung called "anima" and "animus." The subject represses or submerges a caring, core self, while presenting what Jung called a false, desensitized self to the world, a tragically mistaken strategy of evasion that conceals the individual's true nature not only from others, but from oneself.[67] The outer "mask"—passive in Vonnegut's case—is no more a successful response to the hero's sexual wound than the aggression of the Hemingway persona Vonnegut so detests and scorns in the character of Harold Ryan.

In *The Anxiety of Influence: A Theory of Poetry*, Harold Bloom offers a useful frame of reference for understanding the critical moment in Hemingway and Vonnegut's spiritual evolution when they appear to have gone in diametrically different directions, transformations that return us to Vonnegut's caustic portrait of Hemingway in *Happy Birthday, Wanda June*. Bloom argues that to avoid repeating the work of their predecessors—appearing as an "echo" to "someone else's music"—strong writers parody or deliberately misread their literary progenitors. The younger writer fulfills himself by creatively "completing" his precursor, retaining his terms but "meaning" them in another sense, as though the precursor had failed to go far enough.[68] Thus Hemingway and Vonnegut created a hero who feels he has learned the correct way to live in Hemingway's "nada" and Vonnegut's "chaos," what Brett Ashley in *The Sun Also Rises* (1926) says she and Jake Barnes have instead of God, but Hemingway appears to have advocated power and aggression as a right way to live in the world while Vonnegut adopted kindness and restraint as moral imperatives. Hemingway mapped out the spiritual terrain of his new, more virile and stoical hero in terms of the circumscribed world of the bullfight in *Death in the Afternoon* (1932) and the primitive environs of Africa in *Green Hills of Africa* (1935) while Vonnegut defined what he called the "new me," a more optimistic, feminized self in *Breakfast of Champions* (1973), in relation to the imaginative openness of the Museum of Modern Art. It is here that we understand more fully the mystery of Hemingway as Vonnegut's "secret sharer," what Bloom designates an act of "self-purgation." Hemingway is the Jungian "shadow" Vonnegut must not become, symbolic of unconscious aggression and cruelty that Vonnegut believed would eventually destroy the world. As Vonnegut's letters to me confirm, rather than Hemingway reinventing himself in the manner of Harold Ryan in the surprising climax to *Happy Birthday, Wanda June*, Vonnegut saw the real-life Hemingway remaining death bound and fatalistic, trapped in a "forest" of machismo from which he never escaped. With the specter of Hemingway's suicide never far from mind, Vonnegut believed that resisting the pull of his defeatist self was necessary not only to fulfilling his role as canary bird in the coal mine but to life itself.

Vonnegut's fiction from *Breakfast of Champions* to *Timequake* is not only a critical response to a world of violence and death but a rebuttal of Hemingway's response—the Hemingway who equated manhood with heroic comportment and who associated emotional and artistic integrity with the killing of animals. Yet, in dramatic opposition to Vonnegut's view of Hemingway as a brutalized and artistically diminished writer, the quest of the Hemingway hero for healing and redemption is exactly analogous to that of Vonnegut's reformed protagonist, a hero who contradicts the machismo hero of myth from Nick Adams to Santiago. This quest becomes the dominant force in Thomas Hudson, David Bourne, and the narrating Hemingway of *Under Kilimanjaro*.

We shall examine the increasingly open and honest conversation with the suppressed "other" of author and protagonist. If the writers' early works are about flight from the feminine, sins upon women, and the female within, Hemingway's work from *For Whom the Bell Tolls* to *Under Kilimanjaro* and Vonnegut's from *Slapstick* to *Hocus Pocus* are about confession, redemption, and rebirth distinguished by their heroes' willingness to access what Jung called "dangerous knowledge" about himself, knowing "what I myself desire."[69] Jung explained that recognizing and accepting the feminine aspects of the split persona requires a moral effort beyond the ordinary, painstaking, psychotherapeutic work extending over a long period.[70] It requires the courage of the tragic hero, in this case the willingness to acknowledge not only the destructive consequences of the masked anima, but to recognize that the tragedy originates in himself, that he himself has "kept the illusory projection going."[71] Such self-understanding may have come to Hemingway at a slower, more gradual rate, but raising the Jungian "shadow" of self-doubt and feminine denial to consciousness is exactly the achievement of

Kurt Vonnegut and his secret sharer, Ernest Hemingway, a process by which the authors became ever more aware definers of the tragic counterplay between the inside and outside, real and artificial, conscious and unconscious. (Only through psychotherapy with Jung in Paris, Samuel Beckett observed, did he achieve self-understanding of his scurrilous portraits of women in his fiction—a product of unconscious hatred of his mother—and become able to come to full strength as an artist.[72]) Using writing as therapy, Hemingway and Vonnegut each made what Vonnegut calls in *Slaughterhouse-Five* his "duty dance with death," an act of literary exorcism whose threads of suffering and flight and discovery and healing touch on each other at every stitch of the writer's loom.

We could not design a more dramatic climax to this amazing spiritual drama than that which Kurt Vonnegut and Ernest Hemingway chose for themselves in their respective literary farewells: Vonnegut's *Timequake* (1997) and Hemingway's *Under Kilimanjaro* (2005). In a final effort to exorcise Hemingway's ghost, Vonnegut evoked the specter of Hemingway's suicide once more, positioning him intimately within his own immediate family by remarking, "I had recently turned seventy-three. My mother made it to seventy-two. Hemingway almost made it to sixty-two."[73] *Timequake* reaffirms Hemingway as Vonnegut's artistic father. Vonnegut arises from the ashes of Hemingway's deathbed in the magical city of Xanadu to complete the work he chides Hemingway for failing to do, then forecasts his own death "at the ripe old age of 84." Even more symbolically fitting, Hemingway, in his own final work, *Under Kilimanjaro*, experiences a spiritual rebirth exactly like that of Vonnegut in *Timequake*, one that, as with Vonnegut, shows him to be more integrated and at peace with himself than ever before.

# Part 1
# Broken Places

# One

# Family Secrets

## The Absent Mother and Father

■

Children begin by loving their parents; as they grow
older they judge them; sometimes they forgive them.

Oscar Wilde, *The Picture of Dorian Gray*

He who is willing to work gives birth to his own father.

Søren Kierkegaard, *Fear and Trembling*

According to their fictional accounts—what Vonnegut calls "psychological steve-
doring"[1]—Vonnegut and Hemingway's experiences with cold and insensitive
parents constitute early demoralizing wounds that never completely healed. The
childhood traumas that plague Vonnegut's most tormented childhood protagonists, Rudy Waltz in *Deadeye Dick* and Wilbur Swain in *Slapstick*, haunt as well
the young manhood of Nick Adams in such stories as "Indian Camp," "Ten Indians," and "Three Shots." Both Rudy and Nick, as Ray Vince says of Nick, are
twentieth-century Americans "born, raised, and hurt in the middle west,"[2] who
with each successive appearance become the sum of what has happened to them
before and whose wounds and hopes for recovery are nearly always those of their
creators.

I do not assume that Nick Adams and Rudy Waltz are exactly the same person
as the author as if no strategies of authorial distancing were at work to establish
the hero as an independent creation.[3] Yet Vonnegut welcomed my psychoana-
lytical speculations that he used his fiction to summon up deeply repressed childhood experiences that needed to be faced as he confronted the traumatic
experiences of war in *Slaughterhouse-Five*. "You had me dead to rights," he said.
"It seems to me," he explained, "you have solved what has long been to me a mystery: why my work is so offensive to some readers. . . . I now understand that it
is my violation of the commandment that we honor our fathers and mothers."[4]
While Hemingway felt threatened by Philip Young's suppositions that the author
had been psychologically crippled by war and the events of early childhood,

claiming that the critic was trying to put him out of business by psychoanalyzing him, Hemingway was not denying the importance of the unconscious in his work, only that Young was invading psychic territory that belonged to him. Asked if he ever had an analyst, Hemingway explained, "Sure I have. Portable Corona number three."[5] No doubt an adult Nick Adams speaks for his author in "Fathers and Sons" when—reflecting on childhood wounds Nick describes as "not good remembering" but can no longer suppress—he says, "If he wrote it he could get rid of it. He had gotten rid of many things by writing them."[6]

Vonnegut spoke for both writers when he explained in the prologue to *Slapstick* (1976) that "the museums in children's minds, I think, automatically empty themselves in times of utmost horror—to protect the children from eternal grief."[7] Yet Vonnegut created Rudy Waltz, and Hemingway created Nick Adams precisely as Mark Shechner says Joyce needed to create Stephen Dedalus—"to forge some tenable sense of himself from the brittle and painful fragments of childhood,"[8] the first phase of each author's career-long process of fictional cleansing and renewal. Just as the Nick Adams stories portray Nick's evolution from child to adolescent to soldier, veteran, writer, and parent, so *Deadeye Dick* provides the complete history of the maimed Vonnegut protagonist, someone whose most serious psychological wounds originate in childhood, but, as with Nick, require a lifetime to purge.[9]

When Vonnegut speaks in *Timequake* of Kilgore Trout's "ghostly childhood"—Vonnegut's tormented alter ego—he evokes the same adolescent nightmare of family alienation—of sadness, loneliness, and defeat—that Michael Reynolds says turned the Hemingway household into a "bloody family battleground."[10] The ghosts of immediate concern are those real-life parents Vonnegut and Hemingway associate with death and void throughout their careers. Both depressed, unfulfilled fathers died worrying about the loss of their families' modest fortunes, and as Vonnegut says about his mother, Edith, both mothers surrendered, vanished into a "spiritual void," and then "vanish[ed] altogether."[11] What Kathryn Hume says of Edith Lieber Vonnegut applies equally to Grace Hall Hemingway—that Vonnegut's mother so contaminated the author's inner picture of women that the feminine in his early works becomes "an absence . . . through which a chill wind blows."[12] Spilka describes Hemingway's wounded feelings toward his mother as beginning in "passive resentment," then hardening into permanent adolescent hatred.[13] As Trout says, these were memories "he could exorcise only by telling what they were."[14]

Nick and Rudy's common experience with unloving mothers and defeated, will-less fathers cripples their own ability to love, causing them to curse life itself. Rudy, after all, begins his life-story in *Deadeye Dick:* "Watch out for life. I have caught life. I have come down with life."[15] At first the unhappy parents appear to share equal responsibility for their son's fears and insecurities. They are parents who have given up on life as well as each other. Rudy describes his parents as the walking dead: "They were zombies. They were in bathrobes and bedroom slippers all day long—unless company was expected. They stared into the distance a lot. Sometimes they would hug each other lightly and sigh."[16] Nick's parents seem too emotionally distant for even an occasional hug—self-absorbed, spiritually myopic, and oblivious to one another's emotional needs.

Yet while the absence or coldness of both parents is obvious, Nick and Rudy differ considerably as to which parent is most to blame, variance critical to their personal evolution. Nick holds his mother primarily responsible for his family's history of grief, while the greater sins of Dr. Adams go largely unacknowledged by a son desperate for his love and approval. Rudy's attribution of guilt seems more fairly placed, though unlike Nick, he eventually indicts his father as the foremost cause of his family's suffering. In either case nonnurturing mothers and will-less misanthropic fathers so threaten their children with their own bitterness—what Paul Proteus in *Player Piano* terms "lie down and die"[17]—that Rudy emerges from adolescence with "no more feelings than a rubber ball,"[18] and even after the war, childhood nightmares so haunt an older but dazed and wary Nick Adams in "Big Two-Hearted River," that he works hard to suppress them.

No doubt the respective suicides of Nick's and Hemingway's fathers and Rudy's and Vonnegut's mothers, do much to explain why one parent is viewed more sympathetically than the other—why Rudy Waltz judges his father the guiltier parent while Nick's anger toward his mother causes him to rationalize his father's failings and defend him at his mother's expense. Whereas Vonnegut explained, "I learned a bone-deep sadness from parents in full retreat from life,"[19] Hemingway might have said, "I learned to hate them enough to kill." Vonnegut believed that his father's "emotional faithlessness" to his children might not only explain his wife's hatred for him, "as corrosive as hydrofluoric acid,"[20] but it also contributed substantially to his mother's self-inflicted death. In stark contrast Hemingway saw his mother as the main cause of the father's unhappiness, attributing his feelings of abject defeat and suicide to her "utter selfishness and hysterical emotionalism."[21]

Referring to the Hemingway hero's comprehensive wound, Linda Wagner-Martin identifies myriad kinds of loss Rudy and Nick suffer in childhood: deprivations of love, faith, country, and family; of illusions of immortality; of a sense of personal insignificance; and of control over one's fate.[22] From the moment Rudy Waltz's "peep hole" opens in 1932 to the explosion of the neutron bomb that depopulates his hometown, Rudy's world is threatened by the same grisly discoveries, insecurities, and fears that cause Nick to conclude in "My Old Man," "Seems like when they get started they don't leave a guy nothing."[23] In a world that refuses to make sense, physical and emotional breakdown are the norm, turning good people like Nick's father, Ole Anderson in "The Killers," and the former boxer in "The Battler" into passive victims of deterministic forces they feel impotent to resist. While Rudy is appalled by the death of the man in Midland City he most admires, John Fortune, who dies of double pneumonia, and by the death of Fortune's wife from cancer, Rudy is even more devastated by the murders of Gino and Mario Martino, two youthful immigrants with whom Rudy identifies. Closer to home, amphetamines cause the suicide of Celia Hoover, the girlfriend of Rudy's brother, Felix, and Rudy learns that both his paternal grandparents died of carbon monoxide poisoning. Rudy's personal nemesis, however, is Dr. Jerry Mitchell, who tortures cats and dogs while pretending to perform scientific experiments.

These psychological wounds prove as deep and pervasive as the wounds of war to come, scars they bear for life, threatening Nick and Rudy with the same fatalistic malaise that claims their fathers and consequently embitters their dispirited mothers. Yet in Hemingway's story "Indian Camp" and early in Vonnegut's *Deadeye Dick*, Nick and Rudy experience horrors so stupefying as to alienate them from parents too cold and aloof to notice their son's fears—confrontations with death and violence that epitomize yet transcend all other wounds—and create deep-seated feelings of gender disorientation with which Nick and Rudy struggle their entire lives. Mark Spilka labels this the "wound of androgyny," a fear of women associated with birth, suffering, and death and accompanied by secret feelings of vulnerability and impotence related to the father's loss of male identity.[24] Reynolds explains that all his life Hemingway had troubles with women[25] while Vonnegut reported his Aunt Irma saying, "All Vonnegut men are scared to death of women."[26]

It is easy to see that in the disastrous mothers and fathers in *Deadeye Dick* and Hemingway's "Indian Camp," "Three Shots," and "Ten Indians," Vonnegut and Hemingway have given Nick Adams and Rudy Waltz parents ominously like their own, so much so that, as Reynolds says of Nick, the experience and consciousness of the youthful protagonist becomes interchangeable with his author's. Dr. Clarence Hemingway sometimes took Ernest along when making professional visits to an Indian camp far back in the woods, and it is the story of one of these trips that shows Nick's first encounter with violence and death, henceforth associated with childbirth and female suffering. In "Indian Camp" Nick is forced to assist his physician father in a caesarean section of a local Indian woman, performing the surgery with a jackknife and without anesthetics and using nine-foot, tapered gut leaders to sew up the incision. We are told that Nick holds the basin but "is looking away so as not to see what his father was doing. . . . His curiosity had been gone for a very long time."[27] In the meantime, the woman's husband, who suffers from a gangrenous foot and who evidently can no longer bear his or his wife's pain, commits suicide in the bunk above his wife's: "His throat had been cut from ear to ear. The blood had flowed down into a pool where his body sagged the bunk. His head rested on his left arm. The open razor lay, edge up, in the blankets."[28]

Just as Nick has been traumatized by the jackknife caesarean and the husband's slashed throat, Rudy Waltz experiences a similar double horror when, at the tender age of twelve, from the cupola on top of his house, he fires an unaimed round from a rifle in his father's gun collection and accidentally kills a pregnant woman doing housework a mile away. If Rudy's murder of the expectant mother in *Deadeye Dick* is more fictive than Nick's experience with the pregnant woman in "Indian Camp," Vonnegut made clear in his autobiographical preface that the crimes Rudy commits are "payment for all [*his*] sins." "The neutered pharmacist who tells the tale," Vonnegut explains, "is *my* declining sexuality. The crime he committed in childhood is all the bad things *I* have done" (emphases added).[29] Loree Rackstraw's observation that Vonnegut's literary life and life experience are "dynamically entwined" applies equally to both writers. Just as Rudy's shooting of Mrs. Metzger takes place on Mother's Day 1944, the same day Vonnegut's mother killed herself, so the suffering of the woman in "Indian Camp" reflects Hemingway's guilt over his mother's sufferings in childbirth, as well as actual operations he saw his father perform.[30] "So this was mother's day," Rudy thinks, "but to me it was the day during which, ready or not, I have been initiated into manhood."[31] Rudy is jailed, viciously beaten by the police, bathed in ink, caged, and displayed to selected visitors, who are encouraged to punch him out, and even encouraged to kill himself by one of the police officers.[32] Later, lawsuits from the bereaved husband, Mr. Metzger, ruin the Waltz family financially, and Rudy is repeatedly reminded of the tragedy, and reinjured whenever people call him by his nickname, "Deadeye Dick."

From these nightmarish beginnings originates the deadly childhood legacy of fear, guilt, and loneliness, amounting virtually to parental abandonment not only of Nick Adams and Rudy Waltz but of every Hemingway/Vonnegut protagonist from Nick to David Bourne of *The Garden of Eden* and from Paul Proteus in Vonnegut's *Player Piano* to Eugene Debs Hartke in *Hocus Pocus*. The psychological damage to Nick and Rudy by morally obtuse and insensitive parents is particularly notable as it occurs when these archetypal innocents are at their youngest and most vulnerable, most dependent on confident adult authority for a sense of order and meaning in their world.[33] Rudy's observation that he has been "initiated into manhood" is of course tragically ironic. Rather than a classic rite of passage from innocence to maturity, building to a more heightened awareness of self and evil in the world, neither set of parents is morally or emotionally equipped to serve as healthy guides in their child's movement from adolescence to manhood.

At least for the immediate future, neither Nick nor Rudy grows from their terrifying ordeal. Nick learns only that people die, that some kill themselves when they can no longer "stand it," a lesson all the more tragic in light of all the

Hemingway family suicides—his father's in 1928, Ernest's own in 1961, his sister Ursula's in 1966, his brother Leicester's in 1982, and even his granddaughter Margaux's in 1996.[34] Rudy's family members also suffer from mental illness, with which Vonnegut and other family members battled. Vonnegut, whose son Mark suffered from acute schizophrenia, was himself briefly hospitalized for suicidal tendencies. He explained that he came from a family of depressives though he almost always managed to keep working.[35] He said his mother-in-law was also periodically insane. Everyone in Rudy's family is certified to be crazy at some point in the story. Well before his death, Rudy's father loses all touch with reality, and Mrs. Waltz becomes a cynical, hick-town Voltaire near the end of her life. Rudy's parents eventually die of double pneumonia during Midland City's terrible winter blizzard, symbolic of the living death of coldness that claimed his parents long before. Just as Nick hides from pain in various ways, withdrawing into himself for company, Rudy becomes consumed with guilt and concludes that the best thing he can do for himself and others is to want nothing, to be as unenthusiastic and unmotivated as possible so that he will never again hurt anyone.[36]

To transform trauma into healing, the first challenge these wounded adolescents face is to avoid their parents' tragic example of self-blindness and denial of human suffering—retreating into a protective shell of isolation and cynicism as defeating as the misery they seek to escape. To achieve this more authentic initiation, Nick and Rudy must reach a just understanding of their parents' unhappiness and each parent's role in infecting their children with feelings of bitterness and defeat. As to the first of these crises, from the moment the benumbed son and the silent father row back across the lake at the conclusion of "Indian Camp," Nick intuitively adopts Dr. Adams's habit of numbing himself to painful experience, particularly female suffering, by denying its importance or disguising feelings of vulnerability with manly bluff. Sitting in the stern of the boat with his father steering, Nick comforts himself with the thought that surely he will never die. He tries to screen himself from the experience by focusing on what is going on or what is not seen, looking away so as not to see what his father is doing.[37] But he does look, and as we will see, Nick's sense of immortality is undermined by his fear of death and his father's inability to protect him from it.

Apropos of Frank McConnell's observation that "Vonnegut has transferred himself into the sensibility of Nick Adams,"[38] Rudy's need to withdraw into some cozy, womblike hiding place is understandable. Drowning in shame and guilt, believing he has ruined the lives of his family, he decides he is a defective human, one who should no longer be on this planet. Anybody who would fire a rifle over the rooftops of a city, he concludes, must have a screw loose.[39] Consistent with Nick's denial of painful experience, Rudy declares he wants to get into his bed and pull the covers over his head. Rudy maintains his resolve to remain isolated from the outer world, assuming the deliberate death-in-life existence of his parents by remaining "cold as ice" to his high school English teacher and to everyone else. Rudy succumbs to his father's habit of deadening consciousness with a variety of anesthetizing devices, distancing himself, like Nick, from the artistic self both young men hope to become. It comes as no surprise that, symbolic of his parents' destructive emotional legacy, Rudy eventually follows his father's advice to become a pharmacist, dispensing pills for everything.

While the mothers are ineffective nurturers, the weak and misogynist fathers pose a far greater threat to their sons' development, failing as reliable authority figures and revenging themselves on their sons in vindictive ways. Dr. Adams has exposed Nick to scenes of violence and death that burden Nick for life. Though Nick internalizes his horror, his self-deception is shattered by the disillusioning events of the companion stories "Three Shots" and "Ten Indians," where Nick learns that not only is his emotionally constrained father unable to protect him from death and violence, but he is capable of deliberate cruelty. In "Three Shots," which deals with the night previous to the action of "Indian Camp," Dr. Adams labels Nick a coward for fearing darkness, which Nick associates with death and all things feminine. Left alone at camp at night while his father and uncle go fishing, Nick becomes consumed with fear and fires the three shots the men have told him to do in case of emergency. Once again an annoyed Dr. Adams appears oblivious to the deeper causes of his son's distress, telling Nick there is nothing in the woods that can hurt him. As Nick undresses, he sees two shadows of his father and uncle cast by the fire on the canvas wall of his tent, emblematic of archetypal fears of women. When Dr. Adams notices the shadows, he admonishes Nick to dress, as if to cover his own guilt.[40]

In "Ten Indians," with Nick slightly older, Dr. Adams makes a big shadow on the kitchen wall of Nick's home. In this story Nick is thrice betrayed—by the young Indian girl Prudie Mitchell, by his absent mother, and particularly by his strangely antagonistic father. Rather than offering Nick solace and protection at a time when Nick has been emotionally wounded, the unhappy father exacerbates Nick's hurt instead of calming him. As if intentionally inflicting pain, Dr. Adams tells Nick that he saw Prudie earlier that day "threshing around" with Nick's friend Frank Washburn. The story ends with Nick listening to a big wind blowing and awakening with the realization that his heart is broken.

That Dr. Adams and Rudy's even more obviously cruel and distant father, Otto Walsh, are equally disastrous parents comes to us in striking remarks about the father's indifference to the son's welfare—by Nick in "Fathers and Sons" and by Rudy's counterpart, the lonely child protagonist Malachi Constant in *The Sirens of Titan* (1959). In a typical exchange between Malachi and his father that signifies the father's emotional reticence, Mr. Constant gives his son two pieces of advice—to horde his money and to keep liquor out of the bedroom. No wonder that, reacting to a father who confesses he has long been dead to life, Malachi admits that everything he has ever done has been motivated by spitefulness and by goads from childhood.

In "Fathers and Sons" Nick remembers the two pieces of advice his emotionally repressed father has given him, notably implicating Dr. Adams's aversion to sex, which defines Otto Walsh's fear of women and sex as well. "A bugger," Dr. Adams tells Nick, is a man who has intercourse with animals, and though Dr. Adams says he does not know why, "it's a heinous crime." That, Nick says, is the total of direct sexual knowledge bequeathed him by his father except on one other occasion. He explains that his father summed up the whole matter by stating that masturbation produces blindness, insanity, and death while a man who goes with prostitutes will contract hideous venereal diseases; according to Dr. Adams, the thing to do is to keep your hands off people.[41] How eerily this advice repeats the effects on Eliot Rosewater of his father's obsession with purity and his violent aversion to sex in *God Bless You, Mr. Rosewater* and Rudy's decision never to touch anyone again, a warning that associates women with sex and death, inviting years of sexual anxiety and gender confusion to follow.

Referring to his father as frankly vengeful, Vonnegut linked the destructive fathers by describing Kurt Senior as someone who became a gun nut and hunter to prove he was not effeminate, even though he was in the arts, an architect and a painter: "Father believed he could still demonstrate his manhood by fishing."[42] As with the cold and estranged mothers, Rudy agrees these fathers were bad parents to have, men whose feelings of abject defeat cast a pall over the family at large. Like Dr. Adams, Otto Waltz does not talk about intimate things, family things, love things, exacerbating their lack of understanding. He turns out, Rudy says, as "collapsible as a paper cup." Otto finds him so theatrically absorbed by his own helplessness and worthlessness, that if he cares about his son's condition, he gives no sign of it. Like the absent Dr. Adams, who, according to Nick, shared nothing after the age of fifteen, Otto has so little understanding of himself or his son that on his deathbed he claims he has been wonderful with his children.[43] No wonder Rudy concludes that his life must be a big mistake.

Even though it takes time for Rudy to comprehend the extent of his father's guilt in the death of Mrs. Metzger, he knows that his father's beloved collection of guns in the attic of their house—more than three hundred antique and modern weapons—has infected their home with evil.[44] He explains that, from the time he was born, people found his house spooky. Though his father thinks the guns beautiful and, like Dr. Adams, encourages Rudy to love them too, Rudy calls them murder, as dangerous as "copperheads and rattlesnakes."[45] In "Now I Lay Me" Nick too cites the attic of the house where he was born as his earliest memory, but while it literally contains jars of snakes and arrowheads associated with his father's aggression, Nick sees them not as murder, but rather as precious artifacts discarded and burned by his insensitive mother.

Though in these early Adams stories, it is the mother who is literally the missing parent, her conspicuous absence in "Indian Camp," "Three Shots," and "Ten Indians" seems more ominous than the father's blatant sins. Kenneth Lynn suggests Hemingway's disapproving portrayal of Nick's mother in these stories is opaque because the author did not clearly understand his feelings toward her. While we know Hemingway expressed hatred for her openly, referring to his mother as "that bitch"[46]—except for his resentment of having been evicted from Windemere at age twenty-one for laziness, cursing, and accusing her of having hounded his father into his grave—Hemingway never came close to saying why, a telling example, as Reynolds says, of things the boy did not understand and the man did not want to understand. We know that Hemingway expected his independent and creative mother to play roles Grace never enjoyed, those of cook and homemaker, and that he blamed her for depriving his father of his patriarchal position, a form of emasculation that isolated the father from the family and led to suicidal despair. Annoyed that he was not as good a shot as his father, Hemingway even blamed his mother for the impairment of his left eye, believing that her eyes weakened after a bout with scarlet fever and that she passed this trait to her children.

However skewed by personal bitterness, Hemingway's fictional portrait of his mother is unceasingly hostile. During Nick's ordeal in "Indian Camp," Mrs. Adams exists as an eerie nonpresence whose absence nevertheless indicts her for failing Nick when he most needs her love and protection. We feel the estrangement of mother and son again in "Ten Indians," where Mrs. Garner functions as a surrogate mother to Nick. Attempting to protect Nick from the very wound Dr. Adams inflicts on him with the news of the betrayal of Prudie and Frank Washburn, Mrs. Garner, on the Fourth of July, a holiday reserved for family gatherings, invites "Nickie" to her family's dinner. Nick's expression of gratitude, "Thanks for taking me in," might as well be spoken by an orphan. When Nick declines the invitation, he does so because he worries his father is home waiting for him, not his mother. When Nick does return home, it is in fact his father who feeds him supper.

If the author and his protagonist's disdain for the mother is initially indirect, we are aware of Hemingway's notorious portrait of her in "The Doctor and the Doctor's Wife," "Soldier's Home," and "Fathers and Sons," where hostility between husband and wife turns to open warfare, a battle of enemy combatants who force a confused, embattled Nick to take sides, shielding the defenseless father against the offending mother. Mrs. Adams fails to perform any kind of positive female functions in these stories. She represents Hemingway's real-life portrait of the castrating mother whose bullying ways contribute eventually to the father's suicide. Recast almost exactly as the mother's selfishness and the father's abject defeat in "Soldier's Home," where Mrs. Adams proclaims, "I'm your mother. . . . I held you next to my heart when you were a tiny baby,"[47] Hemingway recalled his parents' tragic enmity for one another: "Then the inevitable making up. Loser received by victor with some magnanimity, everything that had been told the children cancelled. The home full of love, and mother carried you, darling, over her heart all these months and her heart oh yes and what about his heart and where did it beat and who beats it now and what a hollow sound it makes."[48]

Krebs, Nick's counterpart in "Soldier's Home," experiences a form of existential nausea when his pious, sentimental mother implores him to get down on his knees with her to pray to God. This is the same obtuse Mrs. Adams who sits in her darkened room with her Bible, oblivious to the son and her husband's needs in "The Doctor and the Doctor's Wife." This scant, three-page story speaks volumes about the tragic estrangement of Nick Adams's family, but it mainly indicts the mother. The story begins with a conflict between Nick's father and a half-breed Indian named Dick Boulton; this scene is followed by a brief interaction between the doctor and his wife and then a final scene when the doctor comes across Nick and the two go off into the woods together. Several references to Mrs. Adams's moral blindness—twice we read that the "blinds" to her bedroom are drawn—suggest that, insulated from the world's harshness by her religious journals spread before her in the darkened room, she appears completely insensitive to her husband's ordeal, telling her husband he must be imagining Boulton's belligerence.

At the end of the story Dr. Adams conspires with Nick against the mother, both father and son wanting as little to do with Mrs. Adams as possible. But, as if to protect his father, Nick assumes the parental role and leads him away into the woods to hunt squirrels. Though Nick, who addresses his father as "Daddy," is still too young to understand his father's complicity in their family tragedy, he has begun to perceive his father's unhappiness solely in terms of the mother's selfishness. Perhaps he thinks he understands his father's painful retreat into silence and suicidal depression, seeing him emasculated by a domineering wife indifferent to her husband's emotional needs. At the apex of his father's struggle with Dick Boulton, Dick's son Eddy hangs a saw up by one of its handles "in the crotch of a tree,"[49] a telling image of Dr. Adams's feelings of castration. Nick may sense that his father is feeling so defeated as to commit suicide. Earlier the doctor has taken his shotgun out and sat with it on his knees as if taking solace in its power to end his troubles. The demoralized doctor is clearly fonder of his gun than of his wife, the implications of which Hemingway explored as late as *Under Kiliman-jaro*. At this point fear of his father's impotence, however unconscious, becomes as much a permanent fixture in Nick's troubled psychic life as the legacy of failure and defeat Rudy Waltz describes as his permanent life's companion. As Rudy observes of Otto, Nick is appalled that Dr. Adams does nothing effective to defend himself.

As the one place where they connect, the woods seem to offer Nick an opportunity for bonding with his unhappy father. In "Fathers and Sons" an older Nick reminds himself that whatever he has learned about his father's weaknesses over time, he will always be grateful to him for giving him his first gun and teaching him to fish and shoot, passions that had never slackened. Their love of nature seems to be an advantage over Rudy Waltz's complete alienation from his father. Yet we see that Nick's fateful alliance with his father and his father's masculine proclivities, most disastrously a flight from the feminine, contrasts markedly with Rudy Waltz's choice of more feminine pursuits, Rudy's more successful achievement of psychic health. In his analysis of Hemingway's early stories, "Reading Hemingway without Guilt," Frederick Busch argues that Dr. Adams presents Nick with a dangerous set of alternatives to life's treacheries: either fall prey to the terror of living and therefore kill yourself or "soldier on" with aggression and what might be called manly honor.[50] The costs of a lifetime of "soldiering on" become increasingly clear with time, culminating with Nick's reappearance as the battered, suicidal Robert Cantwell in *Across the River and into the Trees*.

As with the smug and often insensitive Mrs. Adams, the morose and cynical Mrs. Waltz scarcely evokes Jung's caring, archetypal mother, the "Great Mother" or "Mother Goddess" who protects and transforms.[51] Like Nick, Rudy associates his mother with the darker, destructive aspects of nature, the darkness inside Rudy's home, Hemingway's omnipresent "shadows," what Ann Putnam and Susan Beegel identify as the "fearful other," a disintegrative force rather than one that promotes wholeness of self and community. Just as Mrs. Adams hides in the dark of her bedroom when violence threatens the Adams household, so Rudy's mother takes to her bed when trouble starts. Rudy's sister-in-law suggests that Rudy was born defective, possibly strangled by his mother's umbilical cord. His brother Felix tells their mother that she must be the worst mother a child ever had, that she never did anything a mother's supposed to do. Rudy calls her "a cold and aggressively helpless old bat."[52] She is the first person he encounters after shooting Mrs. Metzger, and he opines, "She wasn't about to hug me or cover my inky head with kisses."[53] When Felix goes off to war, Mrs. Waltz shakes his hand by way of encouragement and then blows a kiss when his train was a half mile away. She is so incapable of imagining what Rudy might want that, after he shoots Mrs. Metzger, his mother does not even get out of the doorway so Rudy can come inside.

The failure of the Hemingway/Vonnegut father and son to connect, except through aggression, has disastrous consequences for both sons throughout their lives, both as it alienates them from fathers they desperately want to please and, more forebodingly, as it alienates them from women the misogynist fathers have taught them to loathe and fear. When the returning soldier in "Soldier's Home" repeats three times that he wants to live alone without consequences, to live so that girls can no longer touch him, he invokes the fathers' treacherous legacy of abuse Jung termed the "deprecation and denial" of women,[54] the Hemingway/Vonnegut hero's earliest and deepest wound. Try as they might, neither Nick Adams nor Rudy Waltz will ever again live free of the "consequences" of the feared and scorned mother, forever associated with pain and suffering. "The secrets were out," Michael Reynolds says: "The son, sex, and death, the screaming mother all bloody in birth."[55]

There is really only one female in the family Nick and Rudy care for, the sister Nick says he "liked the smell of"[56] and the sister Rudy desires in *Slapstick*, incestuous feelings central to each author's untold story. Apropos of Spilka's contention that Hemingway's secret sexual desires were always there beneath the iceberg waiting to thaw, Krebs's relationship to his sister as her "beau" and she as "his girl," displays Hemingway's early fascination with incest and gender transformation. In the meantime the association of the feminine with pain and suffering, accompanied by fears of the father's loss of male identity, cause Nick and Rudy to become increasingly cynical toward love and marriage, which they know only in terms of anger and betrayal, fleeing not only the company of women in general but rejecting the feminine in themselves. According to Millicent Bell, the unspoken fear is that either one will somehow kill love and marriage overall, or it will kill you, as had happened to both authors' parents. In either case Bell says, "death and destruction arrive in the end."[57] Thus originates the tragic psychic imbalance that becomes Rudy and Nick's habitual life condition, a fractured soul they must work the rest of their lives to heal.[58]

In "The End of Something," "Three Day Blow," "Cross-Country Snow," and "Hills like White Elephants," stories that place a premium on male primacy and survival, we see that, because of his mother and his supposedly unmanned father, Nick determines that what happened to his father will not happen to him. Marriage is viewed as a "trap," a spiritually numbing experience that threatens male autonomy. Nick eludes marriage through male bonding and the adoption of primarily masculine interests and values. Vonnegut might well have had these tales of denial and flight in mind when he remarked that the greatest reward for a character in a Hemingway story is the celebration of male bonding, the feeling one man has for another free of the complicating presence of women. According to Joseph Flora, the significance of Nick's dismissal of Marjorie in "The End of Something" is twofold: the breakup is a choice Nick has made, as opposed to the isolation of his earlier childhood, and it portends how distant and removed Nick later is from female companionship.[59] The ease and efficiency with which Nick severs affections with Marjorie becomes particularly alarming when we recognize that, unlike his father and mother, Marjorie wants to share Nick's favorite pastime. She loves to fish, especially with Nick, and she manages the physical details of their fishing adventure with as much knowledge and skill as

Nick, rowing the boat and holding the line in her teeth as the line runs out from Nick's reel.

In the distinctly masculine cottage in the woods in the story "The Three Day Blow," a habitation conspicuously devoid of female presence, Nick continues to deny the deeper motives of the breakup with Marjorie, just as he later resists connecting the physical wounds of war with the psychological wounds inflicted by his parents. Though painfully aware of his loss, rather than thinking further, he decides to get really drunk, echoing his father's response to female suffering in "Indian Camp" that none of it was important. Satisfying himself that the breakup with Marjorie was inevitable, an act of nature he was helpless to resist, the story ends as the two boys take their fathers' guns to join Nick's father down in the swamp where he is hunting, comforted by the thud of the doctor's shotgun and the illusion that Marge no longer matters.

"Cross-Country Snow" again finds Nick safely away from the complicating presence of women, happily bonding with his friend George on a Swiss skiing trip, sharing intimate thoughts that confirm Nick's views of familial life as a mediocre and limited experience, a suffocation of soul. The young men compliment one another on their skiing prowess, agreeing there is nothing better to talk about. "Don't you wish we could just bum together?" George says wistfully, "drink and ski and fish all over Europe and not care about anything else."[60] The "anything else" assumes a familiar threatening shape as Nick suddenly wonders why he had not noticed their waitress is pregnant. Illustrating Frederic Busch's observation that the unifying theme of these stories is the invasive nature of women, especially pregnant women, Nick does not notice the girl's condition because it invokes fears that his own expected child will force him out of this wonderful existence of exhilarating physical sensation, restricting his athletic recreational time with understanding male companions like Bill or George and back into a life of domestic responsibility in the states.[61]

As in "Cross-Country Snow," the "trapped" and unhappy couple in "Hills like White Elephants" bears out Nick's fears that a marriage with Marjorie would have meant an end to male freedom and romantic adventure, transforming them to barrenness and sterility when the complications of pregnancy threaten. Though the boy in the story is never named, we clearly recognize Nick's avoidance of painful emotion when he tells the girl he just cannot think about things as they are. "You know how I get when I worry."[62]

At first look Rudy Waltz's response to his cold and domineering mother suggests that his sexual wound runs deeper and seems less repairable than Nick's. Sexual experiences for him are either unknown or purely perfunctory. The only womb that interests him is that which offers some cozy hiding place—a state of blankness or indifference to anything pertaining to bodily experience, certainly bodily pleasure. Even though Nick's early sexual encounters with local Indian girls are impersonal, leaving him as lonely and directionless as Rudy, his penis works fine—so far. Rudy so fears contact with the opposite sex that, even by the age of eleven, he has given up bringing girls home altogether. After the murder of Mrs. Metzger, he fears entering his locked house, likened to a fortress because he must pass through the darkness associated with his mother's coldness. He feels so neutered and disembodied, so dead to his body, that thirty-eight years after the shooting, he wonders if he might possibly be a homosexual. He cannot be sure because he has never made love to anyone. He cannot get waited on in a restaurant because he feels so disembodied as to be invisible, unable to love or be loved by men or women.

For both protagonists, fear of the mother and flight from the feminine holds terrible consequences for their future development. The splitting of self into separate, warring beings, the masculine-feminine division of soul in which the extroverted animus overrules or annihilates the feminine, threatens a loss of moral identity and precludes greater creative possibilities for the artist.[63] The fear in themselves of feminine weakness and the assumption of a false masculine persona takes on increasingly greater significance in years to come, threatening both boys with the fate of their painfully conflicted fathers—the doctor, the man of healing, devoted to curing people but also in love with guns and killing—and the father, Otto, who dispenses pills and aspires to be a painter but who also worships guns and violence. Rather than suppressing a caring, core self, while presenting a false, desensitized self to the world, Nick and Rudy must learn to embrace rather than deny or submerge the anima, seeking to understand and cultivate the inner feminine instead of viewing it as a landscape to be avoided, taken, or destroyed.[64] Rudy's passive outer mask is no more a successful response to the hero's sexual wound than Nick's increasing toughness. Yet, while Rudy Waltz's sexual dysfunction appears more severe on the surface and more difficult to cure, it may be Rudy's deeper understanding of his father's culpability in the family's tragic history of alienation, and his greater willingness to discuss feelings of sexual inadequacy that constitute his more successful exorcism of parental ghosts.

What Rudy understands about his father, Otto, is exactly what Nick tries to ignore about Dr. Adams—that Otto is a coconspirator in the son's contempt for and flight from the mother. In "The Doctor and the Doctor's Wife," Dr. Adams's failure to act on his wife's desire to see Nick causes Nick to follow his father into the woods to hunt, a subtle enough betrayal on Dr. Adams's part, but one that resonates the rest of Nick's life. Rudy by contrast intuits that the perversion of Otto's artistic ambitions into a passion for beautiful guns and a flamboyant enthusiasm for Adolf Hitler may signify a failure in the bedroom as well as that of provider and moral guide for his wife and children, an absence of fire power Otto transfers to the love of guns. We see that Otto has tainted love with violence from the onset of his marriage, having bought his arsenal of firearms during his six-month honeymoon in Europe.

Though Nick sees his father as a victim of his mother's bullying, the more likely scenario is that, as with Otto, financial collapse and abortive creative or professional ambitions cause Dr. Adams to vent his frustration in forms of aggression he consciously or unconsciously inflicts on his wife and son—a devotion to firearms, emotional cruelty, or feigned indifference, even a vengeful effort to subvert the son's artistic aspirations, which he sees as decadent. Nick is more concerned that his father is a better shot as a hunter than that he might be an emotional or sexual failure to his wife.

Even the matured Nicholas Adams of "Fathers and Sons" fails to acknowledge the destructive association of guns and sex, love and death. Nick's memories of sex with the Indian girl Trudy become indistinguishable from the pleasures of killing squirrels, an even more portentous association when we see that the twenty-gauge shotgun he kills with, the one his father gave him, adumbrates Dr. Adams's death by gunshot and is like the gun Hemingway later used to end his own life. Though Nick fails to appreciate their true import, how tragically prophetic Nick's words become: "He could thank his father for that."[65]

The failure of Eros for fathers real and fictional causes them to discourage the artistic aspirations of their sons. Hemingway's father wanted Ernest to go to a good Congregationalist college or at least to work at something practical. Described as a taciturn, duty-bound man, Clarence prompted his son to specialize in the sciences in order to develop resourcefulness and self-reliance—to do something toward the scientific interests of the world. Jeffrey Meyers reports that Clarence preferred his son to hunt rather than read.[66] Otto Waltz's advice to Rudy to stay away from the arts similarly reflects the frustrations of Vonnegut's father, Kurt Senior, an architect and painter, when economic difficulties forced him to do menial work at the Atkins Saw Company—during years, Vonnegut said, that would have been his most creative. That Kurt Senior's new employer made weapons of some sort constitutes a real-life case of the father's life force subverted by the forces of death. Like Clarence Hemingway, Kurt Senior insisted that his son study something useful in the sciences, that he would in fact send his son to college only if he studied chemistry or biology rather than becoming a writer.[67]

It is worth noting that, whether the loss of self-esteem experienced by Clarence and Kurt Senior was more self-inflicted or more caused by disappointed wives, like their fictional counterparts, Mrs. Adams and Mrs. Waltz, Grace and Edith were talented, cultured, high-energy women who were financially well-off before they were married.[68] More to the point, it is the mothers' creativity—Edith's desire to write and Grace's voice and piano virtuosity—that passed to the sons. Vonnegut took pride in making his mother's dreams of becoming a writer come true, while Hilary Justice explains that Ernest's exposure to music in his mother's home and even his novice experience playing cello in his school orchestra, provided him with "an aural and visceral understanding" of musical patterns that later manifests in his prose.[69] So it is no surprise that in the fictional version of the father's self-betrayal, Otto has been told by his mother that he might be the next Leonardo da Vinci. Instead Otto sees the studio built for him transmogrify into the ominous gun room of Rudy's future childhood nightmare, the scene of what Vonnegut called "the deathly still attic of our house in Indianapolis."[70] Otto's art tutor turns out to be a drunk who leads Otto into a progression of whoring and drinking, and when Rudy examines some of his father's artwork, he notices that everything his father depicts looks like cement. Hence the pitifully frustrated Otto warns Rudy to plug his ears whenever anyone tells him he has an artistic gift of any kind.

The question of the hero's vocation as artist, as it is prepared for in these dangerous adolescent years, is central to any examination of Nick and Rudy's relative progress in managing childhood trauma. Actually Rudy had long been accustomed to venting the artist pent up within himself through a variety of muted creative acts: scat singing, tinkering with imaginative recipes, improvisation, and daydreaming. Each is a formative experience that helps Rudy offset the aridity and paralysis of his death-in-life existence. But it is the nurturing female influence of Rudy's high school English teacher that encourages him to develop his artistic gift, a process of feminization that also occurs early in the Waltz household. While Nick's hunter-father initiates Nick in the Michigan woods through masculine rituals of fishing and hunting, Rudy gravitates to the family's kitchen for solace and instruction, pursuing more traditionally feminine pastimes such as cooking, baking, washing dishes, making beds, washing, and ironing. "It still makes me happy as I can be," he says, "to prepare a good meal in a house which, because of me, is sparkling clean."[71] As opposed to Nick's emotional reticence, Rudy says that, after shooting Mrs. Metzger, he suddenly began to cry about what he had done and all that had been done to him. He grieved so noisily that dogs barked at him.

But it is Rudy's experience as a fledgling dramatist that symbolically frees him from his father's noxious influence. With reference to Lacan, John Bleikaster explains that successful initiation requires eradication of the father, at least subconsciously, as a prerequisite for establishing independent identity. Rather than literally murdering his father as Nick imagines doing, Rudy writes a play, *Katmandu*, that enables him to declare his father's responsibility in the cycle of violence that has institutionalized his mother and devastated the family. The curtain rises on his play just as his father dies back in Midland City, symbolic of Rudy's use of art to exorcise the father's malevolence. No doubt Vonnegut's decision to remove the "Jr." from his name was a way to singularize himself—to prove and proclaim his difference from his troubled father. Rudy realizes that to grow as a writer he must make painful past experience the focus of his art. He has a trick for dealing with his worst memories, he says. He insists that they are all plays, and that he is in the presence of art. He subsequently writes four plays he calls "wheels within wheels," or plays within the novel, all dealing with critical moments in his family's cycle of violence, transforming chaos into order and pain into understanding, just as Vonnegut's preface informs us that he has transformed real life people and events into healing, personal truth.

The upshot of these contrary responses to the father's aggression is that one son's exorcism of family ghosts, Nick's, remains tragically incomplete, while Rudy frees himself from his father by testifying against his father's criminal negligence in a way that Nick is prevented from doing because of his hard-and-fast loyalty to his father. At the same time Rudy's more charitable understanding of his mother opens him to complexities within his own being. Learning to view her as the paradoxical mother of medieval allegories, a redemptive and transformative force as well as a force that poisons and devours, Rudy makes significant progress in achieving the union of opposites Jung saw as necessary for healing the anima-animus wound, the integration of a fully conscious, psychically balanced self. As a creative writer, Rudy understands that resolving his painful dilemma will take him a life time to resolve—that part of him will remain Deadeye Dick. But thanks to the transformative, feminizing powers of art, he is able to announce that to have been a perfectly uninvolved person, a perfect neuter; he should never have written a play. After the death of his father, Rudy remarks that he would be paired off with his mother as though they are husband and wife. Like the author himself, Rudy has accessed the repressed female in him to the extent that Vonnegut declares, "My, how feminine I have become."[72]

By contrast, in the two stories that complete the Adams saga, "Big Two-Hearted River" and "Fathers and Sons," Nick's disdain for his mother remains absolute. Reflective of what Ann Putnam calls the writer-hero's resistance to mysterious silences and guarded memories, Nick's fear of the mother figure in these stories—and of the feminine in himself—not only conceals those "secret sorrows" Nick and his author must bring to light but, as John Hemingway argues in *Strange Tribe* (2007), prevents Nick from realizing powerful maternal instincts necessary to his art, even a desire to fuse with or be the mother herself. For now, however, such secret longings, along with thoughts of the father's cruelty, must be relegated to the undercurrents of the unconscious.

Susan Beegel and Michael Reynolds suggest that such a deeper, personal analysis would require Nick and his author to admit to the father's criminal negligence in ways neither were prepared to do, requiring not only reconciliation with the scapegoat mother but rejection of the beloved father associated with deeply ingrained ideals of masculinity that Nick and Hemingway felt compelled by inclination and education to fulfill. Nick's dilemma is that he can neither testify against nor identify with the father, who ironically fails to achieve the standards of manhood he inculcates in his son. Beegel observes that Nick/Hemingway's defense of the father and deprecation of the mother was enforced not only by a stringent Oak Park ethos but by the feminization of American culture and the endangerment of traditional masculinity. Reynolds explains, however, that Oak Park's conservative, patriarchal culture was sufficiently unforgiving to still Hemingway's artistic conscience, demanding total allegiance to its masculine, chauvinistic norms. There was the early reading of romantic fiction that featured models of manly behavior. There was the family tradition of the glorification of hunting and the rugged out-of-doors represented by his father and grandfather, including his grandfather's Civil War experience. There was the staunchly conservative cultural milieu in Oak Park that encouraged, if not legislated, aggressive, self-conscious manly behavior and heroic comportment, symbolized by the character and philosophy of Theodore Roosevelt and his emphasis on vigorous physical exhibitions of manhood. Roosevelt's influence on Hemingway's early character seems especially telling. Roosevelt was a sort of surrogate father who called for rougher, manlier virtues and for moral and personal courage.

In the most representative of all the Nick Adams stories, "Big Two-Hearted River" and "Fathers and Sons," we know that Nick is a writer whose identity fuses with his author, just as the identities of Rudy and Vonnegut connect climatically at the end of *Deadeye Dick* in the image of an artist-priest with the power to raise ghosts from the grave. Judging from Nick's reflections about the literary life, old friends, and his love of hunting and fishing, we know that Nick's thoughts and experiences in these stories are Hemingway's own. By the end of "Big Two-Hearted River," we encounter Nick at exactly the moment his mature career as a writer begins, off to start the story Hemingway himself has written. In "Fathers and Sons" Nick is slightly older, approximately the age of Rudy Waltz when Rudy writes *Katmandu* and breaks from his father's pernicious influence. But whereas Rudy's fledgling efforts at art body forth an existential vision of life, an open script in which he can write his own existence rather than serve as a robot character in someone else's drama—his parents' for instance—Nick refuses to undertake Rudy's more successful exorcism of his lamentable father or to acknowledge the beneficent influence of his mother, continuing to play the part his father has scripted. More forebodingly than in any other Adams story, Nick refuses to talk or write about buried desires and fears, that dangerous knowledge he and his author must discover and reconcile. Linking Nick's reticence to his author, Malcolm Cowley reminded us that Hemingway was a writer who wrote not as "he should or would" but as he must, subject to personal demons.[73]

While Vonnegut explicitly connected Rudy Waltz's childhood nightmare with the horrors of war, the mysterious silences of "Big Two-Hearted River" reflect

Nick and his author's disconnect between the soldier's suffering in the war vignettes of *In Our Time,* and Nick's adolescent miseries at home, their unwillingness to explore the deeper, more personal meanings of the warfare within the Adams/Hemingway households. Though Nick cannot identify the "tragic adventure" signified by the "swamp" during his fishing excursion, the swamp's shadowy depths auger threats of various kinds, its foremost danger suggesting "entanglements of all things feminine" Nick dares not face—the threat of impending fatherhood, marriage, and familial strife.[74] Such domestic priorities dispute the exclusionary male world of fishing and hunting that protect Nick from thinking about the darkness in nature and in himself, which he associates with the castrating mother and the unhappy father. Unlike Rudy, who learns to accept the mother as an ambiguous being inspiring both beauty and terror, Nick fears a mother he dreads and desires, precluding reconciliation of any kind. From this view the feminine is always a fearful other, a being to be taken or mastered rather than to be understood as a vital aspect of one's self.[75]

The contrary pulls in Nick's painfully divided psyche compete in strange and complicated ways. The "tragic adventure" Nick is determined to avoid in the swamp suggests knowledge of the painful paradox in nature and within himself. Nick's schizophrenic sensibility—the caring, nurturing part of him—versus the self-destructive masculine—emerges at the end of the narrative when he identifies with the dazed rabbit he helps on the trail, pulling ticks from its head and placing it under a sweet fern bush. Moments before, he has felt happy about the trout he released back into the stream, whose pain he caused, telling himself the trout is too big to eat. These empathetic moments suggest an artist who is vulnerable and gentle, contradicting the impulse to cruelty that emerges when Nick uses grasshoppers for bait, crushing or slamming them with his hat, "threading the hook under his chin, down through the thorax and into the last segments of his abdomen."[76]

All the signs of Nick's attempts to mask the depth or source of his psychological wounds are here: withdrawal, fear, isolation, and repressed emotion. As Nick thinks of ways to avoid the complicated self-knowledge that awaits him in the uncertain currents of the river, it seems clear that Nick has become terminally wary not only of emotional relationships necessary to his writing, but of words themselves. As Putnam explains, to keep faith with the writer's sacred obligation to tell the truth no matter the cost the universe exacts, language, a source of both terror and salvation, is the world Nick must ultimately enter. It is the act of telling, Putnam says, that breaks the male code of silence and surrenders to the fertilizing possibilities of the feminine. For now, however, Nick's quest for the simplicity of experience Krebs craves in "Soldier's Home" is stronger than his desire to write. It is easier to think of fishing, hunting, and bullfights than to examine the fractured soul that lurks in the tangled shadows of the swamp. Facing the "tragic adventure"—fishing the river's parabolic shadows and dangerous undercurrents—is the key to Nick's emotional restoration and maturation as a writer, but Nick decides he must leave everything like that behind, "the need for thinking, the need to write, other needs."[77] Unlike Rudy, who chooses to confront his dark past and regenerate himself through language, Nick rationalizes that there were other days when he could fish the swamp.

Like Rudy, Nick in "Fathers and Sons," now a writer and parent himself, has had considerable time to form a more balanced and just understanding of his parents' open warfare and to use his art to analyze rather than distance himself from his family's tragic past. Nick is now "Nicholas Adams," ready to assume his own identify as man and artist. Yet it is clear the thirty-eight-year-old writer feels compelled as ever to defend his father at his mother's expense, suggesting that for Nick/Hemingway, the failure of child-parent relationships may be too deep to heal. Rather than expose his father's failings, Nick continues constructing a self the father would admire.

While Nick admits that his father was cruel as well as abused, he prefers to remember how his father had given him his first gun ("someone had to") and how he has inherited his father's love of hunting and fishing, rather than think about the relationship between the father's frustrations and tendencies to cruelty and, as Rudy does, ask whether his father may have been more victimizer than victim of the vilified mother. Rather Nick insists that, even if his father was cruel, it was because he had much "bad luck." If he had contributed at all to the "trap" of marriage that had emasculated him and led to his death, he had contributed only a little. Nick tells himself that he should get rid of these painful memories as he has gotten rid of other things by writing about them, recalling Rudy's miniplays employed to exorcise family ghosts. But just as his author explained his decision not to write the "Oak Park" novel he had planned, Nick reiterates that while these memories would indeed make a good story, there were still too many people alive for him to write it. He could always write about his father later, he tells himself. Better simply to get rid of the mother, as the author had declared "was the only thing for a man to do" when married to an unjust and overbearing woman with whom he had nothing in common.[78] Apropos of Hemingway's remark in *A Moveable Feast* that even when ignoring them, "families have many ways of being dangerous,"[79] Jung observed that the ideal of ridding oneself of the feminine in favor of an exaggerated masculine identity can only have disastrous consequences for the aspiring artist. Men who valorize masculinity at the cost of the feminine, Jung said, know neither themselves nor those around them and may suffer unconscious phobias, obsessions, and bad temper. Just ask their wives, Jung said, forced to help their husbands perpetuate a false masculine identity to disguise the feminine these men fear in themselves. Jung's observation that the adoption of an artificial masculine persona may even lead to "a limp sexuality"[80] takes on special significance in light of Jake Barnes's condition in *The Sun Also Rises*. Getting rid of the devilishly cumbersome feminine is what Hemingway continued to do with intrusive heroines such as Brett Ashley and Catherine Barkley, along with assertive women writers in *Green Hills of Africa*, the pesky old woman interrogator in *Death in the Afternoon*, and of course those actual wives, who too soon wore out their welcome.

A truer explanation of Nick/Hemingway's avoidance of a thoroughgoing analysis of the mother's victimization and the father's destructive passive-aggression came many years later in the confessions of David Bourne in *The Garden of Eden* that he betrayed his art by denying or lying to himself about his father's transgressions. David reiterates Nick's belief that an honest recounting of the father's terrible secrets, which he had for years put off facing, was indeed a good story, which this time he determines to complete. Equivalent to Rudy's miniplays, David's account of the cruelty and self-deception in his hunter-father is so awful it robs his father of status and dignity. David now knows why it was a story so disillusioning—a tale of a father who kills for pleasure—that he had never been willing to tell it.

The evidence is that Nick will pass on to his own son the disastrous lessons about manhood his father has bequeathed to him, just as Hemingway passed on such masculine ideals to Jake Barnes and Frederic Henry. In "Fathers and Sons" Nick remembers fondly threatening to kill Trudy's older brother Eddie, who plans to sleep with Nick's sister; Nick planned to use his father's gun and considered himself manly for pardoning Eddie. We might dismiss such bravado as adolescent immaturity, except that the requirements for manhood of such later heroes as Jake Barnes and Frederic Henry—self-conscious virility and a penchant for violence—are disturbingly similar. In the meantime Nick will take his own impressionable young son to pray at the tomb of Nick's grandfather, the Civil War hero who is the family's quintessential model of manly comportment. When Nick tells his son they will have to go, it is problematic as to whether Nick means to go in the spirit of Rudy's visit to his family's grave—that is to acknowledge and repudiate the family's legacy of aggression and madness—or to honor the father and grandfather's masculine ideals.

Already, in Nick and his author's failure to deal honestly with the suppressed fears and longings of childhood, we see grounds for Vonnegut's critique that Hemingway was trapped by machismo, contributing to personal and artistic defeat. Explaining his view of Hemingway's tragically early decline, Vonnegut praised what he felt was Hemingway's most durable contribution, his first forty-nine stories—citing "Big Two-Hearted River" and "A Clean, Well-Lighted Place" as his favorites—but decrying the fact that by the age of thirty-nine, Hemingway was virtually through as a writer. Though, Vonnegut said, Hemingway promised to give us twenty-five stories more, "He wouldn't give us even one more."[81] "It seems likely to me," Vonnegut declared, "that he believed his life to be the most memorable of all his stories, in which case that gunshot was a form of typography, a period. 'The End.'"

In Nick Adams's reincarnation as the wounded soldier, Jake Barnes in *The Sun Also Rises* and Frederic Henry in *A Farewell to Arms*, we see greater evidence of the Hemingway whom Vonnegut condemned for equating manhood with heroic comportment. By contrast we see Vonnegut's willingness in *Mother Night* and *Slaughterhouse-Five* to explore suppressed sexual desires and to confess sins against the feared "otherness," leading to a more durable and authentic self. Since Hemingway explained that his strategy of omission was to let the reader supply things left out, it is impossible for the reader to know how much Hemingway understood about the guarded secrets that constitute the underwater part of his work. If, as I suspect, there were things about himself he masked from himself as well as from the reader, it is only when Hemingway and his profoundly wounded protagonist similarly ford the deeper stream, the stream of consciousness as well as the stream of life, bringing repressed experience to light, that they achieve the greater self-knowledge that allows Rudy and Vonnegut to mend their rent souls.[82]

# Two

# Hemingway's *Sun*, Vonnegut's *Night*

## The Spoils of War

■

Undressing, I looked at myself in the mirror. . . . Of all
the ways to be wounded. I suppose it was funny.

Jake Barnes in *The Sun Also Rises*

The Second World War was over—and there I was at
high noon, crossing Times Square with a Purple Heart on.

Eliot Rosewater in *God Bless You, Mr. Rosewater*

In *Fates Worse than Death*, Vonnegut explained that he and Hemingway were natural adversaries because their wars were radically different in mood and purpose
and because, unlike himself, Hemingway was not a soldier in the strictest sense.
Vonnegut contended that by World War II, Hemingway's portrayal of war in *A
Farewell to Arms* and *For Whom the Bell Tolls* had become passé. While writers
such as Joseph Heller, James Jones, and Vonnegut himself viewed war as absurdly
barbaric, Vonnegut saw Hemingway's treatment of war as unanalytical and relatively naive, corrupted by the same attraction to violence that glamorizes big game
hunting or bullfighting.[1] "It must be plain to everyone," Vonnegut wrote, "that
the Ladies' Auxiliary for Men Engaged in Blood Sports has been disbanded for
quite some time."[2] We know now, he said, that there is nothing romantic about
war; it is only the "meaningless butchery" of ordinary people and there are no
potential human enemies anywhere who are anything but human beings almost
exactly like ourselves: "How amazing."[3] Evidently with Hemingway's "ignominious suicide" and notions of "honorable death" in mind, Vonnegut explained that
our present understanding of the nature of war as uncompromisingly "repulsive,
stupid and dehumanizing" means that writers such as he and Heller learned to
prefer life over death for themselves and others at every opportunity, "even at the
expense of being dishonored."[4] We are reminded of Penelope's rebuke of Harold

Ryan in *Happy Birthday, Wanda June*, when Harold's manly honor demands he shoot Woodly for insulting him or die happily in the effort. Death is just death, she tells him, "the absence of life—no honor at all."[5] We endure, Vonnegut said, "all sorts of insults and humiliations and disappointments without committing either suicide or murder."[6]

Vonnegut contended that, while he was a true soldier, a rifleman in time of war, Hemingway was a terrific war correspondent, but not a true combatant, someone who had submitted to training and discipline: "In the Spanish Civil War and then in World War II, Hemingway took no orders and gave no orders. He came and went wherever and whenever he pleased. He actually hunted German submarines for a while in the Caribbean—in his own boat and of his own accord."[7]

Never mind, however, that Vonnegut wound up a witness to horrors in a different war from Hemingway or that his wounding differed slightly from Hemingway's in kind. If one injury was more visible than the other, they were equally complex and psychologically damaging, intensifying the debilitating wounds of childhood, conscious and unconscious. At age eighteen, while serving as a Red Cross ambulance driver on the Italian front, Hemingway was literally blown up by an Austrian trench mortar, receiving something like 237 shell fragments. He rendered assistance to another wounded man and was hit a second time by machine-gun bullets. After extensive physical therapy, he returned to the front but suffered from hepatitis and was hospitalized until the armistice was signed on November 3, 1918. In a letter to a Rinehart editor in December of 1951, Hemingway explained the relationship of his personal wound to that of Jake Barnes, the "genesis" of *The Sun Also Rises*. Suffering from a genital urinary wound that became infected, Hemingway wondered, he said, what a man's life would have been like if his penis were lost and his testicles and spermatic cord remained intact. So he took a boy, Hemingway said, like one he knew, and made him into a foreign correspondent in Paris, exploring the problems of someone who was in love with him while there was nothing that they could do about it.[8]

James Nagel has argued in *Hemingway in Love and War* that the shock of Hemingway's physical wound was compounded, if not acceded, by the loss he felt when he was rejected by Agnes von Kurowsky, his hospital nurse during convalescence and the model for the fictional Catherine Barkley in *A Farewell to Arms*. Nagel points to a "Dear John" letter from Agnes, who was seven years older, breaking off the relationship and dismissing Hemingway in maternal tones as a boy. Agnes said she felt more like "a mother than a sweetheart," adding: "You're just a boy—a kid."[9] Hemingway never showed anyone the letter. Scholars are divided as to the real nature of the Agnes-Ernest romance, as they are about the long-range effects of Agnes's abrupt and somewhat patronizing rejection. We may safely surmise, however, that the vulnerable and impressionable nineteen-year-old could not have been happy being dismissed again by someone calling herself "mother."

As is often the case with Hemingway's submerged "secrets," it is not possible to know whether Hemingway consciously or unconsciously kept the more personal and sorrowful implications of the Agnes-mother connection from the reader. Was this a purposeful flight from painful self-knowledge, a strategy for submerging taboo sexual desires that might classify the author as something other than normal, healthy, and manly, thus limiting his creativity, as Vonnegut would argue? Or to the contrary, did the artful use of the "iceberg," its silences and absences, enrich his work by intensifying the unstated underwater portion of his story, creating provocative metaphoric images that compel active reader response? What we know for sure is that, either way, like Vonnegut, Hemingway was exorcising demons that might otherwise have prevented him from writing at all and that there was a decidedly greater movement toward consciousness and personal revelation as his work evolved.

In his preface to *Mother Night*, Vonnegut wrote that, as an American prisoner of war in Dresden, he had not only experienced the largest massacre in European history, but also saw firsthand the insane bigotry and paranoia behind the Nazi's persecution of the Jews. As a private and a battalion scout, he was forced to work as a corpse miner, burying the dead after high explosives were dropped on Dresden by American and British planes on the night of February 13, 1945, just about twenty-seven years after Hemingway's nightmare at Fossalta. Vonnegut explained that incarceration in an underground meat locker kept him from seeing the fire storm that swept over the city, turning people into artifacts—pieces of charred firewood two or three feet long, or "fried grasshoppers."[10] Later "we were put to work as corpse miners, breaking into shelters, bringing bodies out. And I got to see many German types of all ages as death had found them, usually with valuables in their laps. Sometimes relatives would come to watch us dig. They were interesting, too."[11]

Howard Campbell in *Mother Night* and Jake Barnes in *The Sun Also Rises* are engaged in the same struggle with guilt and pessimism as their authors, and they write from the same numb and detached point of view, suggesting that the authors are again using thinly disguised characters to exorcise personal demons. The kind of impersonal language Vonnegut used, or the absence of language altogether, masks psychological pain too fearsome to acknowledge. As to their more immediate war wounds, it took years and successive attempts before either writer could face such experience directly. Though Vonnegut, like Hemingway, played down the long-term trauma of his war experience, J. G. Keogh and Ed Kislatis contend that for Vonnegut the shock of personally witnessing the war's greatest massacre, nearly two hundred thousand civilians incinerated, had to be exorcised over a long period of writing. Vonnegut remarked, "I came home in 1945, started writing about it, and wrote about it, and wrote about it, and wrote about it, and WROTE ABOUT IT."[12] Thus *Slaughterhouse-Five*, where Vonnegut faced the experience head on, releases his Dresden tensions, which spread out over a lifetime, intensifying from novel to novel. Similarly it took Hemingway more than a decade to deal directly with Fossalta, and his wound, reproduced in *A Farewell to Arms* exactly as it happened, recurs throughout his work as Dresden does for Vonnegut.

A case can be made that putting their nightmares to paper in *The Sun Also Rises* and *Mother Night* was as necessary to one writer as the other—survival through the healing powers of imagination. Vonnegut cited the example of the French soldier-novelist Louis-Ferdinand Celine, who said that only by writing about his war wounds could he cure them. With reference to his own designs as a healer-writer, Vonnegut explained that "Celine was a brave French soldier in the First World War—until his skull was cracked. After that he couldn't sleep, and there were noises in his head. He became a doctor, and he treated poor people in the daytime, and he wrote grotesque novels all night."[13] Metaphorically identifying with Celine's head wound, Vonnegut cited the plight of the sleepless soldier as his and Hemingway's common foe, noting that Celine and Hemingway died two days apart.[14] Vonnegut added that he and Hemingway and others wounded or dead that are close to him—his sister, his first wife, Jane—are "now trying to get some sleep with the lights on."[15] Vonnegut agreed with Hemingway that "no art is possible without a dance with death."[16]

Just as Celine testified about his personal trauma, Vonnegut and Hemingway knew that facing their "head" wounds directly in *A Farewell to Arms* and *Slaughterhouse-Five* was an assignation they are fated to keep, fulfilling their writer's obligation to tell the truth not only about the more immediate wounds of war but about the way the horrors of war compounded and complicated the wound of androgyny—their fear of and flight from women and from the feminine within. We need only compare the deep emotional suffering of Hemingway's sleepless soldier in "Now I Lay Me," "In Another Country," and "A Way You'll Never Be" with Vonnegut's portrait of psychically maimed Eliot Rosewater in *God Bless You, Mr. Rosewater* not only to appreciate how war rendered both veterans senseless but to see their failure to understand the flight from women as their deeper and more threatening neurosis.

In "Now I Lay Me," Nick dwells on his mother's unmanning of the hapless father. Suggestive of the real-life father and son's resentment of Grace's independence, Nick's dire night thoughts focus on the new house designed and built by his mother and on his father's demoralization when she burns his specimen snakes and arrowheads while housecleaning.[17] The "blackened" artifacts suggest the burned-out land and blackened grasshoppers of "Big Two-Hearted River," evidence that "Now I Lay Me" is also about the hurtful memories of childhood as well as the scourge of war. When Nick appears reluctant to accept the cynical advice of an Italian major that marriage to a wealthy Italian woman will solve his problems, we know that Nick's hesitation relates less to his immediate war wounds than to fears of that dominating mother who undermined his father's sense of manhood. The ironic use of a childhood prayer in the story's title suggests Nick's increasing disbelief in God and the efficacy of prayer that his devout mother presses on him in "Soldier's Home." No doubt Nick's forgetting the words reflects his contempt for his mother's sentimental piety, as well as awareness of nature's indifference to suffering, symbolized by the constant sound of silkworms eating in the night.

"A Way You'll Never Be" reminds us again that Nick has been profoundly demoralized by wounds deeper and earlier than the war. As in "Now I Lay Me," Nick stresses his inability to sleep without a light of some sort. But now the combined traumas of childhood and war so shatter Nick's mind, they not only cost him his sleep, they threaten sanity itself. Helmets "full of brains" have become to Nick a not uncommon sight.[18] When coupled with Nick's multiple physical wounds (like his author, he has been blown up in the night and hurt in "various places"),[19] the sight of too many smashed heads and mutilated bodies causes him to ask, "I don't seem crazy to you, do I?" He knows the truth. He girds himself against emotional onslaughts to follow—sudden painful confusion or uncontrollable emotional ranting—by warning himself: "He felt it coming on again."[20]

Though Nick and/or his author may resist connections between his mother's perfidy and his father's weakness and the immediate psychological devastation of battle, Nick's wild and disjointed discourse about blackened grasshoppers—insects that at one time played a very important part in his life, juxtaposed with unconscious references to women who have betrayed him—evoke the ruined terrain in "Big Two-Hearted River" that implicates the destructiveness of both parents and war. When an incoherent Nick insists at the end of his grasshopper rant that there is one thing his fellow combatants must remember—"either you must govern—or you must be governed"[21]—he no doubt has in mind unruly women such as his mother, Luz in "A Very Short Story," or Trudy from the Indian camp, inconstant females who constitute the "feared other," and whose "peril" to him causes him to wake in the night soaking wet, more frightened than he had ever been in a bombardment. Nick's fears of mental illness invoke Hemingway's condemnation of Phil Young for trying to psychoanalyze him and, as Hemingway said, put him permanently out of business. After being "certified as nutty," Nick muses, "No one ever has any confidence in you again,"[22] fears born out by Nick's friend Paravicine, who indeed has no confidence left in his friend once he understands the extent of Nick's mental breakdown. The title of the story, "A Way You'll Never Be," might well describe the neurotic condition of the wounded soldier if he continues to resist fishing the murky waters of the unconscious. Yet, as if Hemingway were becoming tired of his own self-defeating evasions, too many suspect injunctions against "talking so much,"[23] he risks confessing weakness and fear in this story in the knowledge that if he is ever to get rid of these demons, he must confront them head-on, not—as Vonnegut wrote in *Slaughterhouse-Five*—dance round them, "decorating them with streamers" and "titillating" them.[24]

In "In Another Country," Nick joins veterans who meet in a Milan hospital for therapy. Carcasses of dead game hang in store windows, a ghoulish symbol for the mutilated soldiers. The presence of dead game suggests manly hunters somewhere out of sight, an association that along with images of birds on the wing, and the attending doctor in whom Nick and a wounded Italian major have no confidence, may evoke Nick's physician father and wounds more serious than Nick's injured knee or the major's withered hand, "something that had happened" that people who did not know him would not understand,[25] something that neither medals nor the rehabilitation machines would cure. When Nick lies awake in bed at night afraid to die, it is perhaps the offending mother he associates with impotence and death he thinks of, underscored by the bitter major's insistence that whatever Nick does in the future, he must not marry, since it will only produce loss and sickness of soul.

In *God Bless You, Mr. Rosewater*, the novel that connects *Mother Night* to *Slaughterhouse-Five*, we witness the same buried fears of childhood and trials of war that plague Hemingway's broken hero. Like Nick, Rudy Waltz's incarnation Eliot Rosewater may be more desperately in trouble than ever before. While the combined neuroses of childhood and war cost Nick his sleep, they render Eliot unconscious for an entire year. Just as Nick's mental deterioration manifests in uncontrollable bouts of madness that leave him completely disoriented, Eliot experiences "the big click" that renders his memory blank and requires treatment in a mental hospital. Just as Nick becomes painfully confused as to where he is and what his purpose is, Eliot fails to recognize the faces or voices of those around him. Eliot's friend Noyes Finnerty concludes that because of the undisclosed and unresolved "secrets" behind Eliot's eyes, he, like Nick, may never be the same.

As with Nick, the problem for Eliot in finding a cure for the psychic damage of war is that his emotional problems run deeper than he, or even his psychiatrist, suspect. Reminding us of Nick's confession in "A Way You'll Never Be" that only by getting "stinking" can he combat his fears, Eliot discovers his anxieties are so severe that no amount of booze seems to make him drunk. Eliot's exasperated doctor complains that, while Eliot has the most massively defended neurosis he has ever attempted to treat, all he talks about is American history. Like Nick and like Eliot, the doctor sees no connection between the traumatizing influence of Eliot's parents and the more immediate specter of war, connections they must examine closely if they are ever to understand the psychic disturbance responsible for their nervous collapses. The deeper source of Nick and Eliot's suffering emerges when the doctor asks Eliot's father about the senator's lifelong hysteria over nudity, evident when the anal-retentive senator insists his revulsions are shared so far as he knows by decent men everywhere, and advocates stamping out modern degeneracy by creating a system of justice as violent and repressive as Caesar's.

Eventually the doctor sees that the senator's almost violent aversion to the physical causes him to pervert healthy sexual desires by diverting them to the quest for money and power, responsible for the vicious cycle of lovelessness, particularly toward women, passed down from grandfather to father to son. That Eliot suffers from his father's constrictive obsession with purity becomes clear when the doctor suggests Eliot's sexual energies have misfired as well, alienating him from a mother and perhaps a sister whose beneficent influence contrasts markedly with the father's cruelty, but for whom Eliot harbors guilty erotic feelings he far from understands, the dangerous and forbidden "secret" behind Eliot's eyes. Memories of war so magnify earlier childhood wounds, Eliot's actions become increasingly compulsive and antisocial, and despite following his mother's efforts to help the poor, the amount of good Eliot does in *God Bless You, Mr. Rosewater* is seriously in question. Tony Tanner believes Eliot's utopian zeal so displaces Eliot's deeper psychic need that it leaves him "no sex at all."[26]

If we conflate the mentally ill veterans of "Now I Lay Me" and *God Bless You, Mr. Rosewater* with the precariously sane Howard Campbell in *Mother Night* and Jake Barnes in *The Sun Also Rises*, it is a wonder Barnes and Campbell, both writers now, maintain the will to live at all, let alone write about their traumatic pasts as alienated adolescents and psychologically impaired soldiers. Much as with Barnes, life has become so pointless for Campbell after the war that he describes himself as a "meditative invalid" and a "citizen of nowhere."[27] Agreeing with Resi Noth that there is nothing left of him but "curiosity and a pair of eyes," he tells her he does not write anymore because he no longer has anything to say. "Dead men," he says, "do not write very well."[28] The sign on Campbell's gutted, ratty attic apartment aptly describes Campbell and Barnes's inner desolation: "Nobody and nothing inside."[29] Any doubt that Jake is the same disturbed soldier who fears losing his soul if he goes to sleep in "Now I Lay Me" or being certified as "nutty" in "A Way You'll Never Be," should be dispelled when we learn that Jake too cannot sleep without a light on. The toll of war at home and abroad creates in Campbell that same state of nervous collapse that sends Eliot Rosewater to a mental hospital for an entire year.

As postwar exiles in bohemian Paris and Greenwich Village, Jake and Howard are still in a world that is a world at war—if not in the literal sense, certainly in the constant fight against despair. Campbell describes his abysmal fifteen-year underground existence as "purgatorial," while Robert Penn Warren characterizes Barnes's life in Paris as a nightmare barely held in abeyance. Both are spiritually perilous worlds in which Campbell and Barnes move as if through "an enemy territory."[30] Campbell speaks for both traumatized veterans when he describes himself as "frozen" in place by loneliness and fear, a paralysis of the will in which the benumbed individual requires someone or something else to help him move, to provide him or her with a reason for moving at all.

Though Jake Barnes's missing penis seems to establish him as the more severely wounded, both he and Campbell are physically as well as psychologically impotent. Just as Jake's unfortunate wound has made life for him scarcely more than bearable, preventing him and Brett Ashley from becoming true lovers, so shame and guilt rob Campbell of sexual feeling and the ability to love. When Campbell's friend George Kraft tells him all he needs in this world to free him from his postwar malaise is "a woman" to help him get writing again, Campbell replies that he is too worn out for a woman to do him any good. After Campbell's most recent love, Resi Noth, commits suicide, he finds himself so unloved and life so pointless, he loses the will to live entirely. Brett Ashley is as good as dead to Barnes by the end of their story, leaving him similarly withdrawn and cynical.

These wastelandic casualties are even more inclined than Nick Adams and Rudy Waltz to numb themselves to their complex, omnipresent trauma. When, after the war, the American intelligence agent Frank Wirtanen offers to find Campbell a fake identity to help him hide from his past, this mimics what Campbell and Barnes have done for themselves. Just as Barnes fortifies himself with drink, Campbell is tempted by a large quantity of morphine accidentally included with war surplus clothes and furnishings, but he declines only because he understands that he was already drugged. Warren explains that for Barnes, the battlefields of Verdun prepare for the bars of Paris and the escape into sensation of Jake and his dissolute expatriate friends.[31] Considering the horrors Campbell experiences at war's end, it is no wonder he wants to disappear from sight, believing people are still out to hurt or kill him. He explains that, when he was captured in April of 1945, he was forced to observe firsthand the horrifying sights of the first Nazi death camp the Americans saw—the gallows, the whipping post, the gutted and spavined dead in heaps.

Perhaps their most dangerous strategy for forgetting or anesthetizing themselves to painful experience concerns Barnes and Campbell's adoption of what Marc Baldwin calls a "discourse of silence,"[32] the habit of not talking about emotionally troubling experience that becomes for people such as Jake, Brett, and Count Mippipopolous a tacit principle of the Hemingway "code." Pressed to explain his loneliness to George Kraft, Campbell says he never thinks about it. When Wirtanen accuses Campbell of having been one of the most vicious sons of bitches who ever lived, Campbell replies that was not him. When Brett Ashley asks about Jake's wound, he tells her he never thinks about it either. According to Baldwin, through his noncommunication, Jake reserves a dominant position for himself within the narrative, while concealing dangerous or forbidden knowledge from himself and others.[33]

Whether we ultimately view their respective artistic efforts as creative progress or creative atrophy, Barnes, the apprentice journalist, and Campbell, the established playwright, return to the typewriter to write the stories we read in *The
Sun Also Rises* and *Mother Night*. Like their authors, both writers hold the importance of art sacrosanct, underscoring their artistic imperative to tell the truth
about the tangle of forces that have wounded them. When Howard's friend
George Kraft declares that future generations will judge all men by the quality of
their creations, "that nothing else will matter,"[34] he speaks not only for Howard
and Vonnegut, but for Hemingway's view of art in *Green Hills of Africa:* that writing is the most important thing a person can do, that if the writer writes with
"absolute conscience," then "nothing else matters."[35] "Countries come and go and
the people all die, and none of them were of any importance permanently, except
those who practiced the arts."[36] In *Green Hills of Africa* Hemingway took up Jake
Barnes's adulation of Ivan Turgenev where Jake left off, praising Leo Tolstoy and
Stendhal as well for describing the Russia of their time with such fidelity to pic-
torial reality that Hemingway saw all that they saw and felt all they felt.

The fact is that, because Barnes and Campbell create their own story, neither
traumatized writer's retrospective narrative is completely trustworthy. Jake's biases
toward Robert Cohn and Brett Ashley become increasingly apparent as his story
progresses, revealing more of Jake's inner torments than insight into Cohn and
Brett, disqualifying him as a reliable judge of others. While Campbell's story is
more inclusive than Jake's, its veracity is compromised by Vonnegut's editorial
tinkering, foregrounding its existence as construct rather than representation of
actual experience. Faced with the narrative complications of Vonnegut's metafictional apparatus, readers must determine reality on their own. Campbell's "confessions" are "smeary with revisions," translated from German to English, reworked
in part by a poetess-interpreter, then "emasculated" by an editor whose "cuts"
may never be fully known. Despite the obvious difference between Hemingway's
fidelity to representational reality and Vonnegut's postmodern destabilization of
"truth," Hemingway's interest in problematic truth telling increases as his fiction
evolves.

While Campbell acknowledges that his judgments obviously are not what they
should be, he nevertheless proves more faithful than Barnes to that lofty artistic
principle to which both aspire—writing with "absolute conscience." Though
Campbell, like Jake, is initially as reluctant to tell his story, by the time Campbell
is imprisoned and begins his "confessions," guilt and genuine remorse compel him
to testify with complete honesty about the sins he has committed toward humanity in general and toward women and the feminine in himself in particular. For
starters Campbell's tale is more complete than Jake's and more cognizant of the
way the immediate horrors of war compound and extend the wounds of childhood. We hear little of Jake Barnes's wartime experience prior to his life as an

expatriate in Paris and nothing of those troubled, priggish parents, who in "Soldier's Home" fail to understand the nature or depth of their son's despair, let alone their contribution to it.

On the other hand, Vonnegut portrays not just Campbell's hellish existence in New York City after the war, his years as an American agent in Germany during the war, and his ultimate imprisonment for alleged war crimes as a Nazi propagandist, at which point he tells his story, but also the similarly warping effects of his moribund mother and father, those corpselike parents Howard describes as dying of broken hearts. Campbell remembers the absent, war-mongering father rarely at home, whose favorite book was a picture history of World War I with pictures of men hung on barbed wire, mutilated women, and bodies stacked like cordwood, and the talented artist-mother, whose frustrated dreams turned her morose and suicidal. Reminding us of Rudy Waltz's mother in *Deadeye Dick*, who turns off electric lights and lights candles, Howard's mother has a penchant for turning out all the lights, and in the ghastly yellow glow of lit candles, Howard and his mother both look like corpses. From then on, Howard explains, he ceased to be her companion. He tells us that his father's repetitive job with the General Electric Company, like Otto Waltz's, so used up his energy and creative spirit, he had little time and imagination left for anything else. Just as Vonnegut in *Slaughterhouse-Five* connected the horrors of Dresden with those of Billy Pilgrim's Tralfamadorian nightmare, so with equally ingenious concision he fused the Dresden of *Mother Night* with Campbell's memories of his terrible mother and his own death-in-life existence in New York City. On his walk home from the Empire State building, Campbell imagines that the eerie, artificial light from a match in a dark hallway might have been from "the doors of cells in a jail in a burning city somewhere."[37]

What Campbell's supposed editor, Kurt Vonnegut, says about Campbell's confessions—that the demands of art alone were enough to make him lie and to lie without seeing any harm in it—is precisely the understanding Campbell achieves in revisiting the events that cost him the woman he loved along with his moral and artistic integrity. The epiphany that informs Campbell's painful but uncompromising confessions comes to him when he recognizes the perverse habit of mind that allowed him to survive the madness of war. "I've always known what I did," he explains, "I've always been able to live with what I did. How? Through that simple and widespread boon to modern mankind—schizophrenia."[38]

Apropos of Vonnegut's stated moral—"We are what we pretend to be, so we must be careful about what we pretend to be"[39]—Campbell repudiates the notion that he could pretend to be one thing to the world, the Nazi propagandist he plays as an American spy, while burying and hiding an essential part of himself within the confines of his own mind. He had hoped to be merely ludicrous, but he had underestimated the power of unquestioning faith and the eagerness of so many people incapable of thought to believe him—"to believe and snarl and hate."[40] Campbell then wonders if the Nazi in him does not have some basis in reality, whether his pretense has not exposed the capacity for cruelty and moral blindness within the soul of every man and woman.

An anguished Campbell knows well the tragic consequences of his schizophrenic defense against guilt and responsibility, which he calls "a wider separation of [his] several selves than even [he] can bear to think about."[41] He remembers broadcasting in code the news of his wife's disappearance and possible death without knowing what he was doing, leaving him unable to mourn. He understands that the false self he projected to the world both as a dramatist of melodramatic plays and as a Nazi propagandist explains how a household as divided as the one composed of Jones, Father Keeley, Vice Bundesfuehrer Krappauer, and the Black Fuehrer, a Jew, a Catholic, and a black man, each devoted to racial purity and each capable of homicidal violence could exist in relative harmony. That was how, Campbell explains, his father-in-law could contain in one mind an indifference toward slave women and love for a blue vase, how Rudolf Hoess, commandant of Auschwitz, could alternate calls for great music over the camp loudspeakers and calls for corpse carriers, and how Nazi Germany could sense no important differences between civilization and hydrophobia. Campbell likens such perfectly contradictory states of mind—humane and cruel, creative and destructive—to a totalitarian "thought machine" formed by paranoia and a repressed libido and operating in accord with its own bizarre sense of reality and time. Campbell admits that some of the teeth in his own thought machine were missing, but insists that he never knowingly rationalized the importance of those that were gone.

For Howard Campbell it is what his so-called fairy godmother, Frank Wirtanen, calls the "music of conscience" that furnishes Campbell with the reason and courage for "moving on," testifying to the sins he has committed toward humanity in general and toward women in particular. For Jake Barnes it is a more suspect tutor, the young matador Pedro Romero, to whom Jake looks for moral guidance, and the violence of the bullring that excites Jake's literary imagination. The standard view of Jake Barnes is that of a matured and spiritually evolved hero whose emulation of Romero's performance in the Pamplona bullring provides a way for Jake to recover his manhood—living the more disciplined and purposeful life that Romero's style of bullfighting represents. Jake identifies with the torero because the torero is a man who learns to live with fear and death, just as the crippled soldier has to learn. In Arthur Waldhorn's view, while nothing can restore what has maimed Jake physically, he may at least compensate for feelings of impotence by adopting the masculine world view and militant set of ethics Jake learns from Romero, stressing courage and grace in the face of violence and death.[42]

But *Mother Night*, a novel that mirrors Jake Barnes's postwar experience almost exactly, invites a very different reading of Jake's development under the moral tutelage of Pedro Romero. Vonnegut's announced moral about character as self-construct prompts us to consider whether Jake's adoption of the matador's machismo, and his intentional exposure to death and violence in the bullring, does not intensify the conflict in his nature between gentleness and aggression, compassion and cruelty, separating him still further from the feminine in himself necessary to his growth as a writer. I suggest that Pedro Romero's primordial baiting and slaying of bulls constitutes the most critical moment in the Hemingway hero's moral development to date and that nothing proves more damaging to Jake's hopes for a whole and healthy psyche than his identification with Romero's efforts to control, dominate, and destroy his adversary while he prepares him for killing. If, as Waldhorn argues, Jake's sexual wound is that of the fated Fisher King, whose infertility is restored by the courage and daring of the Grail Knight, Romero, then it is reasonable to assume that the ecstatic, even "religious" emotion Barnes feels at the sight of the chivalric Romero discharging his pent-up rage on the savagely charging bull is sexually charged in nature. Jake's momentary recovery of the detached phallus (or chalice) suggests a reinstatement of patriarchal authority stripped from Dr. Adams by the castrating mother in "The Doctor and the Doctor's Wife." In Thomas Strychacz's words, however, Romero's mode of asserting his manhood is a "system of authority"[43] more destructive than Jake perceives.

Following this logic, it is equally reasonable to assume that the dreaded adversary on whom Jake and the morally perverse Grail Knight seek vengeance through intimidation and violence is the secretly feared and hated feminine, associated, as is the bull, with nature and death, and that the satisfaction that comes from controlling, dominating, and killing the bull seems a victory not only over death, but the *bull*-ish mother. Perhaps unconsciously, this is what Jake feels when Montoya speaks of "the shocking but really very deep secret," the "something lewd" about the bullfight that would not do to expose to outsiders,[44] the story he withholds from himself as well as the reader. As the impotent Barnes watches with steadily building emotion the potent Romero dealing out suffering and death, manipulating and dominating his adversary with almost arrogant self-confidence, the "tail" of the bleeding bull goes up and Romero knows he/she "wanted it again." Romero appears to give it to him/her, offering his body in the illusion that in this bloody courtship to which the tormented, humiliated, and exhausted bull is "blind," "he and the bull were one."[45] But rather than love making, Romero surprises the bull with a climactic sword thrust that provides Jake with an orgasmic high he can never achieve in life.

The Freudian implications of what Howard Campbell refers to as a "fandango of paranoia and masochism"[46] seem clear: as with Campbell's father-in-law—a specialist in slavery, destruction, and death—death produces sexual completion for Jake that life could not. Noth, as murderous and conscienceless as Adolf Eichmann, dies with an erection when he is hanged from a budding apple tree, "rewarded with what he wanted most in all this world . . . rewarded with death."[47] When, if ever, Jake develops the awareness and courage to tell the forbidden story of the dark mother so feared and hated, he will understand as Campbell does that the aggression and blood lust of the bullring results from the same deflected libidinal energy that causes Dr. Adams to load his shotgun while listening to his wife's castrating voice in her "darkened room," the same "substandard libido" Campbell attributes to totalitarian madmen such as Lionel Jones, Bernard B. O'Hare, and August Krapptauer—life-hating schizophrenics unable to distinguish civilization and hydrophobia, imbeciles "that punish and vilify and make war gladly."[48]

While Campbell becomes agonizingly sensitive to his divided soul, Jake Barnes appears relatively unaware of the war within, the separation of his several selves. As if to comment directly on the destructive consequences of Barnes's strong man facade, Jung argues that to achieve self-realization—a successful integration of the male and female parts of himself—it is essential for a man to distinguish between what he is and how he appears to himself and to others, a process of "seeing behind the mask." Yet Jung informs us that it is just such a condition of unconsciousness that makes a man ambiguous to himself and incapable of conceiving his weaknesses. People really do exist, Jung says, "who believe they are what they pretend to be." Their self-deception is so consequential that the exaggerated masculine persona fails to understand what it most desires, never knowing what it is about, leading to tyrannical behavior, loneliness and isolation, and even impotence.[49]

Campbell knows the dangers of becoming the war-mongering, Jew-baiting self he pretended to be, but Barnes's impersonation of Romero's machismo threatens to turn him into the belligerent, tough guy he emulates without understanding its myriad destructive consequences. Jake's remark that he likes to see Cohn hurt suggests a burden of jealousy, anger, and guilt Jake fails to analyze or understand, just as he fails to understand that his hostility toward the homosexuals who dance with Brett reflects fears of his own effeminate weakness. Jake says he knows he should be tolerant, but he wants to hit them nevertheless. In my conversations with Hemingway's first wife, Hadley, in Winter Haven, Florida, during the early 1970s, Hadley spoke of Harold Loeb, the source of the fictional Cohn, as a man who was completely kind and gentle, remarking that "poor Harold" never understood the meanness of Ernest's fictional portrait of him.

Because Barnes remains unconscious of, or at least inarticulate about, these unexplained hostilities, his response to Cohn, both directly in the story and creatively as the story's author, remain strangely inconsistent. Suggesting Jung's notion that a fractured psyche produces a multiplicity of contradictory impulses, inviting the absence of objectivity and prejudice toward the "other," Jake projects his fears of feminine weakness in himself onto Cohn. What Jung identifies as "a fear of insidious truths, of dangerous knowledge, of disagreeable verifications," leads to Jake's directing of deprecating "utterances" toward Cohn, "only to revoke them in the same breath."[50] One moment Barnes strikes out against Cohn, and the next he feels guilty. Pulled one way by his determination to be hard, he castigates Cohn and then pardons him with a show of compassion. Though he liked seeing Mike Campbell punish Cohn, Jake wishes Campbell had not done it because afterward it made him disgusted at himself. Cohn speaks with an air of superior knowledge that irritates Jake, but he tells Bill, "The funny thing is he's nice, too. I like him."[51] Jake has never seen a man in civil life as nervous as Cohn, but while Jake enjoys seeing it, he feels bad for feeling that way.

Jung's explanation that there is little hope such morally schizophrenic individuals will perceive these contradictions themselves buttresses Vonnegut's own critical insight into the larger harm of Jake's "emotionally toned projections," suggesting that Jake's kind of feelings of inferiority underlying hostility may cause one to project "one's unknown face,"[52] one's heart of darkness, onto the world— as for instance the Joneses and the O'Hares do in *Mother Night* and as we see Romero doing by projecting his own blood lust, the pleasure he takes in dominating and killing his adversary, onto the malevolence of bull and the world of the bullring. As Arnold and Cathy Davidson remind us, in this humanly constructed game of nature's "kill or be killed," the bullfight is not at all a fair fight to the finish between man and beast. It is a ritual ceremony enacted by a matador who has trained for years to encounter bulls that have been bred and raised to charge the cape he holds.[53]

If the bullfight is a great tragedy, as Hemingway contends, it is more that of Bernard O'Hare's psychopathic fantasy of good triumphing over evil, which inspires his hatred of and violence toward Campbell, the same self-righteous aggression that justifies the Nazi slaughter of Jews. Marc Baldwin suggests it is the same fiction of man's triumph over nature in the bullring that glorified male machismo and violence in the defense of America's manifest destiny to become a world power and that justified the brutal domination of Africa's "lower races" portrayed so magnificently by Conrad's *Heart of Darkness;* bullfight apologists sanctify horrors under the guise of a religious experience to make the senseless and ugly goring of horses and the subsequent slaughter of the bulls "look like a purposeful and beautiful dance."[54] In this light the jocular, racial remarks Jake and his friends direct toward Cohn suggest a dangerous, underlying bigotry as potentially horrific as Campbell's Jew-hating speeches as Nazi propagandist, disguising the capacity for homicidal violence of such insane nationalists and unabashed bigots as O'Hare and Dr. Lionel Jones. Mike Campbell, Brett Ashley's fiancé, seems hardly bothered by the fact she sleeps with other men, as long as "they weren't ever Jews."[55] During the scene where Jake takes Mike, Bill, and Brett to watch bulls being led out of their cages into corrals, Mike Campbell baits Cohn unmercifully, insisting Cohn ought to love being a steer, since he's so docile and is always hanging around. Though we hear nothing from Jake, his silence is self-incriminating. Earlier, when Jake's friend and fellow expatriate Harvey Stone calls Cohn a moron to his face, a case of arrested development, Jake's silence suggests tacit agreement. Baldwin argues that when Jake several times tells Cohn, "Go to hell," he virtually condemns Cohn to "an afterlife of otherness among the eternally excluded."[56]

In contrast to Vonnegut's prioritizing of self-awareness as the basis for Campbell's moral development, Barnes's admiration and imitation of Romero's aggression and stoical reserve in the bullring will neither encourage the introspective habit of mind required to mend his anguished soul nor serve him well as a writer. Jung observed that without understanding the destructive, unconscious promptings of the false masculine self, the unaware individual "behaves more or less like a primitive," like someone not only incapable of controlling aggressive impulses but singularly incapable of moral judgment.[57] Like Manuel Garcia, the matador Hemingway apotheosized in his earlier story "The Undefeated," Romero is a profoundly primitive individual for whom thinking is less important in the bullring than instinct, which will tell him unfailingly what to do—how to control and dominate his opponent and how to kill. The tragic effect of Barnes's aversion to self-analysis—a retreat from self-understanding that correlates with Nick Adams's refusal to fish the deeper currents of "Big Two-Hearted River" or Krebs's withdrawal into solitude and cynical despair in "Soldier's Home"—later surfaces catastrophically in the embittered and aging Robert Cantwell.

As if we needed further evidence that Jake willfully hides his vulnerable self behind the matador's mask, he admits that he cries in the night, one of the cardinal sins for which Cohn is condemned. Jake's night terrors become particularly understandable in light of Jung's discussion of unconscious fears resulting from loss or denial of the anima, or primal mother. Because the mother is the first bearer of the "soul image," someone who protects her son against the dangers that threaten from the darkness of his psyche, separation from her invites not only an infinity of sufferings resulting from her loss but an unconscious reaching back to the mother who shielded his childhood from terrors of night. Surely it is this primal fear that "bursts in" on Nick Adams, Jake Barnes, and Frederic Henry in the night with "annihilating force"[58] when they feel their souls slipping away from them. Jake, like the narrator of the Nick Adams stories, may prefer to keep his mother mute, but as in "Ten Indians," her unacknowledged presence is as sure to complicate Jake's quest for psychic wellness as that buried neurosis Eliot Rosewater's doctor calls the most massively defended he's ever attempted to treat.

As to the effects of Jake's flight from self-awareness on his aspirations to become a writer, Baldwin asks whether Barnes's determination to simplify complex or threatening realities by adopting the matador's moral stoicism, his "code of silence," does not perpetuate his normally benumbed state, limiting self-understanding and complicating Jake's reliability as narrator.[59] People such as Jake, Brett, Bill, and the count, who have been deeply hurt by life but refuse to acknowledge the depth of the hurt, contrast with Cohn, who has a habit of talking openly about his suffering. But Baldwin asks what may be hidden from readers by a narrator who highlights what he wants them to see and blurs or omits what he does not, a narrator who will not and—at times perhaps cannot—give utterance to a wide range of thoughts and feelings because of his stoical mask, particularly about parents Jake evidently wants nothing more to do with.

While neither money nor patriotism interests Howard Campbell, he confesses that the opportunity to star in a real-life drama of pure good at war with pure evil is too irresistible to refuse. The corrida offers the same opportunity for "some pretty grand acting" and potency-inspiring demonstrations of bravery that Campbell admits inspired his melodramas and attracted him to the role of Nazi propagandist.[60] In Jake's eyes, Romero is the "authentic" hero—a "hundred times braver than ordinary men"—whom Campbell knows he himself secretly longed to play.[61] The Pamplona bullring becomes, in Thomas Strychacz's words, "a theater of manhood-on-display,"[62] a drama of life and death that Romero performs as self-consciously as any other actor, ever aware of and bound to please an evaluative audience that directs boos at bullfighters lacking virility and grand applause for those worthy of being dubbed men. Hemingway identified himself and his art with the bullfight as theater; he wrote to Ezra Pound: "I take great and unintellectual pleasure in the immediate triumphs of the bull ring with their reward in ovations," something "literary guys have to wait until they are 89 years old to get." The "Plaza," he said, is the only remaining place "where valor and art can combine for success."[63]

According to Melvin Backman, we get additional macho theater when the superior boxer Cohn punishes Romero with his fists, knocking the matador down repeatedly, and Romero displays what Backman calls the bullfighter's "hard male core" by refusing to quit the fight,[64] a scene as melodramatically conceived as Bernard B. O'Hare's perception of himself as St. George and Campbell as the dragon, pure good triumphing over evil, or George Kraft's fantasy of Campbell as Don Quixote, himself as Sancho Panza, and Resi Noth as Dulcinea.[65]

In this arena where men violently demonstrate their manhood or its absence, Barnes becomes unusually articulate about performances that are "real" rather than "fake." He explains to Brett that whereas other bullfighters use tricks to fake the appearance of danger, Romero's bullfighting gave real emotion because he "kept the absolute purity of line in his movements and always quietly and calmly let the horns pass him close each time."[66] Though we see Howard Campbell similarly concerned with separating the "fake" from the "real," his entire narrative is a lesson in postmodern simulacrum—that is, an understanding that such distinctions arise not from eternal truths but rather from human self-determinations. In response to the belief of homicidally insane Nazis such as August Krapptauer and Adolf Eichmann that there is only one truth—that of the supremacy of the white race—Campbell knows their dreams of racial purity are as deadly a pretense as his playacting the Nazi propagandist, for which he and they must be held responsible. Such, Campbell concludes, was their "paltry understanding of the God-like human act of invention."[67] Barnes is more certain that he can rely on objective reality as criteria for discerning truth and falsehood in art as in bullfighting—keeping faith with Romero's "absolute purity of line"—and as a basis for identifying good people from bad. Brett is "good," one of "us," because like Jake and Bill Gorton, she takes a serious interest in the bullfight and thrills to the qualities of Romero's manly performance. But Robert Cohn—and to a degree Mike Campbell—are "bad" because "they" lack the composure and self-possession of true aficionados.

The problem with Barnes's certainty that he can identify unerringly the fake from the real of Romero's bullfighting is that, in light of Campbell's critique of moral absolutes and hierarchies of values that divide individuals and nations from one another, Jake's certainty bears a disturbingly close resemblance to the moral absolutism that motivates the quest for racial purity by white supremacists such as Bernard B. O'Hare and Lionel Jones, bigoted, homicidal maniacs ready to commit mayhem to eradicate what they decide constitutes evil. The same paranoid logic that causes Bernard O'Hare to focus on Howard Campbell as the source of all his and America's moral failings—his efforts to keep the American blood stream pure—causes Romero to rationalize the ritualistic slaying of bulls and Jake to represent his dislike of Cohn as something less onerous than bigotry. The same belief in racial purity that ironically excludes Campbell's household of white supremacists from each other holds Jake's group of dissolute expatriates together, while at the same time differences of gender, race, and religion divide them and cause them to humiliate and dominate each other as Romero does to his bulls.

Romero explains to Brett that he must kill his friends the bulls before they kill him first—the hostile, always threatening "other," whether in the form of dangerous bulls, unmanly homosexuals, haughty, misbehaving Jews, or dominating women. Robert Cohn is excluded from "Club *Afición*," a haven for bullfight enthusiasts, particularly white Christian men, supposedly because of what Jake portrays as Cohn's tendency to self-pity and sentimentality and because Cohn lacks the tragic life experience and stoical resolve of Jake, Brett, and Count Mippipopolous, but the likelihood is that Cohn is denied membership to the ingroup because of his Jewishness. Secret, narrow, and exclusive, this fabrication of aficionados bears a striking resemblance to Campbell and Helga's "Nation of Two," whose members Howard says became "as content as any narrow minded religious nut anywhere."[68] Jake's admittance demands a spiritual examination the answers to which only truly devout lovers of the bullfight will know. The secret, paranoid, Jew-hating club to which O'Hare, Lionel Jones, Father Keeley, and August Krapptauer belong swears loyalty to the same moral absolutes that define Jake's group—that its members be pure of heart and passionate in their beliefs. Krapptauer's divisive and malignant sort of truth, Campbell says, would be with mankind forever, as long as men and women listened to their hearts instead of their minds. O'Hare hopes to vent his myriad frustrations by focusing on a single, undiluted enemy, just as Jake compensates for feelings of inner helplessness by watching Romero focus and discharge his pent-up aggressions on the object of the bull, a definite, threatening enemy whom it is possible to hate and destroy.

It is all too true that what George Kraft says to Campbell applies to Barnes as well—that what Campbell needs to begin writing again and to write truthfully in a way that may redeem the betrayed feminine in his life. Near the end of his confessions, Campbell concludes, "The part of me that wanted to tell the truth got turned into an expert liar! The lover in me got turned into a pornographer! The artist in me got turned into ugliness such as the world has rarely seen before."[69] Whereas Jake Barnes ultimately aligns Brett Ashley with the world's destructive forces that constitute the conspiratorial "they," Howard Campbell knows full well that the uncaring, pathological part of himself, which finds playing at war and creating melodramatic contrasts between good and evil so compelling, has betrayed the women in his life and tragically subverted the artist within.

Campbell understands how his willful enablement of the Nazi war effort has helped turn Helga and Resi into those "ghostlike . . . God-awful old and starved and moth-eaten" women they see themselves as after the war, disembodied, will-less, and unable to feel.[70] The victims of war or of other forms of totalitarian machinery that uses them for inhuman ends, they become like those nameless, sexless, and shapeless female prisoners of war etched so deeply into Campbell's memory, "squinting, lumpy, hopeless, grubby ragbags . . . pretty as catfish wrapped in mattress ticking."[71] No matter what he feels he really was beneath the Nazi exterior, he knows Helga and Resi tragically believed he meant the things he said about the races of man and the machines of history, so they were happy to entertain the troops. Remarking that was how he lost her, Campbell unconsciously associates Rudy Waltz's murderous father's love of guns and worship of Adolf Hitler with his own responsibility for Helga's suffering. Explaining that Helga often entertained the troops within the sound of enemy guns, he asks, "Enemy guns? Somebody's guns, anyway."[72]

As noted earlier, Arthur Waldhorn concludes that the novel's final words confirm Jake's growth. Countering Brett's belief that, if not for the war, she and Jake might have achieved real love with the sarcastic retort "Isn't it pretty to think so,"[73] Jake trades off false hope and romantic illusion and thus salvages integrity, discipline, and control, precisely the attributes of Romero's manly style of bull-fighting. But in support of Vonnegut's critique, Earl Rovit argues that rather than making Jake a wiser and more complete person, someone who comes into his own as a creative artist, Jake's attraction to violence and gore in the bullring encourages his tendency to belligerence and stoical reserve, creating a wider separation of Jake's "several selves" than ever, placing in doubt the possibilities of a healthy, creative response.[74]

In agreement with Spilka and Strychacz, Svoboda explains that we can best understand Barnes's contradictory, ultimately dismissive attitudes toward Cohn and Brett as the author's own painful ambivalence, a simultaneous attraction and repulsion toward the feminine in himself, a need to express what could not be told, except obliquely, beneath the narrative's surface. As Svoboda does, we need only observe the difference between the negative portraits of Cohn and Brett in Jake's story and Hemingway's notebook intentions for both characters, which project them as heroes,[75] to recognize that the author's satire of Cohn's unmanning and the depiction of Brett as a man-eating "Circe" represent the war within the author, one part that wants to acknowledge the feminine in himself and the other overriding part that must deny the feminine as weakness, the dreaded "other." Just as Barnes is of two minds about Robert Cohn, so he waxes uncertain about Brett, a simultaneous attraction and repulsion Spilka cites as a reflection of Hemingway's childhood twinning with his older sister Marcelline.[76]

Clearly Brett possesses the heroic qualities that critics such as Linda Miller, Kathy Willingham, and Linda Wagner-Martin see in her. Wagner-Martin cites Hemingway's original vision of Brett, excised from the final manuscript, as a woman "clearly positive, brave, imaginative, and loving,"[77] perhaps the novel's central figure. Whereas Jake is unable to love Brett or anyone else (an admission Svoboda explains Hemingway deleted from the final manuscript),[78] Brett is made to look callous by marrying a man she does not love, presumably for his money and title, to look self-indulgent and unsympathetic in her inability to just live with Jake out of love and to seem promiscuous in her ongoing need to fornicate regardless of the pain it causes others. It helps Jake's case against that "damned Jew Cohn" to show that, while Brett initially sympathizes with Cohn, she too finds him repulsive. She hates him herself, she confesses to Jake. Ironically Jake's attempts to incriminate her as sexually deviant, a sister to the harlot Georgette with whom she is paired, says more about his gender phobias than her looseness.[79]

Spilka asks whether Jake's perceptions of Brett's perverse desires do not describe his own deepest yearnings as well. He suggests that this pattern in Hemingway's fiction of the rejected feminine, from the girls Nick treats so casually to the harsh mother figure to Brett, Cohn, and Catherine Barkley, surely indicates something is going on that requires delving beneath the surface. In light of the exchange of sexual roles in *The Garden of Eden*, where David Bourne imagines himself as one of the lesbian lovers in a mysterious stature by Rodin, Jake may imagine playing such a female role with Brett Ashley.[80] Jung notes that one of the mythic mother's infinite variety of representations is that of "a hermaphrodite,"[81] the ideal image of the fully gender-integrated soul. Similarly, analogous to but more disguised than George Kraft's open homosexual overtures to Campbell, with whom he bonds as Jake does with Bill Gorton—Campbell eschews boundaries of any kind—Jake's subliminal comparison of penis sizes in the form of counting trout during their fishing expedition anticipates more blatant homoerotic tensions in *The Garden of Eden*.

No wonder that as the embodiment of multiple taboo sexual desires, Jake/Hemingway exalts Brett to the level of Dionysian goddess, surrounded by wreathed dancers when the fiesta at Pamplona explodes, and she walks through the crowd, her head up, as though the fiesta were being staged in her honor. Jung explains that the elevation of the female to the status of goddess exists as an archetypal paradigm for protecting society against erotic desires. As expressed in Dante's *Divine Comedy*, the image of Woman is exalted into the heavenly, mystical figure of the Mother of God, the "Virgin Mother." While Lady Ashley is certainly no virgin and more pagan than Christian, she does become a vessel of devotion for the men around her, a "siren" who invites unruly passions and therefore must, for her sake and the protection of the men who lust for her, be elevated to a position of holiness and sublimity.[82] This underscores the notion that Jake/Hemingway's repressed libido results from profound frustration over the woman he fervently desires but cannot have, especially if that woman represents repressed erotic fantasies for a mother or sister. As Jung explains, in the face of such overwhelming passions, the boundlessly desired object is unveiled as an idol and man is forced to his knees before the divine image, delivered from the curse of the object's spell. That this particular goddess presides over a wasteland of infertile, wounded lovers—Brett is denied entrance to Chapel Perilous because she possesses demonic as well as spiritual traits—deepens and enriches her mythic qualities, especially as they explain Jake's portrait of Brett as both goddess and witch. In Jungian thought the notion of Brett as persecutor rather than "caldron of renewal" has roots in mythologies that precede Christian consciousness, religions also erotic in origin, but which protect against the tyranny of forbidden primitive passions by devaluing rather than elevating the object of love.[83]

While Howard Campbell's vigorous self-scrutiny frees him from what he identifies as a deathly "freeze," a form of moral paralysis he writes into cynical couplets declaring that everything was probably all for the best, Barnes's flight from thought and language into primitive violence and ritual petrifies him at his very roots, essentially the time of his Midwestern childhood when he learned from his father the habit of noncommunication that precludes the introspection and self-understanding necessary to emotional and creative growth. One thinks of Woodly's characterization of Harold Ryan in *Happy Birthday, Wanda June*, when Harold represents himself "as man was meant to be—a vengeful ape who murders," "a living fossil. Like the cockroaches and the horseshoe crabs." "Evolution has made you a clown," Woodly says. "Simple butchers like you are obsolete!" When Ryan asks whether he was ever of any use, Woodly replies, "Never, for when you began to kill for the fun of it, you became the chief source of agony of mankind."[84] Perhaps Jake's identification with the forces of violence and death renders the truths of his story worse than unreliable, but rather those of the conscienceless storyteller Campbell labels a "pornographic liar," the moral pornography of the writer Jake admits being, who enjoys picturing the bedroom scenes of his friends.

In a sense both *Mother Night* and *The Sun Also Rises* represent what Campbell calls an "adventure in the dark,"[85] a venture by both authors into the most forbidden parts of themselves, where—as Faust's Mephistopheles says in Vonnegut's introduction—light disputes with Mother Night. By referring to Barnes as "an aspect" of his beloved, Brett Ashley, Spilka anticipates a major artistic development in Hemingway's later work, in which he, like Vonnegut, used characters allegorically to represent the split-off parts of his and his protagonists' complex psyche. In this view, for instance, Hemingway becomes an amalgam of Cohn and Barnes and Barnes and Brett, and Vonnegut becomes a combination of Campbell and Helga and Kraft and Resi, as well as such loathsome psychic dwellers as Lionel Jones, Krapptauer, and Bernard B. O'Hare. Vonnegut's allegorical journey takes him into "the basement darkness,"[86] which represents the potential evil in himself as well the literal dwelling of racist psychopaths. Dante or his mythic brethren Orpheus is the prototypal spiritual hero both writers are destined to become, men whose person and art are transformed through the rescue of the sacred feminine in themselves. But for now the descent of Vonnegut and Campbell results in spiritual enlightenment, while Hemingway and Barnes, who identify with Romero's courage to stare down ferocious bulls, are yet unprepared to travel deeply enough into the darkest part of themselves to understand the hidden sexual wound that haunts Barnes in the night and leads to the self-destructive dismissal of the regenerative anima.

However autobiographical these novels are, the question of the authors' "progress" cannot be answered strictly in terms of their protagonists' situations at the end of these stories. Rather, as becomes even more critical in tracing the creative/spiritual evolution of Vonnegut and Hemingway in *Slaughterhouse-Five* and *A Farewell to Arms*, it is the symbolic relationship each protagonist bears to his creator that explains the authors' relative success or lack of success in dealing with pain and suffering, especially their success in recognizing mistakes they have made in creating false selves by which to meet a hostile world. While Hemingway identified closely with the demoralized Barnes, declaring in the galley proofs of *The Sun Also Rises* that "he made the mistake of having been Mr. Jake Barnes,"[87] Vonnegut used a method of narrative framing to establish his authorial identity independent of Campbell's, in which case Campbell is less a manifestation of Vonnegut's own fatalism than a projection of the schizophrenia of self resulting from traumatic experience.

Vonnegut framed *Mother Night* by speaking from a distance about the novel and its relationship to his own experience. Then he moved into a half fiction through the "Editor's Note," in which Vonnegut acts as the editor of the fictitious autobiography written by Howard Campbell. Finally he moved into Campbell himself and the actual narrative fiction. Vonnegut's introduction rejects Campbell's belief in a core self, described in the "Editor's Note" as "a very good me, the real me . . . hidden deep inside."[88] Perhaps it is Vonnegut's postmodern awareness that reality, like storytelling, is "all play-acting," a game the writer makes up, a creative plaything that can create humane new perspectives as well as deaden the imagination, which saves Campbell from moral disaster and Vonnegut from the fatalism whose ultimate toll on Campbell is suicide. In Vonnegut's view, if Hemingway could have put the words "so it goes" into the mouth of a scapegoat protagonist like Billy Pilgrim or Kilgore Trout, perhaps he would have been able to differentiate himself from the tragic fate of Barnes and Campbell, portentously that of his own tragic death.

# Three

# Duty Dance with Death

*A Farewell to Arms* and *Slaughterhouse-Five*

■

Do not all the achievements of a poet's predecessors
rightfully belong to him? Only by making the riches of the
others our own do we bring anything great into being.
Harold Bloom, *The Anxiety of Influence*

I will stop only a time with the night . . .
I will duly pass the day O my mother, and duly return to you.
Walt Whitman, *The Sleepers*

While in his autobiographical first chapter of *Slaughterhouse-Five* Vonnegut reminds us how difficult his Dresden nightmare had been to write about, sufficient time had evidently passed since their Dresden/Fossalta traumas to allow both writers to approach their "duty dance with death" in earnest in *Slaughterhouse-Five* and *A Farewell to Arms*—to put their wartime nightmares to paper rather than "dance" around them[1] as they had in *Mother Night* and *The Sun Also Rises*. Despite Vonnegut's description of their differences—the thousand years Vonnegut said divided him from Hemingway—probably no two works more aptly demonstrate the common art and vision of these literary warriors than *A Farewell to Arms* and *Slaughterhouse-Five*.[2] While *Mother Night* and *The Sun Also Rises* testify to the painful psychic fragmentation of the wounded soldier after the war—and the search for positive values and ways of ordering their lives in a hostile, postwar environment—*A Farewell to Arms* and *Slaughterhouse-Five* show us closer up why the violence and meaningless butchery of war so traumatized and demoralized Jake Barnes and Howard Campbell.

Though Vonnegut said people with such excruciating wounds risk further destruction in looking back, the fate of Lot's wife, who turned to a pillar of salt, he welcomed the gain in awareness and self-possession, identifying with the speaker in Theodore Roethke's poem "The Waking"—who takes his "waking"

59

slowly, but learns by going where he "[has] to go."[3] On the other hand, Vonnegut's satirical representation of *A Farewell to Arms* as a novel in the spirit of Howard Campbell's melodramas, romanticizing war and creating heroic roles for the knightly Frederic Henry and the fair maiden Catherine Barkley, suggests that Vonnegut saw the mask of machismo hardening into the permanent caricature of Harold Ryan in *Happy Birthday, Wanda June*. Though Frederic Henry is a far more complex and interesting character than the self-parodying, masquerading matador Philip Rawlings of *The Fifth Column*, Henry possesses enough of Rawlings's disconcerting bravado to remind us of the macho posturing Vonnegut derided in Harold Ryan.

Vonnegut observed that in *A Farewell to Arms* Frederic and Catherine have too much fun drinking and fornicating for the novel to be taken seriously as an antiwar book, but it is clear that Frederic's and Billy Pilgrim's war wounds are those of their authors, similarly complex and traumatic. Reminding us that the wounded soldier unable to sleep is one of the central themes of Hemingway's work, Frederic Henry, like his immediate predecessors Jake Barnes and Nick Adams, not only suffers sleepless nights but fears shutting his eyes in the dark lest his soul leave his body. Billy Pilgrim's exposure to death and violence induces something worse than sleeplessness, that state of "catalepsies" that lands Eliot Rosewater in an asylum. Given the severity of psychological damage both Frederic and Billy experience, Celine's "cracked skull" seems a particularly apt reference for their metaphorical head wounds. Violence and the meaningless butchery of war so traumatize and demoralize Henry and Pilgrim that each develops a similarly despairing, naturalistic view of existence as perpetually warlike. They are dangerously pessimistic men whose shattered consciousness and flight from complexity and social responsibility reflect their author's own sense of vulnerability and disillusionment.

In the authors' mutually powerful portrayal of the slaughterhouse of war—the brutality of battle, the impermanence of love, and the impossibility of any metaphysical solution for Frederic Henry or Billy Pilgrim—it would at first seem to be the feelings of futility and helplessness war created in both writers, rather than solutions to the violence of war, that occupied them from first to last. Frederic Henry is psychically as well as physically shot to pieces by the end of his story, and Billy Pilgrim emerges from his underground bomb shelter "a broken kite on a stick," headed for a mental hospital. The panorama of death and violence that defines Billy Pilgrim's world prompts Vonnegut to say that, "even if wars didn't keep coming like glaciers, there would still be plain old death."[4] "War time is all time," Arthur Waldhorn explains about Hemingway's world, a metaphor for the "hostile implacability" of the universe toward living and loving. In such a savage, predatory world, Waldhorn says, "when men occasionally fail to destroy one another, nature leaps into the breach."[5]

Reminiscent of the scene in which Frederic Henry likens human beings to ants burned alive in a camp fire, the slaughterhouse where Billy is kept as a prisoner in Dresden becomes a grotesque image of human beings dehumanized by war, hanging like butchered animals on hooks. Billy also sees himself as a "bug trapped in amber."6 In his famous denunciation of the phony ideals for which the war has been fought, Frederic Henry decides that war so dehumanizes individuals that they become no different than butchered cattle. "I had seen nothing sacred," he says, "and the sacrifices were like the stockyards at Chicago if nothing was done with the meat except to bury it."7 Hemingway sees no more spiritual significance to these inglorious deaths than to the deaths of horses and mules in "A Natural History of the Dead," which brings to mind Howard Campbell's contention that the mutilations of war left him feeling like a pig taken apart in the Chicago stockyards. After the explosion of a munitions factory, Hemingway commented on the ghoulish carcasses of mules and horses as well as men, women, and children, or rather on their exploded fragments. "The first thing that you found about the dead," Hemingway reported, "was that, hit badly enough, they died like animals."8 Philip Young summarizes Hemingway's world at war as "one in which things do not bear fruit, but explode, break, decompose, or are eaten away."9

For both protagonists everything eventually dies or goes to pieces. Frederic Henry declares late in *A Farewell to Arms* that there is simply no defense against the ravages of death; the world has to kill people to break them. Billy Pilgrim would certainly concur: "So it goes," Billy wearily laments about the endless death and violence around him, now as always without cessation or sense. The shell that wounds Frederic Henry is flung blindly just as the plane crash that kills everybody but Billy happens randomly and senselessly. Catherine's death—a freak biological accident that defies any sense or meaning or justice in the world—is as arbitrary as that of the death of Edgar Derby, who enters the war out of pure motives and whose efforts to provide helpful leadership to Billy and his fellow prisoners proves futile in protecting Derby from the stupidity and absurdity of war.10 While Dresden goes up in flames, Derby is arrested for taking a teapot and shot by a firing squad.11

Hemingway's work constitutes a study of death and violence that amounts to a lesson in mortality,12 but if one counts deaths that are predicted or imagined as well as those that have actually occurred, there is a greater proliferation of corpses in *Slaughterhouse-Five* than in any other twentieth-century novel. Though spared Frederic Henry's physical wound, Billy Pilgrim is eventually driven mad by the killing machines of war, which tear and mutilate the body and create such sadistic creatures as the revenge-crazed Paul Lazzaro, who carries a list in his head of people he is going to have killed after the war, and the equally rabid Roland Weary, from whom Billy learns about wounds that will not heal, about "blood gutters" and such tortures as having your head drilled through with a dentist's drill, and about being staked to an anthill in the desert.

For both Frederic Henry and Billy Pilgrim, there comes a moment when the madness of war overwhelms them. For Henry, after the desperate retreat at Caporetto, any remaining notions of patriotism or devotion to duty are nullified by countless instances of cruelty, betrayal, and incompetence among his own fellow soldiers, climaxing in needless executions; Henry is mistaken for a German imposter and nearly executed himself. Overwhelmed by similar displays of human warpedness and injustice, Billy Pilgrim experiences a final unbalancing he likens to being stretched on the rack when he remembers the night Dresden was destroyed—the firestorm that "ate everything . . . that would burn, that turned the city into a desert and people into little petrified human beings."[13]

Billy's experience consists of the same maddening contrasts between human ideals and the grotesque realities of war that force Frederic Henry to seek a separate peace and Helga Noth and Howard Campbell to retreat into their "Nation of Two": "bucolic interludes sandwiched between bouts of violence . . . and sanctioned public murder."[14] Thus both men, as Robert Penn Warren says of Frederic Henry, cut themselves from the confused world, which symbolically appears for Frederic as the routed army at Caporetto. When Frederic makes his baptismal plunge into the Tagliamento, he comes into the world of the man alone, no longer supported by and involved in society.[15]

Threatened with annihilation and potentially disabled by fear and cynicism, the Hemingway and Vonnegut heroes face precisely the same dilemma: how to manage existential despair so great that insanity or suicide pose real threats. Billy and Frederic hunger for the sense of order and assurance that most seem to find in religious belief, but they cannot find grounds for such belief. How then do they avoid the complete dispiritedness for which they appear headed and retain faith in the value of human effort, which nevertheless dooms noble human beings such as Catherine Barkley and Edgar Derby? However, Warren and Loree Rackstraw agree that for Frederic and Billy successfully confronting the existential void means more than personal survival. It means staying alive with decency in a world that has crippled them, giving moral significance to the confusions of living.[16] It is how each author defines "moral significance" that divides them. Hemingway acquired ideas about how to live humanly, with courage and stoical bearing, from the world of the bullfight, a religious ceremony glorifying death and violence in the service of domination, whereas Vonnegut formulated ideas of conduct from Christ's Sermon on the Mount, adopting kindness and restraint as moral imperatives. The contrast seems striking in light of Hemingway's story "Today is Friday," about Christ's Crucifixion. While the story says nothing about ideals of charity or compassion, it conspicuously praises Christ's manly bearing—his courage and ability to endure suffering. Wendolyn Tetlow offers a useful way to distinguish the two modes of conduct. In Hemingway's case the world as essentially cruel and predatory is "accepted and assimilated."[17] Violence is justified because that is what it takes to prevail in a violent world, to prove that you are tougher and more courageous. Vonnegut chose to repudiate animal instinct, encouraging a loving rather than adversarial relationship with nature.

Throughout *A Farewell to Arms* and *Slaughterhouse-Five*, however, the only way Billy Pilgrim and Frederic Henry find to deflect pain is to continue the dangerous evasive strategies of their younger selves, to retreat from consciousness and responsibility, which nullifies or at least postpones psychic healing. Frederic masks feelings of vulnerability behind a tough-guy stoicism that borders on cruelty, the schizophrenic fabrications of Pedro Romero and Jake Barnes; and Billy, his emotional fuses completely blown, practices a numbness of response that leaves him as robotically dazed and compliant as Howard Campbell. The authors' ironic, understated styles convey the protagonists' escape into what Millicent Bell calls "the dreamless sleep of apathy"—a screen of simple words and short, declarative sentences meant to numb emotional pain and protect the hero from further horrors.[18]

In their mutual strategies of disengagement from war, the adoption of false selves and dangerously escapist fantasy worlds is foreshadowed by the presence of playacting that Howard Campbell finds so lethal if taken as real, many instances of masquerading and game playing. Life is theater for Frederic, and Billy can relate only to imaginary scenes and people. In the prison-camp performance of "Cinderella," Cinderella's boots fit Billy perfectly—"Billy Pilgrim was Cinderella, and Cinderella was Billy Pilgrim."[19]

No wonder that, like Jake Barnes and Howard Campbell, Frederic Henry and Billy Pilgrim are led by their self-protective masks to disengage from war completely. Henry seeks refuge through flight to Switzerland with Catherine in what he calls their "separate peace," a womblike condition in which the lovers determine to survive by being loyal to a world composed only of themselves. In turn Billy Pilgrim hallucinates the "morphine paradise"[20] of Tralfamadore, an equally dubious utopia, in which he secludes himself with the movie star Montana Wildhack, who—like Catherine—becomes pregnant. Montana's promises of sanctuary and new life prove as abortive as the flight to Switzerland by Hemingway's doomed lovers in *A Farewell to Arms* and the withdrawal of the lovers into their "Nation of Two" in Vonnegut's *Mother Night*. Not only do the Tralfamadorians—with their earthly combination of ferocity and spectacular weaponry and their talent for horror—not improve Billy's vision, but Billy's flight from the responsibilities of "wakeful humanity" leads directly into what John Tilton calls "a spiritual oubliette."[21] Billy trades his dignity and self-integrity for an illusion of comfort and security, becoming a machine like his Tralfamadorian captors.

Just as delusively Frederic and Catherine's flight from outer reality results in what Millicent Bell calls "an almost animal-like isolation and state of numbness and ennui,"[22] a loss of selfhood exactly like Billy's, canceling any hope of new life. Many readers view the "separate peace" the escaped lovers make in Switzerland as an opportunity for Frederic to practice what Catherine has taught him about the value of selfless love. Without question Catherine displays the wisdom, courage, and honesty appropriate to her role as Frederic's tutor. It is Catherine, Sandra Spanier explains, who gives Frederic ample lessons in the heroic declaration that "a man can be destroyed but not defeated." Frederic, says Spilka, is "tenderized" by love and made to care like the caring Catherine, in whom his selfhood is invested.[23] For a while at least, Frederic abandons hunting, sports, and war for a world circumscribed by the lovers' bed.

But reminiscent of the dangerously closed, private, and self-indulgent "Nation of Two" that Howard Campbell and Helga Noth seek in *Mother Night*, Spilka and Millicent Bell agree that the rapture of Frederic and Catherine is never more suspect than in their supposed Switzerland utopia. As an adequate solution to the moral and social evils from which they seek to flee, their personal version of Howard Campbell's romantic fantasy with Helga and Resi remains problematic at best. What Resi says to Campbell echoes Catherine's sentiments to Henry almost exactly, bearing out Campbell's warnings about the myopic nature of "uncritical love." The prospect of life without Howard finds Resi saying, "I am sorry I have nothing to live for. . . . All I have is love for one man . . . but he is so used up he can't love any more."[24] Catherine tells Frederic, "My life used to be full of everything and now if you aren't with me I haven't a thing in the world."[25] Frederic and Catherine's supposed Edenic escape invokes Vonnegut's satire of Hemingway's aversion to marriage and settling down, avoiding a life of civilian responsibilities—becoming a father, getting a regular job. Neither Hemingway nor Frederic Henry, Spilka says, is ready to assume such unromantic possibilities.[26]

Under the impress of war, Strychacz argues, Frederic's caring about Catherine develops too rapidly to be anything more than self-conscious role-playing, more "sexual excitement"[27] than attentive love, as the priest has defined that more transcendent experience. "If I ever get it," meaning true love, Frederic tells the priest, "I will tell you."[28] As with Jake Barnes, we wonder if that moment ever comes. In its place Frederic daydreams of being with Catherine in a hotel room, where he conceives of her as a magnificent whore, evoking the image of Billy Pilgrim with his face pressed to Montana Wildhack's swelling bosom in a similar masquerade. "I was not made to think," Frederic acknowledges. "I was made to eat. My God, yes. Eat and drink and sleep with Catherine."[29] When Catherine agrees to flee with him to Switzerland, he says, "You're a fine girl. Let's get back into bed."[30] Whereas Henry's animal appetite never lags, his capacity for caring is suspect.

Linda Wagner-Martin argues that love for the Hemingway hero generally means erotic desire blended with the concept of courtly love. Catherine, she says, exists as lady to Henry's knight errant.[31] Bolstering Vonnegut's point that Frederic and Catherine represent a good-looking couple having too much fun outside wedlock and having to quit in the full flush of romantic feeling, Wagner-Martin sees blocked desire as the energizing element of Hemingway's romantic treatment of sexual love: "The intensity of the lover's passion is directly related to the extent to which their love is doomed."[32] A genius at replicating the conventions of popular romance, Hemingway created the moral fantasy that love is all-sufficient and that, even if the story ends in death of one or both lovers rather than a permanently happy marriage, it ends in such a way as to suggest that the love relationship has been of lasting and permanent import.[33]

Bell calls Frederic and Catherine's relationship a failure of responsible adult love, a "universe of two" that continues to constrict in "their drift toward death."[34] As Frederic reads wistfully about the war in the Swiss newspapers, we see few signs that his feelings for Catherine differ much from those of the flippant, casual lover who likens love to a game of bridge, little evidence of the selfless love Catherine and the priest represent. Catherine dies while Frederic worries about what to have at his next meal or what wine to order. His dead baby looks to him like a skinned rabbit, and he says he has no feeling at all for the child.

While Billy Pilgrim's disguises leave him dazed and without identity, his passivity seems in Vonnegut's view to be less morally objectionable than Frederic Henry's mask of stoical toughness, misogyny, and occasional cruelty. Apropos of Vonnegut's moral to *Mother Night*—that we are what we pretend to be—Frederic's soldierly masquerade becomes unnervingly real. What Strychacz calls Henry's "shifting articulations of identity"[35] return us to Vonnegut's essential critique of *A Farewell to Arms* and to the authors' contrary views of what it means to fill the existential void "decently" or "humanly." We have noted that in *Mother Night* Vonnegut accuses Hemingway of glorifying war—of heroic posing and the idealization of manly toughness—and of associating honor with death and killing. Are these criticisms still more pertinent to *A Farewell to Arms* and, if so, what do they portend in understanding differences in each writer's vision of life and war?

Certainly Hemingway's many descriptions of war wounds in *A Farewell to Arms* portray war as anything but romantic or glorious. Scenes showing the random horrors of death and suffering on the battlefield not only rival but exceed Vonnegut's in realistic detail. Wagner-Martin points out that Hemingway's readers cannot escape the recognition of "relentless blood and dreadful death" and the frustration of medical knowledge to save lives.[36] At the moment of Frederic's own terrible wound, when he learns it was a mistake to think you just died, he describes the suffering of a particularly brave Italian soldier named Passini, hit by the same trench-mortar shell: "His legs were toward me and I saw in the dark and the light that they were both smashed above the knee. One leg was gone and the other was held by tendons and part of the trouser and the stump twitched and jerked as though it were not connected." Passini screams in pain until, Henry reports, "Then he was quiet, biting his arm, the stump of his leg twitching."[37] Henry tries in vain to make a tourniquet but notices that Passini is "dead already. I made sure he was dead."[38] At the dressing station, Frederic sees doctors working "red as butchers."[39] After a doctor indifferent to Frederic's pain finishes probing and bandaging his wounded knee, he finds himself in an ambulance, placed beneath a hemorrhaging soldier in the cot above him. Frederic tries to move out of the way, but cannot avoid the steady stream of blood from above, turning him "warm and sticky."[40] One would be hard-pressed to view Frederic Henry's famous denunciation of the usual base motivations for war, his contempt for the patriotic platitudes that send young men off to die, as less than a protest of war. When we hear the battle police during the retreat from Caporetto speaking of "the sacred soil of the fatherland" and the "fruits of victory" as they execute their own soldiers,[41] we understand Frederic's disgust.

Yet, if there is validity to Thomas Strychacz's argument that Hemingway's episodes of war function as an alibi for the violence that is being celebrated, Vonnegut's concerns are not wholly misplaced. In Strychacz's view Hemingway's descriptions perform the double task of exploring the guilty pleasures of militarism, decrying, for instance, the pain of brave soldiers whose suffering and death nevertheless bring them glory.[42] The merciless killings during the retreat are terrifying, certainly not an endorsement of the glory of battle or the nobility of death; yet they inspire in Henry exactly the self-conscious machismo Vonnegut disparaged in Harold Ryan, codelike exhibitions of toughness, bravery, and stoical fortitude, a markedly different response to war than that of Billy Pilgrim.

It is not difficult to view Frederic Henry's capacity for violence in light of Harold Ryan's assertion in *Happy Birthday, Wanda June:* "You've got to fight from time to time or get eaten alive."[43] According to Robert Penn Warren and John Killinger, Frederic Henry's violence simply represents an appropriate response to "the great nada."[44] Yet the naturally combative Frederic fights not only to survive, but because he likes it, taking pride in himself as a tough guy who enjoys intimidating other men and even inflicting pain. When he bloodies the face of an Italian officer with a single blow, takes pleasure in scaring the professor he boxes with in Lausanne, or relishes seeing the Italian artillery captain cower when he and Frederic want the same seat on a train, Frederic takes the same pride in his masculinity as he does watching himself shadowbox. There is little difference between this Frederic Henry and the Harold Ryan who thrives on physical threats and enjoys "twitting weaklings"[45] or who proclaims that the core of his life was the pleasure of watching someone make the choice between fleeing and fighting— or of making the choice himself. "This is a moment of truth," Harold Ryan tells his buddy Shuttle contemptuously when Shuttle will not fight him, "and you're almost crying."[46]

We know that, when Frederic dispatches the suffering Passini, he acts from pity. But a far darker emotion surfaces—a seeming enjoyment of killing—when he shoots fleeing Italian officers who resist Henry's orders to help dig a car out of the mud. He describes the killing as coolly and indifferently as if he were shooting quail, consistent with an ideology of violence that increasingly desensitizes him and that he perversely enjoys. "I shot three times," he says, "and dropped one. The other went through the hedge and was out of sight." "Did I hit the other one at all?" he asks someone. When Bonello puts his pistol against the head of one of the fallen soldiers, Henry responds coldly, "You have to cock it."[47]

If Vonnegut's portrait of Hemingway as the bellicose Harold Ryan indicts Hemingway for the kind of aggression that shows up in Frederic Henry, Ryan and Henry also share an unnerving propensity for heroic braggadocio. There are several episodes where Hemingway appears to undercut the kind of heroic posing Vonnegut detests. When Frederic says, "Nothing ever happens to the brave," Catherine smartly answers, "the brave die of course."[48] Yet her view that the truly brave are quiet about it evokes a concept of heroic fortitude that seems staged and pretentious. We see that Frederic suffers, but his valor requires he deny its seriousness. When he describes his swollen and bleeding forehead as nothing, says he waits to have his knee wound dressed because there are much worse wounded, and understates the ordeal of the retreat on foot and then swimming the Tagliamento with "this knee," there is an unmistakable element of self-congratulation reminiscent of the false bravado of the British prisoners of war in *Slaughterhouse-Five*. Henry's shows of courage seem as stage managed for applause as Campbell's melodramas or Pedro Romero's feats of daring in the bullring.

While Vonnegut's criticisms simplify complexities of text and characterization in *A Farewell to Arms*, they nevertheless illuminate essential differences in each writer's management of war wounds at almost identical phases of their careers. Vonnegut's suffering war hero Billy Pilgrim constitutes the antithesis of Hemingway's tough, violent, and sometimes brutal Frederic Henry. Like Norbert Woodly, Harold Ryan's peacenik counterpart in *Happy Birthday, Wanda June*, Pilgrim represents Vonnegut's dicta that "there's no time for battle, no point to battle any more." Woodly, Penelope says, represents the new heroes who refuse to fight. "They're trying to save the planet."[49] Billy's gentleness and subsequent refusal to participate in the world's destructiveness contrasts conspicuously with what we see of Frederic's truculence and enjoyment of physical confrontation. We see Billy as a latter-day Christ who cries at the sight of a suffering German horse, a moment that begs comparison with Hemingway's narrator's impersonal response to the crippled baggage animals thrown in the water to drown in "On the Quai at Smyrna."

Billy's natural gentleness and innocence, appropriate to his role as chaplain's assistant, hardly prepares him for the idiocy of battle, any more than Frederic

Henry's boyish exuberance prepares him for war's destruction. Yet, if anything, Billy grows more docile, while Frederic becomes increasingly militant. While Frederic is self-consciously virile, Billy is loath to discover that his wife associates sex and glamour with war. Rather than show off his personal sexual prowess, Vonnegut jokes in the opening chapter that the war has made his own phallus inoperable—a "tool" that "won't pee anymore."[50] All in all Billy experiences war as an interminable nightmare of victimization and madness in which everyone around him exhibits some form of insane, mechanically conditioned behavior. Hemingway's denunciations of war are more problematic, war viewed as a process of tempering the writer's craft and sensibility, a stage upon which to enact what Warren calls "the lessons of lonely fortitude,"[51] shows of courage and strength necessary to endure in a world that kills and maims with impunity.

Whereas Frederic Henry thinks to himself, "One had so many friends in a war,"[52] we are hard-pressed to think of Billy as similarly blessed. On the one hand, we encounter the mindless hating and killing superpatriot machines of Howard Campbell, Colonel Wild Bob, and Bertram Copeland Rumfoord, whose glorifications of war and exhortations to battle appear ludicrous alongside the pitiful suffering of Billy and his comrades. In addition to the death of Edgar Derby and the execution of Private Eddie Slovik, shot for challenging authority, Billy represents Vonnegut's view that, despite all the popular movies glorifying war and soldiering starring manly figures such as John Wayne or Frank Sinatra, it is usually the nation's young and innocent who are first sent to be slaughtered. One cannot escape the ironic contrast to war movies made of *A Farewell to Arms, For Whom the Bell Tolls,* and *Islands in the Stream,* starring masculine figures such as Tyrone Power, Humphrey Bogart, Gary Cooper, and George C. Scott, or the more pointed irony that, whereas Billy is appalled at the execution of Slovik, Frederic Henry, sans pity or remorse, performs just such an execution on a fleeing Italian officer.

In an episode reminiscent of the chaotic retreat at Caparetto in *A Farewell to Arms,* but conspicuously devoid of Frederic's bravado, Vonnegut's portrait of the demented Colonel Wild Bob exhorting his beaten soldiers to battle epitomizes Vonnegut's refusal to glamorize war in any form. As Billy joins the "river of humiliation" of marching prisoners being spat on by their German captors, violent, "bristly men" with "teeth like piano keys," he hears "Wild Bob," who has lost an entire regiment of mostly children, speaking patriotic nonsense to Billy. He tells Billy and the agonized, uncomprehending soldiers around him that there were dead Germans all over the battlefield who "wished to God" they had never heard of Billy's outfit, "the Four-fifty-first."[53] Other than the fatherly ministrations of Edgar Derby, the only other representation of heroism in the novel occurs when Billy encounters the British prisoners of war, who are described in hilariously parodic terms. The Brits have put up a sign reading "Please leave this latrine as tidy as you found it,"[54] signaling an obsessive pretense of order and cleanliness as mad as the war itself. While Vonnegut comments on the ineffectiveness of war protests, the antiwar element in this novel is direct and powerful. Vonnegut tells his sons not to work for companies that make war machinery and to express contempt for people who think we need machinery like that. True to his promise to O'Hare's wife, Vonnegut demonstrates that wars are fought by children, subtitling his novel *The Children's Crusade*. Ironically Frederic and Catherine hope their son will be a lieutenant commander or, better yet, a general. Billy's son, on the other hand, a decorated Green Beret, achieves the military distinction Frederic and Catherine have in mind, but as a mindless, former high-school dropout and alcoholic, he hardly qualifies as a poster child for war. One telling image, a war movie run in reverse, demonstrates the power of art to subvert the destructive process of war. Fires go out; dead or wounded soldiers are made whole; bombs fly back into planes that fly backward to friendly cities; the bombers are dismantled and minerals used for bombs are returned to the earth.

In defending Frederic Henry's penchant for violence, Warren argues that tough taciturnity constitutes the supreme value of "code initiates" such as Frederic, Catherine, the priest, and Rinaldi, a secret community of people who recognize "nada" as life's essential condition and what is required to live in it. Like Jake Barnes, Brett Ashley, and Count Mippipopolous, Frederic, Catherine, the priest, and Rinaldi are set off against the world "like a wounded lion ringed around by waiting hyenas."[55] Hemingway eventually questioned the wisdom of such exclusive, secret communities in *For Whom the Bell Tolls* and *The Old Man and the Sea* (where he attempted to bring his individual hero back to society), just as Vonnegut did through advocacy of "extended families" in *Slapstick* (1976) and *Jailbird* (1979). But in *A Farewell to Arms* the hero's dependence on toughness for meaning and what Thomas Strychacz calls "a narrow but very potent cultural code of emotional restraint" demands the stoic endurance, the stiff upper lip of the disciplined bullfighter or soldier, which "makes a man a man."[56] When Rinaldi confesses to Henry that "this war is killing me," Henry rebukes him for the code sin of self-pity, what Warren calls "sensitive shrinking."[57] When Rinaldi asks, "Can't I even have human impulses?," he forgets the code imperative that, along with toughness, what makes one "human" is the refusal to complain or even think about unpleasant experience. When Rinaldi corrects himself—"By God, I am becoming a lovely surgeon"—Henry absolves him: "That sounds better."[58]

While Catherine may be right that the truly brave are quiet about it, Henry's manly masquerade again invokes Vonnegut's warning that we become who we pretend to be, in this case someone desensitized to suffering and disinclined to introspection and critical analysis. It is indeed a different notion of humanness Howard Campbell has in mind when he remarks, "It might make me seem more *human* at this point, which is to say more sympathetic."[59] The same denial of emotions that allows Frederic to end Passini's suffering or to cope with Aymo's death—"He died while I was stopping up the two holes"[60]—converts to the callous shooting of the fleeing Italian soldiers. It may underlie the meanness of spirit behind Frederic's racist remark that "Othello was a nigger."[61] Suppressing painful experience—Frederic's constant reminder to himself that his head was "not to think with"[62]—discourages self-awareness in much the same way Jake Barnes and Billy Pilgrim's numbing processes rob them of consciousness and human dignity, preventing both men from understanding their deepest desires and fears. When Rinaldi tells his war brother there are things he knows but cannot say, Frederic responds, "You are better when you don't think so deeply."[63] Tired from thinking so much, both Rinaldi and Henry resort to the mind-numbing consolations of alcohol, "all that manly drinking" Vonnegut associates with masculine posing and male camaraderie. "I will get you drunk," Rinaldi tells Frederic, "and make you a man again. . . . It burns out the stomach completely. . . . Self destruction day by day . . . just the thing. . . ." Not coincidentally does Rinaldi tell Henry that he, Rinaldi, has no married friends because they do not like him.[64] We hear echoes of *Happy Birthday, Wanda June* when Harold Ryan accuses his sidekick Shuttle of unmanliness—"You're hollow, like a woman"—and Shuttle replies that "you aren't going to have any friends left, if you don't watch out."[65]

Frederic Henry's coolly defiant fatalism at the novel's close hastens what Strychacz calls Henry's "desperate urge to complete the mask [of machismo] he now mainly inhabits."[66] Opposed to the standard view that Catherine's death means "rebirth" for the existential hero,[67] Sandra Whipple Spanier sees that, as the agent of Frederic's education, Catherine induces Henry's realization that human destiny is in the hands of an invisible and arbitrary "they," who will kill you in the end.[68] Life is a fixed race, Henry concludes. All life cycles end in death, particularly the love cycle that produces a dead baby and a dead mother[69]—"a dirty trick" he does not want to talk about.

Frederic Henry's mental paralysis results from the same feelings of futility that underlie Billy Pilgrim's incapacitating pessimism. Billy resigns himself to the supposed wisdom of his inner-space friends that events are inevitably structured to be the way they are and hence do not lend themselves to warnings or explanations. Lulled by the Tralfamadorian anesthetic of fatalism, Billy becomes a moral sleepwalker who substitutes forms of moral escapism for necessary self-analysis. His tranquilized existence on Tralfamadore—a variant of the "affective failure" Millicent Bell attributes to Frederic Henry[70]—may insulate Billy from pain, but his illusion of comfort and security leaves him cut off from reality and unable to act in the real world. Since the Tralfamadorians teach Billy that death does not matter since no one really dies, he in fact resigns himself to his own death at the hands of Paul Lazzaro, a form of self-fulfilling prophesy.

Just as neither Frederic's aggression nor Billy's passivity offers a meaningful adjustment to the trauma of war, so their adoption of what Earl Rovit calls "studied forgetfulness"[71] prevents them from understanding submerged fears we have identified as the Hemingway hero's deeper wound, a secret and ambivalent language about repression and infantile longings, mother love, and a desire for merging with the feminine. This deeper, more personal wound evokes the loveless marriages, nonnurturing mothers, and defeated, will-less fathers of Hemingway's Nick Adams stories and the painful adolescent experience of Vonnegut's Rudy Waltz and Wilbur Swain. Until Billy and Frederic Henry face taboo fears and desires that link the traumas of childhood with the wounds of war, they invite the fate of Nick and Rudy, and that of their immediate predecessors, Jake Barnes and Howard Campbell, the former impotent, the latter suicidal.

Yet while *Slaughterhouse-Five* and *A Farewell to Arms* both end on a note of despair, it is Vonnegut's greater willingness to explore buried or denied fears and desires that explains the relative affirmation of Vonnegut's text, and that highlights Vonnegut's critique of *A Farewell to Arms* as a novel that retreats from consciousness and authorial responsibility. We must first of all remember that the hero's deeper wound—feelings of ambivalence toward, if not a fear and hatred of, the feminine—results from their authors' own profoundly conflicted feelings of loss and betrayal, the personal reason for writing that underlies all their work.

For both writers, war becomes an objective correlative for successive personal tragedies, confirming their feeling that death as readily as life is the consequence of sexuality, stirring feelings of hostility and guilt toward their parents, emotions they felt powerless to restrain but compelled to write out. For Hemingway the loss of Agnes Von Kurowsky's love, the ensuing loss of Grace Hemingway's regard and approval, the frustrations with Duff Twysden, the loss of Hadley's love through separation and divorce, and his father's suicide all combine to intensify his most buried anxieties about death and sex.

Similarly many personal blows shaped the pessimism of *Slaughterhouse-Five*. Billy Pilgrim and Eliot Rosewater share a mental ward partly because of what they have seen in war but also because of unresolved hostilities toward their parents, feelings of fear and guilt associated with the financial failures and emotional collapse of Vonnegut's father, the suicide of Vonnegut's mother, the Allied firebombing of Dresden, the death of Vonnegut's sister, Alice, from cancer within days of her husband's death in a train crash, and a sense of futility about the Vietnam War that significantly deepened Vonnegut's sadness. These are the real-life events that produce the hidden agenda of these novels, taboo desires and fears submerged or denied because they are filled with threatening emotional complications. Just as we see of Nick Adams and Rudy Waltz, then of Jake Barnes and Howard Campbell, it is this conflicted state of mind that causes Billy and Frederic Henry to reject women who represent female parts of themselves, particularly the mother figure who in real life has forsaken them, yet for whom they feel repressed infantile longings.

By contrast Vonnegut's iceberg has sufficiently thawed to allow the protagonist's long-building mother neurosis to emerge more revealingly than ever. The mother Vonnegut chides many times for her coldness and insensitivity in earlier works appears prominently in *Slaughterhouse-Five* in scenes that expose severely repressed oedipal desires. Just as Billy is being undressed and deloused as a prisoner of war, feeling his penis shriveled and his testicles retracting, he thinks of his mother. "And Billy zoomed back in time to his infancy. He was a baby who had just been bathed by his mother. Now his mother wrapped him in a towel, carried him into a rosy room that was filled with sunshine. She wrapped him, laid him on the tickling towel, powdered him between the legs, joked with him, patted his little jelly belly. Her palm on his little jelly belly made potching sounds. Billy gurgled and cooed."[72] Billy's long-suppressed desire for his mother emerges in guilty reactions to his mother's presence at his hospital bedside after he commits himself to a mental hospital during his senior year at the Illium School of Optometry. He feels himself getting much sicker at her approach and pulls the covers over his head until she goes away. He becomes disoriented at the sight of her lipstick-smeared cigarettes on the bedside table.

Billy recoils from his mother because, like the mother in *Deadeye Dick* and the mother in Hemingway's fiction, she is insipid, materialistic, and morally obtuse, but he is mystified that his embarrassment and weakness in her presence should be so strong simply because she gave him life. We are reminded of Paul Proteus's oedipal breast and womb fixations in *Player Piano*, which cause him to confuse his wife's bosom with his mother's, and his vision of an angry, punishing father as he dreams of awakening in the night alongside his mother-wife. Billy fails to associate fears of his father's aggression (throwing him into the deep end of the YMCA swimming pool, then taking him to the rim of the Grand Canyon) with oedipal desire for his mother conveyed by the womb/vortex imagery of rims and dark and foreboding holes. It is notably at his mother's touch that Billy wets himself. Montana Wildhack, a surrogate mother in Billy's Tralfamadorian fantasy, later causes Billy to have wet dreams.

In Montana Wildhack, Billy produces an imaginary woman, an onanistic dream who can do him no harm. Catherine Barkley, however, is a real part of Frederic Henry, partly the mother-goddess carrying associations of maternal solicitude and sympathy, but also the terribly real mother he is bound to fear and reject.[73] Confined to his hospital bed, Frederic lives out Billy Pilgrim's fantasy of being tended like a baby in its bassinet, comforted by female caretakers, and particularly the caring, maternal Catherine. For a while his wounds allow Frederic to enjoy his childlike vulnerability free of associations of weakness, fragility, or more troublesome yet, feelings of being female. Even the lovemaking that takes place in his hospital room at night is pleasantly passive; he assumes the conventional female position as Catherine lies on top. As a nurse with the capacity to nurture and guide, Catherine's tender ministrations return us to the subverted potential of Brett Ashley to fulfill her mythic role as fecund healer and archetypal transformer. Spilka explains that Catherine's efforts to teach Frederic the value of womanly caring manifests the same trait Grace Hemingway expected of Ernest and taught him to show his sisters. It was an ideal formed also by Clarence Hemingway's medical world, where male and female caring intermix, and by his own experience as a caring Red Cross corpsman who recovered from war wounds in a Milan hospital.[74] From Millicent Bell's perspective, Frederic's efforts to access the feminine through Catherine are as inauthentic as Pilgrim's fantasized relationship with Montana Wildhack. Frederic, Bell explains, only delusively attaches himself to an "otherness,"[75] the bountiful mother the hero must harmonize with rather than attempt to master or destroy.

Yet, while Henry and Pilgrim both fail at this point in their mutual struggle with the suppressed feminine, it is again the subtle difference in narrative frames that most importantly distinguishes Vonnegut's more positive vision from Hemingway's. While both retrospective narratives distance the teller of the story from the protagonist, the Frederic Henry who narrates *A Farewell to Arms*, presumably after the same ten-year interval that defines Hemingway's writing of the novel, bears significantly closer resemblance to his author than does Billy Pilgrim to Vonnegut. As we have seen, Vonnegut enacted his duty dance with death by repudiating the conscienceless apathy of his hero, opening himself to the female within. Hemingway, on the other hand, resisted humanizing awareness that might mend his wounded psyche, retreating from the feminine while sanctioning aggression as a way to live "humanly" in the world.

Apparently it is Catherine Barkley's evocation of Grace and Hemingway's fear associated with marriage that caused Hemingway to suppress the feminine aspect of his own make-up, bidding "farewell" to the androgynous fusion of masculine and feminine Catherine as he had Brett Ashley. Spilka and Bell see Catherine so absorbing male identity that the author offers her as a sacrifice to male survival, supporting Vonnegut's criticism that Frederic's tears at Catherine's death are tears of relief rather than remorse, since he has been saved from the domestic trap of marriage and fatherhood and the burden of becoming the caring, empathetic Frederic that Catherine tries to nurture into being. Frederic decries the biological trap that kills Catherine and her child; yet it appears this is a trap his creator, not fate, not the dreaded "they," has set, a form of self-fulfilling prophesy that invites the unconsciousness and flight from the feminine by Frederic and his author by the novel's end. Spilka concludes that, because Frederic Henry shows less tenderness to Catherine than Jake Barnes does to Brett Ashley, something in Frederic, and by extension something in his creator Ernest is dying—namely his identification with women in their suffering rather than their "bitchy independence."[76]

When Frederic declares that, even after Catherine's death, there are still things he cannot tell, we may surmise that this statement includes a deeper analysis of the forces underlying masculine pretense. Continuing to equate the female mother with suffering and death, the protagonist retreats into further pessimism and an increasing propensity for violence, failing what Bell calls "the responsibilities of response."[77] Spilka observes that for the next ten years, Hemingway turned to the problem of shoring up his own male identity.[78] Conversely, whereas Hemingway killed off the extremely female Catherine so that he might save his male identity, Vonnegut eliminated Billy Pilgrim as a symbolic repudiation of male aggression, more specifically, the passivity that allows aggression to happen. Vonnegut was careful to dissociate himself from Billy as from no character before, signaled by the fact that the author speaks to us directly in the important first chapter about the impact of the war on him and that, with references such as "I was there," and "that was me," he personally turns up in the narrative four times. Billy, like Frederic, may choose to close his eyes to unpleasantness, but Billy's regress is Vonnegut's progress. The true hero of *Slaughterhouse-Five* is the author himself, as Vonnegut reveals in *Breakfast of Champions*: "I see a man who is terribly wounded, because he has dared to pass through the fires of truth to the other side, which we have never seen. And then he has come back again to tell us about the other side."[79] If Hemingway dodged the responsibilities of thoughtful response, Vonnegut embraced what Doris Lessing has called "the ambiguities of complicity,"[80] causing the reader to think carefully about degrees of responsibility for violence and injustice.

With the help of Phoebe Hurty, that mother surrogate who at the spiritual crossroads of his life helped him develop the necessary moral sense and faith in human development to survive the Great Depression, Vonnegut no longer identified women with death and destruction. Rather Phoebe Hurty represents the feminine will to love and service, the projection of anima we see in Catherine Barkley, but here it is embraced rather than dismissed. Whereas Hemingway's rejection of Catherine precludes the possibility of inner wholeness, Kathryn Hume argues that Vonnegut's exorcism of the mother that so contaminated his picture of women allowed him to accept the creative female principle in himself and to espouse "a more active response to the hurts of the world."[81]

It is perhaps the great *personal* depression Vonnegut survived that *Slaughterhouse-Five* and *Breakfast of Champions* (1973) are most about, and that best explains Hemingway as Vonnegut's bête noire, the troubled and troubling secret sharer of Vonnegut's literary imagination. Vonnegut purposefully targeted Hemingway as he did Billy Pilgrim, Kilgore Trout, and Kurt Vonnegut Sr., as the embattled author's chief scapegoats, carrying his heaviest burden of trauma and despair.

Vonnegut's willingness to look deeply into his own "Mother Night" showed him that Billy Pilgrim's passivity, Hemingway's fatalism, and Frederic Henry's violence all represent the same universal will to destruction. With the specter of Hemingway's suicide never far from mind, Vonnegut believed that resisting the pull of his defeatist self was necessary not only to fulfilling his role as canary bird in the coal mine, but to life itself.

In *Hemingway: The 1930s*, volume 4 of his authoritative biography of Hemingway, Michael Reynolds confirms judgments I made twenty-some years earlier in *Hemingway's Spanish Tragedy* (1973): that the author's assumption of an increasingly belligerent, tough-guy public persona threatened to harden permanently into the caricature of Hemingway later portrayed as Harold Ryan in *Happy Birthday, Wanda June*, obscuring the more complex human being beneath. In the wake of *Happy Birthday, Wanda June* (1971), Vonnegut's fiction from *Breakfast of Champions* to *Timequake* became not only a critical response to a world of violence and death, but a rebuttal of the Hemingway who equated manhood with heroic comportment and associated emotional and artistic integrity with the killing of animals. As if to bear out Vonnegut's fierce indictment, not only did Hemingway not say "farewell" to violence and aggression with the death of Catherine Barkley, in the immediate works to follow *A Farewell to Arms—Death in the Afternoon* (1932) and *Green Hills of Africa* (1935)—he defined himself and his literary aspirations in markedly masculine terms. In *Green Hills of Africa*, as if to revenge himself on that cruel mother for birthing him into the Garden of Eden he could only lose, Hemingway not only takes delight in killing big animals for pleasure, he determines to become an even better killer than the beasts of the jungle. In Spilka's view, these texts become a veritable handbook for manly violence and heroic behavior, the crux of Vonnegut's critique of Hemingway as a hunter and lover of blood sports. Hemingway, Reynolds says, invented the man he wished to be or have people believe he was from his earliest days in Oak Park, a warrior, an outlaw, a rough character capable of extreme violence, a man always in control, always all-knowing, competent; never weak, uncertain, self-doubting, insecure, or afraid of anything. It was a mask, Reynolds suggests and Vonnegut believed, that was no longer removable.

# Four

# Spiritual Manifestos

*Breakfast of Champions, Death in the Afternoon,* and *Green Hills of Africa*

■

I realize today that nothing in the world is more distasteful to man than to take the path that leads to himself.

Herman Hesse, *Demian*

The gratitude for this release of the Unconscious (the so-called "catharsis" or psychic house-cleaning), is the poet's main reward.

Dr. Hans Sachs, *The Creative Unconscious*

*Breakfast of Champions, Death in the Afternoon,* and *Green Hills of Africa* represent Vonnegut's and Hemingway's appraisals of themselves at midlife and midcareer, a time of change and renewal. Vonnegut's metaphor at the start of *Breakfast of Champions* applies to both writers: at age fifty Vonnegut informs us that *Breakfast of Champions* represents "crossing the spine of a roof—having ascended one slope"[1] and that he is thus writing as an act of "cleansing" and renewal "for the very different sorts of years to come."[2] In an act of rebellion against his old, more pessimistic self, he has determined to turn his fictional world on its head, dismantling the familiar trappings of his literary cosmos, including waving good-bye forever to all his old characters, "setting them free."

In a strikingly similar manner, Ernest Hemingway devised a new, more confident relationship to his world and a more bold set of rules for ordering the meaninglessness, the "nada" that cost him youthful ideals and, like Vonnegut, left him vulnerable to the impersonal mechanisms of a godless universe that created the wounds of Fossalta and Dresden.

These respective manifestos solidify each author's notion of what living "decently" or "humanly" in the modern world entails. Yet, whereas the quest of author and protagonist for understanding and wholeness had so far been relatively the same, we now reach that point in Vonnegut's revision of Hemingway that Bloom calls a "Clinamen," a "corrective movement" implying that the precursor was accurate to a certain point, but then should have "swerved" precisely in the direction that the new work moves.[3] Each writer created a hero—literally himself—who feels he has learned the correct way to live in the world that has crippled him, but in an act of psychic breaking with his literary parent, Vonnegut opened himself to what he believed is a "range of being" (Bloom's term) just beyond his precursor, adopting kindness and restraint as moral imperatives. Antithetically the narrating Hemingway of *Death in the Afternoon* and *Green Hills of Africa* appears to advocate power and aggression as a right way to live in the world, signs of which we have seen in the embittered Jake Barnes and Frederic Henry.

It is here, in the aggressive masculine persona manifest in *Death in the Afternoon* and *Green Hills of Africa*, that we come to understand more fully the mystery of Hemingway as Vonnegut's demonic self. As Vonnegut wrote about Eliot Rosewater and Billy Pilgrim, both he and Hemingway had found life meaningless, partly because of what they had seen in war and partly because of childhood traumas they have yet to fully understand, so they were trying to reinvent themselves and their universe. But as Vonnegut's letters to me confirm, rather than Hemingway reinventing himself in the manner of Harold Ryan in the surprising climax to *Happy Birthday, Wanda June*, Vonnegut saw the real-life Hemingway remaining as fatalistic as ever. Vonnegut fashioned the character of Kilgore Trout, a representation of Vonnegut's own most demoralized self, precisely to repudiate his own pessimism, by which the voice of hope has been canceled out by its negative counterpart, the cynical strain in his work that has constituted the critical emotional malady of his main characters and that turned him into a writing machine, writing as he was seemingly "programmed" to write. It is this same fatalistic malaise that explains Vonnegut's career-long efforts to distance himself from his ghostly doppelgänger Ernest Hemingway, which Vonnegut felt led to Hemingway's demise as a writer and ultimately to suicide.

José Castillo-Puche observes that Hemingway's initial attraction to Spain and to the bullfight came just as the author was looking for a ruling philosophy of life and just as he was formulating the essential principles of his craft. Castillo-Puche points out that in the matador Ernest saw a superhuman power that was more than religious—"something almost divine," a power capable of successfully combating in a symbolic way the brute forces of nature.[4] *Death in the Afternoon* proposes not only to be, as Salvador de Madariaga says, "the great book of the bullfight,"[5] a liturgy of life and death, but a book about the values Hemingway was learning in Spain. Rather than merely providing artistic commentaries about this or that famous bullfighter or making apologies for what is accidental and brutal about the bullfight, Hemingway praised the bullfight as the embodiment of something better than giving in to futility and submission in the face of adversity, the fate of so many earlier characters in Hemingway's fiction, including of course his own father, Clarence Hemingway.

The world of Nick Adams, Frederic Henry, and Jake Barnes, and the Spanish world of *Death in the Afternoon* are the same. Violence, suffering, and death are the rule; only, instead of another fictional projection of Hemingway, in *Death in the Afternoon* it is the author himself who takes the reader on tour through the world of the bullfight, expounding as he goes on the world's injustice and on the Spaniard's fatalistic philosophy of life, which corresponds with his own. Hemingway says that death and mutilation are just as prevalent in the Spanish world as elsewhere. They turn on you here to kill and break you as surely as they turn on Frederic and Catherine in *A Farewell to Arms*. In one place Hemingway describes the tragic end of a young torero who fell prey to the deceit and cruelty of life. He laments that the twenty-year-old matador was killed before he ever got going. They worshipped him in Valencia, Hemingway says, before "they" ever had time to turn on him. The bull that killed him never left him until the horn had broken up the skull "like it might break a flower pot."[6] Evidently nothing happened in the years since the writing of *A Farewell to Arms* to change the author's belief that man's chances for survival are shaped largely by forces beyond his control. There are no happy endings in life. All stories, if continued far enough, end in death. There is no remedy for anything in life.[7]

Though Hemingway's outlook on life appears as grave as ever, he takes comfort in the fact that the Spanish take suffering and death to be a daily part of their lives. They go to the bullring to see death "being given, avoided, refused and accepted," the value of which Hemingway is clear about. What gave the bullfight continued importance in Spain, he reports, was that it kept before men's attention their struggle with the brute forces of nature, to control them to their own ends, in which their human ingenuity gave them the assumption of victory if they spent their best effort. One's adversary is given shape and purpose, and the strict requirements of the fight give man the chance to focus and discharge his pent-up aggressions on the object of the bull.

Even death itself becomes bearable, even meaningful, within the ritualized purposes of the bullfight. If the matador dies, he has the chance to die nobly, fighting bravely and with integrity. Pain and mutilation are justified because one understands that they are a necessary part of the symbolic life-and-death struggle. "I believe that the tragedy of the bullfight is so well ordered and so strongly disciplined by ritual," Hemingway says, "that a person feeling the whole tragedy cannot separate the minor comic-tragedy of the horse so as to feel it emotionally."[8] The pain suffered by the horses is not important. Protecting the horses, Hemingway says, is a "romantic thing that the spectators like."[9] Hemingway mocks such people as "animalarians,"[10] suggesting that those who identify with animals are less likely to empathize with human beings, a curious proposition indeed.

Far more fascinating to Hemingway than the Spaniard's acceptance of death was his manner of facing it. What the Spaniard mainly went to see in the course of the bullfight Hemingway describes as the feeling of rebellion against death that comes from its administering. Because the Spaniard is a man in rebellion against death, the author informs us: "He has pleasure in taking to himself one of the Godlike attributes; that of giving it. This is one of the most profound feelings in those men who enjoy killing." It is "true enjoyment of killing which makes the great matador."[11]

What Jake Barnes, Frederic Henry, and Ernest Hemingway find so attractive invokes Vonnegut's indictment of Hemingway's humanity—namely the matador's chin-protruding defiance of death in the bullring and, more unsettling, the association of honor and courage with the enjoyment of killing. The fatalistic philosophy of life that turns Frederic Henry violent, insensitive, and cruel by the end of *A Farewell to Arms*, Hemingway celebrates in *Death in the Afternoon* as the moral element in the Spanish character that, according to the Spanish philosopher Angel Ganivet, is something powerful and indestructible within a man that makes him "firm and erect." The least we can say of such person, Ganivet says, "is that you are a man."[12]

Ganivet explains that, along with this feeling of heightened potency, the feeling of rebellion against death in the bullring and the enjoyment of killing that attends it breed a fierce desire to dominate and to exist as one's own authority, constituting oneself as judge and jury, and feeling absolutely certain that one holds the "truth" in the fullness of its glory. Ignoring others, the individual assumes the defiant pose of the matador, erect and unyielding, arrogant and dominating.[13] In *Death in the Afternoon*, Hemingway exalts the virtues of one matador in particular, Maera, whose tough shell nothing can possibly penetrate. "He was the proudest man I have ever seen," Hemingway says. "When the bulls did not come to him . . . he went to the bulls,"[14] exhibiting the same courage, toughness, fortitude, and desire to dominate his opponent that define Hemingway's future heroes Harry Morgan, Colonel Cantwell, Robert Jordan, and Santiago.

The climax of the matador's demonstration of valor in the bullring, Hemingway says, comes during the brief, last seconds of the fight when the matador and the bull are both ready for the kill. In the moment of the final sword thrust, what the matador calls his moment of truth, courage and the need to dominate show themselves clearest. Thus in Maera's last fight, during his moment of truth, his honor demanded that he kill in a certain way, a way that emphasized his courage and ability to dominate. Hemingway explains: Maera's "honor demanded that he kill him high up between the shoulders going in as a man should, over the horn, following the sword with his body."[15]

The emphasis on the importance of death expertly delivered as a source of honor amplifies Penelope's angry reminder to Harold Ryan in *Happy Birthday, Wanda June* that death is simply death, with nothing honorable or glorious about it, whether in the bullring, on the battlefield, or in relationships with people such as Penelope or Norbert Woodly who dare question patriarchal authority. But it is Hemingway's praise of the matador's ability to function as a "skillful killer," the matador's love of killing as his greatest virtue that draws Vonnegut's strongest censure of Hemingway in *Happy Birthday, Wanda June*. Hemingway explains sympathetically that the great killer must have a sense of glory far beyond that of the ordinary bullfighter. He must be a simple man who not only takes pleasure in managing the bull better than other men but who takes "spiritual enjoyment in the moment of killing."[16] Underscoring Vonnegut's condemnation of Harold Ryan's blood lust, Unamuno, abjures the "flavor of blood and tragedy" he finds in many aspects of Spanish life and finds distorted the notion that killing in a certain way might serve as a source of value.[17]

Maera, who was "proud, bitter, foulmouthed and a great drinker," anticipates Hemingway's personal exhibitions of manhood in *Green Hills of Africa*. Having been deeply moved by the displays of manhood by such men as Maera and Pedro Romero, Hemingway seems bent on sharing the matador's proximity to death and on imposing the same rigid rules of conduct on his favorite pastime, hunting, and on his trade, writing, as those that guide the performance of Maera and Romero in the bullring. He says he has learned the necessary rules and what precautions to take to last and get his work done. On his violent hunting expedition to the plains of East Africa, he attempts to explain these rules and to justify his life and art in terms of the matador's exaltation of violence and the tough taciturnity developed in Barnes and Frederic Henry. Hemingway transfers the bullfighter's values to his own art in setting up terms for greatness: daring, courage, and a desire to dominate. Hemingway's pride as a writer compels him to look at fellow writers as one matador looks at his rival on a Sunday afternoon: competitively, as an enemy to be beaten or destroyed. From now on he sizes up his opponents as the matador sizes up his bull, determining what he has to beat in order to retain his ranking as torero numero uno.

### Green Hills of Africa

In *Green Hills of Africa* Hemingway identifies as closely as possible with the matador, proposing that in many respects writing is to be considered as dangerous a profession as bullfighting. Just as the matador must understand and learn to control such variable circumstances as the wind, the nature of his bull, the nature of the terrain, his own nerves, and so forth, Hemingway claims that it is almost impossible for a writer to survive all the negative influences that threaten to destroy him, most notably women and money, which come in pairs. Very likely with his divorce from Hadley and his marriage to the wealthier Pauline in mind, Hemingway remarks that "our writers when they have some money increase their standard of living and they are caught." They "have to write to keep up their establishments, their wives, and so on," and once they have betrayed themselves, they write slop.[18] About women writers, Hemingway has nothing but ill to say: not only are women first among the forces that bring writers down, they make bad writers themselves.

Hemingway lists the things that ruin writers early as "politics, women, drink, money, and ambition"—or the lack of these things.[19] A few years later, Hemingway dramatically illustrated—through the title character of "The Short Happy Life of Francis Macomber" and Harry, the dying writer in "The Snows of Kilimanjaro"—the threat of women and money to a writer's integrity.[20] Both stories are about cowardly or corrupted men who have traded what was once most dear to them—liberty and integrity—for security and comfort. Spilka observes that the relations between such men and women are brutally damaging; there is no room for tenderness and consideration of the selfless love proferred by Catherine Barkley in *A Farewell to Arms*.[21] Confirming the idea of the bullfight as a battle of genders, Francis Macomber attempts to regain his moral manhood by assuming the aggressive stance of the torero. Just as the matador proves his integrity and courage in the bullring by defying the onrushing bull, Francis Macomber kneels in the path of the oncoming buffalo and thus attains a kind of fearless self-trust and happiness he has never known before. He achieves a moral rebirth by acting bravely during his supreme moment of truth.

In *Green Hills of Africa*, the results of Hemingway's animosity for fellow writers are everywhere in evidence. Not as bad as critics—"the lice who crawl on literature"—those writers who do not share his particular artistic tendencies, or those with whom he feels in competition, are nevertheless chastised. Holding writers such as Thomas Wolfe in contempt for not having been to war, Hemingway wonders if it would make a writer of him, "give him the necessary shock to cut the overflow of words and give him a sense of proportion," if they sent him to Siberia or to the Dry Tortugas.[22] Wolfe evidently missed "the pleasant, comforting stench of comrades" that only the pleasure of writing can match.[23] Hemingway's anecdote about F. Scott Fitzgerald in "The Snows of Kilimanjaro" has been called the public burial of Hemingway's longtime friend, and Fitzgerald was deeply offended. The original version has Hemingway's writer-hero musing on his own life among the American rich, remembering "poor Scott" and his romantic awe of them. The anecdote concludes that, when Scott found out they were not a special glamorous race, it wrecked him.

While the norms and standards for writing that Hemingway sets up in *Green Hills of Africa* seem meritorious, his concept of the author as killer-matador who derives both emotional and aesthetic pleasure and pride from killing well provides the most persuasive argument yet that Vonnegut, as a healer and man of peace, and Hemingway, as a devotee of blood sports, went indeed in very different directions at this critical moment of their writing lives. The writer as killer-matador is what the other half of *Green Hills of Africa* is about: Hemingway pursuing the beautiful kudu bull, drawing his rifle sights on a buck, dispatching it with accuracy, and releasing the tension that approximates the final sword thrust of the torero.

Hemingway's affinity with Maera is shown in their strikingly similar attitudes toward killing. Both were self-engrossed in the sense of glory the matador derives from killing with emotional and artistic integrity. Both, according to Hemingway, were great killers because they "love to kill" and because they believed that killing is its own reward. Hemingway's interrogator in *Green Hills of Africa* is bewildered to find that the author derives as much pleasure from hunting kudu as he does from writing well. Like the matador, Hemingway has strict ideas about how things should be done, and underlining every passage is his fierce pride in displaying masculine skill and courage. So intent is he in carrying out his masquerade as a matador with clenched teeth and sucked-in belly that he evokes the caricature of Harold Ryan in *Happy Birthday, Wanda June*, where the Hemingway-like Ryan relishes violence and confrontation as ways to prove his worth as a man.

Hemingway's identification with the matador-killer shows up unmistakably in a passage that links him to his portrayal of Maera dispatching his bull in *Death in the Afternoon*, killing "high up between the shoulders, going in as a man should, over the horn, following the sword thrust with his body."[24] Hemingway describes the bull he must kill as having to put his head down to hook, "like any bull, and that will uncover the old place the boys wet their knuckles on and I will get one in there and then must go sideways into the grass," just as Maera shrugs over the horn after the kill.[25] Later, patting Hemingway on the back, the guide pays Hemingway the highest tribute he could have received: "You god damned bull-fighter."[26]

When Hemingway feels guilty over a wounded and suffering animal he fails to kill, he reminds himself of the matador's primitive credo forming in the war-damaged minds of Jake Barnes and Frederic Henry, that the instinct to kill is both profound and natural, that "killing is its own reward." Man is both hunter and the hunted, he reasons; he gives only what he takes, meeting aggression with aggression. "I did nothing that had not been done to me," he says. "I had been shot and I had been crippled and gotten away. I expected always to be killed by one thing or another, and I, truly, did not mind that anymore."[27] When the author's conscience bothers him again, he rationalizes that since the natural devouring and self-devouring process that goes on nightly will continue with or without his participation, he might just as well indulge his primitive appetites as one who takes pleasure in the beauty of violence and death. "They all had to die," he says, "and my interference with the nightly and the seasonal killing that went on all the time was very minute and I had no guilty feeling at all."[28] Hemingway's denial of guilt in the wake of obvious guilty feelings confirms what Maxwell Geismar calls a "misplaced irritation which runs through the book, of which we never seem to find the true object; all the unhappy evidence of a morality which is disputing, by all sorts of indirection, its own moral values."[29]

The meaning of this suspect morality comes to us in the form of Max Eastman's analysis of Hemingway's attraction to violence as a hunter and bullfight aficionado, his ecstatic adulation over killing and dominating. Eastman could be speaking for Vonnegut when he writes in "Bull in the Afternoon" that "it is not death Hemingway writes about or travels to see, but killing." Eastman condemns the matador's theatrical pose as he torments and kills his bull and his appetite for killing—for courage, dominating, and blind cruelty, summing up Hemingway's attraction to the bullring in these words: "We took this young man with his sensitive genius for experience, for living all the qualities of life and finding a balance among them—and with that too obvious fear in him of proving inadequate—and we shoved him into our pit of slaughter, and told him to be courageous about killing. And we thought he would come out weeping and jittering. Well, he came out roaring for blood, shouting to the skies the joy of killing, the 'religious ecstasy' of killing—and most pathetic, most pitiable, killing as a protest against death."[30]

In terms of Vonnegut's critique, we must wonder whether Hemingway's comparison of the challenges and dangers of writing to those of the bullfight does not suggest perils the author neither fully comprehended nor was prepared to meet head-on. Such devotion to cruelty and death dealing reminds us of Howard Campbell's declaration in *Mother Night* that he and Resi have become the greatest death worshippers the world had ever seen. When the Hemingway hero—such as Jake, Frederic, or Ernest—feels himself made "firm and erect" at the sight of the matador controlling, dominating, and finally killing his adversary, is the author not perhaps avenging himself on the bullish mother who so gores the father's masculine self-esteem that the father impales himself upon his own sword? Or did Hemingway have in mind the father Nick Adams once drew down on and wished to kill in "Fathers and Sons"?

Thomas Strychacz suggests that the sword thrust that dispatches antagonistic bulls correlates with the author's phallic pen, which sanctions killing as a manly occupation and dismisses still another difficult female from consideration in the form of Hemingway's old-woman adversary in *Death in the Afternoon*, the woman who disputes the author's enthusiasm for violence in the bullring. Hemingway's descriptions of bullfights, Strychacz contends, approximate the act of writing: both reflect a "predilection for virile masculinity," a style that is lean, hard, muscular, tough, and hard-boiled. It is as if, Strychacz says, pen and penis were one entity, affording the writer "a particularly courageous and manly role."[31]

## Breakfast of Champions

In one striking way, Vonnegut's literary interests in *Breakfast of Champions* and Hemingway's in *Green Hills of Africa* strike a common chord. Just as Vonnegut writes about the abuse of Mother Earth by greed and the promiscuous overdevelopment of machines, Hemingway registers his own disgust with a machine-dominated world, expounding on the ignorance and greed that have turned the American wilderness into a literal wasteland. Rather than living in harmony with nature, Americans, he says, ruined the country by cutting down the trees, poisoning the water, and depleting the soil. Anticipating the dismay of the author's most disaffiliated American, Harry Morgan, Hemingway goes on to condemn the "venality and cruelty" of those who have turned the Gulf Stream between Key West and Cuba into a cesspool of ill-smelling garbage, defiling the blue waters with bottles, used electric-light globes, condoms, corsets, and the rotting corpses of dogs, cats, and an occasional rat.[32]

Kilgore Trout learns that the river in Midland City (whose art festival he is headed toward throughout the novel for a fateful meeting with his creator, Kurt Vonnegut) contains a washing machine, a couple of refrigerators, several stoves, an infinity of Pepsi-Cola bottles, and a 1968 Cadillac. Sacred Miracle Cave, Midland City's primary spiritual attraction, has been covered over by industrial pollution. The underground stream passing through the cave forms "bubbles as tough as ping-pong balls," soon to engulf the statue of Moby Dick and invade the Cathedral of Whispers, where thousands of people have been married.[33] The critical difference between Hemingway's disgust and Vonnegut's sardonic vision of a nearly uninhabitable world— where humankind has turned the surface of the earth into a asphalt prairie, the atmosphere into poison gas, and the streams, rivers, and seas into sludge—is that Hemingway finds the despoliation of the American landscape unsalvageable; he declines, as he says in *Green Hills of Africa*, "any further enlistment" in social battles, making himself responsible only to himself and his writing.[34] Let others save the world, he says—writers such as Ralph Waldo Emerson, Sinclair Lewis, John Dos Passos, and of course, Vonnegut— writers who change into "Old Mother Hubbard" as they grow older or, like women writers, "become Joan of Arc without the fighting."[35]

Not coincidentally saving the world is the purpose to which Vonnegut as shaman summoned his best creative energy in the years ahead and the reason he directed his satirical missiles at Hemingway. Vonnegut's newfound optimism led him to condemn any absolute entity or theory that undermines the individual's control over and responsibility for his own destiny and that of the planet, including all theories of philosophic, religious, or chemical determinism.[36]

Hemingway asserts primitivist sympathies in *Green Hills of Africa* when he lets his interrogator know that killing kudu gives him more pleasure than the life of the mind. By contrast Vonnegut believed that the solution to a dehumanized machine world lies not in Hemingway's anti-intellectualism, his retreat to a more primitive, nonmechanical relationship with the land in such places as Spain, Key West, or the wilds of Africa, but in intelligently and humanely directing our course into the future. Vonnegut knew only too well the uphill nature of his struggle, that he must battle his own despair along the way, which returns us to his quarrel with Hemingway's fatalism. I suggest that Vonnegut had Hemingway in mind when, from his perspective as hunter and fisherman, the truck driver who takes Kilgore Trout to Midland City becomes suicidal over the country's poisoned marshes and meadows. In Vonnegut's eyes Hemingway's programming as matador, a man with a love of violence and killing, made him little different than those war machines guaranteed to shoot rockets at and drop explosives on other human beings. It is the tragic susceptibility of people to anti-humanitarian proposals, Vonnegut argued, that perpetuates the misery of those "who couldn't get their hands on doodly squat" and that has been responsible for the worst of America's sins—slavery, genocide, and criminal neglect.[37] In dramatic contrast to the fatalistic strain in *Death in the Afternoon* and *Green Hills of Africa*, Vonnegut declares in *Breakfast of Champions* that he will no longer continue as a writer seemingly programmed to write pessimistically about death and violence.

Robert Merrill faults reviewers of *Breakfast of Champions* who fail to see the novel as a condemnation of fatalism rather than an affirmation. It is only when we understand Vonnegut's use of Billy Pilgrim, Kilgore Trout, and by extension Ernest Hemingway, as expressions of the author's own predilections to pessimism that his main purpose in *Breakfast of Champions* becomes clear. As we have seen of Vonnegut and Hemingway, the identities of Vonnegut and Kilgore Trout are so similar that what is said about the one often applies to the other. As Vonnegut's more embittered and cynical Trout self, Trout is given Vonnegut's social conscience and artistic goals but also pessimism so great that it negates his artistic mission and vitiates his moral zeal. Like Vonnegut, Trout thinks of his artistic mission as being the eyes and ears and conscience of God.[38] But years of neglect and a growing sense of a life not worth living have made Trout temperamentally unfit for the task. He laughs now at attempts to reform the world, believing the whole mess futile. He no longer harbors ideas about how things on earth should be as compared to how they are. Trout in fact has been turned into a proper Tralfamadorian, believing there is only one way for earth to be—the way it is. Trout says he used to be a conservationist who bemoaned the killing of eagles from helicopters, but he gave it up—developing an attitude that reminds us of Hemingway's shooting terns, slender sea birds, for fun. Now when a tanker fouls the ocean, killing millions of birds and fish, Trout laughs and says, "More power to Standard Oil," or whoever.[39]

It is Trout's role as an irresponsible author that explains Vonnegut's view of Hemingway as a writer like himself who has harmed readers with his own pessimistic belief that human beings are no better than robots in a meaningless world, fostering apathy that in turn fosters aggression. We recall for instance Jake Barnes's cynicism at the close of *The Sun Also Rises*, Frederic Henry's feelings of futility at the end of *A Farewell to Arms*, and Howard Campbell's despairing realization in *Mother Night* that his Nazi broadcasts have given "shape and direction" to his listeners, turning them into homicidal monsters. Vonnegut sees how natural it would be for people to behave abominably after reading about people such as Frederic Henry or Dwayne Hoover in books. It is a novel by Trout about people as machines that causes Dwayne to become unfeeling and violent, sending eleven people to the hospital.[40] This, he says, "was the reason Americans shot each other so often: It was a convenient literary device for ending short stories and books." Thus Vonnegut determines to have nothing to do with traditional storytelling with its heroic characters and well-made plots in which good always triumphs over evil. Let others bring order to chaos, he says, "I would bring chaos to order, instead."[41]

Like Trout, Hemingway exists for Vonnegut as a fragment of Vonnegut's own divided psyche, a conflict of mind where potentially crippling pessimism vitiates his moral energy and humanistic zeal and prevents him from carrying out with sufficient vigor his guiding purpose as an artist, to serve as an alarm system to warn society of its technological abuses and dangers to man and nature. If we had not gotten the message of Vonnegut's troubled, dual orientation through previous novels or through obvious parallels to Trout and Hemingway, the author tells us directly that his mounting fear and despair actually made him ill—that his machine-induced nightmares were dreadful enough to result in a state of suppressed schizophrenia that led him to contemplate suicide (his mother's fate, Hemingway's fate, and Hemingway's father's fate) as a solution.

While the recognition that a large part of him was dead machinery discouraged Vonnegut's view of himself as a writer in control of his life and work, it ironically proved his salvation. The act of recognition inferred an imaginative faculty capable of resisting subversion by the machine within and machines without. Vonnegut came to see this awareness according to the vision of Rabo Karabekian as an "unwavering band of light," a sacred, irreducible living force at the core of every animal.[42] This epiphany set in motion the essential drama of *Breakfast of Champions* and perhaps of all Vonnegut's work, his spiritual rebirth, in which he determined to repudiate his former pessimism and in which the tragically repressed voice of hope in his work gained ascendancy over its negative counterpart.

So the final view we are afforded of Vonnegut's arduous climb to his rooftop, the spiritual climax to his "first" career, is his achievement of faith in the inviolability of awareness, especially human awareness, which, if properly cherished and cultivated, may yet redeem us and our planet from the technological horrors of the twentieth century. From this faith came his decision to cleanse and renew himself for the years ahead by performing the most daring and rebellious act of his writing life, the setting free of all his literary characters, including the omnipresent Kilgore Trout. Only the moral inertia Vonnegut associated with the Trout-Hemingway part of himself had to be overcome before he could steer his fictional course, as well as his own life, in a more sane and vital direction. Whatever happened, he vowed that he would no longer serve as anyone's puppet nor put on any more puppet shows of his own.

If at this critical turning point in their careers, Kurt Vonnegut was more successful than Hemingway in managing their common legacy of parental unhappiness, suicide, and the horrors of war, Vonnegut was not so naive as to suggest that freedom from the traumas of childhood and war is ever absolute or that he had solved all his problems. Recall that the author wanted to make his head as empty as it was when he was born "onto this damaged planet fifty years ago."[43] It was not until Vonnegut's final, climactic novel, *Timequake*, that the author finally freed himself from the noxious Trout-Hemingway influence. Nor did Vonnegut exorcise totally the image of that saddened worn-out father, whose fatalistic voice became Trout's and Hemingway's, or that of his "suicide mother who babbled of love, peace, wars, evil, and desperation."[44] Lynn Buck notes that the usual hostility between the protagonist and his father is projected through the racist, homophobic Dwayne and his homosexual son, Bunny, candidates for a "booby hatch."[45] Bunny is accused of trying to kill his father with hatred and then redirecting his hatred toward his mother. Vonnegut clearly struggled to understand the relative blame of each parent for creating the hellish home life portrayed in *Slapstick* and *Deadeye Dick*, guilt Vonnegut took on himself. At the beginning of *Breakfast of Champions*, Vonnegut describes human beings who have been turned into emotional and physical grotesques, standing directly beneath a clock his father designed. Like Trout and the disembodied Billy Pilgrim, Vonnegut still feels estranged from his physical self, which he associates with his father's love of guns, the violence of Dresden, his mother's suicide, and the world's destructiveness in general. Anticipating the painfully neutered condition of Rudy Waltz in *Deadeye Dick*, Trout says he "had hoped to get through what little remained of his life without ever having to touch another human being again."[46]

Nevertheless the author's mother surrogate Phoebe Hurty has triumphed over the Philboyd Studge in him, the voice of hope over the voice of despair. And we experience the first fruit of the author's spiritual rebirth in his next two novels, *Slapstick, or Lonesome No More* (1976) and *Jailbird* (1979). His subject here is the same—the damaging excesses of the machine on the human spirit—and he writes of desolated cities and the depletion of nature, of loneliness and spiritual death—but his voice is more persistently affirmative than ever before. And in *Jailbird* the protagonist is joined by three powerful female guides who personify psychic healing and creative optimism: his wife, Ruth, Sarah Wyatt, and Mary Kathleen O'Looney. Yet while Vonnegut continued to view Hemingway as a writer whose machismo diminished his artistic growth, Hemingway's work from *To Have and Have Not* to *Under Kilimanjaro*, like Vonnegut's from *Slapstick* to *Hocus Pocus*, is similarly about confession, redemption, and rebirth, distinguished by the hero's increasingly open conversation with the suppressed "other," and his willingness to access what Jung called "dangerous knowledge" about himself, knowing "what I myself desire."[47]

# Part 2 The Androgynous Turn

**Five**

# From Jailbird to Canary Bird

*To Have and Have Not* and *Jailbird*

■

The poet is haunted by a voice with which
words must be harmonized.
                        André Malraux, *Man's Fate*

Call me but love and I'll be newly baptized.
                        Romeo in *Romeo and Juliet*

If Jake Barnes speaks for Ernest Hemingway when he says about Brett Ashley, "I
had not been thinking about *her* side of it," Jake likely says more about himself
and his author than he or Hemingway intended. Linda Wagner-Martin suggests
that particularly early on, Hemingway and protagonists such as Barnes and Frederic Henry are more interested in women as sex partners than as people—that
part of being macho is being sexually adept, being able to impress women with
their sexual prowess.[1] I suggest that what Barnes begins to notice about "*her* side
of it"—not just the erotic possibilities of the female for male pleasure, the focus
of Vonnegut's satire of Harold Campbell's *Memoirs of a Monogamous Casanova*, but
a profound sensitivity to the female as autonomous and valuable in herself—
became the key to Hemingway and his protagonists' growth from *To Have and
Have Not* (1937) on.

It is this deepening awareness of what the tough-guy persona cost the women
in his life, and moreover how the submerged feminine in himself threatened what
Jung called a loss of moral identity, disastrous both to Hemingway's person and
his art, that is the focus of part two of this book, "The Androgynous Turn." Just
as Kathryn Hume locates the increased affirmation of Wilbur Swain in *Slapstick*
(1976) and Walter Starbuck in *Jailbird* (1979) in their more productive relationships with women, it is the discovery and embrace of the love and optimism of
loving women such as Helen Gordon in *To Have and Have Not*, Maria in *For Whom
the Bell Tolls*, and Renata in *Across the River and into the Trees* that allows Hemingway and protagonists such as Robert Jordan, Robert Cantwell, and Santiago to

91

reject the escapism of their earlier selves and, as Hume says of Vonnegut's new hero, to respond more positively to the hurts of the world.

Later in this part of the book, we will see that, just as the emergence of Vonnegut's "new me" in *Breakfast of Champions* climaxes in the more optimistic, feminized self of *Bluebeard*, so what Nancy Comley and Robert Scholes call "el nuevo" Hemingway,[2] the more conscious and gender-integrated Hemingway of the posthumous fiction, emerges in *Islands in the Stream, Under Kilimanjaro*, and particularly *The Garden of Eden*, a novel Debra Moddelmog says inspired "the most extensive reevaluation" of a writer's reputation and life "ever undertaken."[3] These critics argue correctly that this new Hemingway was a writer whose androgynous impulses not only contradict the machismo Hemingway of myth, but whose complex female protagonists and problematic treatment of gender suggest that the female voice in Hemingway was always the most interesting and critical aspect of his life and work.

Yet, while Mark Spilka and others find a degree of conscience, introspection, and self-criticism in the posthumous works so advanced the new hero is unrecognizable from those of the past, as if brand new,[4] I suggest the hero's awakening to the destructive consequences of the masked anima—and to a willingness to access that dangerous self-knowledge so long hidden beneath the iceberg's surface—begins in earnest and shows steady progression in *To Have and Have Not, For Whom the Bell Tolls, Across the River and into the Trees*, and *The Old Man and the Sea*—the same quest for self-understanding—and for cleansing and renewal—that separated the "new" Vonnegut from his older, more pessimistic self. If Hemingway's posthumous novels and stories more overtly represent the courageous "confessional" works Gertrude Stein called for, "the real story of Ernest Hemingway"[5] that Vonnegut's critique misses, we see that in Hemingway's final four published novels his efforts to resolve the psychic struggle of anima versus animus prove startlingly analogous to Vonnegut's.

Among the notable achievements of the "new me" of Vonnegut's and Hemingway's second careers is both authors' defining new directions in their art by identifying with humanity as a whole, what Walter Starbuck calls his involvement in "the Family of Man,"[6] an invigorated social conscience that denounces public apathy and commits itself to the illumination and curing of America's crimes of injustice and violence against those who are without political power or great wealth. These crimes "for money and power's sakes,"[7] described in *God Bless You, Mr. Rosewater* as the force that turned the American dream "belly up," play equally important roles in Hemingway's *To Have and Have Not* and Vonnegut's *Jailbird* as the heroes embrace the long-suppressed feminine.

Both novels portray the tragic consequences of a heartless economic system that classifies honest, industrious, citizens such as Harry Morgan as bloodsuckers if they ask for a living wage and compassionate souls such as Walter Starbuck as insane if they show empathy for the poor. Walter is appalled that people consider his ideal of universal brotherhood the product of a diseased mind, a vision of common people pooling their resources as brothers and sisters, creating a friendly and merciful society in which the only ones excluded are those who have taken more wealth than they need. Walter understands that the dispassionate, uncaring system he longs to correct maintains itself through the avarice and cruel indifference to suffering of money-grabbing men such as his surrogate father, the crusty Harvard-educated industrialist Alexander McCone. The predatory lawyer "Bee-Lips," Robert Simmons in *To Have and Have Not* has his hands in other people's pockets more often than his own; he is a "buzzard" who would pick the bones of his own mother.[8] Just released from jail for his "preposterous contributions to the Watergate" scandal, Walter Starbuck finds so many lawyers in prison that his favorite joke becomes, "if you found yourself talking to somebody who hasn't been to law school, watch your step. He's either the warden or a guard."[9] While Harry Morgan is not literally a "jailbird," he risks prison or worse by using his fishing boat to run illegal liquor, swearing he will do what he must to keep his children from going hungry, except digging sewers for the government for less money than he needs to feed them.

With the help of the mayor of Cleveland, Ohio, President Grover Cleveland, local bankers, and the local police chief, Walter's benefactors, Alexander McCone and Sons, authorize the massacre of dozens of homeless, nonunion have-nots picketing the McCone Bridge and Iron Company. Pinkerton sharpshooters kill fourteen unarmed men and women while McCone looks on approvingly from his office window. Harry Morgan encounters one such corrupt and greedy capitalist in the form of Frederic Harrison, a government man mixed up in the prices of things people eat, making them more costly. The mafia-like Chinamen who deal in guns and death describe their transactions with Harry—the smuggling of fellow Chinese promised freedom but brutally abandoned or killed—as "plenty big business."[10]

The world of *To Have and Have Not* is as morally and physically ruinous to Harry Morgan as the world of *Jailbirds* is to Walter Starbuck. Starbuck feels he commits moral suicide by supporting the political and economic machine that jails and ostracizes him. His betrayal of youthful ideals—testifying against a friend during the McCarthy hearings, then helping Nixon officials hide illegal campaign money in his office—fills him with such self-contempt he "strangles on shame,"[11] seeing little hope of reversing the corruption of a free-market system that produces ragged regiments of bag ladies and dope fiends and child batterers. When Walter is wrongly arrested for theft and placed in a padded cell in the basement of a police station, he exclaims that his childhood heroes Sacco and Vanzetti never cracked up—but he finally does. Walter reflects Vonnegut's own frustrations as social reformer. A "canary bird" inspired by a passion for mercy and justice, Walter feels that his "wings" have been broken and that he might never fly again.[12]

Harry Morgan, as a degraded and humiliated member of the have-nots, is similarly victimized by the unjust laws and authoritarian institutions that entrap and imprison Starbuck. Robbed of dignity and turned into an angry and violent outlaw, Harry must endure his rich and rude client Robert Johnson's absurd pretense of superiority, which is based on money alone.[13] In what might have appropriately been called "The Fire Sermon"—after part 3 of T. S. Eliot's *The Waste Land*—Hemingway's brilliant closing chapters of *To Have and Have Not* portray the betrayals of the American dream from top to bottom. With a deftness of touch reminiscent of Fitzgerald's linkage of the vacuous Daisy Buchanan and her brutally insensitive and spiritually vacant husband, Tom, at the top of the social ladder, with the quintessentially soulless and vulgar George and Myrtle Wilson in the ash heaps below, Hemingway's spiritually defrauded wastelanders wind up literally side by side at the end of the novel, as a workingman's fishing boat and a luxurious yacht tie up alongside one another in the Key West yacht basin. Rich and poor, Hemingway's hollow men reap what they sew: sterility and death, death-in-life for those who numb themselves with alcohol or pills or cynical despair, and literal death for the suicides when the money or the abused and corrupted bodies give out. In what Vonnegut in *Bluebeard* called "The Republic of Suicide," Hemingway wrote of the myriad macabre ways people kill themselves when the American dream becomes a nightmare; their only drawback is the mess they leave for relatives to clean up.[14]

When Henry Carpenter, a Harvard graduate like Eliot Rosewater and Walter Starbuck, finds that his trust fund from his wealthy mother is running out and that he is being investigated by the Internal Revenue Bureau, he sums up the ruthless economic system he administers, in which—when scotch and soda no longer serve—suicide is readily available. Carpenter has neither remorse nor pity for the "suckers" he has swindled; yet he misses the tragic irony that he has been as much defrauded by the dream that equates money with happiness as Morgan or poor Albert Tracy, Morgan's fisherman helper who lies dead beside him. We are told that the money on which it was not worthwhile for Carpenter to live was one hundred and seventy dollars more per month than that which the fisherman Albert Tracy was supporting his family on at the time of his death, three days before Carpenter kills himself.

T. S. Eliot's chessmen are all in place, Fitzgerald's unseeing God surveying the spiritual horror with pitiless indifference: the suicidal Carpenter; the rude and bored Wallace Johnston, another wasteland idler, with money from "silk mills," known for abusing his help and bribing them to keep his homosexuality secret; a sixty-year-old insomniac grain broker who thinks in terms of "deals, sales, transfers and gifts," who ordinarily quiets his nerves with "Scotch high balls," but whose organs are so corroded he can no longer drink; and the alcoholic, "professional son-in-law" of the rich Dorothy Hollis. As Dorothy's cuckold husband lies passed out and snoring, oblivious to her affair with "Eddie," "tight as a tick" in an adjoining cabin, she muses in Molly Bloom–like fashion on the uselessness of both men, but unlike the passionate Molly, Dorothy has feelings of futility that make her as uninterested in her mechanical sex life with John and Eddie as Eliot's typist with her "carbuncular" clerk, whose "caresses" are "unreproved, if undesired." As Dorothy sits admiring herself in her dressing-room mirror, brushing her "lovely" hair in "a hundred strokes," her vanity requires no more response than Eliot's typist, smoothing her hair "with automatic hand," or the aristocrat in "A Game of Chess," brushing her hair out "in fiery points." Though Dorothy herself is "no bargain," she, like every woman in Hemingway's novel, is clearly the victim of a cold and brutal economic system that shapes and uses women as sexual playthings or economic commodities. Her longings for sincere love are so betrayed by the spiritually and often physically impotent men around her that she resigns herself to "Bitch-hood" and drugs herself to sleep to keep from going crazy.

However self-justified, Morgan's recourse to violence fuels Vonnegut's charge that Hemingway values violence and machismo over gentleness and intellect. Whereas Vonnegut symbolizes the ascendance of Walter Starbuck's kinder and more optimistic self by having him exchange his prison uniform for civilian clothes, Morgan determines "to soldier on" in the manner of Frederic Henry, relying on his "cojones" rather than more rational means to assert his worth and help his family. Deciding that economic circumstances justify any sort of mayhem to exact justice, Harry puts to use what he has learned on the police force in Miami about his pump gun and his Smith and Weston thirty-eight special, which flops against his leg like a large penis. Though he loses an arm during a gun fight with Cuban police while smuggling liquor, he is "still a man" as long as he has "two of something else."[15] The problem is that, beyond symbolizing a capacity for courage and self-reliance, Harry's fierce pride in "those other two" activates the same violent macho posturing and enjoyment in inflicting pain that reflects the darker side of Jake Barnes and Frederic Henry.

Evidently having to provide for his family by smuggling booze or Chinese men into the United States justifies breaking the neck of a man who perhaps meant Harry no harm. With the same cool indifference as that exhibited by Frederic Henry when he shoots fleeing Italian soldiers, Harry grabs Mr. Sing by the throat with both hands and bends his neck back until it cracks. Mr. Sing, Harry says, "was flopping and bouncing worse than any dolphin on a gaff."[16] The scene recalls Harold Ryan's boastful account to his son in *Happy Birthday, Wanda June* that he choked a soldier to death with piano wire while serving as a guerrilla fighter in World War II. Harold tells Paul, "Your father was quite a virtuoso with piano wire. That's nicer than a knife, isn't it—as long as you don't look at the face after-wards. The face turns a curious shade of avocado."[17]

Starbuck and Morgan are both associated with Christ's suffering. But whereas Harry is spiritually bankrupt, Starbuck's suffering ennobles him, creating a more honest and mature idealism. Walter accepts personal responsibility for the forces that corrupt the American dream, shows genuine contempt for those in prison who boast of fortunes made swindling poor people, and emerges from his tomb-like imprisonment not a "jailbird" but a regenerated shaman. His devotion to three women—his wife, Ruth, and his two former sweethearts, Mary Kathleen and Sarah Wyatt—redeems Walter's tragic past and creates his role as an agent of illumination and spiritual healing. Walter both gives and receives love by taking Ruth and Mary's suffering upon himself. He is the Christological age of thirty-three when he and Ruth marry; devoting himself to restoring Ruth's men-tal health, he declares "My optimism became bricks and mortar and wood and nails."[18] He repays the redemptive love and spiritual potential of "Mary" Kath-leen O'Looney, the primary shaper of Walter's new shamanlike identity, by continuing her unselfish dedication to honesty and kindness at RAMJAC. Appro-priate to what Kathryn Hume calls *Jailbird*'s "Christian mythic exostructure,"[19] Mary Kathleen's death makes Walter's salvation possible. Though she dies in Walter's arms, weary of trying to improve the world, Walter rises from her under-ground tomb to assume her spiritual identity and to carry on her moral commit-ments.[20] Corporate infighting drives Walter "mad" at times, and other greedy conglomerates threaten RAMJAC's new humanitarian purposes, but he boasts of significant sponsorship of the arts and of single-handedly extending the moral life of RAMJAC by placing more good people in positions of executive power.

As Josef Benson suggests, if Hemingway were writing in *To Have and Have Not* only about a man forced by fate to be aggressive and cruel in a world that is unforgiving, then readers might follow Vonnegut's lead and chalk up Hemingway as a racist, a sexist, and an example of a man whose writing is now dated.[21] Ger-mane to our inquiry into Hemingway as Vonnegut's "dark beast," the secret sharer of Vonnegut's embattled literary imagination, a surface contrast of Walter Starbuck's hard-won optimism with Harry Morgan's defeatism appears to justify Vonnegut's view of Hemingway as the dangerously fatalistic self Vonnegut felt he must renounce to avoid Hemingway's crippling depression and suicide. It is such hopelessness that defines Harry Morgan and his wife's death wish by the end of the novel, feelings of spiritual as well as material defeat that Marie expresses by remarking that no one returns from the dead. Describing herself as "dead inside," Marie's lament, "So that's the way it goes," sounds forebodingly like Billy Pil-grim's "so it goes." "Nobody's," she says, "going to tell me that there ain't noth-ing now but take it every day the way it comes."[22] She knows Harry feels the same way, deciding that at the end he was just worn out. Given that Harry's limited imagination and his militant bearing preclude any recourse to violence except violence itself, his conclusion that "they" do not give you any choice indeed suggests he has to do what he has to do, play the fatal endgame of Frederic Henry. Harry's death by water is as ignominious as Gatsby's or Eliot's Phlebas's, attended by Marie's inefficacious "murmur of maternal lamentation"[23] for the living dead and the sinned upon feminine.

The mood of Walter Starbuck's story is so subdued we might mistake him as even less hopeful than Morgan or Billy Pilgrim, echoing Billy's fatalistic cry "so it goes" with "it's all right" about the sociopolitical madness around him. Contributing to Walter's "air of defeat" are his memories of war and what he discovered at age twenty-two when he returned penniless from Europe to find that his father's architectural firm had gone defunct and that his mother had taken her life; soon thereafter the first atomic bomb was dropped on Japan. But if Harry Morgan's aggression ironically emasculates him, Walter's adoption of kindness and respect restores his potency, uniting him with the community of sufferers and prophets including Christ, Joan of Arc, Sacco and Vanzetti, Laurel and Hardy, and particularly Mary Kathleen O'Looney.[24] It is of no little consequence that, relative to Vonnegut's ongoing quarrel with the pessimism in himself, he should resurrect the exemplar of his more cynical voice, Kilgore Trout, alias artist Bob Fender, a fellow jailbird, to accentuate the triumph of the canary bird who affirms versus the Trout self that denies. For now, rather than a harbinger of despair, Trout/Fender's genteel humanity provides an "alternate universe"[25] for Walter. As a tailor of Walter's new identity, Fender mends the hole in the crotch of Walter's pants (restores potency) and as a fantasist, warns Walter of the perils of "not giving a damn," which, like Vonnegut, Walter sees as the most serious threat to the planet.

Still more efficacious to Walter/Vonnegut's quest to overcome feelings of futility and to adopt a more caring and hopeful identity is the supposedly demented Mary Kathleen O'Looney, bag lady but once political activist and Walter's college sweetheart, whose powers of psychic healing and creative optimism prove Walter's salvation. Directly counter to the defeatism that helps doom Harry and Marie Morgan, it is Mary Kathleen who informs Walter that he can be as powerful as he wants to be, making him determined, as Kathryn Hume says, to show "what an individual can do to alleviate the pain inherent in the human condition."[26] Walter's increased affirmation clearly relates to his more productive relationship with these wise and merciful women, "more virtuous, braver about life, and closer to the secret of the universe" than he has ever been.[27] Perhaps the most important name on the list of redemptive females above is that of Walter's own mother, whom he lists prominently with the four women he believes sacred to him. Walter is not only no longer "petrified" of women such as his mother for placing impossible demands on his manhood—expecting him to be a brave soldier, a great lover, and a wonderful wage earner. He now determines to make amends for his responsibility for the "publication of some of the most scurrilous books about women ever written."[28] It seems more than coincidental that Vonnegut should compare a song inspiring men to overcome their fears of women—sexual inadequacy in particular—with one sung by lion hunters on a night before a hunt.[29]

But there is ample evidence in *To Have and Have Not*, as Josef Benson argues, that Hemingway's purpose in this little-appreciated novel is more to indict than to celebrate the machismo and violence of lion hunters or bullfighters, testosterone-crazed (or sexually inadequate) men like Harry Morgan, whose aggression is so disastrous to themselves and others. What if, this time, as Vonnegut did in *Mother Night* and *Slaughterhouse-Five*, it is Hemingway who distanced himself from the hunter-killer in himself by repudiating Morgan's brutality and fatalism as Vonnegut did by renouncing the formerly noxious Trout in *Breakfast of Champions*? By no coincidence does Robert Jordan in *For Whom the Bell Tolls* open himself like Starbuck to the possibilities of recreating himself and pursuing dreams of a more just and harmonious social order by promising to write a book about women after the war. We may assume the book Jordan has in mind is precisely the one Hemingway has given us in *To Have and Have Not*, with its richly complex portraits of women such as Marie, Helen Gordon, and Dorothy Hollis who "pay, and pay, and pay" for male aggression. He soon followed these depictions with the portrayal of Maria in *For Whom the Bell Tolls* and Renata in *Across the River and into the Trees*, works that, like Vonnegut's, honor the healing powers of women.

Benson points out that the use of multiple narrators complicates and undercuts the authority of Morgan's masculine point of view. With the phallic pen removed from Morgan's hand, the absence of language becomes his greatest impotence. We have in Harry a protagonist who not only does not want to think but cannot. While Vonnegut established ties to his protagonist in *Jailbird* stronger, more intimate than ever, spending approximately half of his thirty-eight-page prologue explaining Walter's failed parents as his own, Morgan has fewer autobiographical connections to Hemingway than any other protagonist. Morgan's past least resembles his creators; he is the least artistically inclined, and his simple, unintuitive mind makes him as unlikely to be a dependable conduit for truth telling as the self-absorbed and unaware writer Richard Gordon. Perhaps Hemingway in fact found his Trout-like scapegoat for aggression and despair in Morgan-Gordon, the brute in the writer, the schizoid artist-killer, embroiled in interminable contradiction and moral confusion.[30]

However, the foremost case for *To Have and Have Not* as a product of feminine enlightenment comes in the author's portrayal of either women damaged by authoritative masculine behavior or women wiser, kinder, and more psychically whole than their male counterparts, who parody violent macho posturing.

Whereas in Brett Ashley, Hemingway did little more than give lip service to the totalitarian machinery of government and war that kills the spirit of women like Brett (as it does Vonnegut's Helga and Resi Noth), Marie Morgan, Dorothy Hollis, Helene Bradley, and Helen Gordon offer a veritable education in the way women pay for masculine domination and insensitivity. In this case the "haves" are men and the "have-nots" are women, and Harry's epiphany—"no matter how a man alone ain't got no bloody fucking chance"—refers to the problematic social limitations on women as well as to the brutalizing power of animus untempered and unmediated by the protective, nurturing force of anima. As Harry says, "It had taken him a long time to get it out and it had taken him all of his life to learn it."[31]

As epitomized by the truculent, bitter marriage between Helen and the writer Richard Gordon, masculine pretense assures that Richard's inner world remains in darkness, in "shamefaced silence" about the real nature of his desire for his wife/mother.[32] I take this reading from Jung's assertion that the supposed super potency of men like Harry and Richard may cover up feelings of sexual inferiority for which their wives are forced to compensate. Such men, Jung contended, require their wives to provide them with proof they are the strong men they outwardly pretend to be, rather than the weaker, more emotionally needy men their wives know in private. Richard may enter Freddy's bar "plenty cocky"—the preening rooster with "barnyard" morals his wife knows him to be[33]—but twice in one day women expose the desperately insecure man behind the mask. First his mistress, Helene Bradley, accuses him of having no regard for women and, reversing the male role Harry has in mind in his advice to Albert to slap his wife when she gives him hell, slaps Richard repeatedly. Then Helen deflates his ego by calling him a talentless, "picknose" writer who whores for money and by saying her new friend John MacWalsey is the good man Richard is not. Richard's casual infidelities so sour Helen that she sarcastically rejects his sentimental notion that two people can be everything to one another, the illusion that shatters for Frederic Henry and Catherine Barkley—and for Campbell and Helga Noth. "Love was the greatest thing, wasn't it," she tells him. "Love was what we had that no one else had or could ever have . . . and I was your whole life."[34] Confirming Helen's estimation of Richard's inability to love anyone but himself, his final thoughts of her are purely physical. Unlike Marie, neither mistress nor wife will grant Richard illegitimate authority over her by encouraging his masculine facade. This refusal so shatters Richard's heroic image of himself, it is as if he is left with no self at all, no "true personality" in Jung's terms.

Helen's contrasting close and fruitful relationship with the economics professor John MacWalsey makes a strong case that Hemingway had indeed begun to reevaluate ideas of manhood based on dominance and assumptions of male superiority, an illusion whose exposure dooms Richard Gordon to a life of drink and self-pity but which, at his final breath, provides illumination and a measure of spiritual redemption for Harry Morgan. Whether consciously or inadvertently, Hemingway found in Helen and MacWalsey the androgynous ideal secretly ensconced in his iceberg, which allowed him to pursue its potential for new personal and creative growth. Both individually and together, Helen and MacWalsey embody the complementing male and female parts Jung posited as the ideal of a healthy, integrated soul. MacWalsey is kind, generous, intelligent, and thoughtful, where Richard Gordon is vain, self-absorbed, and, like Morgan, morally blind and incapable of honest introspection. MacWalsey is in fact exactly the new, more feminized hero Penelope Ryan calls for in *Happy Birthday, Wanda June*, the new hero "who refuses to fight."[35] "What kind of a country has this become?" Harold Ryan asks in alarm. "The men wear beads and refuse to fight—and the women adore them. America's days of greatness are over."[36] Exactly as Penelope is drawn to the doctor and peacenik in Norbert Woodly because he abjures fighting and hates pain, so Helen prefers the educated, empathetic professor MacWalsey, who, as Harold puts it, would rather "be a woman and run with women"[37] than hunt or fish, who thinks with his brain instead of his body, and who refuses to fight when Richard Gordon hits him. "I don't fight," MacWalsey tells Gordon, using words instead of fists, Woodly's "weapons" of compassion and unselfishness. Like Harold Ryan, Gordon feels cheated of satisfaction, "mocked, insulted," as Ryan complains to Penelope. Penelope tells her mystified husband she hopes Woodly never hunts, never kills an animal or harms another human being. MacWalsey so worries about Gordon he assists him home, hates himself for causing him emotional pain, and wishes he could do more to relieve his suffering.

I suggest that, if there is a genuine hero to this story, it is Helen Gordon, who, like Marie Morgan, is confident and strong, but who, unlike Marie, refuses to play the man's "game" that renders her a "slave" of destructive male fantasies of control and domination, like that of the woman whom the drunken vet invents for Gordon to bolster Gordon's morale, "the finest little wife in the world," a woman much like Marie, who is so devoted, so "carried away with [him]," if he "got a whim, it's her law."[38] When the vet's friends say they've never seen this wonderful wife, the vet explains that sometimes he thinks she is maybe Ginger Rogers, waiting quietly for him to return. "Keeping the home fires burning," someone retorts.[39]

Marie Morgan probably does not fear being knocked around by Harry, but she fits Jung's description of wives who need to convince themselves as well as others that their husbands are the heroes they pretend to be in public. To offset Harry's anxiety about his missing limb—a potential symbol for limp sexuality—Marie assures him that she can think about him anytime and get excited, that the way he is built, "she could do it all night and never sleep."[40] There are no more men like Harry. Marie's importance in supporting Harry's masculine image takes on familiar meaning when we see her assuming the role of mother, a role Jung explained that the wife inherits from the husband's mother, the first bearer of the "soul-image," and whose continuing protection he seeks. Marie cuts up his food "as for a small boy,"[41] reprimands him for swearing at "her table," and watches over him as he sleeps, "just like a baby."[42]

If anyone's "cojones" are real—that is, emblematic of genuine courage, self reliance, and moral probity—the honor belongs to Helen. Unlike Marie or Harry or Richard, or the battered, despondent vet, people who, as Harry decides, have no other choice but to "take it," Helen has the will and spunk to give it out as well. If, as we may assume, this pretty, blond woman in the white sweater who turns heads in Freddy's bar is modeled after the real-life Martha Gellhorn, perhaps the androgynous "Marty," a journalist herself, was ultimately less negative an influence in Hemingway's life than he let on, but of all his wives provided the best example of the manly woman he secretly admired and perhaps desired to be. As Helen does for MacWalsey, Martha occasioned a dramatic turn in Hemingway's life that anticipated the author's achievement of a more integrated, more balanced relationship of the gender opposites within himself, and the enlarging humanistic sensibility that informs his next novel, *For Whom the Bell Tolls*. MacWalsey is so moved by the strength and honesty of Helen's love, it changes him too, forever. Determining he must live up to the image of the aware and compassionate man Helen's androgynous example inspires, he will no longer blame others for his problems, or rely on the anesthetic of alcohol to numb his pain.

# Six

## Anima and Animus in
## *For Whom the Bell Tolls*
## and *Slapstick*

■

God guide the hand and mind of Dr. Wilbur Rockefeller.
Eliza in *Slapstick*

Oh, Sweet Blessed Virgin. . . . Take care of him for me.
Maria in *For Whom the Bell Tolls*

Judging from the evidence of *Jailbird* and *Slapstick* and *To Have and Have Not* and *For Whom the Bell Tolls*, both writers survived what Vonnegut in *Breakfast of Champions* called the "spiritual crossroads" of their careers—a battle with personal despair—and, with the help of their work as therapy, learned to create for themselves that "humane harmony" whose absence may nearly have driven them crazy. Wilbur Swain, like Vonnegut, has learned to resolve personal and social fragmentation by creating fantasies that encourage communal bonding rather than narcissistic withdrawal. Having reevaluated the vision in *The Sun Also Rises* and *A Farewell to Arms* of what it means to live "decently" or "humanly" within the existential void of the modern world, Robert Jordan, like Hemingway, finds salvation not in isolation from others but in collaboration with a brother-sisterhood that cannot be disavowed or ignored if we are to truly live with grace.

Whereas Hemingway once appeared to derive his world view from the bullfight and his personal and artistic values from the image of the dominant, conquering matador, the humanity of his vision of life and love in *For Whom the Bell Tolls* suggests a universe in harmony with itself, whose major symbols are the life-giving and spiritually regenerative sea, the Gulf Stream, the islands of the Caribbean, and the creatures of the ocean world. Joseph De Falco describes what he calls a vision and a system of aesthetics of a different order once Hemingway "adopted" the Gulf Stream as a major metaphor and abandoned his long-favored use of the bullfight: a major shift to the affirmative mode, and "new fresh ways" of rendering reality in his work. DeFalco says, "To express themes of human solidarity and brotherhood led Hemingway away from the sophisticated rituals of the bullring to the pastoral primitiveness of the Gulf Stream." This universe is shared, DeFalco explains, by Jordan, Colonel Cantwell, and Santiago, where man's "willed actions have meaning in a way they do not for a compromised Jake Barnes or a despairing Frederic Henry."[1]

This more integrated and harmonized universe is shared as well by Wilbur Swain, whose major goal—explained in the first two pages of *Slapstick*—is "to bargain in good faith with destiny"[2] and to treat people with "common decency,"[3] an aspiration that describes the dominant impulse in Jordan, Cantwell, and Santiago as well. Apropos of Spilka's observation that Hemingway learned to listen to "devilish and adoring muses within himself"—learned, that is, what a woman is and suffers—it is the presence of adoring sisterly or sisterlike muses in these works of Vonnegut and Hemingway that inspires the hero to "bargain" in good faith with the feminine both without and within, no longer to flee or hide from it through strategies of numbing, drugging, or masking. Swain emerges from his amazingly intimate bonding with Eliza, Wilbur's literal sister, and Jordan from his with Maria, Jordan's surrogate sister, changed men, more whole and optimistic and with a deeper capacity to love.

Vonnegut and Hemingway's protagonists grow and heal in similar ways as a result of Eliza and Maria's nurturing influence, spiritual as well as physical, the most surprising of which is the power of these wise and loving muses not just to heal the protagonist's personal wounds—such as apathy, flight, anger, and denial— but to lead them to desire and actively seek the healing of an entire society. Salvation for both Jordan and Swain comes in learning to identify their personal "destiny" with that of humanity as a whole, epitomized by Hemingway's idealistic inscription from John Donne: "No man is an island . . . ; any man's death diminishes me, because I am involved in Mankind; and therefore never send to know for whom the bell tolls; it tolls for thee." Jordan declares, and is ready to sacrifice his life for, an ideal of universal brotherhood that he explains in relation to his companion, Anselmo, as follows: "Neither you nor this old man is anything. You are instruments to do your duty. . . . there is a bridge and that bridge can be the point on which the future of the human race can turn."[4]

While we see Wilbur Swain and Robert Jordan making admirable progress in addressing those deep-seated psychological wounds we have called "androgynous," it is clear that both continue to struggle with the dangerous habit of moral evasion of their predecessors and that those wounds and those evasions are those of their authors. The anger and hatred that wells up in Jordan from the cruelties and betrayals of war lead inevitably to painful memories of childhood battles with his tyrannical mother and weak-willed father. The two forms of "bitchery,"[5] the two kinds of "heads business"[6] coalesce when, eyeing a disabled soldier, Jordan says he knows about cripples. With thoughts of his own father's suicide fresh in mind, Hemingway had Jordan focus particularly on his father's cowardice. Worrying that he may have to take his own life rather than be captured and interrogated, Jordan tells himself, "I don't want to do that business that my father did," choosing instead to bolster his courage by remembering his grandfather's courage in the Civil War.[7] Jordan remembers being embarrassed by his father's sentimental piety when he went away to school for the first time, the "damp religious sound of the prayer" and the "awkwardness" of the kissing.[8] He remembers the grandfather's arrowheads that his mother burned, then thinks of the grandfather's Smith and Wesson his father used to kill himself, which, when he dropped it in the lake, made bubbles as large as a watch charm.[9] The reference brings to mind Vonnegut's frequent use of spiral and clock imagery to describe the circular, age-old impulse to aggression and death, which the young Robert Jordan / Nick Adams evidently feels, if only subliminally. A wiser, more aware, and forthright Hemingway/Jordan in fact comes closer than ever to understanding the relative complicity of Nick Adams's cold and unloving parents in creating the wounds of childhood. Jordan realizes that his judgments about his father's cowardice originate from a youthful and immature mind, but more important, he wonders if it were not, after all, the paradoxical mother, threatening but strong, who provided what the father lacked, not just courage but an androgynous force vital to his creativity. It seems clear that in the androgynous, compassionate warrior Pilar—a gypsy version of Grace Hemingway—the author experienced new dimensions of imagination and heart that include a better understanding of his mother's complexity, if not the forgiveness he afforded his father. Yet Jordan's preoccupation with his grandfather's soldierly demeanor at the end of the novel, his concern with manly comportment, and his continuing need to defend his father at his mother's expense suggests that, when he looks down into the river's swift currents in the "cool dark" below, there are still those shadowy places, entanglements of the feminine he must investigate more fully to complete his human and artistic reconstruction. In a moment of black humor, when Maria asks Jordan if the purpose behind his father's committing suicide was "to avoid being tortured," Jordan answers, "Yes."[10]

Judging from Swain and Vonnegut's need to portray "love" as less important than "common decency," it appears they too have considerable work to do to overcome fears of feminine vulnerability and reconcile themselves with parents viewed as monstrously destructive. Pointing to Laurel and Hardy as chief sources of instruction in his childhood, Vonnegut's autobiographical preface explains that he finds it natural to discuss life without ever mentioning "love," that based on past experience love just does not seem important to him. His favorite relationships have been those in which he treated somebody well for a little while or maybe even for a tremendously long time, while they treated him well in turn. He cannot distinguish between the love he has for people and the love he has for dogs. In short Vonnegut found love so troublesome, even "poisonous," he would rather have "common decency"[11] instead.

But both authors were so sly in their management of such abstractions that readers must join these increasingly rational and analytical narrators in sorting out such equivocal terms as "love," "truth," and "desire" for themselves. It is in fact their mutual understanding of self-limiting, even dangerous, moral absolutes that philosophically unites Swain and Jordan and determines their creative progresses, opening them to more imaginative and emotionally enriching relationships with women.

Jordan knows that his devotion to duty is far more complicated than he first makes it sound. When questioning the notion that he has only one thing to do, he sets in motion an inner dialogue that constitutes the hero's new capacity for vigorous self-scrutiny. When Jordan assures himself that the importance of the cause will enable him to do anything he is ordered, the self-critiquing Jordan "feels a little theatrical," a product of too much "Latin bravado."[12] Just as Vonnegut castigates Starbuck and Wilbur Swain for blindly doing the will of others, so Hemingway holds Jordan accountable for unquestioned allegiance to his superiors when those orders are as inhumane and dehumanizing. While he hopes to maintain his innocence by arguing that the responsibility of an act is that of the one who orders it, Jordan's evolving moral sense causes him to ask: "But should a man carry out irresponsible orders knowing what they lead to?"[13]

In *Hemingway's Spanish Tragedy*, I described this new kind of conflict in Robert Jordan, Robert Cantwell, and Santiago as a kind of morality play between the forces of compassion and restraint on the one hand and aggression and destructive male pride on the other. Allen Josephs calls this split Spain's genius and its devil, "two-Janus-faces of the same being."[14] In the course of this agonized psychic interplay, the hero's fatalistic acceptance of the Spaniard's view of the world as endlessly unjust and destructive leads him to sanction the destructive impulse to cruelty and death dealing in himself and in the world around him. But at more rational moments, the hero seems at one with Vonnegut's reflective, self-searching protagonist in recognizing that these aggressive impulses are preludes to moral and physical disaster. As Hemingway's own stirrings of conscience increase over the years, so the conflict in the mind of the hero becomes more severe, self-conscious, and articulated.[15]

Vonnegut's explanation that the absence of affection and the fear of physical contact of Wilbur and Eliza Swain's parents is that of his own family gives us pause. Does his discourse on the limitations of love not mask lingering fears that the deeper, more demanding feeling of love may simply be beyond him as well? We think of Harold Ryan's answer to his wife, Penelope, when she asks him to tell her that he "loved" her once, that love at least existed somewhere in their lives: "Testimonials of that sort are—are beyond my range. I don't do them very well,"[16] except this time it is Vonnegut who bears comparison with Ryan rather than Hemingway. Vonnegut confessed that, when one of his adopted sons said on his twenty-first birthday, "You know—you've never hugged me," his emotionally challenged father hugged him for the first time. "It was very nice," Vonnegut said. "It was like rolling around on a rug with a Great Dane we used to have."[17] About his older brother, Bernard, the Felix of *Deadeye Dick*, Vonnegut admitted, "We have hugged each other maybe three or four times—on birthdays, very likely and clumsily. We have never hugged in moments of grief."[18] Vonnegut was too honest not to acknowledge the connection between his continuing discomfort over physical intimacy and that of his protagonists throughout his work— caused by unloving, ineffectual, emotionally sterile parents. It is precisely his willingness to revisit the childhood nightmare of Rudy Waltz, Walter Starbuck, and Wilbur Swain that won him the affirmation of the novel's opening epigraph: "Call me but love, and I'll be new baptized."

Vonnegut declared that his story is about "desolated cities and spiritual cannibalism and incest and loneliness and lovelessness and death, and so on" and that it depicts him and his "beautiful sister as monsters."[19] Clearly the first cause of this pyramid of catastrophes is the "spiritual cannibalism" of parents who symbolically eat their children alive, creating the loneliness and lovelessness of Wilbur and Eliza's childhood, the desperation of incestuous love that comes from that, and the larger horror of desolated cities—the ruins of Manhattan, where almost everyone has been killed by a mysterious disease called the "Green Death." Vonnegut tells us directly that he writes of his grief for his sister, Alice, who died of cancer at the age of forty-one, among strangers in New Jersey. That tragedy was compounded by the death of Vonnegut's brother-in-law just days earlier in a train crash. Alice's death is projected into the novel in the fate of Wilbur's twin sister, Eliza, killed in a bizarre accident, an avalanche that leaves Wilbur in a fit of depression and drug addiction lasting thirty years. Among other revelations about the importance of his sister to his work, Vonnegut confessed that Alice was the person he had always written for—the secret of any wholeness and harmoniousness in his work. In *Slapstick* Vonnegut paid homage to her—making good a debt of love and inspiration by dedicating his own slapstick "opera" to her.

Vonnegut used the occasion of his sister's death not only to portray the intimacy he felt for her but to continue venting his anger at parents whose power to alienate their children is so great it turns them into monsters. Obsessively materialistic, viewing intelligence as a liability in their champagne world of power and appearance, Wilbur and Eliza's parents are so stupefied and humiliated by the ugliness of their strange Neanderthal children, they entomb them in a spooky old family mansion on an isolated mountaintop in Vermont. Visiting the twins once a year on their birthdays, proffering affection with "bittersweet dread," the parents are the true grotesques of this piece. By the age of fifteen, Wilbur observes that he and his sister are more than unloved; their parents wish their children would hurry up and die.[20]

The fact is that, in the power created by the gender joining of these fraternal twins, Vonnegut found the long-sought cure for his and his hero's "head wound," a paradigm for psychic balance at the heart of their mutual quest to heal the wounds of childhood and war. Functioning as an intimate unity, thinking and feeling as an androgynous whole, they became, Wilbur declares, the geniuses they know themselves to be. Symbolic of the yin and yang of Jung's complementary aspects of soul, Wilbur's contribution is practical, analytical, and functional, while Eliza's talents are intuitive, expressive, and visionary.

Eliza and Wilbur's creative genius frightens and repels their parents more than ever, unleashing a new form of cruelty. Wilbur and Eliza are turned over to the family psychiatrist, then separated for good as Wilbur is whisked off to a school for severely disturbed children and Eliza is exiled to an expensive institution for the feebleminded. The forced separation not only destroys the harmony and wholeness of their single healthy mind, but it is also a separation so complete that Wilbur must be reminded over the years of his sister's existence somewhere in a world very different from his. Eliza's eventual death causes Wilbur years of destructive behavior in which he pretends to talk to his dead sister and finally considers suicide.

The rest of Wilbur's disaster-filled story might suggest that *Slapstick* is the bleakest, most demoralized of novels, the sort Vonnegut is accused of writing. The nation is bankrupt, and people are dying by the millions of the Albanian flu and that mysterious plague the "Green Death," a disease psychological in origin that infects its victims with will-lessness and apathy. But Wilbur's story, like Robert Jordan's, is not only about moral escapism or a failure to cope but also about the salubrious effects of loving women and sister-muses; and about the healing, self-reflexive process of art that allows Wilbur and Robert Jordan to experience new dimensions of imagination and heart.

Wilbur and Eliza twice experience something shocking and remarkable relative to the hero's long-repressed taboo desires. On the first occasion, while they are still children, knowing that, at their parents' request, a "cruel axe man" is about to split them in two, the twins wind up with more than their heads together: "the two of us . . . wound up under the table—with our legs wrapped around each other's necks in scissors grips, and snorting and snuffing into each other's crotches."[21] Later, during their final visit together, Eliza initiates something she has planned for a long time, binding and gagging their parents so they cannot interfere and then enticing Wilbur into an orgy of coupling and "writhing embraces" that lasts a week. The experience at first seems to leave Wilbur emotionally shattered.[22] The deeper consequence appears, however, when Wilbur twice hears his sister's voice, once when he graduates from medical school and again when he becomes president of the United States. Hovering over him in a helicopter during his graduation party, Eliza appears to Wilbur as an allegorical angel, showering him with these lines from a Shakespearean sonnet:

> Even for this let us divided live,
> And our dear love lose name of single one,
> That by this separation I may give
> That due to thee, which thou deservst alone.

Properly moved, the normally emotionless Wilbur says, "I shouted something daring; and something I genuinely felt for the first time in my life. . . . 'Eliza! I love you!' I said. . . . 'Did you hear me, Eliza? . . . I love you! I *really* love you!'" Then Eliza says, "I will say in turn something that I really mean, my brother— my twin. . . . God guide the hand and mind of Dr. Wilbur Rockefeller Swain."[23]

It is the abiding memory of Eliza's love for Wilbur and Alice's for Vonnegut, that allows Wilbur and his author to survive and lead creative, harmonious lives without them, empowering Vonnegut in his role as shaman and Wilbur, as a literal physician healer and later as president, to help overcome the crisis of fragmented identities and loneliness that threatens society at large. Symbolically appropriate to curing his own childhood afflictions, Wilbur becomes a pediatrician, and we learn that in the midst of their incestuous orgy, at the point of greatest intimacy, Wilbur alternated passionate embraces with his sister with passionate sessions at the typewriter, giving birth to what he calls his intellectual center of gravity, a manual on child rearing that is surely the counterpart of the life stories composed by Wilbur and Vonnegut, the fruit of that therapy and that invention by which the sickness of childhood has been transformed by art into something harmonious and whole. It is no coincidence that, when Wilbur attempts to reunite his mind with that of his dead sister in order to recreate the genius they had been in childhood, it is through an electronic device called a "Holligan" that bears a striking resemblance to a typewriter. The Holligan has obvious Freudian characteristics. Wilbur would have crawled into it if he could, and someone observes that, straddling the Holligan, he looked like "the biggest baboon in the world trying to fuck a football."[24] The experience is more crudely incestuous than the brother-sister love affair between Maria and Robert Jordan, or Nick Adams and Littless in "The Last Good Country," but both are emotionally nourishing and clearly encourage wholeness and growth.

As president, Wilbur puts to work his and Eliza's scheme to bring together people without great wealth or powerful friends into membership of thousands of artificial "extended families," in effect a social extension of his and Eliza's personal cure for alienation. Families are decided not by background, wealth, or social position but by new middle names that allow them to claim relatives all over the world. As with the chastened but still steadfast ideals of Walter Starbuck,

Wilbur's vision of extended families offers no panaceas—no "Garden of Eden" or womblike hiding places from complex human problems. Rather Wilbur's goals are modest, humane, democratic, and almost comically practical. His foremost hope is to increase the individual's sense of personal worth and power in determining his or her own destiny. Even as relative anarchy, disease, and economic collapse grip the country, with everybody being someone else's relative around the globe, people have become less lonely and more merciful. There is no such thing as a battle between strangers anymore. An antidote to the Green Death has been found, and Wilbur observes that the machines have decided to stop fighting. In a battle, Wilbur observes, people were deserting and surrendering and even embracing.

Except for Billy Pilgrim, each of Vonnegut's earlier heroes shows potential as a healer of self and then a healer of others. But Wilbur demonstrates the greatest potential yet to re-create himself through art. The faith that eludes previous heroes, but which now produces Wilbur's equilibrium, is the discovery of art and life alike as protean, open-ended structures—a faith much like the one Hemingway's Robert Jordan finds. Furthering the existential education of Rudy Waltz, Wilbur learns to manipulate such structures creatively by combining harmonious minds—thus answering the challenge of the universe, which Wilbur hears saying to him, "I await your instructions. You can be anything you want to be. I will be anything you want me to be."[25] Wilbur's narrative itself was experienced first as a daydream and then transformed into the story of this novel. Invoking the specter of Hemingway's infamous "they," Patricia Waugh suggests that, in such metafictional narratives as *Breakfast of Champions* and *Slapstick*, novelists have discovered a surprising way out of their dilemmas and paranoia. Rejecting the limitations of conventional forms of literary representation in vogue before World War II, writers such as Vonnegut, Waugh says, understood that reality or history no longer consists of eternal verities but a series of constructions, artifices, and impermanent structures.[26] When we turn to *For Whom the Bell Tolls*, we see how Waugh's observation serves more to identify Hemingway's own evolving epistemological sophistication than differences between Hemingway's realism and Vonnegut's fictional self-consciousness. The stifled gifts of invention of Jake Barnes, Frederic Henry, and Harry Morgan give way to Robert Jordan's creative, self-conscious use of language as renewal and celebration.

In perhaps the most resoundingly affirmative resolution to any Vonnegut novel to date, Wilbur Swain leaves this poem at his death, hoping someone will use it for his epitaph:

> And how did we then face the odds,
> Of man's rude slapstick, yes, and God's?
> Quite at home and unafraid,

Thank you,
In a game our dreams remade.[27]

Like Robert Jordan, Wilbur has learned to resolve personal and social fragmentation by using his more optimistic and humanistic view of life's creative possibilities to encourage communal bonding rather than narcissistic withdrawal. In the closing pages of *Slapstick*, Vonnegut embodied his optimistic faith that human beings can be anything they want to be in a final act of gender joining, Wilbur's mating at a time when he has thrown off his addiction to drugs, which eventually produces a granddaughter named "Melody." "Melody," Vonnegut explained in the prologue, "is what is left of my memory of my sister—of my optimistic imagination, of my creativeness."[28] In that spirit Melody arrives on the scene amid the desolation of New York City with a Dresden candlestick as a gift, climaxing an incredible journey eastward in search of her legendary grandfather and climaxing as well, I think, Vonnegut's long obsession with Dresden. She is surrounded by lifesaving equipment and vital living presences. She is pregnant; members of her extended family feed, warm her, and point the way; she possesses a compass, an alarm clock, and a needle and thread for weaving—the first for direction, the second for awareness, the third for weaving the loose ends of fictional yarn we are told Wilbur has left behind into more stories of wholeness and harmony such as *Slapstick*.

Through much of *For Whom the Bell Tolls*, it appears that Nick Adams's decision to avoid fishing the deeper waters of the unconscious continues to hold—that is, to use Vonnegut's expression, "to empty," thus "protect" himself, from "horrors" earlier than those of the immediate battlefields of war. Jordan repeats Nick Adams's belief that he can rid himself of bad experience by writing about it. "Once you write it down," he says, "it is all gone."[29] Yet, while Hemingway's latest psychically embattled hero does not survive the literal war in Spain, his courage to face long-suppressed fears of his war with vexing parents wins him the grace of Wilbur Swain's spiritual rebirth. As opposed to Nick's flight from painful self-knowledge, Jordan's androgynous turn seems to make it clear that Hemingway and his matured writer-hero have begun to view the tragic effects of machismo from Vonnegut's own critical lens, becoming the more dependable and courageous truth teller Hemingway had set out to be in *Death in the Afternoon*—writing not with tricked or deceived emotion about suffering he taught himself to suppress but with honesty and truth about what he really felt rather than what he was programmed to feel. I suggest Hemingway in *Death in the Afternoon* told us much more than he understood at the time when he condemned writers for blurring or shutting their eyes to scenes of unbearable pain. If to protect himself from potentially overwhelming grief the author were guilty of the very deception he deplored in disingenuous writers or cowardly bullfighters, it is "the real thing" that he was working so hard to get that he achieves in *For Whom the Bell Tolls*. It is not as much literal death, the more observable violence of the bullring, Jordan confronts but the inner violence of a fragmented psyche resulting from exaggerated machismo and the denied anima.

Just as with Wilbur Swain, Jordan's inward war between hope and despair corresponds to the literal civil war raging around him in Spain. Republicans war with fascists while the forces of restraint and aggression battle for Jordan's soul. All the members of Pablo's band display extremist tendencies, with the bloodthirsty Pablo at one pole and the tender-minded Anselmo at the other. Just as Swain's optimism is threatened by apathy, so Jordan is torn between cynicism and withdrawal, and love and engagement, as in his good companionship with Anselmo and his love for Maria. Jordan's devotion to the Spanish people is such that he wants desperately to believe in the justness of their cause. He tells himself, "This ideal gave you a part in something you could believe in wholly and completely and in which you felt an absolute brotherhood with the others who were engaged in it. It was something that you had experienced now and you gave such importance to it and the reason for it that your own death seemed of complete unimportance."[30] Yet Jordan's optimism is constantly undercut by the betrayals and frequent reversions to bestiality of those around him, and the pathological aspect of much that is irrationally aggressive within him. The intensity of Jordan's inner turmoil is so great, he might summarize his condition in the words of Wilbur Swain when Wilbur taps his head and says to a soldier, "You should see what it looks like in here."[31]

Jordan is so actively devoted to the establishment of a more harmonious human community that for a long time he tries to rationalize shameful acts of violence and cruelty among his comrades that undermine their cause. The killing of fascists by Pablo and his mob is perhaps more coldly brutal than any previous episode in Hemingway's work, a blood letting little different from mass murder; yet Jordan works hard to convince himself that the executions were necessary. He would like to put his conscience on hold for the duration of the war, to suspend all "thinking" that might undermine his ideals and clash with what he perceives to be his soldierly responsibilities. As the war effort worsens and he admits to lying more and more about things he no longer believes, he develops a strategy of conscious exaggeration and deceit that he not only argues is necessary for the war's prosecution, but which he comes to enjoy. The problem is that Jordan's pretend self encourages the self-deception he must resist to become the writer he aspires to be after the war.

Despite Jordan's massive disappointments, he does not lapse into the self-pity of Harry Morgan or the destructive cynicism of Barnes and Frederic Henry. Jordan's story, like Swain's, is about the forces that allow Jordan, like Swain, to become more merciful and self-confident and to achieve rare feelings of love and wholeness. That Jordan, who calls himself the "windy bastard," becomes his own severest critic mitigates against an otherwise unnerving authoritarian manner. Confessing there are things he knows nothing of that he thought he knew, he worries that "he had gotten to be bigoted and hidebound about his politics as a hard-shelled Baptist" and that his mind employed "clichés" both "revolutionary and patriotic" without criticism.[32] The things he comes to know in this war are not so simple, including his faith in the Spanish people and the purity of the republican cause, notably the trustworthiness of what Agustin calls the lunatic asylum of guerrilla fighters around them and the insane leadership of officers such as André Marty, whose incompetence represents the futility of the war effort in general. Commenting about his orders to blow up the bridge, Jordan laments, "What do I know about why this attack is made? Maybe it is only a holding attack. Maybe they want to draw those troops from somewhere else. Perhaps they make it to draw those planes from the North. Maybe that is what it is about. Perhaps it is not expected to succeed. What do I know about it?"[33]

Particularly important to our understanding of Jordan's moral growth is the way the novel's problematizing of truth illuminates Jordan's awareness and management of the separate selves of his inner world. However much he desires to dominate and control those around him, his every opinion and every assertion of truth is complicated by an opposing or qualifying truth, "riven with contradictions," as Strychacz puts it.[34] As much as he wants to believe that "now" (*ahora*) is all that matters and that one can have as good a life in three full days as in a lifetime, his skepticism causes him to wonder if that is not nonsense.[35] Questioning his faith in anarchy, he thinks, "So he believed that, did he?"[36] Wondering if "patriotic imagination" has not skewed his perceptions, he says, "Karkov said it was true. But then he had written it for Russian papers so he probably wanted to believe it was true after writing it."[37] Karkov believes Félix Lope de Vega's *Fuente Ovejuna* was the greatest play ever written, and "maybe" it was, "but he, Robert Jordan, did not think so."[38] He says he would like to know how it "really was at Gaylord's" but knows his belief, what he holds to be true, is all he has.

Despite Jordan's understanding that he must make difficult moral choices that are always subjective and personal—what Kierkegaard calls the existentialist's "earnestness"[39]—he is forced to question his most ensconced convictions about war, killing, religion, and the humanity of the Spanish people. In the tortured debate between Jordan and Anselmo about the right to kill, Jordan wants to ease his conscience by believing that killing the enemy is the only means of ensuring the cause of peace, while the wiser, gentler Anselmo argues that killing teaches nothing, that it only breeds hatred and a desire for revenge. Both men agree that killing in Spain is done too easily, and admitting to Anselmo that for a very long time he himself has been "tainted" by a love of killing, Jordan declares that those who like it "are disturbed in the head."[40] A sign of Jordan's increasingly sophisticated understanding of semantic manipulation, he recognizes that calling killing "successful assassination" makes the act no more palatable. Though he struggles to believe in the rightness of the republican cause, his attempts to rationalize killing as a necessary means to a noble end wear thin. He knows that the killing he feels required to do will harden him even more, much as bullfighters are warped over time. Pilar explains to Pablo that she has lived too many years with bullfighters not to know how they are after the corrida.

Hemingway connected the blood and gore of the bullring with the horrors of war through the slaughter of fascist prisoners organized by Pablo. We recognize the blood lust common to the killing of men and animals alike when the massacre begins and someone yells, "Let the bull out."[41] When Don Faustino, a former aspiring matador, announces that he is coming out, we hear that it was the same impulse that had made him announce himself for the bullfight. Jordan recognizes too that the absurdity of war requires killing people labeled "enemy" whom one otherwise might befriend; people are divided only by arbitrary political alignments. Andrés reasons that, if his father had not been a republican, both he and his brother would be soldiers now with the fascists. Anselmo observes about the fascists at the bridge, "I have watched them all day and they are the same as we are."[42] Essentially reiterating Howard Campbell's belief that nothing so encourages aggression as artificial boundaries, Jordan observes that there are as many sorts of Spanish as there are sorts of Americans. Josephs explains that Pilar's tale of the cruel and hateful execution of the fascists has its precise counterpart in Jordan's account of the Ohio lynching of a black man. Nothing confounds Jordan's efforts to simplify the Spanish people more than the character of Pablo, sometimes cowardly and cynical, but at other times brave and sincere.

In my first analysis of Jordan, I showed that no Hemingway protagonist to date had been more willing to examine the darker side of his nature. It was Hemingway's focus on Jordan's painfully conflicted nature, which is complex, divided, contradictory, and tragic, that made him such a convincing character. What I, along with Vonnegut, however, had not seen was what the female scholars in *Hemingway and Women* and critics such as Spilka and Eby clarified as the deepest and most personal part of Hemingway and his protagonists' multifaceted natures, their buried or suppressed feminine. I recognized the existence of contradictory or disharmonious selves, but not that the mask and the man beneath the mask would have been more revealingly described as the mask and the woman beneath the mask, Jung's "eternal feminine."

It is here that Spilka's probing of the hero's "androgynous wound," the more personal and delicate sexual depths of Hemingway's iceberg, helps us appreciate the way Jordan's healing of psychic fragmentation approximates that of Wilbur Swain. Just as Vonnegut and Wilbur's growth are affected by their abiding memory of intimacy with Alice and Eliza, so Hemingway and Jordan are guided and inspired by their sisterly muse. As Spilka explains, Hemingway had begun in *For Whom the Bell Tolls* to explore the taboo sexuality—incest and the transformation of gender roles—that anticipated the gentler, more feminized Santiago and the more gender-integrated figures of Thomas Hudson and David Bourne. In Hemingway's sisters Marcelline and Ursula, we have the gender equivalent of Vonnegut's Alice, whose love both sensual and spiritual influenced the author over a lifetime. It was Ernest and Marcelline whom their mother dressed and groomed as "twins," and it was brown-eyed, brown-haired Ursula, always Ernest's favorite, who in Eliza-like fashion made the incestuous overtures to her brother intimated in *For Whom the Bell Tolls* but so overt and portentous in the posthumous story "The Last Good Country." As Spilka says, these buried tensions were always there for the discerning and willing reader to thaw, the difference being that the thawing of the iceberg, the gradual release of guilty desires from Hemingway's secret hidden depths is now what the fiction is about at its deepest and most personal level.[43] Kenneth Lynn observes that, whether Hemingway and Ursula were ever really physically intimate, as in "The Last Good Country" and "A Soldier's Home," their closeness would seem to have become incorporated into the larger drama of sexual desire that causes Krebs and Nick Adams to relate to their sisters as paramours.[44] Lynn reports that, like Vonnegut and Swain, Hemingway, Nick, and Krebs and their sister are equally angry with their families, loving each other but not their parents. Parallels between Alice and Ursula extend even to the fact that each died an early death from cancer.

In the bountifully erotic albeit spiritual Maria, we see a sisterly female like Eliza with whom Jordan desires to merge identities. Their three nights of rapturous lovemaking—their "hot-aching, rigid, close together"[45]—evokes the five days of "writhing embraces" of Wilbur and Eliza both in erotic intensity and the power to heal the protagonist's fragmented soul. As Pilar observes, "You could be brother and sister by the look," to which Maria replies, "Now I know why I have felt as I have. Now it is clear."[46] Anticipating the prolonged incestuous gender games between Nick and Littless in "The Last Good Country" and later Catherine and David Bourne in *The Garden of Eden*, Jordan thinks of his true love, Maria, as his fantasy wife but also as his sister and his daughter. Like Catherine and Littless, Maria lets her surrogate brother know she is happy to switch identities if her sibling lover wishes it.

Gail Sinclair and Debra Moddelmog suggest that Jordan's Spanish family—the matriarchal mother, Pilar; the wise grandfather, Anselmo; the disgraced and ineffective father, Pablo; and especially Jordan and Maria as sister-brother lovers—reflects Hemingway's evolving feelings about his own failed biological family and about his growing sensitivity both privately and fictively to the presence of a nurturing, guiding, maternal self that subordinates its needs to those of others.[47] "We are all thy family," Maria tells the orphaned Joaquin—to whom, as with Jordan, she feels both brother and sister. Jordan's family of freedom fighters mirrors Hemingway's real family so closely that Spilka likens gatherings in their sheltered forest home to "a Hemingway family picnic in the Michigan woods"[48]; yet as Sinclair and Moddelmog demonstrate, what Moddelmog calls Jordan's "queer" family—analogous to Vonnegut's concept of the "extended family"—distinctly improves on Hemingway and Jordan and Maria's biological families in every respect. Anticipating Vonnegut's call for an "anti-loneliness plan,"[49] artificial families as a cure for loneliness and isolation, Pilar, the family "psychiatrist," quips, "Everyone needs to talk to someone. Before we had religion and other nonsense. Now for every one there should be some one to whom one can speak frankly, for all the valor that one could have one becomes very alone."[50] Pilar's loving declaration to Joaquin—"For what are we born if not to aid one another"[51]—proves the spiritual twin to Vonnegut's announced moral to *Bluebeard*, "We are here to help each other get through this thing, whatever it is."[52]

Apropos of Vonnegut's argument for artificial families as a cure for damages to America's past created by loneliness rather than sin, Moddelmog suggests that the "queerness" of Jordan and Maria's cave-home not only provides the caring community their biological families fail to provide but subverts traditional, inherited notions of love and sexuality by "blurring the boundaries between nonerotic and erotic, sanctioned and taboo bonds."[53] With Jordan and Maria's brother-sisterly coupling in mind, Josephs suggests that in this powerful fusion of the sacred and the sensual, where anima and animus are finally balanced, there is no such thing as "inappropriate" behavior. All behavior is appropriate and consequentially all things are possible.[54] The morning after Jordan and Maria first make love, Jordan feels emotionally liberated as never before.

If, as Spilka suggests, the tough, outspoken gypsy Pilar is an inversion of the mother Ernest would have preferred, Hemingway took a significant step forward in dealing with complex, even oedipal, feelings for Grace, whom Pilar in many ways resembles. Though Pilar is wise and frank about sexual matters in ways Hemingway's mother was not, the two women share remarkable similarities both physically and spiritually, and Grace may very well have shared Pilar's complicated lesbian yearnings.[55] Pilar establishes herself as Jordan's mother-lover by telling him she could have taken him away from Maria when she was young. She sanctions the killing of her husband, Pablo, so that Jordan may assume his place as head of the family and possibly wed the mother. Spilka detects in the erotic threesome—Mother Pilar's simultaneous attraction to Jordan as son-husband and to Maria as daughter-lover—a desire for the ménage à trois of *The Garden of Eden* and the hero's interest in playing the female role. According to Moddelmog, Hemingway's psychological explorations here are doubly admirable, risking as he did the emotional turmoil of dangerous self-knowledge and heightening his understanding of the creative as well as the destructive aspects of unconventional desire.

Spilka argues that in ending his story by separating Jordan from Maria, Hemingway once again betrayed the transformative possibilities of androgynous love. To the contrary, analogous to Wilbur Swain's designation of Eliza as *his* "allegorical angel," it is Maria's as the "androgyne of classical methology"[56] that completes Jordan's humanity by uniting the two halves of his divided soul. Just as Wilbur says about his "blushing bride" Eliza, "I could no longer tell where I stopped and Eliza began,"[57] so Jordan believes his transcendent love making with Maria makes them one being, so close that neither can tell that one of them is not the other. Maria agrees: "I am thee, and thou art me and all of one is the other." Reflecting what Jung called the "spiritualization of eroticism,"[58] Maria's fertilizing, transformative powers as combined Virgin Mother and Spanish earth goddess register dramatically in a veritable rite of healing and renewal. As Maria presses against Jordan, her breasts are like "small hills" rising out of a "long plain" where there is a "well," and the country beyond "was the valley of her throat where his lips were. He lay very quiet and did not think and she stroked his head with her hand."[59] "I will keep everything clean," she promises Jordan, "and I will obtain olives and salted codfish and hazel nuts for thee to eat."[60] When at novel's end Jordan feels his heart beating against the pine-needle floor of the forest, Jordan's integration with Maria and the Spanish earth completes itself.

Despite Spilka's criticism that Hemingway relegated Robert Jordan's struggles with machismo to the novel's subtext, it is precisely what Josephs cites as the creative and fertile "overthrow of the authoritarian masculine"[61] that defines Jordan's moral progress in relation to earlier heroes. In reference to Jordan's observation that he was learning fast at the end, nothing guides his integration of self and "other" more than his hard-earned knowledge and subsequent cultivation of what I call Hemingway's "doctrine of plentitude," which is associated with Maria's physical and spiritual fecundity, the knowledge that for every rapture there is an offsetting dread. For instance there is the life-affirming "plenty" Maria offers him in the form of transcendent lovemaking and the deathly "plenty" that had been done to her by fascists. Reflecting the complex and contradictory nature of Hemingway's own art, Jordan hears singing inside the cave about nature's bounty—the beneficence of sun and moon. Yet in the space of a few minutes, Jordan's buoyant mood is undercut by knowledge of nature's perfidy, a coming frost, the cry of an owl hunting, the sound of distant firing, and the gypsy Rafael's insistence that Jordan must kill Pablo.

If life is the ecstasy of Jordan and Maria's lovemaking, it is as well the omnipresence of the fascist planes, "shaped like sharks," the "mechanized doom" that kills El Sordo, the earth rolling and lurching under him at the moment of his death, a grotesque inversion of "La Gloria," the life-affirming eros of Jordan and Maria. But this is ultimately a novel about creative transcendence, a profoundly mythic tale of new life out of sacrificial death, the saving realization for which comes to Jordan when, envisioning Madrid "just over the hills there . . . rising white and beautiful," he declares, "That part is just as true as Pilar's old women drinking blood down at the slaughterhouse. There's no one thing that's true. It's all true. The planes are beautiful whether they are ours or theirs."[62] Jordan's reconciliation to plentitude's painful duality, a paradox Jordan knows he now carries within himself, allows him to feel, as he says, "completely integrated," first with the Eden, the defiled Spanish earth that has betrayed him even as he reaffirms his love for it by touching the palm of his hand against the pine needles where he lies at the moment of his death, and second with his beloved Maria, his Eve, the embodiment of ideal plentitude, the reunion with whom represents not only a healing of the hero's masculine-feminine wound, but a reconciliation with all women—lover, wife, sister, even the daughter Jordan and his creator will never have except through the fertility of imagination.

In light of Vonnegut's uneasiness about Hemingway's pessimism, Jordan's renunciation of cynicism may prove to be the most important convergence to date of Vonnegut and his secret sharer's management of the dreaded "head wound," the equivalent in *Slapstick* to Wilbur Swain's denunciation of personal and public apathy. When Jordan finds himself growing cynical about the futility of the war and morbid with thoughts of his own death, he chides himself that he has lived fully. Rather than submit to the fatalism of Raphael's "no hay remedio," Jordan's awareness of the inevitability of loss and death compels him not only to face ultimate truths about himself with searing honesty, but to become skilled in the artful management of time—Jordan in life, Hemingway on paper—knowing how to extract the maximum value and pleasure from sensuous experience, what Thomas Hudson calls the "palliative measures,"[63] by paying complete and focused attention. While Jordan's love for Maria is ultimately spiritual or sacred, he understands that loneliness and even death may be abolished by the fullness of her body warm against him.

The war tragically separates Jordan and Maria just as Wilbur and Eliza's cruel parents separate them. Totalitarian forces alienate and dehumanize individuals in the name of profit and control. In the meantime what Josephs calls Jordan's "hedged optimism" has been sorely tested by the treachery and cruelty in the world around him, and in the novel's closing moments, it is partly the manly pride of the matador and of his beloved grandfather Jordan relies on for the fortitude to endure the pain of his hemorrhaging broken leg and to hold off enemy soldiers so his friends may get away. But, while Jordan steels himself against death in the macho manner of Harry Morgan or Pedro Romero, Strychacz is right that masculine authority and the will to power is the "terror" from which this novel "recoils."[64] Though Jordan longs for a shot of the old "giant killer" to bolster his courage, it is neither booze nor cynicism nor machismo that sustains him at the end but the knowledge that his "plentitude" with Maria has amounted to a full and fulfilled life. He hates to leave this world, but it is one worth sacrificing for.

Just as the quality of Maria's devotion inspires Jordan to sacrifice his life on behalf of others, so his love for her allows her to survive and lead a full life without him—though not really without him. Just as Wilbur passes on Eliza's capacity to nurture, care, and respect to his granddaughter, Melody, the child Maria may carry assures the continuity of life in the very face of destruction.[65]

In fairness to Spilka, what we have discussed as the novel's complex aesthetics requires that we no more insist on one reading of this richly problematic text than another. Josephs and Strychacz show us that *For Whom the Bell Tolls* is the perfect place to appreciate Hemingway's complicating narrative strategies, whose inventiveness not only rivals the acclaimed experimental storytelling of rivals such as Fitzgerald and Faulkner but also anticipate the self-reflexive polyphonic texts of postmodernism. Like the characters, says Strychacz, we "hazard interpretations" that reflect our own values and interests. Later we will learn more about the continuities and discontinuities of modernism and postmodernism that help account for differences as well as likenesses in each writer's work. In *For Whom the Bell Tolls* we see evidence of Hemingway's postmodern awareness that reality, like storytelling, is "all play acting," a game the writer makes up, a venture in self-creativity. By no coincidence perhaps does Ihab Hassan suggest the inaugural date for the inception of postmodernism as 1939, the year before the publication of *For Whom the Bell Tolls*.[66] Foregrounding art and life as mutually playful constructions, Jordan blurs the line between reality and illusion by parodying Gertrude Stein: "A rose is a rose is an onion"; "a stone is a stein is a rock is a boulder is a pebble."[67] As an increasingly self-conscious storyteller, Jordan warns himself to stop making dubious literature when he finds himself lying about his enjoyment of killing. Much as Wilbur Swain senses life as illusion or story, Jordan imagines he plays a part from something he has read or dreamed, "feeling it all move in a circle,"[68] proposing reality as a hermeneutic conundrum that denies closure. Just as Wilbur first experiences his transformative narrative as a daydream, Jordan imagines a better future for himself and for humanity, not as absolute reality but as becoming like a dream he must help make real. The bridge he must blow is a "bloody dream bridge."[69] Maria herself may be something he "made up," someone he has "dreamed" from cinemas he has seen.[70] Reminding us of André Marty's use of the word "story" "as you would say lie, falsehood, or fabrication,"[71] Jordan associates the smell of cyanide with that of bitter almonds in detective stories.[72] In contrast to the earlier hero's denial of the feminine—a masculine sensibility Hassan associates with the hieratic, phallic nature of modernism, associated with paranoia, moral absolutism, domination, control, and violence—Hemingway's movement toward postmodern narrative strategies aligns him with the feminine anima, a turn to linguistic play, indeterminacy, difference, parody, and androgyny.[73] Like Vonnegut and Wilbur, Hemingway and Jordan deconstruct epistemological certainties, embracing plurality in lieu of fascist authoritarianism, suggesting that they too learn how to creatively manipulate life and answering the existential challenge that contends with fatality: "I await your instructions. You can be anything you want to be."[74]

# Seven

# A Soldier's Confessions

### *Across the River and into the Trees* and *Hocus Pocus*

■

Must a written book be brought forth in which everything
is contained from which the ashes should be judged?
Vonnegut, "Mass Promulgated"

In the fountains of the heart, let the healing fountains start.
Archibald Macleish, *J.B.*

To judge from Vonnegut's transparent parody of Hemingway's *Across the River
and into the Trees* (1950) in *Hocus Pocus* (1990), Vonnegut was attempting to distance himself further than ever from his imagined nemesis, making good his
assertion that differences in their respective cultures and war experiences made
them natural adversaries—"a thousand years apart" in mood and purpose.[1] Contrasts between the authors' two battle-scarred army colonels—Vonnegut's Eugene
Debs Hartke and Hemingway's Richard Cantwell, veterans of the Vietnam War
and World War II respectively—appear deliberately designed to prove Vonnegut's
case that the Vietnam War made Hemingway's portrayal of war in *Across the River
and into the Trees* irrelevant. What made the Vietnam soldier particularly "spooky,"
Vonnegut said (read Eugene Debs Hartke), was that he never had romantic illusions about war, never had Hemingway's need to return from war with the shocking news that war was repulsive, stupid, and dehumanizing.[2] Rather, Vonnegut
explained, the Vietnam veteran was the first American soldier to know from childhood that war was a meaningless butchery of ordinary people like himself and
that death was plain old death, the absence of life.

   Much about Vonnegut's satire in fact suggests these wars epitomize a difference in historicist sensibility that not only separates one author from the other,
but the first half from the last half of the twentieth century or modernism from
postmodernism. From this perspective, though both writers and their protagonists share a violent, fragmented, decentered universe, exhibiting the same sense
of crisis and loss of belief in religious absolutes, Vonnegut, according to Jerome

Klinkowitz, aligned himself with a "postmodernist will toward unmaking, which disassembles . . . modernist structures of authority,"[3] while Hemingway as modernist attempted to encounter the real—to perceive the essential and "true" or, as Alan Wilde observes, to reach toward the heroic in the hope of recuperating a lost wholeness.[4] Evoking Yeats's famous image of a world in which the center no longer holds,[5] Ihab Hassan sees postmodernism tending toward "artistic Anarchy in deeper complicity with things falling apart."[6]

John Clark might well have Vonnegut's postmodern antihero, Lieutenant Colonel Eugene Debs Hartke, or Hemingway, in mind when he asserts that the function of such heroes is "to question, alter, and replace . . . society's mythologies and idols" by debunking the traditional heroes of conventional culture.[7] As Vonnegut intended, Hartke may be read as a deliberate deflation of Hemingway's Colonel Richard Cantwell and his heroic stance as well as a reflection of a postmodern world, in which Cantwell's ideas of heroism seem no longer desirable, if possible. Vietnam veterans such as Hartke, Vonnegut explained, no longer believed that dishonor was a fate worse than death; the military death of one man might easily mean the death of everything.[8] As Clark observes, once the idea of the hero is disparaged, "we tend to renounce ideas of tragedy—our mode becomes mocking, parodic."[9] What the modernist treats seriously, the postmodernist ridicules. Disassembling, or "unmaking," Hemingway's heroic or tragic structures in *Across the River and into the Trees* seems to be exactly the purpose of Vonnegut's *Hocus Pocus*, which he described as "a sardonic fable in a bed of gloom."[10]

While both aging, embittered soldiers share an existential view of war as a violent distillation of the ceaseless combat of life, providing intense awareness of one's existence, Vonnegut mocked what he viewed as Cantwell's perception of war as a potentially virtuous activity if it is fought well. For Vonnegut, as Peter Reed explains, war provided the ultimate measure of man's folly, his inhumanity, his inability to match means and ends, and his incapacity to maintain an ordered control over his destiny.[11] While Cantwell shows signs of fulfilling what John Raeburn calls the romantic view of the "artist hero" as a sacrificial figure,[12] a genuine fighting man devoted to his "trade,"[13] Vonnegut remained true to his promise to Mary O' Hare in *Slaughterhouse-Five* by writing a book uncompromising in its exposure of the horrors of war and the idiocy of manly bravado. Richard Cantwell touts soldiering as an honorable profession, "the oldest and the best,"[14] even though most of its practitioners are unworthy. Eugene Hartke, on the other hand, is coerced into becoming the professional soldier he never wanted to be, transformed from promising musician and future journalist into "The Preacher," "a puritanical angel of death."[15] He refers to his chance encounter with Sam Wakefield, the officer who recruits him for West Point, who bears a remarkable resemblance to Hemingway, as the biggest mistake of his life. Hartke notes that

Lieutenant Colonel Wakefield had been wounded in World War II and would eventually "blow his brains out."[16] "I think exhaustion got him," Hartke says. Wakefield's suicide note—"My work is done"[17]—exactly reflects Vonnegut's view of Hemingway at the time he was writing *Across the River and into the Trees* and *The Old Man and the Sea*—that Hemingway was not an old man "but obviously felt like one, felt that his work, thus his life was done."[18]

As a teenager, Hartke is interested only in playing music; yet his plans to continue making music while studying journalism at the University of Michigan are shelved after he is pressured into accepting appointment to the Academy by a father desperate to salvage his own damaged pride. After he graduates from West Point a newly commissioned second lieutenant, Hartke is so astonished by his own transformation that he asks himself, "Can this be me?"[19] He rises to the rank of lieutenant colonel during the Vietnam War, where he proves to be as ubiquitous as Cantwell in World War II. By contrast, however, Cantwell begins his career avidly as a sixteen-year-old in the Montana National Guard, priding himself that even as a boy he fought in World War I against Erwin Rommel and defended Italy, where in 1918 he received the wound that took away his sense of immortality. Whereas Hartke finds his soldierly identity a distortion of his real self, Cantwell's darker persona appears gratified by the physical attributes of his profession, eyes "metallic" like "old used steel" and a nose "like a gladiator's." The distinction sharpens in their respective response to people who stare rudely at their uniforms. Cantwell, spoiling for a fight, retaliates with a salute and sarcasm. Hartke, in full dress uniform after his return from Vietnam, reacts with embarrassment rather than disdain when someone remarks, "My goodness! Is it Halloween?"[20] Hartke believes himself to be the "freak" he is thought to be, deciding not to give some draft-dodging student "burst eardrums" and a "collapsed windpipe" to think about, when in fact he has much deeper reasons for unhappiness—inability to find a job and win back the love and respect of his children. By contrast, though Cantwell sees the act of two sailors who had been drinking and who whistle at Renata as harmless enough, he beats them bloody, which excites him sexually. Cantwell's uniform *is* his identity, fixed and brutal and a source of pride.

Vonnegut accentuates Cantwell's and Hartke's differences of temperament by having Hartke remark that he would have given anything to die in a war as meaningful as World War II. He muses that in World War II civilians and soldiers alike felt pride in their participation, whereas none of the dying soldiers in Vietnam had illusions that he had somehow accomplished something worthwhile. Hartke contends his war was about nothing but the ammunition business and belonged only to those "stupid and dirty enough to have fought in it."[21] Rather than a victorious invasion, Hartke's war ends in ignominious retreat. He is the very last of the Americans evacuated from the roof of the American embassy during the fall of Saigon.

Despite Vonnegut's protests, *Hocus Pocus* and *Across the River and into the Trees*, like their aging, beat-up protagonists, are far less opposite than alike. Each novel is the memoir of an old and demoralized soldier struggling to come to terms with his life as he faces death. And both are confessions in which women provide the inspiration that leads the protagonist to confront the past that haunts him. Rather than representing significantly different aesthetics, both texts conform to Irving Howe's view of modernists in search of "a moral style" to substitute for the failed traditional values and beliefs of a society fallen into "moral disorder."[22] What more and more we learn about Vonnegut and Hemingway's evolving interest in fiction as self-creativity is that neither can be easily pigeonholed as a modernist or a postmodernist. They differ from traditional realism by producing characters increasingly adept at deconstructing old patterns. The metafictional feats of Vonnegut's later novels find analogues in Hemingway's through many self-reflexive references that challenge representational reality, and both authors disseminate their speaking voices over intertextual space that includes real-life experience and their fictional lives as traumatized adolescents and battle-scarred soldiers.

Yet rather than making radical departures in theme and technique, neither Vonnegut nor Hemingway turned his back on his realist and modernist forebears by rejecting narrative and representational art. They remained aware of the limitations of conventional realism while finally accepting a substantial real world and a stable level of reader familiarity.[23] If Vonnegut's moral style tends more toward fabulation than Hemingway's verisimilitude—more toward abstraction than mimesis—their efforts to recuperate a lost wholeness, psychic and social, and their intensified capacity for vigorous self-criticism fueled by a heightened feminist sensibility suggest a shared moral and artistic vision that increasingly closes the gaps between them.

I suggest the key to understanding the heroic achievement of Hemingway's oeuvre from *For Whom the Bell Tolls* and *Across the River and into the Trees* onward is to investigate its meanings as a single tapestry, the ways in which the rich thematic interplay among these and texts to follow produce constant interchange and circulation of meaning, intercourse that is organic and fluid rather than static or linear. Rose Marie Burwell explains that the last two novels published in Hemingway's lifetime, *Across the River and into the Trees* and *The Old Man and the Sea*, were conceived as parts of a big "Land, Sea, and Air" book that was to include the posthumously published *Islands in the Stream* (1970) and *The Garden of Eden* (1986). Though this "dream" conception never came together in its entirety, the "Land" section, which dealt with the war in Europe was reduced and incorporated into *Across the River and into the Trees*; the "Sea" section, which initially had four parts, became *The Old Man and the Sea* and the three sections of *Islands in the Stream*: "Bimini," "Cuba," and "The Sea Chase." Burwell explains that "Miami," a section omitted from *Islands in the Stream*, was later published as the posthumous story "The Strange Country" (1987).[24]

Of particular importance to the case for viewing Hemingway's late work as a single opus—an intensely autobiographical work that Reynolds believes Hemingway intended as his most personal and important literary legacy—Burwell explains that, beginning with *Across the River and into the Trees* and Hemingway's ten months of covering the European theater during World War II, the author's ever-expanding work focuses on the creative problems of a protean artist who is sometimes a writer named Robert Davis or David Bourne and sometimes a painter named Thomas Hudson or Nick Sheldon.[25] Unsurprisingly, as with Vonnegut's most evolved hero, Rabo Karabekian in *Bluebeard*, Cantwell also sees the world in the light of painters who provide perspective and inspiration for his spiritual odyssey, not only Titian, but Giotto, Hieronymus Bosch, Piero della Francesca, Andrea Mantegna, Michelangelo, Tintoretto, Edgar Degas, and Diego Velásquez. Cantwell's driver tells him Titian's wonderful paintings of women would be out of place in the local war museum—replete with mementos that recall the attic of Nick Adams's family home—arrowheads, war bonnets, scalping knives, different scalps, petrified fish, and the skin of a hanged man. Particularly notable, it is a painting of the Madonna-like Countess Renata, a painter in her own right—that takes Cantwell most deeply into himself, providing the source of transformative insights that change him from a warrior to a man of peace.

Michael Reynolds and major critics of the posthumous works, such as Burwell and Robert Fleming, argue persuasively that Hemingway treated wounds in these highly personal novels and stories as tormenting, albeit more subtle than the one at Fossalta, and grows more honest with himself about his deepest needs and anxieties. Yet they believe that, because of Hemingway's progressive depression, the author could only go so far in dealing with a lifetime of guilt. Reynolds and Burwell tell us that around the time Hemingway was writing *Across the River and into the Trees* and his short story "Black Ass at the Crossroads," the author in fact hit a new low in depression and that his physical and emotional problems were greater than ever.[26]

At the approximate time and setting of his novel and story, while Hemingway served, albeit illegally, as an armed combatant in Germany with the field commander he wished to emulate, Colonel Buck Lanham, the author was so depressed as to be suicidal. Burwell explains these were particularly unsettling years of frustration and guilt in Hemingway's relations with difficult wives, Martha Gellhorn and Mary Welsh, and with twenty-year-old Andriana Ivancich, the complex daughter-sister-lover-muse he allegorized as his erotic twin in *Across the River and into the Trees*. Neither Martha nor Mary was as willing to play the role of agreeable, uncomplaining wife as Ernest would have liked. In particular Martha was contemptuous of what she saw as Ernest's schoolboy scheme to hunt German submarines in the Caribbean, complaining that it detracted from her writing as well as his. The author's resentments of Martha so escalated that their mutual editor Charles Scribner had to force Ernest to delete scurrilous passages about her from the galley proofs of *Across the River and into the Trees*, and by the time of its publication in 1950, Mary had become so discouraged by Ernest's "over-drinking," "carelessness," and "brutality," she had made plans to leave him.[27] Burwell explains that Hemingway's depression was exacerbated by the realization that neither wife could bear him the daughter he craved and that his newfound love with Adriana was destined to cause him endless frustration and heartbreak. The agonizing love Hemingway felt for Adriana—his need to love and be loved by, even married to, this girl he so adored but was denied by the barriers of age and culture—produced the inspiration and heart of this underrated novel. When Renata asks Cantwell, "What happens to people that love each other?" it is undoubtedly the author's feelings for Adriana that Hemingway had in mind when Cantwell responds, "I suppose they have whatever they have, and they are more fortunate than others. Then one of them gets the emptiness forever."[28]

Reynolds feels the tragic implications of the unfinished works went deeper yet, that they became both a cause and the consequence of Hemingway's post-1946 depressions. That is to say, having written so much and so well on something so complicated, Hemingway feared that he would be unable to finish these books and became depressed to the point that he could not finish them.[29] I suggest that, despite Hemingway's battles with depression (like Vonnegut's own struggle), a better understanding of the symbiotic relationship of Hemingway's late work not only disputes Vonnegut's jaundiced view of Hemingway's late years but offers a portrait of creative courage and growth that merits the appellation "epic grandeur," the term Matthew Bruccoli used to describe the redemptive totality of F. Scott Fitzgerald's life and work.[30]

Ironically Hemingway/Cantwell's willingness to reopen and confront old wounds by revisiting Fossalta in middle age—a traumatic experience Carl Eby sees rooted in Hemingway's childhood[31]—suggests the courage and possibilities of psychic repair of Vonnegut's return to Dresden. As Kathleen Robinson explains, we now know it took far more than ten years between the wound at Fossalta and its treatment in *A Farewell to Arms* for Hemingway to deal with it adequately. Accordingly *Across the River and into the Trees* becomes the "denouement" to *A Farewell to Arms*, in which the hero's understanding of that early trauma prepares him for the still more confessional work ahead. Rather than seeing *Across the River and into the Trees* as a novel given short shrift by critics, Robinson sees the book as occupying a pivotal position in the Hemingway canon. Via Cantwell's remorse over the hopeful youth he once was,[32] Hemingway recognized how the traumatic effects of his wound—the burying, repressing, or disguising of painful experience—kept him self-victimized. The masculine facade not only subverted

the feminine, the vulnerable Nick Adams or Renata in him, but prevented potentially healing self-knowledge of the masked soldierly identity of Jake Barnes and
Frederic Henry, who fail to explore the wounds of childhood and war as honestly
as Robert Jordan and Cantwell. In Robinson's view, the hero is doomed to repeat
the violent, often unkind behavior of the traumatized soldier until and unless he
understands (the process of this novel) the necessity of accessing memories that
testify to the tragic costs of war and the hardened soldierly mask.[33]

What I argued in *Sanity Plea* about the essentially moral vision of *Hocus Pocus*
applies equally well to *Across the River and into the Trees*—that in spite of each
protagonist's calamitous past history, which includes childhood trauma, family
insanity, and deforming experiences as soldiers, no Vonnegut or Hemingway protagonist chose to explore his shadowy inner world so directly or to nurture awareness and moral responsibility more avidly than Eugene Debs Hartke or Colonel
Richard Cantwell. The key to the creative affirmation of both stories resides in
the protagonist's determination to hold himself accountable for transgressions
against others and against the split-off feminine aspect of self. While Eugene
awaits a literal trial for supposedly masterminding a prison break at the New York
State Adult Correction Institute, he determines to conduct a hearing of his own,
both moral and psychological, in which he weighs the sane things he has done,
the hopeful, caring, merciful side of his nature, against his insane deeds, the cruel
and aggressive acts of an unfeeling, cynical, or indifferent self. He will compile a
moral account book he hopes will prove his sanity—that he could be compassionate despite his worst sins—setting the lives he has taken and the lies he has told
against his life-enhancing deeds.[34]

Invoking Hemingway's iceberg of sparse dialogue and suggestive prose, Hartke
writes his defense on scraps of paper, containing short, cryptic notations. When
Eugene fills one up, no matter what its size or how brief the reference (for example, "Cough," "Vietnam," "Losers!"), he can satisfy himself that he has written
enough about "this or that"[35] to suggest its meaning. Once again the authors'
postmodern inclinations come to the fore. Hemingway's self-conscious withhold-
ing of information coincides with Vonnegut's editorial tinkering, foregrounding
the story as a product of authorial invention. Eugene and his "editor" identify
Eugene's memoirs as pure fiction, a game or trick. Eugene's "truths" are prob-
lematized by imperfect memory and by his editor's own selective storytelling.
Cantwell's "truths" are similarly personal, elusive, and multifaceted. He reports
war stories that "could or could not be faulty intelligence,"[36] and hesitates to
speak with certainty about things he could not possibly be sure of and about
which he has been wrong so many times. The man who puts the morning paper
under his door may or may not be a former fascist. How does he know? Renata
tells him that his interpretation of her portrait is not really her, but the way he
likes to think of her. While he hopes his sins of faulty truth telling are only those

of exaggeration, he confesses to enjoying liars in full flower. Yet despite such artistic contrivances, both texts in the quest for psychic balance offer plausible, modern narratives—confessional memoirs that allow the long repressed feminine artist to ascend.

While it is the entire last half of the twentieth century that has potentially unbalanced Eugene, he remarks that he has been "zapped" during the "darkest days" of childhood[37] and refers to both childhood and Vietnam as battlefields. Despite Eugene's acceptance of personal responsibility for his crimes—the corpses he created, the slaughters he planned and led—he locates the most immediate source of the "something wrong" with him in what he calls his "family image problem," a father who "whores" for Dupont, "as full of excrement as a Christmas turkey,"[38] and a "blithering nincompoop" of a mother so vacuous she agrees with every decision his father makes.[39] After all, Eugene says, "If my father was a horse's fundament and my mother was a horse's fundament, what can I be but another horse's fundament."[40] He finds his parents' lack of integrity so deeply troubling, he suggests that an appropriate epitaph would be, "OK, I admit it. It really was a whorehouse."[41]

Despite Eugene's confession that he has been an all-too-willing participant in the cruelty and carnage of war, it is clear that his freakish parents bear a major responsibility not only for the temporarily insane, psychopathic killer he becomes but for spawning the expert liar whose elaborate destructive fantasies carry over to his role as public-relations officer in Vietnam.[42] Eugene is a genius of "lethal hocus pocus" whose justification for all the killing and dying becomes "as natural as breathing."[43] Vonnegut perhaps had Hemingway in mind as a dangerous father figure when Hartke fantasizes that his own father was a war hero killed on safari in Tanganyika, one of his many lies to impress women in the bedroom.

The association of Hemingway and Eugene's cynical father as men whose work fosters pessimism and violence continues Vonnegut's concern, first highlighted in *Mother Night* and *Cat's Cradle*, with fiction as a form of play that can be constructive or destructive, and his belief that artists have a moral obligation to produce art that discourages aggression and promotes awareness and compassion. He saw all wordplay or fiction—"hocus pocus" —as practical joking, albeit with the power to encourage compassion and engagement as well as cruelty and violence. Vonnegut referred in *Fates Worse than Death* to the "hocus pocus Laundromat,"[44] which may turn good to evil or evil to good, calling this a case of "post-modern multiple crossover." Such was the fate of the students at Tarkington and the prisoners at Athena with learning disabilities, victims of destructive lies or fictions passed on to them by materialistic parents and by the romantic success myths that dominate Tarkington's library.

Conducting his self-inquiry at age sixty-one, in the year 2001, from his home in the Tarkington bell-tower library, Eugene indicates that by war's end he was indeed a seriously wounded man both physically and psychologically—a potential "burned out case"[45] prone to "psychosomatic hives"[46] and dangerously tempted by "good old oblivion."[47] It is probably Hemingway as well as himself that Vonnegut was thinking of when the computer Griot finds Hartke so unsalvageable that it projects him as hopelessly depressed, dying of cirrhosis of the liver on skid row. As ripe a candidate for Tralfamadorian fatalism as Billy Pilgrim or for the suicidal depression that claims Sam Wakefield and Ernest Hemingway, Eugene appears to agree when he reads in the story "The Elders of Tralfamadore" how human beings are so dumb and aggressive that the planet's destruction as imagined by Kilgore Trout is inevitable. Believing that the Creator himself wants earthlings to "wreck the joint," the elders make the deadliest weapons and poisons in the universe, annihilating strangers as if doing "him" a big favor.[48]

According to a majority of reviewers of *Hocus Pocus*, those "crazy lunkers" from outer space, the infamous Tralfamadorians, were at it again, reflecting the author's own sense of life's futility. Yet it is precisely Eugene's willingness to face the painful complexities of human identity and the anguish of choice that saves him from the deadly fantasies of Billy Pilgrim and the emotional malaise of earlier heroes. The story's pessimism so concerns Eugene that he is glad he has not shown it to his friend Hiroshi Matsumoto, an act that might have hastened Hiroshi's suicide. According to Eugene, Hiroshi might have left a note saying, "The Elders of Tralfamadore win again." "Only I and the author of that story," Eugene concludes, "would have known what he meant by that."[49]

What Tralfamadorian fatalism "means" to Eugene Hartke and to Kurt Vonnegut is central not only to Vonnegut's affirmation in *Hocus Pocus* but to our understanding of Hemingway as Vonnegut's bête noire, or "secret sharer"—Vonnegut's sense of Hemingway as that dangerous, aggressive, and pessimistic potential in himself that he associates with violence and authorial irresponsibility. Contemptuously Eugene calls "dumb" and "humorless" those who find acceptable the series of side-splitting satires about Tralfamadorians arriving on other planets with the intention of spreading enlightenment. Tarkington's trustees, who call Hartke a pessimist and defeatist for attempting to expose self-serving fantasies, and Vonnegut critics who read Eugene's memoirs as models of despair project their own apathy and cynicism and thus fail Eugene's primary criteria for sanity.

It is not the Eugene who killed with his bare hands and laughed about it who writes these memoirs, but the long-repressed artist for whom this act of creative exorcism and renewal has been so humanizing and illuminating that he can say it was "the old me . . . I think . . . the soldier I used to be."[50] Whereas he once found it easy to mask or distort the truth, he determines no longer to "play hide-and-seek." Yet Eugene's rescue of the thwarted shaman-artist in him would have been impossible without confronting his most serious transgression, his long history of exploiting women too insecure to make emotional demands. Marilyn Monroe would have been perfect, he muses. But appropriate to Kathryn Hume's observation that the increased affirmation of Vonnegut's protagonists after *Breakfast of Champions* correlates with their more sympathetic relationships with women, Eugene's new connection with a community of female sufferers is, as is said of Zuzu Johnson, not only "deep" but "thoroughly reciprocated,"[51] soulful and intellectual as well as ardent or libidinal. Just as Eugene's final thought is of their well-being, their courage and love prove cathartic and liberating to Eugene, opening him emotionally and helping him form a more holistic and creative self. Hence Eugene finds himself "spilling his guts" to Pamela Hall about the Vietnam War and purging himself of unspeakable scenes of cruelty, stupidity, and waste by confessing his nightmares to Harriet Gummer. When Marilyn Shaw, also a Vietnam veteran, lapses into despair after the war, it is Eugene who rescues her drunk and asleep on a pool table and who apparently nurses her back to health. Eugene's eventual colleague at Tarkington, Muriel Peck, reminds him of how kind and patient he has been with his worse than useless relatives, remaining so loyal to his unbalanced wife and mother-in-law that Andrea Wakefield calls him a "saint." Bringing us full circle from Vonnegut's professed inability to "love" in *Slapstick*, when Eugene's estranged out-of-wedlock son, Rob Roy, assures Eugene that he intends to make no demands on his father's emotions, Eugene welcomes that relationship, insisting, "Try me," determining to behave "as though [he] were a really good father."[52]

As Eugene sorts out his tangled relationships with women—especially his habit of fear and flight—his association of the infamously feminine-looking, long-haired Custer, a West Point graduate like himself, with father-Hemingway, bears interpretive fruit that may escape Vonnegut's notice. If we take our cue from Carl Eby's psychosexual analysis of Hemingway's work, Vonnegut's reference has as much relevance to "secret desires" that Vonnegut shares with Hemingway as to Hemingway's own complex sexual longings and taboos. Eby sees Custer as a mirrored image of "the something shameful" that so long hidden must be brought to light,[53] assisted by the hero's subsequent turn to sister-daughter female guides for intimacy and inspiration. Explaining that Custer is far more than a picture on a wall in *To Have and Have Not* and *For Whom the Bell Tolls* or *Islands in the Stream*, Eby demonstrates the "beautiful" general's function as a highly androgynous figure throughout Hemingway's work, alternately admired and disavowed. The significance of this idea regarding the lifelong quest for self-knowledge of Cantwell and Hartke is that "Fanny," as Custer was named by fellow cadets, serves as the perfect icon for ambiguous sexuality that both authors and their cross-gendered protagonists seek to understand and accept in themselves.

Following the reference to Custer, Hartke remarks that he and his father (read Hemingway) "were a demonstration of abnormal psychology" so perverse that Hartke longs for "a whole new planet or death"—Tralfamadore would do.[54]

Eugene's confession that he has never masturbated because of his father and grandfather's belief that it would make him lazy and crazy reminds us of the perverse sexual notions of Nick Adams's father and of Otto Waltz. Not coincidentally perhaps, Hartke empathizes with the young Tarkington college student Bruce Bergeron, who is murdered by "somebody who presumably hated homosexuals, or loved one too much."[55] Hartke/Vonnegut's trepidation magnifies in light of Eby's explanation that Custer also functioned for Hemingway as an icon of "transvestic identity" that Hemingway and Cantwell try to deny—the desire not just to fuse with, but to become, a woman. The transvestic impulse is there, Eby argues, when Cantwell sees Renata's portrait in the mirror instead of his own image and is simultaneously lured and appalled by the transvestic identification.[56] Eby and Debra Moddelmog agree that, as Moddelmog says, turning the female gaze on the male hero's body not only feminizes him but produces homosexual implications.[57] As we learn from the tensions between Nick Adams and Rudy Waltz and their sexually repressed fathers, what is truly "abnormal" is the masculine penchant for hating and killing they have inherited from these militant fathers and sexual neuroses passed down from father to son, rather than their identification with the self-reflexive feminine that Cantwell sees in the mirror and that Hartke knows he has betrayed in his transformation from journalist music maker to pathological killer, dolefully observing, "Can this be me?"

What Hartke acknowledges as his addiction to older women and housecleaning implicates the Vonnegut hero's lifelong taboo feelings for what Eby calls Hemingway's attraction to the "phallic mother," but it is that very awareness that, after a lifetime of disavowal, drives Hartke and Cantwell's confessions as to their respective betrayals of the artist-feminine in themselves. We may look to Eby's interpretation of the lost eye suffered by the Italian writer, lover, and national wartime hero Gabriele D'Annunzio for a deeper understanding of what both Cantwell and Hartke must understand about their repressed sexual desires. Like the figures of D'Annunzio and Custer, with whom Cantwell identifies, both Hartke and Cantwell are lieutenant colonels who bear symbolically castratory wounds represented by D'Annunzio's lost eye. Hartke's immediate counterpart in *Bluebeard*, the consummate artist-hero Rabo Karabekian, has lost an eye in the war. He calls it "his most secret disfigurement."[58] Likewise Eby explains Cantwell's mutilated hand as Hemingway's castratory wounding at Fossalta.[59] Though Hartke's and Cantwell's wounds refer respectively to Dresden and Fossalta, they may be traced earlier to the infantile sexual wounds of Rudy Waltz and Nick Adams, gender anxieties created by association with the father's emasculation and the child's fantasies of sexual union with the mother.

Once again the chief irony of Vonnegut's efforts to distance himself from the Hemingway he saw as trapped and defeated by machismo is that nowhere in their mutual, late career confessions of entangled desire and guilt and spiritual reclamation does their work so connect and illuminate what Edward Stanton calls the "chaos within"[60] than in *Hocus Pocus* and *Across the River and into the Trees* and the accompanying Hemingway story "Black Ass at the Crossroads."

While critics such as Roger Whitlow and David Gordon suggest that none of Hemingway's characters is convincingly repelled by war,[61] the fact is that, if Cantwell/Hemingway fails to censure war as emphatically as Vonnegut does, Cantwell shares most if not all of Hartke's concerns about the hellish aspects of battle and his own complicity in causing human suffering. I suggest that, as with Hartke, it is less a celebration of his soldierly experience that inspires Cantwell's confessions of vanity and cruelty than his efforts to understand the stresses in his tragically divided nature—what Edmund Wilson calls the hero's "discords of personality," his "fears, which he has tried to suppress, his mistakes, which he has tried to justify, the pangs of bad conscience, which he has brazed out."[62] It is Cantwell's awareness that war has brutalized him beyond reclamation, splitting him in two between a self that glorifies war and a self that questions the insidious nature of military programming—that reflects Hemingway's sense of the tragic consequences of his and Cantwell's soldierly masquerade. It has never been more important for readers to understand the profoundly personal nature of Hemingway's work than at this critical moment of creative and spiritual metamorphosis, when the author and his anguished protagonist come face to face with a lifetime of self-betrayal yet sense the possibility of moral and creative renewal in the short time that remains. If there is occasional awkwardness to the novel's style, it reflects the chaos of Cantwell's inner hell, the severity of the traumas Cantwell has sustained since childhood. Spilka observes that the "truculence" in Hemingway's own life at this time brought him perilously close to "paranoid hysterics."[63]

While Hemingway often cited C. T. "Buck" Lanham as the novel's hero, Lanham reminded his friend, "Ernesto, *you* are the hero of every book you've ever written."[64] As Sidney Knowles puts it, *Across the River and into the Trees* "owes little to the mind of anyone but its creator."[65] When measuring the relative success of Hartke and Cantwell in managing their respective "head wounds," let us keep in mind the psychoanalytic perspective of Millicent Bell, whose understanding of autobiography in Hemingway's work informs this study. The deeply embittered experience of this highly intelligent fighting man, who in effect "writes" this story in the guise of a female surrogate, is less about the literal battles of World War II than the author's own inward struggles with the effects of violence and anger on his person and his writing. Carlos Baker rightly saw the novel as darkened by "a strange psychological malaise, as if Ernest were using the pages of his novel as the equivalent of a psychiatrist's couch."[66] The mysterious narrow streets and tortuous canals of Venice becomes a vivid paradigm for the interior landscape of Cantwell's mind. Cantwell's damaged heart and the scarred hand he despises symbolize the hero's wounds in all respects, "all your other wounded places," as

Renata puts it.[67] The "regiment" he loses, the desperate remembrance of "lost battalions and of individual people" reflects failed marriages, battles with friends, mistakes with children, and most traumatizing of all, his memories of the father Nick Adams hated enough to kill and of the bullying mother with whom he will never completely reconcile. And all the wounded, he says, "were wounded for life."[68]

The important break-through for Cantwell is not the literal one in Hurtgen Forest but one that allows these thoughts into consciousness, "mistakes" he has made in his civilian life, for which he assumes responsibility. The dangerous currents of Nick's boyhood trout streams are never far from Cantwell's mind—nor is the Paris that was the setting for the destruction of a marriage to a woman he valued above all others. Reflecting on "the *Trieste métier* of war," Cantwell reminds himself, "Hell, I've felt this way before many fights and almost always at some time in the fall of the year, and always when leaving Paris."[69] In what Rose Marie Burwell calls Hemingway's Proustian vision, these cumulative wounds, the thematic matrix of this novel, are never exclusive and need to be understood as one continuous hurt if the Hemingway hero is to make peace with himself.

If J. Bakker is right that Cantwell really makes no serious attempt to improve his relations with his fellow humans despite his admonitions to be kinder and more understanding,[70] this says less about Cantwell's lack of remorse than what he has become as a result of his many years' association with violence and death—a burned-out old man who looks in the mirror and observes that "the cruelty and resolution showed in his large eyes as clearly as when the hooded muzzle of a tank swung toward you."[71] When he calls himself "the unjust bitter criticizer who speaks badly of everyone," Renata reminds him that he speaks worst of all about himself. He may still be the "tough boy" he calls himself, but it is a toughness tinged with Hartke's sense of regret and a greater stirring of conscience than in any previous Hemingway hero. Cantwell knows very well why his heart of all the muscles should have failed him, or better, that it is he who has failed his heart. Continuing Robert Jordan's capacity for vigorous self-scrutiny, Cantwell asks, "Why am I always a bastard and why can I not suspend this trade of arms and be the kind and good man I would have wished to be?"[72] At least, he decides, "I should be a better man with less wildboar blood in the small time which remains."[73]

Cantwell's plan to be a kinder and more decent man requires nothing less arduous than the allegorical descent into his darkest self, the relentless scrutiny of masculine/feminine drives that have split his soul in two. The person with whom Cantwell will pursue self-enlightenment is Countess Renata, "Queen of Heaven,"[74] who, like Dante's Beatrice, will inspire and guide Cantwell's exploration of the hellish darkness of his inner self.

Just as Dante finds his way blocked by three beasts—a leopard, a lion, and a she wolf—the colonel encounters a coyote, a wolf, and a mule. Declaring himself

"Mister Dante for the moment," Cantwell "drew all the circles"[75] and, as "a descending passenger,"[76] steps into the gondola by which he will cross the river Acheron and navigate the city's "strange and tricky" streets and canals, the labyrinths of the human mind and the hell of killing and cruelty that resides there. Even Cerberus is there, shivering at the colonel's feet. Appropriate to the hero's need to access the underwater knowledge of self beneath the protective iceberg, Cantwell asks the boatman for an oar to help break up the water's ice to forge an open passage. Though Cantwell's sins are myriad, evidently the circle of hell reserved for him is that which draws Vonnegut's Hartke, the fiery abode of those who not only kill but lie about it. Thus Cantwell observes that he and his driver, Jackson—who catches him lying, corrects his exaggerations, and perhaps intimidates Cantwell by observing his strange contradictions—must "move in different circles."[77] Jackson finds Cantwell so "beat up" he calls him "slug-nutty."[78]

Though Cantwell calls on God to help him "not be had," that job falls to the Venetian countess Renata (her name being Italian for "rebirth"), who enters the story "shining in her youth and tall striding beauty."[79] Spilka finds Cantwell's obsession with the adoring, nurturing, and protective Renata a manifestation of Hemingway's efforts to shore up his shaky male identity, as if Hemingway were still working from the predominantly masculine perspective of *Death in the Afternoon* and *Green Hills of Africa*. In *Across the River and into the Trees*, Spilka contends, Hemingway pushed that "middle-aged fantasy to its absurdly immature conclusion."[80] Spilka views Cantwell exactly in the light of Vonnegut's sense of Hemingway as a writer defeated and diminished by machismo, the suppression of the feminine and what Spilka and Burwell call the "postfrontier stoicism" Hemingway made famous—and by which he had continually attempted to define himself and his heroes.[81] Specifically Spilka echoes Vonnegut in citing Hemingway's "shortsighted" denial of the feminine in himself, which "might have enriched and expanded his art, and preserved his life and sanity in old age."[82] I suggest that as right as he is about the nature of the hero's androgynous wound, Spilka's strangely hostile view of Cantwell's "immature" relationship with Renata stems from his failure to understand the allegorical framework of *Across the River and into the Trees*, in which Renata, like Maria in *For Whom the Bell Tolls*, represents the redemptive, feminine aspect of Cantwell's divided soul. Like Eugene Hartke's love affair with Muriel Peck in *Hocus Pocus*, Cantwell's affair with Renata is what Hartke describes as a reciprocal, multidimensioned relationship, one that is erotic and spiritual in equal measure. Both men make love to their women in the outdoors, offering, as Kathleen Robinson says, opportunities for love that is external yet internal. Hartke in fact dreams of Venice as the place to make love to Zuzu Johnson, the wife of the president of Tarkington College.[83] In Venice he would give English lessons, and she would photograph tourists in gondolas. Cantwell sees Renata rising from the sea like the goddess Amphitrite, whose name means one who encircles everything, who calms turbulent waters, and whose abode beneath the sea positions her to understand the nature of Cantwell's submerged or unconscious needs. As the embodiment of Venetian sensuality, she will see to Cantwell's most erotic physical desires, but in her association with Titian's Madonna, she will attend his spiritual needs as well. As Maria does for Jordan, Renata protects, guides, and transforms Cantwell, completing, as it were, the male's female incompleteness. Cantwell has come full circle from Frederic Henry's tragic self-absorption.[84] He not only shows greater courage in facing the complexities of the combined traumas of childhood and war, he allows Renata to succeed at what Catherine Barkley attempts and fails but what Maria begins and Renata fulfills—to expose and redeem the tender feelings Hemingway and his hero have tried to hide.

In this instance it is Spilka and Vonnegut who are "short sighted" about Hemingway and Cantwell's emotional and creative growth. It is not the Cantwell who, like Hartke, killed with his bare hands and laughed about it or the Cantwell who confesses to Renata that he had grown immune to the horror of killing civilians, but his author, whose cathartic telling constitutes the creative exorcism that prepares for the greater spiritual reclamation of Santiago and Thomas Hudson. I suggest Burwell has it right by referring to the "deep, strange merging of identities" Hemingway sought with Adriana Ivancich as the most potent instance of his attempt to experience the feminine aspect of his own creative imagination.[85] The power of that attraction, Burwell explains, is probably intensified by the fact that Adriana's nascent talent combines the poet and painter—additional parts of himself Hemingway longed to merge.[86] When Renata urges Cantwell to write so "someone would know of such things,"[87] it is the softened, feminine part of Hemingway who will do the writing, just as it was Hemingway who ultimately fulfilled Robert Jordan's novelistic aspiration in *For Whom the Bell Tolls*. Declaring them symbiotic halves of one soul, Renata tells Cantwell she will write his story for him.[88]

As with Hartke's enriching relationship with Muriel Peck, Renata inspires and guides Cantwell's spiritual journey in multiple ways. Because Renata understands Cantwell's divided nature, she sees her task as reforming the part of Cantwell capable of brutality and violence while encouraging the man who loves art, music, and literature and who shares her delight in the magic and beauty of Venice. She shows her ailing colonel something of heaven as well as hell, providing him with the courage to examine and disclose his sins, but also enveloping him in the sensual delights of Venice, a "moving feast"[89] of aesthetic, gustatory, and feminine pleasures. Suggesting that it is perhaps an emotional reattachment to the defamed mother that Renata helps Cantwell achieve, her voice always reminds him of the cello, the instrument Grace chose for Ernest to play. The sound makes him feel "as a wound does that you think you cannot bear."[90] While telling Cantwell he needs to tell her things to purge his bitterness, she is careful about managing her colonel's despair—setting the need to confess against his stoical defense. When she senses a bitterness rising up in him that she feels may do him harm, she tells him, "Don't be angry about it. Let me be angry for you."[91] Just "tell me as true as you can," she says, "until you are purged of it."[92]

Renata's gentle but forceful promptings compel the colonel to divulge his worst memories. While Hartke tells of napalm killing Vietnamese of both sexes and ages, Cantwell remembers the German "roasted" by white phosphorous. Hartke speaks of his air force blowing people up no matter whose side they were on, while Cantwell describes the Valhalla Express bombing both sides to leave as few people as possible. What Hartke refers to as readying men to be fed into a meat grinder, Cantwell refers to as running up an excessive butcher bill. Cantwell appreciates what Eugene knows firsthand about the corrupt military machine he helps administer—that public-relations people and Rotary Club generals have turned the army into a business establishment whose military contractors split the profits for their shoddy merchandise with some brother officer. In particular the SHEAF insignia, "a badge of shame" according to Cantwell, reflects his disapproval of the military "business."[93]

In pithy Vonnegut fashion, Cantwell sums up his awareness of soldiers who "know what the score is"—that no one escapes war unscathed: "Don't shit me, Jack."[94] Cantwell tells Renata that in the futility of battle, everything boils down to the fact that you stay in until you are hit badly or killed or go crazy. Since Cantwell is still alive, he must be one of the crazies. When Renata asks Cantwell how many stories like that he has to tell, he says "plenty," repeating Vonnegut's doleful observation in *Slaughterhouse-Five* that he doubts the effectiveness of antiwar books, since wars, like glaciers, kept coming. He could tell "a thousand like that," Cantwell says, "and they would not prevent war."[95] In a Vonnegutian moment of black humor, Cantwell jokes to Renata that perhaps it was not the war but "land crabs" that ate his brother Gordon in the Pacific. "Or maybe he just deliquesced."[96]

Nevertheless Cantwell's continued recounting of the grotesqueries of battle reflects Vonnegut's remark in *Slaughterhouse-Five* that the ones who know war firsthand are the ones who hate war the most. Apropos of Vonnegut's promise to Mary O'Hare that there will be no parts in his book for glamorous macho men like Frank Sinatra or John Wayne, Cantwell tells Renata he hates war monuments and does not believe in heroes. As if to underscore Vonnegut's contention that there is nothing intelligent to say about a massacre, because everybody is supposed to be dead, thus never to say anything or want anything again, Cantwell tells Renata that real soldiers never tell anyone what their own dead looked like, that he is through with the whole subject. But just as Vonnegut summoned the courage of Lot's wife to face his worst fears, meeting his Dresden nightmare head-on, Cantwell looks back with Renata at his most tortured memory—the annihilation of his regiment in Hurtgen Forest, a trauma Renata knows he must relive to complete his exorcism. Cantwell's courage to revisit the death of his troops, "mortared all to hell,"[97] their bodies frozen up afterward, "gray and yellow like wax-works,"[98] climaxes the military portion of his redemptive underworld descent. He reports fire all around him, artillery fire, automatic weapon fire, machine gun fire, interdicting fires, mortar fires. "The hell with it," Cantwell says.[99]

If Vonnegut's condemnation of uncritical loyalty to authority is more direct than Hemingway/Cantwell's, Cantwell admits distrust of duty and blind obedience when doing what he is told results in the needless destruction of his regiment. The fact that Cantwell agrees to spend half of his time in hell with the general who commanded the attack suggests acceptance of at least half the blame for the slaughter that occurs. James Meredith is right that Cantwell loses his stars when he is used as a scapegoat by his leadership,[100] but apropos of Hemingway's portrayal of Cantwell as a Christ figure, the suffering he causes suggests the colonel's tragic self-betrayal as well, Judas and Christ in the same divided soul. In any case Hartke and Cantwell are similarly dehumanized and sickened by the senseless violence and cruelty around them. Cantwell acknowledges that in the army "you obey like a dog,"[101] and Hartke confesses he once actually barked "like a dog" after killing a man with his bare hands.[102] The end of the war finds both soldiers fed up with the human race.

Renata knows that absolution for Cantwell means probing wounds that precede those of his literal war experience, those his "bastardly" cruelty have caused him to commit as well as those he has received. Asking him to tell her about mistakes he has made with women in particular, those he has loved and lost, his hesitation suggests these more personal wounds may be deeper and harder to cure. "They'd bore you," he tells her. "They beat the hell out of me to remember them."[103] When she insists on knowing about them, he assumes the familiar soldierly tactic of attributing his losses to others. "You lose them," he says, "the same way you lose a battalion, by errors of judgment; orders that are impossible to fulfill, and through impossible conditions."[104] Having lost "three battalions" and "three women" in his life, he wonders "where the hell" it ends. But hell is where he is, and to escape this particular mendacious circle, Cantwell must understand that his torment, his history of turning women and children into casualties, will not end until he becomes a less brutal and less selfish human being. Nowhere does this knowledge register more clearly than in his initial efforts to blame the failure of his third and most disastrous marriage on the "ambitious" journalist wife he labels selfish, conceited, and opportunistic. While he likes to think he has "cauterized" that wound, arguing to Renata the journalist wife is forgotten now and for good, he and Renata know better. Telling himself he did not like to remember how "the career girl slept," he admits that "yes he did."[105] When

Renata continues probing Cantwell's "armored" defenses, telling him a woman like that is a "terrible" thing in memory, he confesses his complicity. "Who the hell are you to criticize career girls. What miserable career did you attempt and have failed?"[106] Remembering his anger that his wife "could not even make a child," he becomes circumspect and says, "But who should criticize whose tubes?"[107] Though Cantwell would like to convince himself and Renata that, while he has been a sorry son of a bitch, he was "never anybody's sorrow," his confessions tell a more truthful story about the colonel's history of inconstancy to women, one not lost on Renata when she tells him, "I would probably end up as an unnecessary myself. That is the good thing about you going to die that you can't leave me."[108]

When Cantwell tells Renata that there are lots of things he can never say to her that might be good for him, she recognizes that to complete his quest to reconcile his separate selves, he must confess to a still more guarded betrayal than that of his abuse to wives and lovers. She must help him understand the complex sexual wound that haunts the Hemingway hero in the night. As we began to see through Carl Eby's analysis of Cantwell's fantasy laden secrets and taboos, what Eugene Hartke calls his game of "hide and seek" includes multiple forms of unconventional sexual experience the Hemingway hero secretly longs for, which Renata incarnates and projects in the gift portrait of herself she gives the colonel. Suggesting the portrait's gender ambiguity, Cantwell says to it, "Boy or daughter or my one true love or whatever it is; you know what it is, portrait."[109]

According to Eby, what Cantwell sees in the portrait is the daughter-sister lover he has always wanted, and even more sexually adventurous the possibility of androgynous lovemaking in which he plays the female role. We think of Pilar's injunction in *For Whom the Bell Tolls* that "there is always something like that."[110] When Renata tells Cantwell that she can be his daughter as well as *everything else*, the idea of incest excites them both, the colonel's voice "thickening" with excitement.[111] Two chapters later, holding Renata close and addressing her as David Bourne does Catherine in *The Garden of Eden*, which runs concurrently with *Across the River and into the Trees*, "I love you devil," Cantwell warms further to the father-daughter, brother-sister relationship: "And you're my Daughter, too. And I don't care about our losses because the moon is our mother and our father."[112] As indication that Cantwell/Hemingway has grown bolder about confessing sexual desires of all kinds, Cantwell expresses interest in and sympathy for a group of lesbians sitting next to him in Harry's bar, and later Renata—a "gentle cat" anticipating Catherine Bourne—answers Cantwell's need to know how a woman feels sexually as well as emotionally by doing something cryptic with him in a gondola and directing him to "guess now."[113] Lovemaking that takes them to an "unknown country" is supremely satisfying to both. While commanding once gave Cantwell pleasure, the once egotistical colonel now finds the reciprocity of intimacy and love preferable to the distorted gratifications of aggression and war. "I want you, daughter," he tells Renata, "but I don't want to own you."[114]

As one who, like Catherine, enjoys making up stories, Renata's precocious postmodern understanding of the problematic nature and importance of truth telling makes her Cantwell's ideal mentor as well as confessor, instructing him to use words more responsibly. She understands, for instance, that language precedes but does not objectify reality, that truth is something everybody has to figure out for themselves, largely the product of imagination, fluid and dynamic as dreams, varying with the perception or invention of the viewer, or determined by historical or cultural context. When—sounding like Harry Morgan or Vonnegut's parody of Hemingway, Harold Ryan—Cantwell declares, "You have to be a tough boy in this town to be loved," Renata asks him, "And what is a tough boy?"[115] People perceive the four-leaf clover Cantwell wears as "ivy," but, Cantwell explains, "it was not." It was a four-leaf clover "disguised" as ivy.[116] Towns that looked innocent were really fortresses. Referring to the "silly parlance" of his trade, Cantwell uses nonsense language to parody the guarded order of wounded veterans to which he and the "Gran Maestro" belong: "Love is love and fun is fun. But it is always so quiet when the gold fish die."[117] Before they are done exploring the subjectivity of reality and truth, Renata and Cantwell agree that such words as "love," "happiness," and "beauty" mean what people believe they mean and nothing else. Renata compliments her pupil that he learns fast from his mistakes, that he is becoming less judgmental and more open minded.

In the spirit of reality as creative construct, Renata and Cantwell play at exchanging identities with changes of setting, varying their language accordingly, agreeing for instance that meaning changes when they speak Italian. Renata imagines herself an American westerner. "Put it there, Pal," she says. "This grub is tops."[118] Asking Cantwell what she would say as a gangster in America, he suggests, "Listen, Mac. You hired out to be tough, didn't you?" "That's lovely," Renata says and repeats it "in a voice she had learned from Ida Lupino."[119] That people construct identities based on models from literature or popular culture—one of Vonnegut's pressing concerns—Cantwell borrows thoughts from famous writers: Shakespeare, Blake, Rimbaud, Dante, even Eliot and Fitzgerald. Remembering New York as "shining, white and beautiful," a sentiment from Fitzgerald's "The Crack-Up," Cantwell admits he stole that. Cantwell pronounces his former wife deader than Eliot's "Phoebus [*sic*] the Phoenician." Renata fantasizes a "pretend" life with Cantwell among the rich based on pictures in *Vogue* magazine.

Fiction imitates fiction imitating reality when Renata and Cantwell imagine taking a car trip similar to the one Roger and Helena take in "The Strange Country," but their most significant role-playing occurs when they imagine themselves as other people, demonstrating the reality of "self" as made up. They might be "Othello and Desdemona." Cantwell would be an awfully funny Verlaine. When

Cantwell asks Renata if she wants to change the game to historical personages, she responds, "Yes, let's play that you are you and I am me."[120] Her remark to Cantwell that "everyday is a new and fine illusion,"[121] prepares for the surprising, affirmative aspect of Cantwell's transformation from a fighting man to a man of peace.

Vonnegut is not entirely wrong about the tragic ending to Cantwell/Hemingway's life—that the demands of the fabricated masculine self take a physical and spiritual toll that never completely heals. Yet I suggest that the strength of Cantwell's critical judgments on himself, made possible by Renata's purging of the colonel's bitterness, and her elucidation of the possibilities of human and artistic reconstruction produces the moral achievement Jung associated with the tragic hero—one who recognizes his tragic flaw and takes steps to redeem himself. From Jung's perspective, as the former soldierly persona immune to self-analysis, Cantwell appears as the "passive victim of his affects," one who has "bungled" his own life and the lives of others; yet he remains incapable of understanding how much the tragedy originates in himself and how he continually feeds it and keeps it going. Because such a person remains unconscious of his motives, Jung said, he bewails and curses a faithless world that "recedes further and further into the distance," an illusion that in the end will completely envelop him.[122] Yet it appears that Cantwell's symbolic role in Hemingway's allegorical drama reflects Vonnegut's own point of view—that the cruelty and violence in human nature must reform itself if the planet is to survive, that acquiescence to a world of death and violence leads only to destruction.

Cantwell's recantation of his previous affiliation with soldiering climaxes his allegorical journey when, bidding farewell after the duck shoot in the novel's concluding chapters, Cantwell says to Alvarito, "Consider me not a Colonel."[123] Cantwell makes giant strides in resolving the tragic duality of his identity—compassion and destruction, feminine and masculine—by dismantling the protective "cocoon" hiding his true self and veiling him from the world.[124] "A blind," Cantwell reports, "is any artifice you use to hide the shooter from that which he is attempting to shoot, which, in this case, were ducks."[125] We may understand the "blind" to represent multiple forms of "artifice" we have identified throughout this study as the means by which the author and his protagonist mask their vulnerability: understated style, the secrets in the submerged portion of the iceberg—emotional repression, stoical fortitude. Invoking the protective iceberg, Cantwell declares, "Now here was the frozen lagoon to ruin everything."[126] But this time Cantwell promises Renata he will tell the truth about the "shooter," the "gun handler" part of him that brings his life to a tragically premature close. Calling it "murder" when he kills a drake and his female mate, Cantwell proceeds to speak to the birds not as adversaries—bulls or kudu to be hunted and slain—but, in the manner of the Cuban fisherman whose avatar he is, extensions of himself to be protected and loved.[127]

Making his final "good-bye" to Renata, or the mother with whom she blurs, and to the wives and children he has wronged, Cantwell agrees with Renata that he has seen enough of fighting. He does not want to kill anymore, ever. The shooting is over.[128] Sensing that Cantwell has been cleansed of "wild boar blood," Renata, a "deer in the forest," sheds whatever fear she might have about Cantwell's violent past.

Cantwell's final act on earth, "breaking ice" as he goes, is to care for a crippled bird, "intact and beautiful to hold, with his heart beating and his captured, hopeless eyes," which Cantwell reunites with his female mate, an act of soul joining that mirrors and epitomizes Cantwell's own achievement.[129] When the bird's wounds heal, Cantwell thinks he will set her loose in the spring. References to birds rising and traveling out to sea, the unfrozen sea from which Renata also rises, signify the hero's liberated feminine self, and the sea is that ultimate unifying force in which the hero as Santiago will realize feelings of perfect harmony with the universe and the world within.[130]

# Eight

# Now It's Women's Turn

## The Rescue of Eurydice

■

In the deep still woods upon the Thracian Mountains
Orpheus with his singing lyre led the trees,
Led the wild beasts of the wilderness.

Apollonius of Rhodes, quoted in Edith Hamilton, *Mythology*

A thing which in consciousness makes its appearance as
two contraries is often in the unconscious a united whole.

G. W. F. Hegel, *Phenomenology of Spirit*

While Vonnegut's critique of Hemingway's late work appears unwavering over time, the fact is that Hemingway's progress in healing the traumas of childhood and war in *The Old Man and the Sea* (1952), *Islands in the Stream* (1970), and *The Garden of Eden* (1986) precisely mirrors Vonnegut's progress in *Galápagos* (1985) and *Bluebeard* (1987). Though the movement of these late Hemingway works is more circular than linear, looking at these final versions of Hemingway's artist-hero in the above order crystallizes Hemingway's evolving creative vision, taking us to what is arguably the moral and artistic summit of Hemingway's life and work in *Under Kilimanjaro* (2005).

To complete their quest for psychic healing, both authors needed to face taboo fears and desires linking the traumas of childhood with the wounds of war, accessing the buried or denied feminine. Concomitantly they needed to resolve ambivalence, if not hatred, toward nonnurturing mothers they felt had forsaken or betrayed them and defeated, will-less fathers who threatened them with their own pessimism—the earlier, deeper, and more personal wound that underlies all Hemingway's and Vonnegut's writings. It is their ability to resolve tormenting feelings of hostility and guilt toward the parents, as well as frustrating anxieties about death and sex, that defines the achievement of their late works. I conclude my discussion of the authors' redemptive, reconciliatory vision with *Bluebeard* and *The Garden of Eden* because it is in the fused identities of Rabo Karabekian and Circe Berman in *Bluebeard* and David and Catherine Bourne in *The Garden of Eden* that we encounter the hermaphroditic solution to the authors' quest for psychic healing, the apotheosis of the hero's renascent and harmonized self.

### *Galápagos* and *The Old Man and the Sea*

It is through Vonnegut's merging of Hemingway, Kurt Senior, and that eternal harbinger of doom, Kilgore Trout, as one symbolic father figure—the voice of pessimism Vonnegut battled throughout his career—that we may understand *Galápagos* as Vonnegut's latest and most focused effort to purge himself of his embittered and cynical self. In *Timequake*, Vonnegut's literary good-bye,[1] it is no coincidence that Trout dies in the Ernest Hemingway suite of the writers' retreat known as Xanadu, the city of imagination, or that the Trout whose cynicism drives his wife and son from home in *Galápagos* and leads Leon Trout's mother to suicide, should speak to Vonnegut in the demoralized voice of Vonnegut's own father. Standing in the mouth of the "Blue Tunnel of Death," a sort of limbo between life and death, the morose and artistically failed Kilgore implores his son to give up the ghost, calling his commitment to life, his curiosity, foolish. "Keep moving Leon," he says, "No time to be coy. . . . You come to Papa right now."[2]

Leon's father's fatalism exerts a powerful pull. With a past as brutalized as Vonnegut's other war-scarred, father-persecuted heroes, Leon welcomes a brain that no longer hurts or feels. As a soldier in Vietnam, he fantasizes putting down his weapons and becoming a fisherman, and his depression climaxes when military scientists bring about an apocalyptic nightmare that changes forever the course of human destiny. Fleeing for their lives on a ship called the *Bahia de Darwin*—the new Noah's ark—the future progenitors of the human race wander aimlessly about the archipelago and are finally marooned on the island of Santa Rosalia. Like Leon all aboard the ship bear the scars of pathologically unloving parents, so crippled with fatalism and apathy they view mindless, emotionless life on Santa Rosalia as a blessing. Leon declares that the captain's view of life as a meaningless nightmare with nobody watching or caring what was going on was quite familiar to him.

Yet, while the deadly "father" has become so insanely cruel and vengeful in *Galápagos* that he wishes his own son dead, the novel does not represent, as some argue, Vonnegut's own surrender to the fatalistic malaise he attributes to doppelgängers Kurt Senior and Ernest Hemingway, the feeling that overcomes the weak-minded characters in *Galápagos*. Rather than advocating the mind-numbing pessimism that threatens the will of the narrator, *Galápagos*—as always in Vonnegut's fiction—is a warning against apathy bred by the belief that people are machines or machine parts in irreversible mechanistic systems of control. Hence, in his deadly, soul-threatening "courtship dance" with his father, Leon notes, "I took one step in his direction, but not a second one. I was like a female blue-footed booby at the start of a courtship dance. As in a courtship dance, that uncertain first step was the first tick of a clock, which would become irresistible."[3] Rejecting the noxious Trout, Leon achieves the optimism and the will to declare: "Mother was right. Even in the darkest of times, there was still hope for humankind."[4] Leon's identification with the female in the courtship dance with his father and his portrayal of his mother as the thinking, feeling, and affirming force within himself coincides with Vonnegut's association of the female with creativity in all his novels after *Breakfast of Champions*. Appropriate to the title I have given this chapter, "Now It's Women's Turn: The Rescue of Eurydice," just as Orpheus descends into the underworld and uses his art to charm Cerberus and persuade Hades and Persephone to release his bride and muse from the shades of hell, Vonnegut and Hemingway replicated the task of mythology's most achieved poet and musician in attempting to resurrect the denied or buried feminine.[5] In *Galápagos* it is the Mary Hepburn in himself whom Vonnegut summons to complete the psychic integration of anima and animus and to convert death to life, the "soul" Mary defines as the "part of you that knows when your brain isn't working,"[6] described in *Breakfast of Champions* as the sacred living force at the core of every human being. Mary realizes, however, that these twin psychical realities are equally vital to survival. She tells her students that there was possibly a lot of good to those preposterously active and contradictory big brains—"people playing with all sorts of ideas in their heads."[7] She sees reality—the Galápagos Islands, the universe, and the evolutionary process—as "imaginary," "pretense," a "game," an "invention" of human will and imagination; she sees "significance" as that which the mind's subjectivity assigns. Human beings write these fictions, not the blind mechanisms of nature. Such stories can "end up any which way."[8] Thus Mary generates life out of an experimenter's "curiosity" as to whether it can be done. Her creativity renews life; it does not launch missiles.

The same force that rescues Mary Hepburn by rejecting mindlessness and elevating the soul liberates the creative imagination of Rudy Waltz, Wilbur Swain, Walter Starbuck, and Leon Trout. Leon notes that Mary did not fulfill her creative potential until she achieved her master's degree at the age of twenty-two and became independent from her parents. Only then did she accept responsibility for her identity, passing through suicidal impulses to create, if not Beethoven's Ninth, at least new life for humanity from the verge of absolute sterility and annihilation. Like Orpheus, Leon rescues Mary, uniting his disparate selves—the self that thinks with the self that feels, cares, and creates—providing the will to resist his father's pessimism. (The name "Orpheus" derives from the Greek *orphanos*, "fatherless," "orphan.") Like his mythic counterpart, Leon assumes the role of mystery priest, augur, and seer who heals and transforms.

Just as *Galápagos* features Leon's reconciliation with the typically feared or rejected mother, arguing, "My father was Nature's experiment with cynicism, and my mother was Nature's experiment with optimism,"[9] *The Old Man and the Sea* portrays the natural progression in the spiritual evolution of Hemingway's late hero—a rebirth of artistic potency and integrity afforded both writers by women who represent the agency and embodiment of the authors' resurrected feminine selves. While there are no literal women present in Hemingway's novel, Susan Beegel makes clear that *The Old Man and the Sea* features a complex and powerful feminine persona in its title role, a female protagonist on equal footing with Santiago.[10] Beegel explains that in gendering the sea as female, Hemingway gave us a paradoxical mother figure as instructive and potentially redemptive as Maria, Renata, or Jan in *Islands in the Stream. The Old Man and the Sea* is the story of a man whose marriage to the feminine sea teaches him empathy and compassion and provides further understanding of the father's masculine aggression. Mindful of Orpheus's rescue of Eurydice, Beegel stresses that this is no safe or simple romance, but a tragic love story of separation and loss in which the hero and his author feel a sense of connectedness with the sea as wife or mother and with the feminine marlin that has so long eluded them,[11] expressed in language from the sacrament of marriage: "Now we are joined together" and "Fish . . . I'll stay with you until I am dead."[12]

. It is after Santiago's marlin is firmly hooked that the relationship between Santiago's and Leon Trout's ordeals at sea becomes apparent—both need to understand the complex mother as nurturer and destroyer and to reject the father's destructive masculine ideology. Though Santiago's wife is deceased, so that he no longer has a literal Mary Hepburn to comfort and guide him, Santiago's worship of the Virgin Mary as the eternal feminine underlies the resurrection of life for Santiago just as it does for Leon Trout. A devotional picture of the Virgin of Cobre, the patroness of Cuba, hangs on the wall of Santiago's shack, and his prayers at sea are "Hail Marys," which he finds easier to say than "Our Fathers." Like Mary Hepburn, whose identity is contradictory at times—she is profoundly feminine but consorts with a machine—the Virgin of Cobre is a sea goddess whose medieval roles cast her as tender and beautiful as well as dark and demonic, someone who arouses forbidden and irresistible passions. Such contradictions cause the Hemingway/Vonnegut hero to turn toward and away from women simultaneously. Hence, as Beegel explains, Santiago knows the maternal, womb-like space the fishermen call "the great well" both as a deep hole teeming with life and as deadly and merciless, a darkness of sharks and poisonous jellyfish.[13] The hero's challenge is again learning how to forgive and love this difficult parent, whom Gerry Brenner characterizes as "an idealized, androgynous figure" of indeterminate gender,[14] a saintly mother who offers him succor and regeneration but also the she devil who threatens the essential male self and tempts him with the guilty pleasures of erotic bonding, a so-called perversion punishable by sickness and death. Hemingway was of two minds about the natural world and by extension womankind; he told his friend Bernard Berenson that he viewed the sea as "*la puta mar* that we have loved and has clapped us all and poxed us too."[15]

Like Leon, Santiago thinks of resolving his painful inner confusion by numbing himself in the manner of earlier heroes ("you think too much, old man"), or worse by revenging himself on the primal mother as an object of dread rather than worship, whom he seeks to dominate or destroy. On the one hand, Santiago relates to the animals around him with love and respect. He values the porpoises, "his brothers,"[16] for their mated love and feels sorry for animals in trouble. He especially identifies with the marlin's suffering, feeling its wounds as his own, and sees the separation of male and female as the saddest thing he has even seen. It is when he claims he kills the noble marlin in self-defense, rather than because he enjoys killing, that his justifications wear as thin as those in *Green Hills of Africa*. Like those pathological personalities in positions of power, whom Leon Trout cites, whose explanations for making war always came afterward, Santiago argues he has only done what all animals do in the deadly primal relationship of the hunter and the hunted. He reasons that the sea is a place of inescapable violence where the great law of life is strife and destruction: "everything kills everything else in some way."[17] At once Saint Santiago, the patron saint of Spain, but also Santiago *Matamoros*, killer of Moors, Santiago appears to resolve his inner struggle by declaring he loves the fish but will kill him anyway. The fact is, as Santiago discovers through vigorous self-scrutiny, it is the masculine love of domination and of killing that trumps his desire for love and peace.

This impulse causes Santiago to act out, as Thomas Strychacz says, a veritable theater of manly bearing—demonstrations of physical courage, endurance, and the stoical bearing of pain[18] to kill brutally what he considers to be less honorable or distinguished animals, such as the Portuguese man-of-war jellyfish he genders female and which he loves to crush with his feet on the beach after a storm, hearing them pop when he steps on them. It is also the impulse that causes him to vilify the *galanos*, the evil-smelling sharks he associates with the feminine, which he hacks and harpoons with "complete malignancy,"[19] reminiscent of bullfighters in *Death in the Afternoon* who feel that killing is its own reward. Santiago admits that "you enjoyed killing the *dentuso*."[20] When he drives his harpoon in until he and the marlin become one, Santiago experience a spasm of ecstasy closer to rape than lovemaking, the perverse aggression that allows Vonnegut's Guillermo Reyes in *Galápagos* to experience an orgasm with his radar dish, a sexual release that leaves him happy and drained.

While Santiago wants to believe their mutual condition of existence justifies killing the beautiful marlin, he is neither the nonanalytical primitive Vonnegut has in mind nor the misogynist Hemingway, whose masculine rituals required shooting and killing as meaningful and necessary. Rather, as with Robert Jordan and Richard Cantwell, it is precisely Santiago's willingness to acknowledge his capacity for irresponsible aggression and cruelty that indicates his evolved moral sense, acknowledging personal sins against animals certainly but also women and children. The ascending feminine—a more fertile and active conscience—informs him he has killed the marlin not to feed others but to feed male vanity and demonstrate his superiority to other fisherman, to whom he confesses that he has ruined the marlin and himself by going out so far. While the literal father is absent from the novel, we recognize his destructive presence, the converse of the nurturing, redemptive mother, in the hero's obsessive need to prove his manhood, as Santiago says, over and over and over.

The point is that rather than the adversarial relationship of man and bull, Santiago establishes his moral superiority over earlier Hemingway heroes by learning to relate to the feminine not as a hater or destroyer but as a lover and caretaker, someone like Mary Hepburn, more interested in bringing forth rather than taking life, which explains Santiago's nurturing relationship with the boy Manolin. As a teacher, Mary explains the mysteries of life to young survivors while Santiago mentors his disciple by providing understanding of and sympathy for all the sea's creatures. Just as the androgynous Mary positions herself as both mother and father in performing reproductive experiments that assure the future of the human species, "man-midwife" Santiago achieves continuity of life by delivering Manolin from the sea in a violent birthing, "the cycle of life turning upwards once more."[21] Manolin remembers the old man's saving him from a fish attack by throwing him into the bow of his boat "and feeling the whole boat shiver . . . and the sweet blood smell all over [him]."[22] Like Mary Hepburn—and in the spirit of Maria in *For Whom the Bell Tolls*, and Renata in *Across the River and into the Trees*—Manolin will carry Santiago's legacy forward, ensuring the continuity of life in the face of destruction.

In Spilka's view, by conceiving the world in feminine rather than masculine terms, the hero has traded an ideology of control and domination for one of empathy and caring. Evidently, Spilka surmises, *The Old Man and the Sea* expresses regret for a life devoted to killing animals, a novel that reads "like a long-buried confession."[23] It is a novel, Spilka says, in which Hemingway's attitude toward animals—add, women and children—as "lesser" creatures often cruelly subject to adult control, finally implodes.[24] The author's reverence for nature, Beegel notes, comes through even in the story's lyric prose, the objective correlative for "an emotion of love."[25] Burwell might have Vonnegut and Hemingway both in mind when she concludes that, "if Santiago lived in Africa rather than Cuba, and were a Wakumba hunter rather than a Cuban fisherman, he would be a *mzee*," or shaman, the status to which Hemingway aspires in *Under Kilimanjaro*, an old man with mystical powers.[26]

### Bluebeard, *Islands in the Stream,* and *The Garden of Eden*

Evoking the promise of Nick Adams in "Big Two-Hearted River" that he would one day fish the deeper, more dangerous waters of the unconscious, John Wain remarks about Santiago's achievement: "If man can dig down to his own deepest springs, and find something good there, he can go ahead and die, because the most important business of his life is completed."[27] But, while Hemingway himself believed *The Old Man and the Sea* to be the best he had ever done—the "epilogue" to all he had learned or tried to learn, he knew his idyllic book about the sea and his hero's inner calm only prepared him for the more mature and complex works of *Islands in the Stream* and *The Garden of Eden.*

If, as is commonly argued, Santiago's "crucifixion"—like Leon's decapitation—does not appear to lead to any sort of traditionally Christian rebirth, we should remember that the essential heroes of these texts are the authors themselves, whose characters represent different versions of the writer's self-wrestling with and accepting of the "other" and whose resurrected feminine self in *Bluebeard, Islands in the Stream,* and *The Garden of Eden* represents a quantum leap in psychic healing. For these final versions of the evolving artist-hero—Rabo Karabekian, Thomas Hudson / Roger Davis, and David Bourne—love and reverence for the women in their lives and the feminine artist in themselves produces a renascence of artistic potency and integrity emblematic of the real Eden they seek, not a place but a state of mind, an androgynous balance that harmonizes anima and animus. The erotic content of what Hudson and Karabekian will paint and Davis and Bourne will write, the "perverse scenario," as Carl Eby explains it,[28] exposes the hero's deepest and most carefully guarded secrets, climaxing in a final exorcism of the emasculated father and reconciliation with the impugned mother through identity-merging brother-sister, mother-son lovemaking with female angels/devils.

It is not surprising that in *Bluebeard* Vonnegut should devote an entire novel to Rabo Karabekian, the painter whose work in *Breakfast of Champions* inspires what Vonnegut called the "new me," or that Vonnegut's secret sharer Hemingway should represent his own achievement of wholeness as man and artist through the more conscious and gender-integrated painter Thomas Hudson, whose androgynous impulses offer further rebuttal to Vonnegut's view of Hemingway's machismo. Nothing in Rabo's calamitous past—childhood unhappiness, the horrors of war, and profound depression—differs from that of Vonnegut's former traumatized heroes. Rabo's parents are as unfeeling and materialistic as the parents of Eliza and Wilbur Swain, Rudy Waltz, and Leon Trout. "I can't recall our ever having touched before," Rabo reports.[29] Rabo's parents also hold the arts in contempt and discourage Rabo's artistic yearnings. Having barely survived the attempts by the Turkish Empire to exterminate its Armenian citizens,

Rabo's parents develop terminal pessimism. Rabo looks into the eyes of his father and sees what every Vonnegut hero has seen, a zombie: "There wasn't anybody home anymore."[30]

Rabo, like Leon Trout, holds his father responsible for his mother's schizophrenic collapse and death; she is the mother who "up and died" on him.[31] He accuses the father of cheating himself and his mother by becoming "the unhappiest and loneliest of men," bent on self-immolation.[32] Rabo knows that if he were still alive, the defeated husband and failed artist who authored Rabo's childhood nightmare and even wished him dead would only laugh at his paintings and rejoice in their collapse. And he "wouldn't have razzed just me," Rabo says, "he would have razzed my Abstract Expressionist pals, too, Jackson Pollock and Mark Rothko and Terry Kitchen," painters acknowledged to be among the best the world has ever seen.[33] But though he understands the hellish connection between his father's crippling influence and his own susceptibility to the soulless art of the commercial artist Dan Gregory, Rabo is at peace with himself about this father, who dies wearing his cowboy boots, alone in the Bijou Theater. While he has forgiven his father hundreds of times, this time Rabo is going to accept. There are, he says, "no bodies in his barn."[34]

In the first of several major parallels between *Bluebeard* and Hemingway's *Islands in the Stream* and *The Garden of Eden*, Rabo's most troublesome memories are, he says, his failure as a husband of "the good and brave Dorothy, and the consequent alienation of my own flesh and blood, Henri and Terry, from me, their Dad."[35] The fact is that, like Catherine Bourne in *The Garden of Eden*, "the good and brave Dorothy" hates Rabo's work and literally destroys his paintings. Rabo links their destructive marriage to the traumas of war, labeling Dorothy's mutilations a "massacre." Dorothy undermines her husband's confidence, telling him in spite he could not draw something real if he had to and insisting he take a degree in business education. Somewhat akin to Marita, Catherine's temporary replacement, Rabo's second wife, Edith, does not hate his work but turns him into a social animal and smothers him with kindness. But, as with Thomas Hudson and David Bourne, Rabo's remonstrance to family members is relatively gentle and amicable—that of a man at peace with his transgressions and satisfied that his priorities are finally right.

The efforts of Hemingway's psychic artist projections, Hudson and Bourne, are uncannily similar replications of Rabo Karabekian's efforts to redeem his sins and heal his psychic wounds through art; yet Vonnegut's portrait of the demonic figure Dan Gregory returns us to his primary quarrel with Hemingway as the fatalistic self whose romantic stereotypes and moral absolutes encourages power and aggression. Gregory is that allegorized spook of cynicism and self-doubt who tempts past heroes to suicide—to seek escapist solutions to complexity and moral responsibility. Reminding us of Hemingway's self-confessed guilt about marrying money in stories such as "The Short Happy Life of Francis Macomber" and "The Snows of Kilimanjaro," Rabo's parents have supposedly delivered their son into the hands of the rich and famous illustrator of novels, magazine stories, and advertisements with the hope that Gregory will introduce Rabo to all his rich friends. But the prospective betrayal is Rabo's alone. As the embodiment of the potentially destructive animus in Rabo, Gregory warns Rabo to never have anything to do with a woman who would rather be a man, since women are terrible artists, born to bear children, take care of the housework, and encourage their men. Along with Joan of Arc, the first such "hermaphrodites" Rabo thinks of are Circe Berman and his cook, Allison White, who feed and nourish him, are fiercely independent, and love art as well.[36]

This Lucifer of a "papa"[37] is known as the champion commercial artist of his time, a master of illusions—a perfect copying machine, in fact, with absolute control of its paintbrush. "Nobody," Rabo explains, "could counterfeit better than Dan Gregory."[38] Though technically perfect, there is nothing human about Gregory's art, nothing of the vision of human sacredness and imaginative wonder that in his own work would one day provide so startling an epiphany for Vonnegut in the novel *Breakfast of Champions*. Most troubling of all to Rabo, Gregory's work is dangerously reductive—stagnant and morally simplistic. "Nobody," says Rabo, "could put more of the excitement of a single moment into the eyes of stuffed animals." "Let me put it another way," Rabo says. "Gregory was a taxidermist. He stuffed and mounted . . . great moments, all of which turn out to be depressing dust-catchers, like a moosehead . . . or a sailfish on the wall of a dentist's waiting room."[39] Intending to offer his apprentice a major spiritual lesson, Gregory takes a Springfield rifle off the wall of his studio—a replica of the murderous gun Rudy Waltz uses to kill a pregnant housewife—telling Rabo his work will only be good when it makes such "perfect killing machines" so real he can load it and shoot a burglar.[40] We are reminded of the hellish violence in Thomas Hudson's painting in *Islands in the Stream*, reproduced so realistically that someone throws a mug of beer at a waterspout, trying to break it down.

Rabo knows that the tendency of people to imitate art makes the "lies," the allegedly objective representations of artists such as Gregory, as lethal as bombs or bullets—as dangerous as those toy machine guns with plastic bayonets that look so real. He fills his narrative with examples of lives perverted by the sentimental or romantic mystifications of life by art, such as Nora's declaration at the end of Ibsen's *A Doll's House* that she will make her own way in the world despite having no skills or education or money and no prospect of a job. He worries that young people will believe movie versions of World War II, in which wars are fought by old men instead of babies and with blank cartridges and catsup for blood.[41] The most destructive storytellers, Rabo believes, and those who play at God, or at least justices of the "Supreme Court of Good and Evil."

Neither the romantic illusions Gregory peddles nor his moral and artistic authority are easy to resist. Rabo's early self-concept comes from reading romantic histories and novels and from self-help books about how to get ahead in America.[42] Looking back, he reflects that he was damnably close to becoming what Gregory was—and did become like him in many ways. Rabo admits to remaining capable of the same sort of "commercial kitsch" Gregory used to do—a facility for drawing or painting a likeness of anything his eye could see, putting his perfect mechanical dexterity to work in pursuit of a dishonest commercial success. The reference brings to mind Vonnegut's remark to Rackstraw that he could draw a representational picture quite easily but preferred to complicate and tinker with his drawing to soften the edge of how serious he was about the damage done by man's inhumanity to man.[43] It also reflects Vonnegut's dissatisfaction with his early concessions to commercial success. Rabo's early paintings are clearly an embarrassment, a negation of art, "black holes from which no intelligence or skill can ever escape."[44] The paintings fall apart because of an unfortunate choice of materials and chemical reactions between the paint he uses and certain pollutants in the atmosphere. He reflects that he gave up his boyhood dream of being a serious artist, convinced by Gregory that he would never be anything but "a reasonably good camera."[45] But while in thrall to Gregory, Rabo began to serve a second apprenticeship to the great modern masters in the Museum of Modern Art—the impressionists, cubists, Dadaists, surrealists, and abstract expressionists.

Their intensely psychological canvases speak to Rabo's deepest spiritual needs; they provide a sympathetic analogue to his personal struggles with fragmentation and despair; they confirm his sense that the important realities are those inside himself; and they encourage him to explore his own subconscious for a deeper understanding of the chaos within, showing him ways to transform schizophrenic fragmentation into works of art that are paradoxically beautiful and whole. These paintings are not petrified like Gregory's but "liquid"—open, emotional, complex, and protean, "old stuff in music," Rabo explains, "pure essence of human wonder."[46]

As surely as Dan Gregory represents the loveless, stagnant, counterfeit self against whose artistic authority Rabo rebels, so the mother-sister muse figures of Marilee Kemp and Circe Berman serve as agents of new life for Rabo, providing a symbiotic experience in psychic healing and self-creativity that pries him from petrifying memories—literary exorcism in the form of autobiography—and emotional renewal in the form of a diary that assimilates the past and revitalizes the present. In the spirit of Orpheus's rescue of Eurydice, Rabo saves Marilee from the death dealer who sends her alone to a clinic to dispose of the fetus she carries. He gives Circe new life by freeing her from painful memories of a husband who sees himself as a machine and a father who commits suicide, experiences so paralyzing they make her nearly catatonic, and about which, like Rabo, she must write "to keep grief away."[47] About Circe and his fellow veteran, Paul Slazinger, whose dreadful war injuries and troublesome pessimism land him in a psychiatric ward, Rabo asks, "And which patient needed me most now in the dead of night?"[48] But more than returning the favor, whereas war and childhood alienation have left Rabo a "blank brained, deep breathing hermit,"[49] these powerful surrogate mothers, lovers, sister-muses not only bring this "Lazarus . . . back to life again"[50] from the dark world of male ego, but they restore both Eros and the maternal anima to his feminine starved soul. Appropriate to Jung's argument that psychic healing requires a scrupulously honest dialogue between anima and animus, allowing "the other side" to speak,[51] Rabo, Hudson, and Bourne all welcome the "conversation" Rabo says Circe strikes up with[in] him, allowing her to operate on his masculine ego as though it were a "machine" and she were "a monkey wrench."[52] After all, he says, "let's be honest, I invited her."[53]

As strong, intelligent women who defy sexual boundaries, Marilee and Circe provide exactly the uniting and creative force that illuminates and heals the long guarded and deeply personal wound Rabo calls his "most secret disfigurement,"[54] which is like those of Thomas Hudson in *Islands in the Stream* and David Bourne in *The Garden of Eden*. Serving as what Jung called a "guiding star" to the darkness of the masculine mind,[55] Thomas Hudson's first wife, Jan, and David Bourne's wife, Catherine, join Marilee and Circe to complete the female rescue squad begun by Eliza Swain and Melody in *Slapstick* and by Maria in *For Whom the Bell Tolls* and Renata in *Across the River and into the Trees*, agents of Eros who not only make the hero a whole man but teach his soul to sing. These women possess exactly the balance of masculine-feminine qualities the hero seeks for himself, the Platonic hermaphrodite who becomes the perfect symbol of human completeness. Describing Circe Berman as both voluptuous and opinionated, Rabo says he knew several colonels and generals like Circe in the army, "but they were men and we were a nation at war."[56] Jan Hudson is delightful and charming but commands like "a good general."[57] Catherine Bourne defines herself as a woman who really feels things but, as male, commands and directs like Jan and Circe. She is a master creator who plans the daring sexual experiments she and David enjoy and inspires the narrative of their shared adventures. Women with this masculine and feminine balance, according to Jung, serve as the best path back to the complex primal mother.

In each narrative the author makes clear that the female protagonist and the mother of classical myth are one and the same being; that as well as ardent lover, this androgynous partner is best able to serve as "spiritual guide and advisor,"[58] one who criticizes and corrects the sins of the masculine-self prerequisite for higher consciousness. Willful by design—exactly like Catherine Bourne—Circe in her first words to Rabo, "How did your parents die?"[59] shocks him into revisiting repressed childhood traumas one final time, thereby dealing constructively with the present—a moral imperative that now, like Circe, "nips at his heels like a rabid fox terrier."[60] Telling Rabo she is tired of pretending, she instructs him to tell "Mama" how his parents died. Though he exclaims, "Tell *Mama!* Can you *beat* it?" the incestuous implications are hardly lost on him. He admits, "She had straight black hair and large brown eyes like my mother's" and says she is only "shapelier" because his mother "didn't care" what she looked like, "because Father didn't care."[61] Fusing the identity of both mothers, literal and figurative, Circe responds to Rabo's description of his mother's death by tetanus infection, by saying "so long, Mama" and adding: "At least she didn't have to see her only child come home a Cyclops from World War Two." "There was that word Mama again," Rabo notes.[62] More important, there is that sexual wound again, which this redemptive mother-muse completely understands and for which she will provide a cure.[63]

Jan Hudson and Catherine Bourne may not call themselves "Mama," but their embodiment as mother-sister lover and muse is equally powerful and remarkably similar to Circe's. Carl Eby suggests that Jan's return to Hudson "like a ghost in the night" represents a release of myriad psychosexual feelings associated with the denigrated mother and darkness within. Hudson hopes that thinking about her will encourage her to visit him in his dreams, no longer the feared ogre but a source of "unbelievable pleasure."[64] Evoking Nick Adams's experience in "Now I Lay Me" and "Soldier's Home," where the girls in Nick's life all blur and become the same (the mother Nick simultaneously fears and desires), Hudson's lady friend Audrey Bruce confirms the observation by Hudson's son Tom that "the same girl" appears in all the books by Roger Davis, Hudson's writer-self, calling it "pretty accurate."[65] Like her richly mythic counterpart Circe, Catherine Bourne is as much sorceress-agitator as nurturer-redeemer. Yet her role as bedeviling, paradoxical mother may be the most instructively transformative of all in its revelations of the author/hero's complex sexual identity and its power to feminize the hero's character and art for the better.

Not only will this particular mother not abandon the traumatized hero, but she also possesses the authority to undress him by, as Jung put it, turning the "burning ray of her Eros" upon him.[66] Reminiscent of Countess Renata as sea goddess, Circe is frequently found staring out to sea, which concerns Rabo because to swim, he is forced to take off his eye patch, which hides his terrible and secret wound, the "mess" of incestuous desire and fear of emasculation "under there" that he is embarrassed to expose.[67] Freud and Jacques Lacan both observed that fears of castration represent themselves in the form of a rent, tear, or primal hole, which could only be filled imperfectly by a patch.[68] But just as the force of a more forgiving, feminized consciousness allows the aggrieved Vonnegut and Hemingway protagonists to put their fathers to rest, the lovemaking of Circe and

Marilee Kemp, and of Jan and Catherine proves so simultaneously erotic and maternal that it provides the ultimate acceptance of self and sympathy for the mother, which is critical to psychic healing. Sex with Marilee is so tender and sensual that Rabo has splendid successive orgasms he calls "retroactive" and "prospective,"[69] transporting him into the fluid space-time of those prized abstract expressionist paintings in the Museum of Modern Art, where distinctions of past and present, flesh and spirit, male and female lose their meaning. Marilee makes Rabo a celebrant of Eros, leading him to the bedroom and the ecstasies of erotic love as she leads him to the Museum of Modern Art, but he wonders if he might also be a replacement for the Armenian baby who had been taken from her womb. Thinking of their lovemaking as "sacramental," physically as well as spiritually renewing, Rabo likes this older woman so much and enjoys their intimacy so guiltlessly that he imagines them cleaving together in the Garden of Eden, eating and drinking and enjoying their bodies as they "were on earth to do."[70] There was no vengeance or defilement in it, Rabo says; rather their lovemaking anticipates abstract expressionism. What they do in bed and what abstract expressionists do with paint similarly liberate repressed libidinal feelings from deep within. Reminded of what the painter Jim Brooks said to him about how all abstract expressionists operated, laying on the first stroke of color, then letting the unconscious do the rest, Rabo says, "In Marilee's and my case, the first stroke was a kiss just inside the front door, a big, wet, hot, hilariously smeary thing. Talk about paint!"[71]

Citing Jan Hudson's Circe-like sexual provocations in the earlier version of the *Islands in the Stream* manuscript, Eby explains that it is Jan who teaches Thomas Hudson acceptance of taboo desires by serving both as his erotic and spiritual guide, correcting sins of his masculine self necessary not only for psychic healing but for the more universal, spiritually expansive art he hopes to achieve. As wise and "authoritative" as Circe, Jan understands that, to achieve his potential as painter and writer, Hudson must, like his one-eyed counterpart Karabekian, acknowledge repressed yearnings for broader, more inventive sexual experience, gender-bending relationships that express his bisexual nature. Pressing Hudson to be more adventurous, Jan insists he submit to nontraditional lovemaking she knows he desires, an entrée to "secrets and surprises" she promises will change him forever. It is notably in the darkness of Hudson's studio, the dark associated with secret desires for the mother, that Tom and Jan make love. Suggesting the transformative "kiss" that precedes Karabekian's emotional and artistic metamorphosis, Jan demands that Hudson kiss her not as her male lover, but as her "girl." Despite the late hero's usual pretense of resistance, Hudson admits— as Rabo and Bourne do—that he likes the change from male to female, feeling the masculine defense "destroyed" within and thanking Jan for making him "brave."[72]

The gender-bending games Thomas Hudson experiences with Jan largely through memory, David and Catherine Bourne enact with startling if not shocking immediacy. Catherine's desire for an unconventional relationship starts innocently with getting a boy's haircut, an androgynous transformation that makes her feel she "can do anything and anything and anything."[73] But the boundlessness of "anything and anything and anything" soon escalates to her interest in nonnormative sex, gender inversion that requires David to accept the role of female in bed while she plays the boy she literally and figuratively grooms herself to be. Thus, with Catherine on top, David directs her "searching hand" to himself in an act of digital anal penetration that casts him as the girl and leaves him marveling at the "weight and strangeness inside." "Now," Catherine tells him, "you can't tell who is who."[74] Thanking David profusely for allowing the change, she calls him her "beautiful lovely Catherine" while taking the name "Peter" for herself, a somewhat comic appropriation of her phallic role that nonetheless accentuates the point she implores him to know and understand.[75]

The "change" to which Catherine refers is the one that Maria first effects in Robert Jordan, that Renata nurtures in Richard Cantwell, and that Jan enforces in Thomas Hudson—understanding and accepting the buried feminine that heals the hero's psychic split. It is on behalf of these powerfully transformative women that the renascent Hemingway/Vonnegut hero ventures into hell, that sleepless, nightmare region whose terrors have haunted them since childhood. This final descent yields not only a rescue of Eurydice, a reunion with the eternal feminine that mends their fractured psyche and matures their work, but a final purging of the traumas of childhood and war that occasions the fresh beginnings Vonnegut had in mind for Karabekian by calling his extended family the "Genesis Gang," when "meaning" had yet to be created. To this end Hemingway referred to the resolution of lifelong tensions with his father—which I argue refers to his mother as well—as a good way to end his book, except that it marked a beginning not an ending.[76] Hemingway's resurrection of his younger, more hopeful self in David Bourne and Nick Adams of "The Last Good Country" represents what Vonnegut called a "timequake," reliving past experience that appears to be predestined, but which awareness and the will to change allow characters such as Rabo Karabekian, Thomas Hudson, and David Bourne to reinvent themselves as kinder, more compassionate beings.

Only after Rabo confronts the devilishly clever commercial artist Dan Gregory, does he understand and renounce his sins and heal his psychic wounds. Rabo remembers Gregory as always dressed in black and his art as "diabolical"; Gregory appears to Rabo crouched before a fireplace as if engaged in satanic ritual; his studio, his "indubitable masterpiece," is filled with image-distorting mirrors, pictures of false paradises, and many glowing fires. An Antichrist in artist's clothing, the master of deceptions once appears to Rabo only as a head and hands, declaring he was born in a stable like Jesus Christ and unleashing a "harrowing counterfeit" cry of "an unwanted baby."[77] Gregory's studio teems with hellish omens, human skulls, and a Gorgon's head coated with verdigris, an appropriate symbol for one whose work is loveless and stagnant and turns to stone the humanity of all who look upon it. No wonder that—like Richard Cantwell, Thomas Hudson, and David Bourne—Rabo expresses reluctance to venture further into such a complex and hellish world. Yet aided by his twin female surrogates, Rabo's excursion into Hades proves critical to his final healing, reversing the chronic depression that plagued Billy Pilgrim and completing his artistic apprenticeship.

Thus the spiritual dynamism of Circe and Marilee frees Rabo from a sterile and mechanical creator and allows him to become a more honest and potent creative being. The vigor of Rabo's narrative alone, the energy of Eros, tells us that the Vonnegut hero has said his own final "good-bye" to his most visible psychological wound, a dissociation of mind and body and an inability to enjoy normal male-female relationships. Rabo exalts not only in the fact that his and Circe's house by the seaside, once so dead and empty, gives birth to Circe's book about how to revolt successfully, a book about how poor girls feel about rich boys, and to the memoirs of a painter who discovers what he says had so long eluded him, "soul, soul, soul,"[78] but that they are expecting a baby too.

But it is the amazing painting in Rabo's potato barn that climaxes and confirms his and Circe's achievement: a harmony of self and society, body and soul, man and artist that makes him not only sane but happy. Rabo is Vonnegut's most emotionally fulfilled hero. No wonder that Vonnegut dedicated his life story to his wife, Jill, who is described in *Fates Worse than Death* as Xanthippe, "a life force woman" without whom he says he "probably would have died of too much sleep long ago"[79] and that Rabo devotes the master work he calls *Now It's Women's Turn* to Circe, whose humanity explains Vonnegut's title, *Bluebeard*. By contrasts to the obscenely destructive male of the seventeenth-century fairly tale by Charles Perrault, Rabo notes that it is the female of the species who plants the seeds of something beautiful and edible. She is a creative as well as procreative force that, according to Jung, has "the power to fertilize the feminine side of the man."[80] "The only missile women can ever think of throwing at anybody," Rabo says, "is a ball or a bridal bouquet."[81]

At peace at last, Rabo ends his story praising the unity of body and soul that created a painting such as the world had never seen before. "Oh, happy meat," he exclaims, "Oh, happy soul. Oh, happy Rabo Karabekian."[82] At age seventy-one, high time! Soul clap its hands and sing. Rabo subtitles his autobiography "Confessions of an American Late Bloomer or Always the Last to Learn."[83] Confirming that Rabo's painting is compellingly autobiographical, when Circe asks Rabo if he is in his painting, he points himself out as the one with the crack running up his spine and parting him in half, the fragmented self that the painting, Rabo declares, purges and restores through the reconstructive possibilities of art. Circe is gratified to see that the dominant force in this painting is Eros, not Thanatos, and that women are not only present but act as the painting's supporting pillars. When she searches for images of healthy women, Rabo notes, "You'll find healthy ones at either end—in the corners and at the bottom."[84] As if answering Circe's challenge to provide art with the medicinal power of vitamins and minerals, paintings with grass and dirt at the bottom, Rabo points out that the painting literally expresses organic balance. It is "animal, vegetable, and mineral with colors and binders taken from creatures and plants and the growth beneath us."[85]

Because Circe knows Rabo's spiritual and artistic metamorphosis is *her* work as much as *his*, she is humbled and awed at the prospect of viewing the forbidden contents of Rabo's potato barn, and the sight of Rabo's magnum opus, the gem of his collection, transports her to a state of "postcoital languor."[86] Circe's erotic response to the painting—the "perfectly tremendous whatchamacallit"—suggests its potency-restoring sexual power, climaxing their relationship as spiritual lovers, and intensifying the coupling of art and love as a redemptive force. Circe cannot imagine how Rabo or anyone else could make such a "big, beautiful painting about something so important."[87] What the painting is "about"—"an exorcism of an unhappy past, a symbolic repairing of all the damage I have done to myself and others during my brief career as a painter"[88] climaxes and augments the meanings of Rabo's narrative and of Vonnegut's work as a whole.

It is no coincidence that, as we see in the striking parallel careers of Rabo Karabekian and Thomas Hudson, the more Hemingway and Vonnegut's fictional projections look like their authors, the closer the authors look like one another. Just as Karabekian's underworld descent yields a more aware and accomplished artist, so Hudson's frequent sojourns into nostalgia, the inevitable by-product of female empowerment, produce increasing self-awareness and more expansive and potent art. Hudson understands that nostalgia can kill you, but rather than an escape from pain and personal responsibility, his remembrances of things past allow the author to address questions close to his own heart with a frankness unparalleled in any of the works published in his lifetime. In a reversal of the iceberg principle, Hudson summons lost souls, wives and children alike, to denounce the sins of his darker self, a form of spiritual exhumation I call an aesthetics of "superconsciousness,"[89] a turning inward that produces not only a more mature hero but one more open to the unconscious and able to talk about repressed experience.

As with Karabekian, there is a persistent sadness about Thomas Hudson, but Hudson's detractors fail to see that he, like Cantwell and Jordan before him, is his own severest critic, that his remembrances of things past are not just about happy surface events—for instance young Tom's wonderful experiences in Paris as a baby—they are about what went on "down below." "He could feel it all coming up," he says, "all the grief he had put away and walled out."[90] When Willie feels the confessions loosening Thomas up and in effect creating a new potency, he remarks, "Now you got the old pecker up," and "see what I meant by sharing it?"[91] It seems a further descent into inner darkness beginning with Robert Jordan, intensifying with Cantwell, and deepening with Santiago and Hudson that proves the source of Hemingway's new aesthetic. The great "leaver outer" becomes a "putter inner," continuing the allegorical technique Hemingway called "remate," creating characters who represent an integral part of himself, generally avatars of his more vulnerable feminine self, such as Maria, Renata, Manolin, Thomas Hudson's sons, young David Bourne, and Debba in *Under Kilimanjaro*.

In Burwell's words this "twinning, cloning, or splitting" of characters—"interior reflections of himself"[92]—facilitates Hemingway's descent into the iceberg in *Islands in the Stream* and *The Garden of Eden*, a "hell" Hudson says was "just opening" to him.[93] Facing what Joseph Campbell explained as the perils of "descent,"[94] Hudson risks Orpheus's rescue of the "other" by turning a kinder, more vulnerable face to wives and children he recognizes as "one flesh" with himself and who awaken him to the sins of his darker self. As Jung explained, it is the courage of this moral effort—inspection of the darker, repressed aspects of the "shadow" that constitutes the moral achievement of Hemingway and Vonnegut's later heroes—daring the rare and potentially shattering experience of gazing, as it were, into the relative evil of their own nature.[95]

Just as Rabo Karabekian hopes to regain the affection of his two sons, Henri and Terry, Hudson begins this fearsome journey to the underworld by attempting to recuperate the lost love of his three boys, a repairing of filial love and respect. As an aggregate of their father's complexity—a mix of intelligence, physicality, and caring with a dark side—the children express their individual talents and gifts. As allegorical projections, they enable Hemingway, in Jungian terms, to examine replicas of his "own unknown face."[96] Thomas, the oldest, a happy boy whose face in repose looks tragic, is fiercely loyal and feels a sense of responsibility for each person in the family. Davy, the middle son, "sound and humorous," has a mind and life of his own; he is a "Cartesian doubter" and "avid arguer" who loves to tease, but without meanness.[97] While traits Hemingway either feared or aspired to are seamlessly blended among the three sons, it is Andrew, the youngest, who most resembles his father physically and spiritually—he is a "copy" of Hudson, imaginative and athletic, but "with a dark side to him that nobody except Thomas Hudson could ever understand."[98] Hudson reports that while he and Andrew recognize the badness in each other and are close, he has never been as much with this boy as with the others.

It is through Andrew's spiritual affinities with Hudson's best friend and companion Roger Davis—Hudson's demiurge—that Hemingway explored the masculine ethos undermining his and Hudson's caring, more feminine self, that which alienated them from the women in their lives and denied them greater creative vision, Hudson's as a painter, Davis's as a writer. Establishing them as psychic twins, someone refers to Davis as "a rotten writer and a lousy painter,"[99] the bartender at the Floridita describes them as quarter brothers, and Hudson explains they used to live in the same town and make the same mistakes. Equivalent to the duality that links Rabo Karabekian to Paul Slazinger and Dan Gregory in *Bluebeard*, Roger represents the potential for cynicism, brutality, and violence in Hudson that he has struggled to overcome. Roger admits being "evil as hell" and, as a Harold Ryan clone, enjoys fighting and inflicting pain. About his battering of an obnoxious but defenseless yachtsman, he tells Hudson, "I was taking pleasure in it from the minute it started."[100]

Still more incriminating, Roger—in direct contrast to Hudson and his son Andrew—tells Hudson in familiar macho fashion that he is unafraid of the dark, denial harkening to the death of his kid brother Davy in an overturned canoe, which invokes the death of innocence, fear of the dark, and retreat from consciousness of young Nick Adams in "Indian Camp." The fact is that Davis has spent a lifetime fearing death but refusing to think or write about its connection to his brother's cold drowning—at exactly the age of Nick Adams—or about his subsequent alienation from his mother and father. Though Roger tells Hudson the water was cold for him too, like Nick in "Big Two-Hearted River" or "Fathers and Sons," Roger says he could not say that; while sooner or later he knows he has to tell about his guilt and shame, he confesses he has become too corrupted by denial and violence to write honestly anymore. If he wrote about the canoe and its psychological aftermath, he says, he would probably romanticize about heroes rescuing beautiful Indian girls fit for a Cecil B. de Mille film. What it amounted to, Davis says, is that he came back and his brother did not.

Allegorically speaking, Roger Davis is the pessimistic, brutalized, and female-fearing masculine self, who prevails early on in the hero's psychic war between anima and animus, emerging from an embattled childhood and traumatizing war angry and violent; Hudson's is the becalmed, increasingly reflective and self-critical self, who critiques the "bad" Davis part of himself and exhumes those buried fears and allegedly shameful desires Davis confesses he has never worked out. In a dialogue Hinz and Teunissen call "Hemingway talking to Hemingway,"[101] Davis rationalizes that the violence in him is as inevitable as tidal waves, content that "evil is [his] dish,"[102] whereas Hudson tells him it is time to grow up and assume responsibility for his actions, advising him that all fights are bad, that he has made up his mind not to fight anymore himself because, "when you start taking pleasure in it you are awfully close to the thing you're fighting."[103] When Davis proposes he might be "just enough of a son of a bitch to be a good writer," Hudson retorts, "That's the worse oversimplification I've ever heard."[104] When Davis admits to fearing death but refuses to plumb the darkness in himself—numbing his conscience with drink or other forms of forgetfulness and arguing he might have saved his brother if the water had not been so deep and cold— Hudson counsels him that he cannot just run away all the time and says to forget his plans to head west since Eden is a matter of peace of mind, not a place. It is notable that, hoping to boost the confidence of the demoralized writer, Hudson engages in his self-critiquing conversation with Davis at night, after which both men sleep well, psychically prepared for the next day of underwater fishing.[105]

While Hudson, Andrew, and Davis know they share a "badness" inimical to becoming better human beings and artists, we glean from their descent into dark and dangerous waters—a metaphorical exploration of the complexities of Mother Sea equivalent to Santiago's—the threat Roger poses to the hero's efforts to approach the feminine with respect and love rather than fear and hatred. Masked and armed with spears, Andrew, afraid of everything underwater, ironically welcomes his older brother David, who is never scared, and Davis, professedly unafraid of the dark, as guides and protectors. But because Roger has allowed the boys to become separated from one another, David becomes easy prey to a "bitching" hammerhead shark, slicing toward him in the water, drawn by the scent of blood from David's speared fish. Eddy the cook shoots the shark just in time, but Roger is particularly unnerved and remorseful, perhaps unconsciously shaken by feelings of responsibility for the death of still another David.

When Eddy sees the shark as evil incarnate, he repeats Santiago's mistake of relating to Mother Sea and her creatures as adversaries. The shark, as huge and grand as Santiago's marlin, is to be mastered or overcome. In the spirit of hunters proud of their kill, young Tom, the least affected by the shark attack, wishes they could have saved the jaws as a trophy for their papa. But David's pretend stoicism dissolves into tears, and even more tellingly, Andrew declares he is glad they have not got them, that they would give him bad dreams. Based on the author's son Greg, Andrew, the most sensitive and inventive of the group, capable of imagining other selves, proves most vulnerable to macho posturing, understandable in light of John Hemingway's poignant elucidation of his father's lifelong struggle to become the woman he desired to be. At least symbolically, John reports, Greg's transvestic tendencies merely picked up where the grandfather's literary and nighttime fantasies left off, taking them to their logical conclusion. Like Ernest, John says, Greg struggled for most of his life to deal with his own contradictions and to create a balance between the hypermasculine and the hidden female sides of his personality, a conflict John calls "unbearable."[106]

It is when Andrew's older brother Tom, who knew James Joyce during his father's Paris years, inquires about Joyce's "great secret" that the deeper meaning of those underwater fears that haunt Andrew—but which Roger Davis denies— come to the surface. Tom is worried that, as his headmaster at school has warned, he might have a dirty mind for liking Joyce's portrait of the unbridled sexual desires of Molly Bloom. His father assures Tom that Joyce's work might be sexually explicit but is no more salacious than his own paintings of dark women in the nude, or women in earlier stories by Davis. Tom's amazement that Joyce could be bad without remorse no doubt represents part of Hemingway's own great secret, his struggle with repressive Oak Park puritanism, the prudishness that poisoned his parents' marriage, that caused his mother to label his work "dirty," and that arguably compromised the scope and depth of his artistic vision. Burwell points out that, if a "skin of memory" has grown over his childhood wounds, the damage done to his person and art are never far from Hudson's mind, including the "entrapment" of pleasing adults and becoming implicated in adult cruelty.[107] Now, however, as if to reverse Nick Adams's sense of his mother's moral obtuseness in "The Doctor and the Doctor's Wife" and "Soldier's Home," it is the father's insensitivity that Hudson holds responsible for his wound, the obsessive machismo that has dominated his adult life and wasted his talent.

Remembering early days with his father "in a blind," Hudson reflects that he cannot feel the same about hunting as he did as a boy and has "no wish to kill" ever.[108] As we learn from the surfacing secret desires of Robert Jordan, Richard Cantwell, and Thomas Hudson—which explode into unconventional sexuality of all kinds by David and Catherine Bourne—Hemingway's greatest personal and artistic challenge was to overcome the paralyzing emotional legacy of the unhappy parents, refertilizing his creativity by integrating the split-off parts of his psyche and learning to "be bad" like Joyce without remorse, to view so-called perversion— brother-sister, mother-son love, gender swapping, identity merging—as natural, good, and essential to a deeper, more honest artistic vision.

While Roger Davis resists confronting the darkness in his nature, a betrayal of the female within that denies him greater consciousness and artistic power, it is Thomas Hudson's recuperation of the feminine—his merging with Mother Sea—that liberates his unconscious creative energies and makes him the perfect secret sharer of Rabo Karabekian. Exactly in the manner of Circe Berman, Hudson's former wife, Jan, provides the critical self-knowledge and the energy of Eros that allows him to love and paint in ways that nourish his mind and art.

Apropos of Jan's concern that Hudson be as courageous on canvas as he is in bed, it is the mysterious erotic change produced by the "devil" in her and her sister provocateurs that enlarges and deepens Hudson's artistic vision. He remembers back to a winter in Switzerland when he would alternate between erotic games with Jan at night and painting Alpine glaciers during the day. Referring to Tom both as her "brother" and her "girl" and encouraging him to grow his hair longer and even dye it so they will look alike, using water from the sea to transform his looks, Hemingway's Circe, Jan—Eros incarnate—promises him he will produce something magnificent if he transfers the humanizing, identity enlarging possibilities of untamed Eros on to canvas.[109] Thus does Hudson hope to paint his own magnum opus, the artistic embodiment of this truer, less inhibited sense of self that Eby refers to as "the purest experience of the aesthetic moment."[110]

While there are no literal females in the Bimini section of *Islands in the Stream*, Hemingway's encapsulation of his male community within the strong, nurturing, generative space of Hudson's house, gendered female, but possessing male and female traits, tells another story. With its big open fireplace, connoting domestic warmth, Hudson always thinks of the house as "her"—"Thomas Hudson never saw the house, there on that island, but that the sight of *her* made him happy"[111]— a community structure designed to protect and nurture. Suggesting the generative house by the sea in which Circe and Rabo's creativity flourishes and literally gives birth to new life, all the rooms of Hudson's house allow him to watch his sons while they swim and play, and the enclosed porch with its cooling sea breezes sustains Hudson's painterly work ethic while providing peaceful interludes.

In the manner of Vonnegut's sustentative extended families, the community of men in the house acts out a gentler, more nurturing identity. Helping Hudson orchestrate his sons' visit, Eddie the cook and handyman, Joseph the houseboy, and two black characters embody the androgynous ideal Hudson aspires to, a composite of equal male and female traits. Joseph is idiosyncratic and exotic, equally successful at the masculine and feminine roles of houseboy, personal secretary, housekeeper, maid, cook, handyman, and estate manager. Like Tom, the oldest son, Joseph is staunchly loyal and dedicated to care and nurturance of the family, with a fierce love for the boys. Sounding like a member of Karabekian's "Genesis Gang," devoted to new beginnings, Joseph declares about the boys' arrival: "There won't be nothing like it since they had the big fire. I rank it right along with the Second Coming. Is it nice? you ask me. Yes sir, it's nice!"[112]

The other handyman, Eddy, also cook and sailor, is a simple, childlike character more at home in nature than society, but Hemingway's appropriation of the familiar trope of Mother Nature as paradoxical suggests Eddy's blend of male and female traits. He frets constantly about the boys, taking great care at preparing their food but is nevertheless a tough guy efficient with guns. While Hudson and Davis are similarly complex—tough and caring—Roger's masculine propensities predominate, while Hudson is as likely to engage in the housewifely duties of inspecting each day's menu and making sure the boys are well fed as to exhibit skills as a boat captain, sportsman, or painter. It is in fact his commitment to the female characteristics of sympathy and nurturance that not only sustains the caring community around him but that completes his artistic soul and prepares him for his most complicated and important work.

Potentially titling his painting *The End of the World* or *God's Own Hell of a Waterspout*—a nearly exact replication of Karabekian's autobiographical, multi-framed masterpiece he calls *Now It's Women's Turn*—Hudson is advised he cannot make a picture like that too big, that rather than the "little simple pictures" he usually paints or the "junk" Roger Davis writes, he must "put in everything," the life above the sea as well as below, paint "one to end them all."[113] No matter how horrific or scary the undertaking, he must paint from within the "eye of the storm," expressive of the inner eye and the labyrinths of the human mind typical of Karabekian's intensely psychological canvases. Hudson's own massive canvas suggests the psychic dynamism, the movement, and grandeur of Hudson's inner and outer worlds, the subject, Hudson says always appealed to his imagination, "the coldness of the iceberg,"[114] and the bedeviling paradox of Mother Sea that Hudson's more courageous art brings to consciousness. This time he will paint with the fuller self knowledge of the contraries within and the contraries without it has taken him a lifetime to learn—right and wrong as "identical twins,"[115] creative possibilities of which, he says, are just opening to him.

Emblematic of the late hero's pursuit of the entombed feminine, Hudson's painting mirrors Karabekian's apocalyptic scenes of violence and human suffering, people doomed like the citizens of the Galápagos by dangerous waters filled with sharks and killer whales who feed on those who try to swim away. More important, however, as Karabekian does, Hudson places himself right in the center of the picture, reflective of his own destructive nature and the harm he knows he has wrought on himself and others, including his nearly fatal pessimism. There's "me in the dinghy," Hudson says, "and nothing I can do."[116] In the self-critical spirit of Vonnegut's condemnation of the destructive machismo of the character Bluebeard, the hellish world of Hudson's imagined painting teems with images of the excluded and deprecated "other"—the "bullied" and desecrated bodies of women "stepped on" by egocentric men or "blown out to sea," half dead black men "floating everywhere," and animals "forked" by devils.[117] Hudson understands that all living things are subject to what Santiago calls "the *puta* sea," squalls and water spouts whose wreckage is sometimes unavoidable. But neither Hudson's painting nor his narrative is about the destructive power of Thanatos. Rather it reflects his doppelgänger Rabo's—and most notably Santiago's—awareness of the sacredness of all living things.

"That could make a *hell* of a painting," a friend says, one fit to hang in the Crystal Palace alongside the works of Hieronymus Bosch and Pieter Brueghel.[118] More to the point, Hudson's apocalyptic masterpiece, mirroring Rabo's in every respect, stands beside *Now It's Women's Turn* as an exorcism of past ghosts, an acknowledgment of personal responsibility for harm to himself and others, and an affirmation of Eros critical to psychic healing. While Hudson's all-inclusive vision of the sea's power for good and evil features a myriad of destructive waterspouts, hurricanes, tidal waves, and dense fogs, women are not only the chief victims in this sea of suffering humanity but its redemptive force. Their fate is not the schizophrenic splitting typically experienced by Vonnegut and Hemingway's male heroes—symbolized by the island's "rising waters" that threaten to engulf them[119]—but that of harbingers of hope and new life. Apropos of Eby's illumination of Hemingway's lifelong association of cats with all things feminine and erotic, cats are the only creatures to transcend the holocaust of killer fish and male tormentors, not merely surviving but "clawing the devils" and swimming "as good as you want to see."[120] Eby explains that connections between cats and women pervade Hemingway's novels, but they are particularly noticeable in *Islands in the Stream* and *The Garden of Eden.* Catherine Bourne, for instance, moves under David's hand just "like a cat,"[121] and Hudson associates Jan's erotic lovemaking with her feline qualities throughout the story, experiencing as much pleasure stroking her as his cat, Princessa. He dreams of being as "shameless and wanton" in Jan's bed as Princessa is in hers.[122] Given this association of the redemptive feminine with royalty, it is unsurprising that Hudson should honor his proposed masterpiece by toasting all great women, particularly Queen Mary of England, a nod of appreciation both to Hadley and to Mary Welsh, evoking Jan's spiritual twin, Mary Hepburn.

When Hudson remarks that the great thing about pictures is they made you hopeful, because they do what you always worked to do, he speaks for Hemingway and Vonnegut as well, a point clarified in Hudson's further observation that everything a painter or writer does is part of his training and preparation. What they have trained to do is to achieve the deeper, more feminized art manifest in the marriage of heaven and hell, feminine and masculine, in Hudson's and Karabekian's paintings, the heightened creative possibilities of life and art I call the doctrine of plentitude. Appropriate to Hemingway's planned "Land, Sea, and Air" book, Hudson announces: "The land of plenty. The sea of plenty. The air of plenty."[123] As with Santiago, Hudson sees "plenty" as both the "puta sea" and "the sea of promise"—and it is the tension born of this eternal paradox that Hemingway arranges in a powerful juxtaposition—nada and fullness, pain and pleasure, loss and recovery—that constitutes the mutual canvas of Hemingway's writing and Hudson's painting.

Though the sea deceives at time, it is her complex nature that bonds them to her and her creations and whose paradox they carry within themselves. Like Karabekian's own struggle for self-understanding, this spirit of acceptance carries no sentimental illusions about man's fate. Hudson knows that the same force supporting and filling him during his time of life is that sea into which he must ultimately dissolve. Acknowledging life's necessary cycles, which ebb and flow throughout the story, he feels the "happiness of summer drain out of him as when the tide changes on the flats and the ebb beings in the channel that opens to the sea."[124] Though he wishes that many things about his past were different, better, that he were able to draw like Leonardo or paint as well as Pieter Brueghel, that he would always be healthy, and that he could have his children back alive along with all those who have gone from his life, he knows he cannot have these things. Central to Hudson's life-affirming approach to plentitude is not just his knowledge that for every "bad" there is an offsetting "good," but that the good sometimes requires the bad as a regenerating force and that the existence of the bad may sharpen sensitivity to the good in a way that intensifies one's appetite for experience and one's ability to make art.

When David Bourne declares that writing is the only progress he makes, we know that for him as well as Thomas Hudson and Rabo Karabekian, creative growth and moral growth are entwined and that neither is possible without the help of forceful, androgynous women, including Jan, Catherine Bourne, Marita, and Circe Berman and Marilee Kemp. Years after their divorce, Jan reminds Hudson that it was because of his dark side they parted, but that he is now more caring and selfless than she can ever remember: "You are changed," she declares.[125] This line is weighted with meaning for our understanding of the author as the primary benefactor of his more open and expressive heroes. For those who read the novel's final section as an expression of Hudson's despair and diminished feminine consciousness, I suggest that Hudson's aggression as a German submarine hunter signifies what Carlos Baker regarded as "self-rehabilitation," Hemingway's moral directive to himself.[126] The author faces those masculine sins that have damaged those he loves and compromised his art, that is, gotten "in the way of everything," as Hudson says about his guns.[127]

Rather than likening Hemingway to a modern Odysseus as Vonnegut does in *Happy Birthday, Wanda June*—a man who flees marriage, fatherhood, and domestic responsibility, I agree with Robert Fleming that, in the "Cuba" and "At Sea" sections of *Islands in the Stream*, Hudson's human side again prevails over the destructive Roger Davis part of his character, not a repeat of his father's machismo but a continuance of Santiago's gains in humility and gentleness. As Fleming explains, Hudson's vulnerability and more sensitive self appear not only in sympathetic, self-critical conversations with Jan but also in tender feelings toward acquaintances such as Honest Lil and other acquaintances at the Floridita Bar. Hudson even worries what will become of his pets if he is killed at sea. Just as the transformative power of the mythic Circe changes Odysseus's crew of beaten-up men into seaworthy sailors again, comforting and nourishing them and giving them hope, so she does what she does for Rabo Karabekian, waving her magic wand over Hudson's band of "half saints and desperate men," infusing them with the same warm and supportive qualities that creates the caring, nurturing community of men present in the book's opening section. Fleming observes that Hudson concerns himself with the emotional well-being as well as the physical safety of the men who man his boat, and they in turn nurture and protect him, feeding and covering him with a blanket when he sleeps.[128] When Eddie tells Hudson to please be careful of himself and the ship, we recognize that this is no floundering *Bahia de Darwin*, but the *Queen Mary*, whose feminine virtues promise salvation.

Moreover this infusion of courage and hope in "At Sea," as Circe does for Ulysses, makes possible Hudson's journey into the underworld in his *"undersea* boat," risking the "promising *deep* water" and "searching the *inner* keys." The more than forty references to hellfire suggest the hero's final descent into the iceberg's forbidden depths, in which the resurrection of Eve-Eurydice, whose Circe-like voice comforts and encourages him in his final moments, redeems his myriad transgressions, reconciles him to the vagaries of Mother Sea, and liberates the erotic imagination that fuels his author's amazing artistic undertaking in *The Garden of Eden*. Though Hudson quips that learning not to quarrel with women anymore was as difficult to learn as to learn how to settle down and paint in a steady, soulful way, it seems clear that as for his author, one follows the other, that he has learned more every year, as he says, about the importance of balancing compassion for people with discipline for his work. Just before Thomas Hudson dies, he realizes that he has been dreaming that he will live, which in essence he does. His reincarnation as David Bourne continues the pattern of sacrificial death and renewal in *For Whom the Bell Tolls*, *Across the River and into the Trees*, and *The Old Man and the Sea*, a pattern that generates an increasingly moral and artistically evolved hero.[129]

### The Garden of Eden

When Hudson/Hemingway remarks that everything a painter does or a writer writes trains and prepares him for what he is to do, the author might well have the androgynous commingling of women, writers, and painters in *The Garden of Eden* in mind. This novel's fluid gender alignments epitomize what Hemingway's writing had always been about at its deepest and most personal level. What differentiates the relationship of David and Catherine Bourne from those of their predecessors is not just an intensification of the garden's forbidden fruit—gender inversion and the realization of erotic dreams with real or symbolic sisters and mothers that Hemingway flirts with in *For Whom the Bell Tolls*, *Across the River and into the Trees*, and *Islands in the Stream*—but the author and protagonist's greater consciousness as to the hidden or secret nature of such transgressive sexual desire and its effect on their life and work. It is this deepening awareness that allowed Hemingway his greatest understanding yet of the lifelong gender battle he shared with Vonnegut.

Like Renata in Venice or Jan in Paris, Catherine is a young beauty who helps her wounded husband enjoy the sensuous pleasures of still another garden of plentitude in the seaside town of le Grau du Roi, located in an Eden of sand, blue skies, and sparkling seas along the coast of southern France and northern Spain. But as with these prior flesh and blood, albeit allegorical figures, it is Catherine's role as the protagonist's female inner voice that changes him from inside, serving as his spiritual guide, directing his descent, and critiquing and correcting the sins of the masculine self. Marita observes that, as the creative female principle David needs to complete his quest for integration of self and the world, achieving full potential as a writer, "Catherine is always with him," a mirror reflection, David sees, of his own "strengths and weaknesses" who knows "the faults of *our* defenses."[130] Though David (or his creator) pretends to resist Catherine's Circe-like efforts to change him—he learns that in the quest for psychic wholeness, "Catherine was not his enemy except that she was himself."[131]

Certainly Catherine's reclamation of David's artistic integrity, saving him from the machismo that dominates his work and the timidity that prevents him from opening himself to deeper, more personal revelation, is as daunting as the grand project of *The Garden of Eden* itself, the "vast undertaking" Catherine refers to, the book Burwell sees as so big and important that it separated from Hemingway's planned tetralogy to become its own text. Just as Circe Berman struggles to dislodge Rabo from years of lazy, simpleminded art, Catherine finds David's masculine proclivities so entrenched and automatic that she complains, "Do you want me to wrench myself around and tear myself in two because you can't make up your mind? Because you won't stay with anything?"[132] Her efforts to liberate him from a lifetime of repressed desire and facile masculine creativity so potentially fragments and exhausts her that she considers David—her work in progress—a hopeless cause and momentarily retreats into that same murky unconscious David fears and resists.[133] "I just want to sleep for a long time,"[134] she says. David's strategies of forgetfulness are all too familiar: mind-numbing alcohol, "the old giant killer,"[135] and a retreat from introspection: "He thought that if he did not think then everything that was wrong might go away."[136]

Coupled with honest fears that Catherine's sexual adventurism may lead to moral and artistic disaster, even cost his sanity, David's conservatism is so deeply ingrained that, when Catherine brings the seemingly more conventional Marita into their lives, he does not know for sure which woman he wants.[137] Marita appears to him as the perfect adjunct wife that years of cultural indoctrination convince him he needs, a wife Catherine heroically refuses to become—the supportive, nurturing, but pacifying spouse played by Edith in *Bluebeard*, who—by contrast to the devilish Catherine-like provocateur Circe Berman—renders Karabekian docile rather than encouraging him to think and take risks.

In fact not only does a submissive Marita not exemplify David's deeper feelings, but—from what we know about Hemingway's intentions for her in the Kennedy manuscript—she proves to be Catherine's sexually rebellious twin, "enmeshed" with Catherine and David "like three gears" in his psychic "wheel."[138] When David complains to Catherine, "You only want things for you, Devil," Catherine corrects him, "That's not true. Anyway I am you and her. I'm everybody. You know about that, don't you?" He evidently does, acknowledging: "Each must know what the other thought and probably what they each had told him."[139] Even in the published text, Marita's sexual anarchy enforces David's own taboo longings. Catherine delights in finding that Marita shares her defiance of prescribed gender roles—her eagerness for lesbian as well as incestuous experience. Like Catherine, Marita turns critical not only of David's gender anxieties but of his literary evasions as well. When he balks at exposing his vulnerability by letting her read the story of his father, she responds, "Can't I read it so I can feel like you do and not just happy because you're happy like I was your dog?"[140] As one of Catherine's several mirror reflections, which also include Barbara and Helen in the Kennedy text, Marita becomes even more scornful of the role of dutiful housewife, extending Catherine's critique of David's machismo. "If you kill things unnecessarily," she tells him, "some day there won't be any things to kill."[141]

Faithful to Hemingway's determination in *Death in the Afternoon* to report how he really feels, David admits to wanting Catherine and Marita both alone and together. Like Barbara and Nick Sheldon in the uncut version, Marita joins Catherine in what David describes as "figures in some unbelievable play he had been brought unwilling to attend."[142] When lying together in bed, the women tell the reluctant David they have been waiting for him. The door they open for him, the dangerous space these daughters of Eros invite him to explore, is that imagined moral darkness so long feared and avoided. "That's why I came here," Marita says,[143] in effect to offer David the fullest range possible of human sexual experience. Catherine and Marita's increasingly tanned skin reflects the darkness—the interior wilderness of psychic dangers that simultaneously attracts and repulses David. When Catherine anticipates the author's final descent in *Under Kilimanjaro* by offering to go to Africa with David—a world with "lots of wild places"—and be his "African girl," David's response seems to suggest he is no further along in curing his head wounds than Nick Adams: "It's too early to go to Africa now," he says, "everything is like a swamp."[144] Yet David's wondering how dark she might become speaks more of what he hopes for than what he fears.

While coerced gender roles drive Catherine to distraction, she is not so much literally "crazy," as often alleged by those who would shut her up, as she is, along with Marita, the symbolic expression of David and his creator's fears of inviting personal and creative chaos by giving in to wayward sexual desires. Clearly these mad muses, all of whom ascend from the mist of the protagonist's unconscious—suddenly real and normal again—function as one person with Ernest Hemingway as the provocative, ascending anima that produces a deeper and more expansive creative vision. The names change—Maria, Renata, Jan, Catherine, Marita, Barbara—but as Jung's "guiding star," their task is always the same—to direct and inspire the men in their lives to become more honest about their feelings, and more daring in their artistic expression.

Catherine and Marita's task of enticing David to explore his psychic under-world is made easier when these alleged she devils force him to admit his taboo desires are as insistent as theirs—that, as Catherine tells her one-eyed Cyclops, he is not hard to corrupt, because he really wants it too. Catherine informs Marita that if he ever says no about anything, just to continue on because it does not mean a thing. We know David has been attracted to Catherine's risky forms of sex play from the start, but Marita confirms this by insisting that any girl he will ever be attracted to who does not bore him will have the same complex sexual interests as she and Catherine. Whatever the games—brother and sister incest, sodomy, or the ménage à trois he enjoys with Catherine and Marita—David finally admits he is as excited by them as the women are. "Say it," he tells himself. You like it." "Don't ever say anyone tempted you or that anyone bitched you."[145] Though he refers ostensibly to feelings of sexual transformation pro-duced by hair or skin color, he knows the change in sexual identity runs far deeper: "You know exactly how you look *and* how you are." "Now go through with the rest of it," he tells himself, "whatever it is."[146]

We may assume that David's certain, if reluctant, admissions that he wants and enjoys what Catherine and Marita want represent a critical juncture in the author's own battles with erotic desire.[147] Certainly it is himself Hemingway had in mind when he wrote that, as apprentice to Catherine and Marita's moral in-struction, David takes a chance, declaring perversion to have been around forever and nothing to be afraid of. As if the author needed to hear so-called perversion pronounced healthy and sane as often as possible to believe it, defiance of sexual norms becomes the cause célèbre of his disparate fictional selves throughout the *Garden of Eden* manuscript. To wit Marita remarks about David's conflicted moral life, his perpetual war within, that she did not know it was a battle when she came.[148] As long as it is David's "crazy" wife, the devilishly seductive Eve, who breaks the rules, both he and his creator may indulge all manner of sexual fan-tasies without fear of censure, either from themselves or judgmental readers such as those puritanical Oak Park parents, whose restrictive ideas about sex Hem-ingway and his fictional hero have battled their entire lives. But David's tacit acceptance of the feminine that Catherine's "dark magic" signifies presages new awareness and self-confidence that not only reconcile the gender contraries in Hemingway and his developing hero but augments their power as artists. Cather-ine, described—like Circe Berman and Jan Hudson—as emerging from the sea, can announce to David that Mother Sea—the universal birthing force, light and dark, masculine and feminine, that unites and nourishes all its creations—has done her work.

It is again Hemingway's as well as David's voice along with Catherine's when she declares that the bravest, happiest people are those unafraid to break the rules: "We're so happy when we're natural and do what we feel." "Maybe," she says, "it's how people always were and never admitted."[149] Identifying Catherine and David as "pioneers" whose gender bravery may be "the salvation of the whole coast," their hotel waiter exclaims, "So long as it isn't violent, there is nothing wrong with it."[150] What these evolving, interfused characters finally know and understand is that breaking the rules, defying convention, is prerequisite both to moral and artistic growth. Accepting forbidden erotic longings as healthy and pleasurable is paramount to quelling inner demons—incestuous desires for the feared and impugned mother, and the literal, real-life sister who appears as Littless in "The Last Good Country"[151]—and fears of impotence associated with the emasculated father. As with Rabo Karabekian's more soulful painting and writing, it is precisely David's liberated Eros that produces the greatness of art represented by Rodin's statue *The Metamorphoses of Ovid* and its literary counterpart of harmonized male and female parts, *The Garden of Eden*. David infers the nourishing, symbiotic nature of art and sex by conflating them as similarly precious, orgasmic experiences. When he remarks to Marita about his treasured stories that "it's right you're only allowed so many in your life," and Marita asks, "So many what?" David explains, "So many good ones."[152]

As Jan has done with Hudson/Davis, and Circe Berman with Rabo Karabekian, Catherine compels David to confess betraying his creative powers by avoiding his deepest, most important subject—vulnerability and secret desires masked by macho posturing. She detests the press clippings praising David's recent World War I novel, urging him to explore the complex sexual dynamics of their present lives rather than continue the hunting story he is writing about his early life with his father in East Africa. In a self-critiquing observation that implicates Hemingway's own unfinished work, Catherine accuses David of jumping back and forth from one text to the other, "escaping [his] duty" rather than keeping with the narrative "that meant so much to all of us."[153] Though David shares his author's dictum that lasting and finishing your work is the artist's first priority, he admits he has either not known enough about himself to explain in earlier books what he really believed, or like Roger Davis, has not risked descent into the dark and dangerous waters of the unconscious to understand his "badness" truly. He wonders, for instance, if his famous iceberg theory of omission has not been a convenient way to bury memories that hurt too much to think about. Explaining the intensity in his work in terms of a "camera" that allows him to focus only on what he chooses to see, Catherine asks, in effect, if such narrowed perspective does not defraud his wife and all his friends. David answers that it is only himself he cheats.

The fact is, however, in what may be the finest aesthetic moment of all Hemingway's late work, the author ingeniously fuses the moral rigors of David's hunting story with the exploration of betrayal and inner darkness in the larger narrative. As David informs us, one story generates and comments on the other:

"So you must write each day better than you possibly can and use the sorrow that you have now to make you know how the early sorrow came."[154] Not only do these symbiotic artistic ventures demonstrate David's artistic growth, but tracking his and Catherine's dangerous, complicated marriage requires as much courage as his fictional safari into his father's heart of darkness, the painful story of the way his father's "dirty secret" shaped and scarred David as a young boy. Bourne/ Hemingway takes exactly the literary risks that Catherine's sexual games represent and literally embody. Whether it is Catherine's voice who chides him for avoiding more serious work or the rising feminine in David that directs his elephant story, both narratives allow the "other" side to speak a scrupulously honest dialogue between anima and animus that produces David's best writing.

While David bristles at Catherine's scorn of his fictional portrait of his "despicable" father, he admits she has started him thinking about his father more honestly than ever before, that really she is right, it *was* an "awful" story—"By God it was."[155] Believing he now knows more than ever why he has put off writing it so long—certainly more than traumatized Nick Adams of "Indian Camp" knows or Nick of "Fathers and Sons" is willing to admit—David tells himself it is time to grow up and face what he has to face, not to worry about who might not understand or like what he writes any more than he would refuse to open the door of his darkroom to see how a negative was developing. Just as the forbidden contents of Rabo's potato barn move Circe to postcoital languor, so David's once feared androgynous feelings in the honeymoon and hunting narratives, freed from the bolted door of his workroom, make Marita so happy and proud she kisses David hard enough to draw blood from his lip. Just as with Circe and Rabo, Marita and Catherine's sexual response to David's deeper, more careful work climaxes the relationship between Catherine and David as androgynous lovers, a mingling of masculine and feminine that transforms what was tragically divided and defiled into art that is more fertile and whole.

David's experience combines with Nick's when David recounts the strategy of repression he developed, as a vulnerable eight-year-old on safari in Africa with his father, to protect himself from knowledge of his father's weakness, deciding he must keep his father's dirty secret as his own. David is as appalled and shaken by his father's slaughter of an old bull elephant as Nick Adams is by his father's primitive surgery in "Indian Camp," remarking that this was another of his father's mistakes. But fearful of appearing unmanly and intimidated by his father's insistence that it was simpler and better to forget anything bad that happened, David decided never to share his feelings again. In a remark implicating Hemingway's critical understanding and rejection of the hero's lifelong strategy of forgetfulness and denial, David observes, "he knew this was the start of the never telling that he had decided on."[156] But understanding better how his father's callousness and emotional reticence have threatened his art, David determines "to get things right this time."[157] He will no longer rationalize his father's cruelty and coldness. Instead he will testify to it as Rudy Waltz does to free himself from Otto's tyranny. David speculates that what he calls his father's lack of vulnerability—his emotional deadness and incapacity for guilt—renders him no more capable of caring about crimes against his family than about his betrayal of the elephant, giving it "no more importance than he had given to the fine print on a transatlantic steamship ticket."[158] Hemingway's subtle, ambiguous use of the pronoun "him" in his description of the elephant's terrible death fuses the animal's suffering with David's, suggesting as well the death of childhood innocence: "He had tried to make the elephant alive . . . in his final anguish and drowning in the blood that had flowed so many times before . . . and now was rising in *him* so he could not breathe" (emphasis added). "He looked sad," David says, "the same way I felt."[159]

Whereas David feels his father dealt too lightly with evil, what David knows and chooses no longer to hide—described as "dreadful true understanding"[160]— is that the father's brutal killing of the elephant, David's "brother" looking for his mate, exacts retribution against the offending mother, a betrayal David feels he shares for having put the men on to the elephant's trail. The destruction of the elephant for its tusks and David's potential betrayal of Catherine's quest for more androgynous art and lovemaking become one when David describes his wife as being as "smooth as ivory too."[161]

As he had done with Santiago's fish, Hemingway accentuated the image of male on female violence through describing the elephant's long eyelashes and referring to his ear as the female vagina. When Juma, their tracker, drives his rifle angrily into the wounded, despairing elephant's ear hole, firing twice, David feels he will remember the different colored blood for a very long time.[162] This description appears to critique the glorification of killing in *Green Hills of Africa* and bullfighting in *Death in the Afternoon* when David observes, "The bull wasn't doing anyone any harm. . . . My father doesn't need to kill elephants to live. . . . Fuck elephant hunting."[163] Young Bourne's sympathy for the elephant rather than the cold-blooded hunters culminates in his declaration that "the elephant was his hero now as his father had been for a long time."[164] The father's careless gloating at the elephant graveyard, which the living elephant seems to visit in genuine mourning, leads David to decry the men as "god damned friend killers"[165] and to tell his father he wishes the elephant had killed their tracker Juma instead. While David has resisted Catherine and Marita's desire to read the story, he reiterates Thomas Hudson's understanding of the therapeutic value of confession, deciding "he could not help sharing what he had never shared and what he had believed could not and should not be shared."[166]

Kenneth Lynn suggests that, as with David, Hemingway's loss of respect for his father, whose supposed emasculation so confused and demoralized him, was never resolved, that his anger with the man he feared he might become made him angrier with every passing year.[167] Indeed, when David (and by extension Hemingway) concludes, "All your father found he found for you too . . . the truly bad and the much worse," and "It was a shame a man with such a talent for disaster and delight should have gone the way he went,"[168] David's harsh words, tinged with regret, echo Vonnegut's view of Hemingway's decline and suicide. But David's open rebellion, the virulence of his condemnation of his father's violence, suggests not only a repudiation of his father's cruelty but of his own sins against the "other," what Thomas Hudson decries as selfishness, ruthlessness, and irresponsibility—the misogyny Vonnegut satirizes in Harold Ryan and Dan Gregory. Marita responds to David's revelations about his father's cruelty by asking, "Was this when you stopped loving him?" David answers, "I always loved him. This was when I got to know him."[169]

Just as Rabo Karabekian's forgiveness of his father resolved Vonnegut's lifelong tensions with Kurt Senior, so Hemingway decided Bourne's deeper understanding of the father, whose failings tormented him as they did Nick Adams, was more than a way to end his book; it was a fresh beginning.[170] When David expects to see his father's presence in the mirror over the bar but instead realizes he is alone, we may assume the fictional exorcism of the father is complete—that, like Rudy Waltz and Rabo Karabekian, David has achieved a standard of growth by which he says his "progress" as man and artist may be measured.

While, like Rabo, David did not known how "divided and separated"[171] he was, the rejection of the masculine ethos that enables Rabo to heal, wedding anima to animus, allows David to shed the baggage of misogyny and cynicism he inherited from his father and to achieve rebirth as amazing as that of his gunshot counterpart. But, as with Vonnegut, does Hemingway's fictional rejection of the father's machismo suggest a softening of feelings toward the author's real-life, flesh-and-blood mother, a return to what Spilka calls "his old childhood tenderness"?[172] Or, as Kenneth Lynn and Jeffrey Meyers believe, did Grace remain the "dark queen of Hemingway's inner world" all his life?[173] Hemingway did not see his mother for twenty years prior to her death, and perhaps he felt more relief than remorse at her passing. Certainly Catherine Bourne's angry burning of David's stories and press clippings, supposedly a fictional revisiting of Hadley's loss of Hemingway's early manuscripts, appears critical of women real or fictional. Yet a deeper truth seems to lie in the kind of healing Hemingway and Vonnegut envisioned with their late protagonists, reconciliation with profoundly intelligent, headstrong "Circes" whose androgyny inspired and redeemed their art. I suggest Maria and Pilar, Renata, Jan Hudson, and Catherine Bourne equate with Vonnegut's own "female rescue squad"—powerfully independent women based on real-life wives, whose positive influence inevitably reflects the presence of a strong-willed and authoritative Grace Hemingway.

Even if Hemingway's fictional projections were kinder to those wives in print than in person and although Hemingway fell short of Vonnegut's reconnection with Edith, Hemingway's positive fictional portraits seem to represent heartfelt if grudging efforts to reconcile with the figure of Grace Hemingway. Evidence that the writer gained an increasing sense of confidence in assuming his mother's androgyny in writing and life, the "provisional ending" of *The Garden of Eden* omitted by his editors shows David not only forgiving Catherine for undoing his old work, admitting that his carefully considered revisions represent writing more honest and powerful, but reuniting with her in body and spirit, an integration analogous to Vonnegut's own achievement of psychic healing.[174] If the promise of healing is tempered by the knowledge that the Garden of Eden is perishable—captured in the paradoxical possibilities of the Bourne's last name, which is pronounced "born" or "burn"—Catherine's return and David's warmly caring response celebrate the power of sympathy and creativity as supreme human values. In Hemingway's existential reenactment of Genesis, rather than cursed, expulsion from the Garden of Eden produces the knowledge that salvation lies in cultivation of the garden's sensual delights and possibilities for renewal.

Yet, while David's fragmented selves, like Rabo's, are reconstituted and harmonized by the unifying power of art, the artwork itself—like those Picasso cubist works that Hemingway and Vonnegut admired—provides final instruction in the fusion of modernism and postmodernism that challenges totality and closure. Neither writer rejected the representational art of their realist, modernist forebears, defending the ability of simple-seeming art to make profound statements. As Patricia Waugh puts it, while such fiction does not abandon the real world, its self-reflexive literary forms constitute "a new realism," allowing for "reader familiarity,"[175] helping us understand how concepts of gender and race in novels such as *Bluebeard* and *The Garden of Eden* are constructed rather than fixed or absolute. If Vonnegut's metafictional strategies are more consistently displayed—through parody, self-reflexivity, and interpenetrating narratives and genres—both novels challenge the simple notion that objective representation in language is possible, and both involve the reader in arriving at a final interpretation of the text.

On the one hand, when David Bourne says he hopes to write his elephant story with an accuracy of detail that makes it believable, remembering the actual things that created it, he reminds us of the clarity and sharpness of Hemingway's objective projections of reality, which made him famous. As with *Bluebeard, The Garden of Eden* looks back to major events in the authors' lives that pay tribute to those real-life women who helped them grow as men and artists. Yet, if David's reference to his "camera's eye" suggests Vonnegut's satirical portrait of Dan Gregory as a simple copying machine whose shallow creations were truthful about material things but hid or lied about the chaos within, Hemingway's repudiation of photographic realism in *The Garden of Eden* is as emphatic as Vonnegut's. Both novels replicate the intense psychological canvases of Rabo's *Now It's Women's Turn* and Thomas Hudson's *End of the World* where past and future time fuse to form a pastiche of simultaneous activity.[176]

Coupled with allusions to painters and paintings throughout the authors' later work, these massive, all-inclusive canvases provide the perfect analogue to the kind of writing to which both Hemingway and Vonnegut were ultimately drawn— work not petrified like Gregory's, but complex, open, and protean. Echoing Hemingway's determination to write each book as if it were his last, leaving nothing out, Rabo declares, "Life, by definition, is never still. Where is it going? From birth to death, with no stops on the way." In art that has "greatness," Rabo concludes, "birth and death are always there."[177] Hemingway's interpenetrating texts—as organic, refractive, and revealingly autobiographical as the interpenetrating frames of Rabo's meta-art—produce constant interchange and circulation of meaning, ventures in self-creativity whose blurred boundaries, real and imaginary, flesh and spirit, masculine and feminine, attest to the humanizing possibilities of invention. Such meaning defies closure, inviting the reader to join in a mutual celebration of the transformative possibilities of language, as creators rather than interpreters. The reader reassembles the text—painting or novel—as Picasso reassembled Gregory's militant advertisements. "Make up your own stories," Rabo says, "as you look at the whatchamacallit."[178]

Vonnegut's appreciation of Hemingway's "brushwork," his painterly eye, suggests that however much he objected to Hemingway's machismo—comically evinced in Rabo's remark that his father, Hemingway, and Dan Gregory all believed stored up sperm[179] made men braver and more creative—he recognized that even Hemingway's early work was as defiant of artistic convention, as stylistically innovative as his own. I suggest, however, that what Vonnegut missed is that, offsetting his view of Hemingway's decline, Hemingway's efforts to purge potentially overwhelming traumas of childhood and war, and to atone for sins against himself and others in these late works, perfectly defines the mutually confessional and redemptive nature of Vonnegut and Hemingway's work as a whole. Cross-references to the heroic defiance of the "forbidden" by Lot's wife in *The Garden of Eden* and *Slaughterhouse-Five* suggest that Bourne/Hemingway's exploration of what Ann Putnam calls "the dark moon of the self"—going where they have "no right to go"[180]—was as cleansing and potentially renewing for Hemingway as for Vonnegut. In both "moonlit" stories, the act of turning back like Lot's wife, or like Orpheus, to see what must not be seen, provides the final reclamation of the feminine that fuels David Bourne's and Rabo Karabekian's transformative art in *Bluebeard* and *The Garden of Eden* and prepares for Hemingway's and Vonnegut's farewell stories of personal and artistic salvation in *Timequake* and

*Under Kilimanjaro*. It is precisely the creative and spiritual achievement represented by Hemingway's Santiago, Thomas Hudson, and David Bourne and Vonnegut's Leon Trout, Eugene Debs Hartke, and Rabo Karabekian that gave their
authors, as Vonnegut wrote in *Bluebeard*, every reason to feel "at home . . . a place
I never thought I'd be,"[181] the right to rest from their long psychic journeys and
to feel, as Rabo explains, "twangingly proud and satisfied."[182]

# Nine

# A Literary Farewell

*Timequake* and *Under Kilimanjaro*

∎

In every work of genius we recognize our own rejected
thoughts—they come back to us with a certain alienated majesty.
Ralph Waldo Emerson, "Self-Reliance"

What a book would be the real story of Hemingway, not those
he writes but the confessions of the real Ernest Hemingway.
Gertrude Stein, *The Autobiography of Alice B. Toklas*

That Ernest Hemingway and Kurt Vonnegut should tell their own stories in their
respective literary farewells—*Under Kilimanjaro* and *Timequake*—underscores my
argument that their work is always foremost about themselves. While in the
rebellious spirit of *The Garden of Eden* and *Bluebeard* both texts blur the boundaries of fact and fiction, it is personal memoir that comes to the fore, retrospective assessments of personal and artistic achievement that clarify and punctuate
their work as autobiographical psychodrama.[1] Hemingway's central role in Vonnegut's final defining vision of himself in *Timequake* completes my view that
Hemingway was as important a force in Vonnegut's literary imagination as Dresden or the science-fiction writer Kilgore Trout or the gun-loving nut of a father,
whom Vonnegut described in *Timequake* as looking like Kilgore Trout.

For a while in *Timequake*, Trout, Kurt Senior, and Hemingway merge as
one symbolic father figure, the voice of pessimism Vonnegut battled in himself
throughout his career. Vonnegut's dangerous fathers appear as fatalistic as ever,
progenitors of what Trout calls "timequakes"—a psychic phenomenon that causes
people to relive past experiences on "auto-pilot," will-less and destined to make
the same mistakes over again. Lost fortunes and unrelieved suffering convince
people that free will is more a curse than a blessing. Notable real-life timequakers
such as Vonnegut's mother and father, Hemingway (linked with Vonnegut's
mother in the same sentence), and Hemingway's father turn suicidal, wondering
if such a robotic existence is worthwhile at all. "What was the point?" Trout asks.[2]

Though free will eventually kicks in again, once having lost control of their lives, survivors find themselves unable to adjust to thinking for themselves. Infused with "Post-Timequake Apathy," or "PTA," they choose instead to do nothing, letting the inertia of the moment carry them.

In such a state of mind, rather than reinventing himself à la Harold Ryan, the Hemingway of *Timequake* remains death bound and fatalistic. But in a character transformation more startling than the one in *Galápagos*, Vonnegut's long-suffering, most volatile literary figure, Kilgore Trout, finds himself the sole person not only to understand the destructive nature of "timequake" thinking but to oppose it in dramatic fashion. Armed with a bazooka and seemingly prepared to save the day in the "John Wayne" fashion Vonnegut so often decried, Trout instead becomes an anti-PTA advocate by harnessing the power of language, explaining to those afflicted from the return to free will, "You were sick, but now you're well, and there's work to do."[3] Once order is restored, Trout is venerated by Vonnegut and other literary critics and taken to the "writer's retreat at Xanadu," where he is given the Ernest Hemingway suite, in which he lives out his final days honoring his creator by becoming a healer, a shaman battling the effects of PTA.

No matter how successful Kilgore Trout's metamorphosis, his affirmation is neither easy nor simple. Vonnegut was not so naive as to think that free will, his philosophic focus in *Timequake* and throughout his work, is ever complete or that it solves all human problems any more than do those "big brains" in *Galápagos*. Worrying that the pessimism that drove his own wife and son from home makes him unfit for the task of shaman and that his proposals for reform go unnoticed in any case, Trout wonders whether once and for all he should not stop caring what is going on or what he is supposed to do next. He does not need a timequake, he says, to teach him that being alive "was a crock of shit": "I already knew that from my childhood and crucifixes and history books."[4] Notably it is on Hemingway's bed in the Hemingway suite at Xanadu that Trout continues writing stories that threaten to infect his readers with his own disillusionment, causing them to believe they can no more feel or reason than grandfather clocks. Further reminding us that, like Vonnegut's father and Ernest Hemingway, Trout serves as Vonnegut's scapegoat, bearing the author's burden of trauma and despair, Vonnegut himself worried that scientists are finding more and more evidence to make us believe that genes make us behave "this way or that," just as a rerun after a timequake would do.[5] It is Vonnegut who creates a virtual litany of people—such as his mother and father, his sister Allie, and Hemingway—who hated life and secretly wished for it to end. Vonnegut acknowledges that he, Trout, and Hemingway are all polar depressive, people convinced that only 17 percent of people on the planet have lives worth living.

But if Vonnegut and Trout are still susceptible to the potentially fatal pull of PTA, it is their hopeful voice inspired by their faith in the inviolability of human awareness that prevails in *Timequake*. Trout recognizes that it is not a timequake dragging people through endless knotholes, but something just as mean and powerful, the mind-crippling force of PTA, the moral sickness that steers the characters of *Galápagos*, who have stopped giving "a damn" into an apocalyptic nightmare. As with Vonnegut's seeming advocacy of the consolations of smaller brains in the *Galápagos*, *Timequake* presents us again with counterbalancing texts—the advantages of free will versus the attractions of determinism—that force us into a closer-than-usual examination of the devilish consolations of PTA. But reading closely, using *our* will and *our* "big brains," so to speak, we see that the petrified victims of PTA become as dehumanized and unfeeling at the twin computers in *Galápagos*, Gorbaki and Mandarax.

If Vonnegut opens this book with a list of the living dead, which once would have included himself and Trout, he also speaks of Jesus Christ and the Sermon on the Mount, offering his usual prayer for mercy and respect: "For Christ's sake, let's help more of our frightened people get through his thing, whatever it is."[6] Poisoned with PTA, Hemingway and Vonnegut's mother may have killed themselves, "but not Kilgore Trout." His "indestructible self-respect," Vonnegut declares, "is what I loved most about Kilgore Trout."[7] Trout's literary metamorphosis directs him to write stories that combine traditional humanism with the openness and philosophical pluralism of Pablo Picasso's paintings in the Museum of Modern Art, stories important for their humanness rather than their "pictureness." He expresses his contempt for "cruel inventions," "irresistible forces in nature," and fictions with absolute moral codes, closed scripts that privilege masculine authority and contain romantic plots such as that of *A Farewell To Arms*.

Judging from reviews of *Timequake* and from recent assessments of Vonnegut's artistic purposes in general, Vonnegut's critics, as if awakened from a timequake, no longer persist in reading Vonnegut as a writer of "pessimistic" or "defeatist" novels, but at long last appreciate the nature of his work, in which he battled personal despair and, as an avowed humanist and healer, warned against the perils of fatalism rather than affirming such a philosophy.[8] Not so, however, with Vonnegut's view of his artistic forefather Hemingway. Through Vonnegut's contrary recreations of self—Trout as humanist-shaman, Hemingway as ardent primitivist—Vonnegut offered his final view of the disastrous effects of PTA on Hemingway's life and art and of his own efforts to provide an iconography that turns war to peace, hatred to love, and bigotry to compassion, rather than egging men on to be even more destructive and cruel. Perhaps, Vonnegut wryly observes, the best thing to be when free will kicks in is a Mbuti, a pygmy in an African rain forest, where the painful complexity of human identity ceases to be, a black hole in which people are relieved of responsibility for their actions and no one needs to apologize.

Yet in *Under Kilimanjaro* it is precisely Hemingway's beneficent "timequake" experience in Africa, his reconsideration of personal sins against himself and others, animals included, that identifies the author as a fellow shaman, a healer of self, then, literally, as a healer of others[9]—whose transformation provides an equally dramatic example of people as essentially fictional beings in stories they themselves create. It is the author of *Under Kilimanjaro* who fulfills David Bourne's hopes of being "whole" again as he writes, writing from "an inner core that could not be divided."[10] As we know from Hemingway's myriad physical and emotional trials during the last fifteen years of life, my view of his positive Vonnegut-like metamorphosis must be weighed against the unfinished work—*A Moveable Feast* (1964), *The Garden of Eden* (1986), *Islands in the Stream* (1970), and *Under Kilimanjaro* (2005)—works Michael Reynolds argues were meant to be his greatest legacy but which many critics, including Reynolds and certainly Vonnegut, use to signify personal and artistic decline. The debate over whether the posthumous works add to or detract from Hemingway's stature will not be won or lost here. But it would be as critically negligent to devalue the evidence of creative courage and growth epitomized by all Hemingway's late work as to underestimate the destructive effects of machismo, particularly the heavy drinking that, added to the author's increasingly frequent depression, became such a burden to Mary. David Bourne's observation that "he was not a tragic character" may be off the mark.[11] The willingness of Hemingway and his most recent fictional heroes to access memories testifying to the tragic human costs of the hardened soldierly mask grants them tragic stature. With appropriate associations of Oedipus in mind, even the author's death was a final positive action in his brother Leicester's view, an act ethically and spiritually consistent with the life Ernest lived.[12]

Just as Trout must battle pessimism, Hemingway's continued refrain in *Under Kilimanjaro*—"no hay remedio"—suggests the "bad ass" depression he fought nearly all his life. But rather than encouraging a militant code of ethics such as Harold Ryan derives from the circumscribed and deterministic world of the *corrida*, Hemingway created in *Under Kilimanjaro* his most human and optimistic self, a true-to-life avatar of moral and creative evolution prepared for by Jordan, Cantwell, Santiago, Hudson, and Bourne. As opposed to the aggression and emotional stoicism of Hemingway's earlier heroes, Hemingway does not kill anyone, or achieve "honorable" death, but exactly in the form of these later protagonists, opens himself to the female within, to the more creative and gentle side of his nature, adopting kindness and restraint as moral priorities rather than a militant code of conduct that esteems physical toughness and stoical reserve. More important perhaps, he experiences guilt at infecting anyone with "no hay remedio," as though a "defeatist" or a "collaborationist."[13]

As with Vonnegut/Trout's reformation in *Timequake*, Hemingway recognizes that these contending moral forces are never absolute, but imaginative constructions with the power to either encourage or distort our humanity. His final descent into moral darkness in *Under Kilimanjaro* represents his and Vonnegut's common

understanding of the spiritual life of human beings as inherently "schizophrenic"—
that is, capable of using our creative genius for harm or for good. "I believe in
original sin," Vonnegut says, and "I also believe in original virtue. Look around."[14]
As Vonnegut fills his novel with dichotomized people and conditions, "the best
and the worst of Civilization,"[15] so Hemingway explores the potential for cruel
or humane action within himself, "options" Vonnegut and Trout show are responsible for the atomic bomb, but whose creator, Andrei Sakharov evolves from
an atom bomb advocate to one of the world's most ardent dissidents. Evoking the
paradoxical creative potential in Bourne's last name, Vonnegut cites the example
of Prometheus, who brings fire to human beings so they can be warm and cook,
but who instead use fire to incinerate other humans in Hiroshima and Nagasaki.

We know the tensions between the macho persona and the more gentle and
vulnerable author have always existed in Hemingway's protagonists, but in *Under
Kilimanjaro* this career-long struggle of contending forces comes to the fore as
the primary text. Now it is not Renata, or Jan, or Catherine, but Mary Hemingway who inspires the author's self-conscious allegory of divided selves at war. She
is a gentler, more loving self representing the repressed feminine, who opposes
the self bent on aggression and cruelty. What matters here are not the marauding leopards and lions or menacing elephants the author pursues, but the Jame-
sian beasts of ego and self-love hidden in the tangled thickets of his own mind.
"When I had first been in Africa," he says, "we were always in a hurry to move
from one place to another to hunt beasts for trophies."[16] Now he says, "The time
of shooting beasts for trophies was past with me."[17] He has other work to do, he
explains, which justifies his presence there—to learn, for instance, the individual
animals, and the "snake holes and the snakes that lived in them."[18] In the novel's
opening, Hemingway remarks to those who supposedly know all about his "inner
life" about the "battle" he has fought there and how he has written with an
"absolute assurance" he himself had never felt.[19] "Nobody knows about the
night," his hunting companion Keiti tells him. "It belongs to the animals."[20]
Hemingway responds, "What Keiti said was true; no one knew the night. But
*I* was going to learn."[21] When Mary asks him early on what it is they are to do,
he answers that they are to explore dangerous places in the forest that border the
swamp. Appropriate to his own venture in self-creation, Hemingway makes this
Dantesque descent without his former moral guide and tutor from *The Green
Hills of Africa*, Pop or Philip Percival, who tells him that now he is strictly on his
own. And so the author continues his journey into what F. Scott Fitzgerald called
the "dark night of the soul," an inner safari braver than any he has dared, into "the
darkness . . . where the blood was still fresh . . . until we reached the other end."[22]

Referring to the cleavage in spirit and outlook that divides active hunters
and warriors such as Keiti and the other Wakamba "bad boys," as he calls them,
from those who were nonfighters, those too delicate and gentle and loving to be

trackers or warriors, Hemingway introduces us to contrasts that represent his divided loyalties—white and black, American puritanism and the fecund power of Africa, blood religion versus Christianity, primitive instinct versus social obligation—but no two forces carry more symbolic weight than Hemingway's wife, Miss Mary, "blessed," "Queen of Heaven,"[23] and her spiritual counterpart, Debba, Papa's African mistress, who inspires his tribal loyalties, the dark forces of the blood, the night world of the unconscious.

On the one hand, Debba and Miss Mary represent the dark and the light of Hemingway's complex psychic life that climaxes the author's quest for unity and integration of self—a balance of African and Western values, body and soul, yin and yang that enriches artistic possibilities and creates tribal community feeling analogous to Vonnegut's extended families. If Mary represents the power of love and conscience, Debba represents the mysteries of the senses, the body, the primitive. While Mary is associated with the Christian church, Debba is related to the earth and nature—to the natural world to which Hemingway has always wished to belong. By marrying Debba, he may achieve a symbolic union with Africa, the African world, and its people. Though Debba reminds us more of erotic Catherine Bourne, and Miss Mary of the more domestic Marita in *The Garden of Eden*, both are positive female creations whose emotional vitality suggests Hemingway's successful rejection of Oak Park puritanism, and his exorcism of the cold and withdrawn mother. Wondering how to spend his night, Papa decides it is his pleasure, even his duty to be with both women, Queen of Heaven and Queen of the Ngomas. Free of "timequake" Oak Park moral compunctions, Hemingway makes his own rules, declaring that now he will decide what was a sin and what was not.

In Carl Eby's terms, the androgynous appearance of Debba and Mary provides further evidence of Hemingway's attraction to "transvestic transformation,"[24] Debba as a masculine, sturdy looking woman with pierced ears and tribal marks, and Mary, "his smaller brother," third party to a possible ménage à trois. But Debba is literally the person Catherine has in mind when she tells David his narrative will be so much better when he has a dark girl too, a profoundly fertile, Dionysian woman who inspires taboo sexual experience important to the earthy aspect of his work. Though tribal law forbids sexual contact with Debba, Hemingway defies the elders to make love to her, putting us in mind of the "Elders of Tralfamadore" in *Hocus Pocus*, who preach obedience and aggression. The comic spirit in which Hemingway openly portrays his efforts at fusion with this latest mother-sister-daughter love triangle indicates he is more at ease than ever with transgressive sexual desires.

As attracted to his African fiancée as he is, and as important as both women are to what Burwell calls the "cross-fertilization" of Hemingway's creative imagination,[25] Hemingway's narrative is more about Mary than either Debba or himself, further evidence that, as Doctorow and Spilka argue about *The Garden of Eden*, what seems most instructive is the degree to which Hemingway has learned about what a woman is and suffers and about the "devilish and adoring muses within himself."[26] Through much of the novel, Hemingway's light and dark muses complement one another as civilized inclinations to peace and mercy, love and art, counterbalanced by enriching primitive rituals in which the author plays shaman to Debba's tribe, doctoring people and allowing his "unabashed" "child's heart," as he calls it,[27] to come to the fore.

But the author discovers that the Lawrencian blood religion he forms with Debba, whose tribal laws and rituals require shooting and killing, comes at a price to Mary, calling into question the degree of success he has achieved in understanding and balancing the light and dark in his nature. "In our religion," Hemingway says, "there was not going to be any Game Department," only "slavery by those we had taken prisoner personally" and cannibalism for those who wished for it.[28] Understandably Hemingway reports that Mary hated what she knew of the religion and was ostracized by his group. While Mary is no missionary in the ordinary Christian sense, he explains that she has nevertheless been worshipped by some and has had a great talent for affection and forgiveness. She has too kind a heart to kill animals, her husband says, and so has to be angry to do it. There is something good in her, he says, that works subconsciously and makes her pull off target. She loves to read and watch birds. While one of Mary's main concerns is finding a proper Christmas tree, Debba's greatest thrill is sex with Papa while fingering his pistol holster. When Mary does hunt, she does it to earn her husband's love and respect—despite *his* proclamation that she loves it but wishes to do it without inflicting suffering.

Under Debba's influence, Hemingway becomes openly contemptuous of Mary and the civilized virtues she represents. When Mary encourages the artist in him, imploring him to write something that will make her proud, he responds sarcastically that he will also remember to brush his teeth and put the hyena out. But it is Debba's association with tribal violence, inspiring contrary tendencies to aggression and cruelty that mainly constitutes what the author calls "Miss Mary's sorrow." "I did not know what to do about Miss Mary's sorrow," he confesses, "and I began to know how great a sorrow it really was."[29] He begins to recognize that he is the source of Mary's emotional distress, that she lived all her life never wishing to kill anything until she met him. He confesses he has put as much or more love into his relationships with his guns as into that with his wife or friends. "I had the . . . well-loved, once-burnt-up three times restored, worn-smooth old Winchester model 12-pump gun that was faster than a snake and was, from thirty-five years of us being together, about as close a friend and companion with secrets shared and triumphs and disasters not revealed as the other friend a man has all his life."[30] Is Hemingway thinking of his previous three wives, which the beloved gun has outlasted? That Mary might expect similar sorrow, Hemingway prepares for his descent into real tribal darkness by bringing his guns into Mary's tent and placing them on her bed.

Mary knows both the good and the bad of her strangely complicated husband, and throughout the story, she serves as his severest critic and goad to conscience. When G.C., their game warden, says that he loves to see "the good side of his character," Mary replies, "He hides it carefully." She identifies the good side as "delicate and sensitive—his Proustian side," which comes out unexpectedly.[31] When she cautions him to be good, and he protests, she tells him that he and G.C. are sometimes wicked and fiendish, doing terrible things in the night, and wonders how the pagan killer in her husband reconciles with the valuable man and writer. When Hemingway says that he has to study the animals at night, she accuses him of doing devilish things to show off. When he waxes nostalgic for a past, less civilized world, Mary reminds him that the Wakamba used to eat people in what he and Pop refer to as the good old days. Really angry, she tells him that he and G.C. have the consciences of "bush-whacking delinquents,"[32] that they are just a pair of murderers "condemning things to death and carrying out the sentence."[33] "There's that strange suddenness," she tell him, "and the inhumanity and the cruel jokes. There's death in every joke."[34] Mary further criticizes her husband's need to command, to hold center stage, the "lion-hunting general who knows everything."[35] Reminiscent of Circe Berman and Catherine Bourne, when he repeats that he wants his lion to be confident and not to spook, she belittles the language that accompanies the famous code-prescribed heroic behavior. "Now I'm getting a little tired," she says, "of the phrase, I want them to be confident! If you can't vary your thinking you could try to vary your language."[36] Notably it is when Miss Mary, the voice of conscience and reason, sleeps that he most identifies with the predatory animals in the forest. Only when she is sleeping well does he go out to sit by the fire to stay awake and listen to the night, listening to the lion, or thinking of Debba.

For a long while the hunter-artist's divided loyalties remain unresolved. When Mary questions Papa's motives for hunting and killing, that is, for whom they keep this "hunting racket" going,[37] Hemingway confesses he feels as mixed up as the country. After describing his pride in killing a leopard, he bemoans the terrible odds against the animal and the cat's unbelievable vitality. He wishes he had never signed any contracts to kill and be photographed. Admiring a group of birds in flight, he notes that watching them was better than shooting them. But at the same time, he remembers fondly when he and G.C. would willingly pay a penalty for exceeding their limit. After a particularly self-serving show of macho prowess, showing off for Mary by calling the location of the shot he would try on a feeding ram, he explains how pleasant it was walking through the grass with the white flowers, and what a lovely evening it was.

Nothing silences Mary's humanizing counsel faster—a voice hushed by the noise of hyenas and jackals—than the convenient "timequake" rationalization that there is really no remedy for the world's suffering: "no hay remedio."[38] Sounding much like the boastful hunter of *Green Hills of Africa*, Papa rationalizes his love of hunting and killing in the name of shooting for meat, backing up Miss Mary, or for control of marauding animals. When Philip Percival chides him for killing elephants, calling him "an escaped ivory poacher from Rawlings, Wyoming," Papa absolves himself by arguing, as if to the father he still seeks to please, "Pop, you know I have to do away with them if they are bad behaving and if they ask me."[39] If he occasionally shot animals who just happened to have trophy horns worth keeping and made him happy, all the better. Punctuating his belief that life is naturally predatory and neither he nor anyone else is going to stop it, he tells the story of his dead horse, whose "lips were not there because the eagles had eaten them and at his eyes which were also gone."[40] "I felt badly about Miss Mary's sorrow," he says, "but I could not tell her what the eagles meant to me nor why I had killed these two, the last one by smacking his head against a tree."[41] Rather than challenge the barbarity, our vengeful narrator joins in by shooting both birds with his .22 Winchester, one in the head and another twice in the body. As if reliving the traumas of childhood and war, he describes the sound of the eagles descending on his horse as being like "the sound of an incoming shell,"[42] creating the equivalent of a war zone where death and suffering are unavoidable.

Though Mary informs her husband that nothing ever reaches the "no hay remedio" stage—"Don't ever think it even in your sleep"[43]—Hemingway's aggression and penchant for rationalization infect her innocence as well. While countless times we see that shooting animals leaves Mary filled only with sadness and guilt, perhaps to save her marriage, certainly from insecurity about his love, she tells her husband that his confidence in her shooting has never made her happier. To impress her husband with her toughness and to warn rivals away from his grudging heart, Mary boasts she has killed an "innocent buck deer" at a distance of three hundred yards and eaten him with no remorse and killed "a great and beautiful onyx" more beautiful than any man.[44] Though the reason for Mary's obsession with shooting the equally beautiful lion eludes her, she insists she has to get him. Is this the key to Papa's heart? Is learning to shoot without flinching the fulfillment of the passionate kill that substitutes for lovemaking between her husband and Debba?

How successful is Hemingway's night journey? How far has he progressed in self-knowledge? What, if anything, will he do to remedy a condition he has characterized as hopeless? Notably it is Mary's departure for Nairobi to buy Christmas presents that frees Hemingway from all civilized restraints, signals a shift in allegiance from Mary to Debba, and allows him to complete his transformation to Wakamba hunter and warrior—a time, he says, when he is happier than ever before. Now there are no people, scouts, or game rangers who have sold their Wakamba heritage and no worship of Miss Mary, of whom he says all except converts and believers have been tired for a long time. Symbolic of his new identity, Debba takes hold of his beloved holster and declares herself his true African wife. Honeymooning as we might expect, Papa comments that he hopes to kill a beast sufficiently large, fat, and succulent to do them justice. Lining up a Tommy ram by putting Debba's finger on the trigger next to his, he says, "I felt the pressure of her finger and her hand against mine . . . and I could feel her trying not to breathe. Then I said, 'Priga' and her finger tightened as mine tightened on the trigger . . . and the ram, whose tail had been switching as he fed, was dead . . . and Charo was running out . . . to cut his throat."[45] The sexually transported Debba holds tight to Papa's carved holster in as emotional a moment as these death lovers will have.

Explaining that his newly shaved head makes him look like a member of some ancient lost tribe and priding himself on having become dark enough now to pass as half-caste, Hemingway joins with his Wakamba spiritual brothers in a veritable orgy of hunting, killing, and celebration of warriorlike prowess. His macho inclinations—characterized by such remarks as "a man should be able to kill a leopard before breakfast"[46]—multiply to the point of parody, stressing that a real man should never admit to grief, nervousness, or pain. But it is the following concession to atavistic instinct that marks the climax to Hemingway's allegorical descent. After describing his delight and manly pride in killing a leopard, he bites on a piece of splintered shoulder bone until it cuts the inside of his cheek and the blood of the leopard mixes with his own. "There is no explanation of that," he says, "I did it without thinking. But it linked us closer to the leopard. . . . The new blood tasted like my own."[47]

While the night animal in Hemingway momentarily prevails, we see intermittently and in the novel's conclusion that Mary's Circe-like doggedness has done its work: "We were hunters," Hemingway says, "but this morning we were working for . . . our lord, the Baby Jesus . . . we were working for Miss Mary."[48] In a moment of seemingly genuine remorse for the harm he has done to animals and people alike, Hemingway says he wishes he had never become involved with Debba or her shamba. Along with contrition for bad deeds and notable occasions of pity and kindness, he welcomes opportunities to think about his children and to read and nurture the neglected side of his nature, what he once derisively referred to in *Death in the Afternoon* as animalarian. He determines to spend more time studying birds that nested and sang around the camp rather than shooting them as birds of prey or targets for trophies. Mary had been much better, he says. "She was always seeing birds that I did not notice. . . . I felt how stupid I had been and how much time I had wasted."[49]

Hemingway here seems to have made notable strides over the Hemingway of *The Green Hills of Africa*, who appears far less conscious of a self in conflict, repentant over the slaying of beautiful animals, or sensitive to his more humane potential as artist, husband, father, friend, and caretaker of animals. He knows there are secret places in him that he describes as far from gentle, confessing to terrible nightmares and having to drink to be brave in the night. He acknowledges that his black African driver, Mthuba, is kinder and more caring than he could ever be. When told by G.C. that "only shits got in trouble," he says he knows that he could qualify for that class at times.[50] When Mary asks whether D. H. Lawrence liked to hunt, Hemingway answers, "No. But that's nothing against him, thank God."[51] What? A kind word for another writer, one thought effeminate by some?[52]

Echoing David Bourne's surprising confession in the *Garden of Eden* manuscript, Hemingway confesses that the tough-guy mask is a defense against vulnerability—a cover for things feared, the unconscious source of "these nightmares and mid-night sweats." "I realize now," he says, that "loneliness is best taken away by jokes, derision and contempt for the worst possible outcome of anything."[53] When Mary questions his longings for a more primitive African past, he admits that the old days are gone, but maybe that is not so bad.[54] In a particularly redemptive moment, he takes his finger off the trigger at the moment of a kill, explaining that he might have crouched and crawled in animal fashion but there were too many flowers, and he wears glasses and is too old to crawl anyway.

When Mary returns from Nairobi at the novel's close, Hemingway protests returning to the civilized white world Mary represents, but with the power of anti-PTA determination, her influence is immediately felt. When he asks her to drink from a bottle as the Africans drink—telling her "it's just tribal . . . phases of the moon"[55]—she responds, "You get too tribal for your own good," adding, "I'm tired of it."[56] When she chides him for going out nights by himself, he tells her sarcastically that he will try to make their camp just like Nairobi for her and will be on such good behavior that he might write about it for some religious publication. While they are out under Mary's guidance looking for a Christmas tree, Hemingway assures Debba that they will go and shoot again, but at that very instant Hemingway appears to recognize that his long journey into night has brought him to a crucial impasse. "Today we were in suspense," he declares, "suspended between the old Africa that we had dreamed and invented and the return of Miss Mary."[57] It seems clear that this cleavage of spirit between the darkness and the light in himself, between Miss Mary and Debba remains unresolved—no hay remedio. He must continue exploring the night, he tells Mary, "Because the time is getting short, and he has to."[58] With the knowledge of humanity's ageless sorrow in mind—what was true at first light[59]—he evokes the fall from the Garden of Eden: "a dark night like tonight when the great python would come out of the swamp to the edge of the flats to lie coiled and waiting."[60] Yet if Debba, his night mind, remains with him, he appears more sensitive to and appreciative of Mary, the voice of conscience, than ever before, cognizant of Philip Percival's words at the start of the story to try to be as good as he can and to take care of Mary. It is as if that final night journey has provided a deeper understanding that allows him to emerge more integrated and content.

Suggestive of this new balance, when he tells Mary that he is seeking new knowledge, she tells him his possibilities are wide open. Just as cruel and unfeeling characters in a Trout story become hopeful, caring, and merciful when nurtured by such civilizing influences as books, paintings, and music. Hemingway welcomes the return of civilized graces he associates with the white or European race: *Time* magazine, the British airmail papers, and "the bright . . . light and the fire and a tall drink."[61] For the first time since Mary has gone, he takes a hot bath, thinking to "wash everything away" and "soak it out" with Lifebuoy soap.[62] The predominant images at story's end are of husband and wife at tea over the bird-identification book or just watching animals rather than shooting them. When Mary expresses interest in a rhino and two lionesses, Hemingway says, "Maybe we can just watch them,"[63] and even when they encounter a lion that has been raiding the Masai, Hemingway suggests, but "that was conjecture and no evidence to kill him on."[64] This night, as he and Mary go to bed early, Hemingway notices that they are the same size and that their dimensions are perfect as they make love to each other. A lion roars in the morning, but holding one another hard and gently, and with those contrary forces in balance—man-woman, night-day, animal-human, light-dark—the lion feels far away.

Mirroring Vonnegut's presence in *Timequake*, Hemingway's emergence as himself in *Under Kilimanjaro* is an act of free will, a "man made epiphany"[65] that celebrates the humanizing possibilities of creation by effectively blurring the line between author and text. However problematic one may judge Hemingway's efforts at moral amelioration in *Under Kilimanjaro*, perhaps the most important thing to notice is Hemingway's several Vonnegut-like reminders that all writing is invention, all writers liars, hence that the narrating Hemingway of *Under Kilimanjaro* is but a self-conscious reflection of Hemingway the author sitting in judgment of himself, an author who knows full well the human failings, evasions, contradictions, and half-truths of his fictional counterpart. So what we ultimately have is not as much an author trapped by machismo, but one who, like Vonnegut, climaxes his venture in self-creativity by becoming a more caring man and writer, the most human and complete of all his creations. To borrow a page from Trout's Dr. Schadenfreude, Vonnegut and Hemingway have seemingly laid all ghosts to rest, said their good-byes to the demonized fathers and mothers, and can rest in peace. Like the builder Ted Adler in *Timequake*, both authors can conclude that it was all worthwhile, asking with delight about their powers of invention and reinvention, "How the hell did I do that?"[66]

# Notes

## Introduction

1. Vonnegut, *Mother Night*, 117.

2. McConnell, "Stalking Papa's Ghost," 163.

3. See my essay "Vonnegut's Goodbye." While it contains my initial thinking about Vonnegut and Hemingway, I had not fully appreciated the feminine creative principle that inspires and humanizes the late works of both writers.

4. Vonnegut, letter to author, May 22, 2005.

5. Vonnegut, *Fates Worse than Death*, 62.

6. Ibid., 66.

7. Vonnegut, *Timequake*, 109. Vonnegut obviously subscribed to Carl Jung's view of aggression as a reflection of the psyche's darker self, "the existence of a lower level of personality . . . where one behaves more or less like a primitive . . . singularly incapable of moral judgment" (*Aspects of the Feminine*, 58).

8. Vonnegut, *Fates Worse than Death*, 7.

9. Ibid., 9.

10. Vonnegut, letter to author, May 22, 2005. In my interview with Hemingway's first wife, Hadley, her only complaint against her former husband was that he underestimated her stamina, leaving her behind when he would go on long hikes. Like Ernest Hemingway's androgynous mother, Hadley was a talented pianist and took pride in her female independence.

11. Vonnegut, *Fates Worse than Death*, 9.

12. Vonnegut, *Happy Birthday, Wanda June*, viii.

13. Ibid., 2.

14. Vonnegut, letter to author, May 22, 2005.

15. Vonnegut, *Happy Birthday, Wanda June*, 182.

16. Ibid., 2.

17. Ibid., 21.

18. Ibid., 7.

19. Vonnegut, *Timequake*, 81.

20. Ibid., 80–81.

21. Ibid., 79.

22. Ibid., xiii.

23. Ibid., 23.

24. Ibid., 163.

25. See Langer's *The Holocaust and the Literary Imagination*, an excellent study of the historical forces behind the differences in the tone and mood that separate modernism from postmodernism. I take my understanding of the differences between modernism and

postmodernism primarily from Patricia Waugh, Brian McHale, Ihab Hassan, and Jerome Klinkowitz: postmodernism is a literary ideology that should be defined both historically and theoretically. As they see it, the term infers both continuity and discontinuity, sameness and difference, unity and rupture, and filiation and revolt.

26. Vonnegut, *Fates Worse than Death*, 60. In Bloom's view Vonnegut's hyperbole may be explained as the younger writer's effort to appear original by generalizing away the uniqueness of the literary parent. The larger the newcomer's resentments, Bloom says, the greater may be his or her "creative corrections" (*The Anxiety of Influence*, 30).

27. Vonnegut, *Fates Worse than Death*, 62.

28. Vonnegut, *Timequake*, 70.

29. Vonnegut, *Fates Worse than Death*, 144.

30. Ibid., 146.

31. Vonnegut, *Happy Birthday, Wanda June*, 174. In *Happy Birthday, Wanda June*, Penelope inquires into the sexual roots of Harold Ryan's obsession with heroism and death (139). She tells Harold one reason men like war is that it allows them to manifest their fear and disrespect for women. Mildred, Ryan's deceased wife, once remarked that sex with her husband was all over "ten seconds after he'd said the word 'buffalo.' Then he'd zip up his pants and go outside, and tell true war stories to little kids" (139). The perversion of life-directed processes, of love and creativity, by the instinct to death and aggression is a major motif in the works of both writers.

32. Vonnegut, *Fates Worse than Death*, 61.

33. James Jones, author of *From Here to Eternity*, told Vonnegut that he did not consider Hemingway a fellow soldier because Hemingway had never submitted to training and discipline either in World War II or in the Spanish civil war (Vonnegut, *Fates Worse than Death*, 61). Vonnegut quipped in *Palm Sunday* that Irwin Shaw's *The Young Lions* was such a good book that it made Hemingway mad: "He thought he had copyrighted war" (138). C. T. Lanham reported that Hemingway was "battle-wise" and "smart as hell on the battlefield," while the colonel's army psychiatrist Meyer Maskin characterized the author's "playing at soldier" as a "silly macho thing," which meant other soldiers had to guard him at risk to themselves (Brian, *The True Gen*, 171, 179).

34. Vonnegut, *Timequake*, 130.

35. Ibid., xi.

36. Ibid., xiii.

37. Ibid.

38. Ibid., 51.

39. Ibid., xii. Vonnegut of course "made it" to the age of eighty-four, when on April 11, 2007, he died from an accidental fall at home in New York City.

40. Vonnegut, *Fates Worse than Death*, 66.

41. Ibid., 67. Vonnegut's perception here convinces me he had not read Hemingway's posthumous novels and stories. These works suggest that Hemingway was anything but "through" after *The Old Man and the Sea*, that Hemingway meant them to be his major literary legacy, his most ambitious and personally revealing undertaking.

42. Vonnegut, *Fates Worse than Death*, 183.

43. Ibid., 187.

44. Ibid., 189. As I demonstrate in chapter 5, "From Jailbird to Canary Bird," Hemingway and Vonnegut shared populist sympathies, a respect for the world's have-nots. Vonnegut

referred to them in *Timequake* as "sacred cattle," people who are "somehow wonderful despite their economic uselessness" (141). That Vonnegut's social concerns, however, are more direct and extensive than Hemingway's is a major difference between them.

45. My essay "Images of the Shaman" explores Vonnegut's self-characterization as a kind of spiritual medicine man, whose function is to expose various forms of societal madness. The historical role of Vonnegut's artist-shaman is described by Mircea Eliade as someone proficient in speculative thought—a singer, poet, musician, diviner, priest, and doctor—a preserver of oral traditions in literature and of ancient legends (*Shamanism*, 30).

46. Vonnegut, *Fates Worse than Death*, 182.

47. Vonnegut, letter to author, April 2, 1990.

48. In *Hemingway and Spain* Stanton reiterated my thesis in *Hemingway's Spanish Tragedy* (1973) that Hemingway's identification with the Hispanic code of machismo led eventually to disillusion and despair, to a self who prefers oblivion to a life without physical strength and sexual potency (207). Stanton concluded that Hemingway's suicide was "a personal as well as a Spanish tragedy," that following the moral code of the matador leads to a "blind alley" for both the author and his characters.

49. Vonnegut, *Deadeye Dick*, 208.

50. Vonnegut, *Fates Worse than Death*, 67. Explaining that Hemingway was always shaping and reshaping reality to suit himself—that is, to "soothe himself"—Morley Callaghan referred to the author's "wild imagination working away" during his last days, "seeking the right end to his story, his life" (qtd. in Brian, *The True Gen*, 299).

51. Vonnegut, *Fates Worse than Death*, 39.

52. I allude to Joseph Conrad's story "The Secret Sharer," which explores the psychic duality of Conrad's protagonist, the split between a conscious "ideal" self and a primitive, savage unconscious self.

53. It is best to believe that both writers wanted the reader to view their fictional creations in light of their own values and attitudes. Each, as Jackson Benson said of Hemingway, enlarged, subtracted, combined, transposed, and added new cloth to his underlayment of memory (*The Short Stories of Ernest Hemingway*, 289).

54. Rovit, "On Psychic Retrenchment in Hemingway," 185.

55. McConnell, "Stalking Papa's Ghost,"170.

56. Ibid.

57. See Putnam, "On Defiling Eden," which treats the influences of the feminine in "Big Two-Hearted River" and argues that the story not only "holds the accumulation of all the sorrows from the stories that came before it" (112) but also anticipates Hemingway's paradoxical attitudes toward the feminine and toward nature that emerge in works to come: nature as "beckoning and maternal," a "source of both salvation and rapture," and also "an eroticized other who must be mastered" (114–15).

58. Reynolds, *The Young Hemingway*, 102.

59. Vonnegut, letter to author, November 30, 1982.

60. Putnam, "On Defiling Eden," 129.

61. Vonnegut, *Slaughterhouse-Five*, 21, 22.

62. Vonnegut, *Palm Sunday*, 243.

63. Hemingway, *Death in the Afternoon*, 192.

64. Beegel's observation that omissions from the surface story are like "the ghosts of sensation where an amputated limb has been" (*Hemingway's Craft of Omission*, 92) has major

relevance for our understanding of the potentially negative repercussions of the protagonists' buried or submerged self, "submerging the dread" (114), as Putnam calls it. The danger of such an inner, defensive maneuver is that the mask—passive for Vonnegut, aggressive for Hemingway—may become compulsive and hence more a threat than a safeguard to the sanity it is meant to preserve. Withdrawal from an outer world of people and things into one of phantom fulfillment may lead to a total inability to act and finally to a state of nonbeing and a desire for death. R. D. Laing likened such a fate to living in "a concentration camp" in which the imagined advantages of safety and freedom from the control of others is tragically illusory. By putting a "psychic tourniquet" on his ailing soul, Laing said, the individual's detached self develops a form of "existential gangrene" (*The Divided Self*, 82). Beegel sees at least five categories of omitted knowledge that affect the surface story (*Hemingway's Neglected Short Fiction*, 89).

65. I am employing the concept of "creative evolution" first as explained by Bredhal and Drake in *Hemingway's Green Hills of Africa as Evolutionary Narrative*. In this sense the term describes the process by which each new hero assimilates the lessons and creative energy of his predecessor. Citing the similar interdependence of Vonnegut's work, Kathryn Hume explains that "the artistic and personal problems [Vonnegut] takes up in one story are directly affected by those he did or did not solve in the previous story" ("Vonnegut's Self-Projections," 178). Developing an aesthetic of discovery and renewal, the hero learns increasingly to embrace the feminine rather than to view it as a landscape to be avoided, taken, or destroyed (Putnam, "On Defiling Eden," 113). Exactly parallel to the development of Vonnegut's hero is Hemingway hero's eventual acceptance of the duality of nature and by extension the duality within himself—what Allen Josephs calls the "creative and fertile overthrow of the authoritarian masculine" ("Hemingway's Spanish Sensibility," 98)—that defines his progress in relation to earlier protagonists. Second the author-protagonist's moral growth—the understanding of the feminine in himself, leading to a more hopeful and integrated disposition—expands the scope of the writer's vision and craft.

66. Jung, *Aspects of the Feminine*, 91.

67. The splitting of self into separate warring beings—the outer passive-aggressive persona the hero projects to the world to hide the hidden feminine—constitutes a defense against pain that McConnell called "a studied forgetfulness" ("Stalking Papa's Ghost," 169) and that Vonnegut in *Mother Night* called "that wider separation of my several selves than even I can bear to think about" (136). In Jung's view this painful division between a public persona and a private, submerged identity portends tragic consequences both personal and creative. Denying the feminine creative principle threatens a loss of moral identity and precludes greater creative possibilities for the artist.

68. Bloom, *The Anxiety of Influence*, 14. Bloom explains that the later writer may have believed himself to be more tough-minded, more realistic and less romantic than his predecessor (69).

69. Jung, *Aspects of the Feminine*, 85. Especially applicable to the late work of both authors, in which they open themselves to Eros, Bloom has suggested the uncanny effect is that the new writer's achievements make it seem as though he were writing the precursor's work himself, and vice versa (*The Anxiety of Influence*, 16).

70. Jung, *Aspects of the Feminine*, 165.

71. Ibid., 167.

72. Bair, *Beckett*, 212, 401.

73. Vonnegut, *Timequake*, xiv.

## Chapter 1. Family Secrets

1. Vonnegut, *Fates Worse than Death*, 54.

2. Vince, "War, Heroism, and Narrative," 66.

3. Hemingway's "On Writing" argues that his quest for "the real thing" was a matter of simulation rather than recalling and simply reproducing what he had seen or felt. Such a view obligates us to examine both Hemingway and Vonnegut's characters as complex, independent creations rather than as simple projections of the author. As intriguing metafiction, "On Writing" comments not only on other Adams stories but on the entire corpus of Hemingway's work. Its exuberant tone and fluid imagery project a far more hopeful and healthy character, one aware of the power of art to shape human destiny and less afraid of complexity. Like *Deadeye Dick*, "On Writing" transforms itself into a provocative story about ways of perceiving reality, about the impossibility of determining truth in absolute terms, about the way perception arises from the relative roles we play, and about the way the perceiver determines what is perceived. See my essay "Hemingway's 'On Writing.'"

4. Vonnegut, letter to author, February 12, 1990.

5. Hotchner, *Papa Hemingway*, 139.

6. Hemingway, "Fathers and Sons," *The Complete Short Stories*, 371. Hereafter cited as *CSS*.

7. Vonnegut, *Slapstick*, 15.

8. Shechner, *Joyce in Nighttown*, 238.

9. Kenneth Lynn has reminded us that Hemingway would have conceivably written a full-length novel account of his traumatic childhood as personal as that of *Deadeye Dick* if the subject had not been "too hot to handle" or if he had worried less about hurting his family (*Hemingway*, 26). In my discussion of childhood trauma and therapeutic telling in the Nick Adams stories and in *Deadeye Dick*, the latter plays a dual role. While Vonnegut's novel and Hemingway's stories constitute the most focused portrait of the protagonist's adolescent psychological wounds, *Deadeye Dick* demonstrates that it is only in these writers' later works— Vonnegut's post–*Breakfast of Champions* novels and Hemingway's posthumous novels and stories—that they achieved understanding and forgiveness of the hostile, ineffective father and the cold, withdrawn mother. As is true of Hemingway in the Adams stories, Vonnegut in his early novels appears to have been unwilling or unable to scrutinize his parents' loveless marriage and their inability to provide parental love and guidance. For instance a character in Vonnegut's first novel, *Player Piano*, wonders what a psychiatrist would say about the protagonist's unconscious swipes at an absent father and a mother who withholds affection, asking, "Was our father a bastard?" Paul Proteus answers, "How do I know who my father was? The editor of who's who knows about as much as I do" (85). Like Hemingway's protagonist throughout his work, Paul has night visions of a mother he secretly desires and fears, and an angry, punishing father. The fact that real understanding occurred only when both writers were in their fifties underscores my view that, like their war experience, the struggle to heal childhood trauma took a lifetime of cathartic unburdening of fear and guilt to achieve.

10. Reynolds, *The Young Hemingway*, 64.

11. Vonnegut, *Jailbird*, xi.

12. Hume, "Kurt Vonnegut and the Myths and Symbols of Meaning," 2.

13. Spilka, *Hemingway's Quarrel with Androgyny*, 122.

14. Vonnegut, *Timequake*, 50.

15. Vonnegut, *Deadeye Dick*, 1.

16. Ibid., 108.

17. Vonnegut, *Player Piano*, 166.

18. Vonnegut, *Deadeye Dick*, 144.

19. Vonnegut, *Jailbird*, xiii.

20. Vonnegut, *Fates Worse than Death*, 28.

21. Qtd. in Spilka, *Hemingway's Quarrel with Androgyny*, 57.

22. Wagner-Martin, introduction to *New Essays on* The Sun Also Rises, 5. Vonnegut's ambivalent feelings for his father, the "unfilled prince," fits Hemingway's feelings for Clarence to a tee. Both fathers had promising careers that were "gutted" (Vonnegut, *Fates Worse than Death*, 13) by mismanagement and economic circumstance, and, like their disappointed wives, they lapsed into depression and marital bitterness. Whereas Edith's disengagement is more tragic, Grace, "whose breast milk," Hemingway wrote, "was never Heaven" (*For Whom the Bell Tolls*, 129), disappeared into seclusion across the lake from the Hemingway home and possibly into the arms of a female lover.

23. Hemingway, "My Old Man," *CSS*, 160.

24. Spilka, *Hemingway's Quarrel with Androgyny*, 222.

25. Reynolds, *The Young Hemingway*, 199.

26. Vonnegut, *Palm Sunday*, 57.

27. Hemingway, *CSS*, 69.

28. Ibid. While Dr. Adams apologizes to Nick for the horrors he witnesses, the father appears professionally detached rather than sympathetic. His answers to Nick's questions about the woman's suffering and the terrible death of her husband are typically superficial and inadequate.

29. Vonnegut, *Deadeye Dick*, xiii. If Hemingway had consolidated the major trials of his life, they would bear striking resemblance to Vonnegut's: the suicide of a parent, the trauma of war, the possibility of violent death, the loss of a beloved younger sister, troubled marriages, severe depression, and the festering wounds of parental alienation. In a larger sense both were wounded culturally and spiritually by a twentieth-century America exploited and depleted by machines and material glut.

30. The troubles between Ernest and Gregory probably had more to do with Ernest's embarrassment over Gregory's transvestic tendencies than his mother's difficulty giving birth to him, though Ernest accused Gregory of causing Pauline's death for both reasons. As John Hemingway told us in *Strange Tribe* and as Gregory demonstrated in *Papa*, Gregory in turn debated the good and bad of his father all his life.

31. Vonnegut, *Deadeye Dick*, 61.

32. "Bathed in ink" signifies the paradox of deep suffering converted to art central to both writers. The antithetical meanings of "bathed"—death versus cathartic rebirth— illustrate Saussure's proposition that signs function not through their intrinsic value but through their relative position.

33. Rudy and Nick join the ranks of Huck Finn and Faulkner's Quentin Compson, other spiritual orphans with absent or deadly fathers who cripple their children's search for personal identity. While the theme of absent, impotent, or fragmented parental authority goes back at least as far as *The Odyssey*, the Nick Adams stories and *Deadeye Dick* belong with the most important father works in twentieth-century fiction. See Bleikasten, "Fathers in Faulkner."

34. Suffering from diabetes like Ernest and Clarence and not wanting to become a burden to his family, Leicester shot himself with a revolver after doctors told him both his legs

would have to be amputated (John Hemingway, *Strange Tribe*, 82). At relatively the same age as Hemingway was when he talked of suicide, Vonnegut committed himself to Bellevue for acute depression, "all but terminal," as Rackstraw explains in "Dancing with the Muse."

35. Vonnegut, letter to author, November 30, 1982.

36. Vonnegut, *Deadeye Dick*, 112.

37. Despite ample biographical evidence that the hero reflects the author's own strategy of numbness and retreat—presenting a desensitized exterior to the world—repressed experience serves Hemingway's powerfully effective iceberg aesthetic.

38. McConnell, "Stalking Papa's Ghost," 23.

39. Vonnegut, *Deadeye Dick*, 79.

40. Functioning dialectically, Hemingway's imagery of darkness and shadows assumes different meanings throughout his work. The hero's "shadow" or "darker" self may suggest fear of feminine weakness in himself or creative or destructive primitive passions. Jung associated such contradiction with the paradoxical archetypal mother, both spiritual and erotic, an object of worship and of dread (*Aspects of the Feminine*, 84).

41. Hemingway, *CSS*, 371–75.

42. Vonnegut, *Timequake*, 144.

43. Vonnegut, *Deadeye Dick*, 11.

44. Rudy's childhood home, the scene of endless trauma, is structured like "a human watchtower" (Vonnegut, *Deadeye Dick*, 81), suggesting that, like clockwork, insanity is as sure to come around to him as to his mother and father and their parents. Rudy remembers the Nazi flag hanging on the wall of his living room, and Otto's belief that Hitler's Germany would be the salvation of the world; Rudy also remembers Otto's favorite joke: "Cross a Pole with a Negro, you were certain to get an amusing laborer" (Vonnegut, *Deadeye Dick*, 29).

45. Ibid., 55.

46. Hemingway, qtd. in Lynn, *Hemingway*, 27.

47. Hemingway, "Soldier's Home," *CSS*, 116. Meyers suggests that Hemingway's view of the dominating, castrating mother may be attributed in part to the father's willing assumption of domestic chores—preparing the children's breakfast, buying groceries, cooking, doing the laundry, even serving Grace in bed. Obviously Clarence experienced his son's own feminine-masculine contradictions (Meyers, *Hemingway*, 8).

48. Qtd. in Spilka, *Hemingway's Quarrel with Androgyny*, 195. Lynn reminds us that Nick/Krebs's company at his mother's bedside has other, more positive connotations: that as in Hemingway's case, the mother is a reader of books like himself, which she must have made available to him (*Hemingway*, 183). Grace arranged the Hemingway household to assure that her children would receive maximum exposure to music painting, and literature, even if the books were mainly Victorian. Not coincidentally, perhaps, Howard Campbell's mother in *Mother Night* wants him to play the cello as Grace had Ernest do (Vonnegut, *Mother Night*, 32).

49. Hemingway, *CSS*, 73.

50. Busch, "Reading Hemingway without Guilt," 82.

51. Jung, *Aspects of the Feminine*, 103.

52. Vonnegut, *Deadeye Dick*, 71.

53. Ibid., 142.

54. Jung, *Aspects of the Feminine*, 91.

55. Reynolds, *Hemingway: The 1930s*, 136.

56. Hemingway, "Fathers and Sons," *CSS*, 375.

57. Bell, *"A Farewell to Arms,"* 123–24.

58. Josef Benson has reminded me that in my use of Jung's anima/animus paradigm for balanced psychic life, I am not arguing for an innate psychic structure, an essentialist or reductive view of masculine and feminine traits. On the contrary I suggest the authors moved toward an androgyny of soul/psyche that is salubrious to both men and women. Rather than an absolute condition, I use "femininity" metaphorically to represent the power of transformation and to indicate that part of the self that is more gentle, creative, and giving.

59. Flora, *Hemingway's Nick Adams,* 55.

60. Hemingway, *CSS,* 145. Vonnegut quipped that he could think of only one other book that despised matrimony as much as *A Farewell to Arms*—Thoreau's *Walden.* But this seems a more likely instance of Vonnegut's point that Frederic Henry sheds "tears of relief" at avoiding the domestic responsibilities of marriage—"getting a regular job and a house and life insurance and all that crap. . . . Whew what a close shave" (*Timequake,* 81).

61. Hemingway, *CSS,* 143.

62. Ibid., *CSS,* 213.

63. Jung, *Aspects of the Feminine,* 83.

64. Putnam, "On Defiling Eden," 124.

65. Hemingway, *CSS,* 376.

66. Meyers, *Hemingway,* 12.

67. Correspondence between Ernest and Clarence—letters of March 8, 1925, to August 8, 1927—suggests a more complex relationship than existed between Kurt and his father. Despite the cloying puritanism of both Grace and Clarence, encouraging Ernest to make his work less brutal and more uplifting, Clarence moralized less and rejoiced more in Ernest's early talent. Note the irony, though, in Clarence's example of Midwestern morality when he offered his son his "little wop automatic" while insisting that Ernest respect "all that is good and noble and brave in Manhood, fearing God and respecting women" (letter, June 4, 1920, Kennedy Library).

68. Edith and Grace had sizable inheritances from their fathers, and both men married into wealth and instant social status. The Great Depression ruined Kurt Senior, and poor land investments hurt Clarence. The parents spent less and less time together as time went on.

69. Justice, "Alias Grace," 222–23.

70. Vonnegut, *Fates Worse than Death,* 38.

71. Vonnegut, *Deadeye Dick,* 26–27.

72. Vonnegut, *Fates Worse than Death,* 119.

73. Cowley, "Nightmare and Ritual in Hemingway," 51.

74. Putnam, "On Defiling Eden," 114.

75. Ibid., 124.

76. Hemingway, *CSS,* 175.

77. Ibid., 164.

78. Qtd. in Griffin, *Along with Youth,* 15.

79. Hemingway, *A Moveable Feast,* 114.

80. Jung, *Aspects of the Feminine,* 83.

81. Vonnegut, *Fates Worse than Death,* 66.

82. While I argue that it is only when the hero develops the courage and will to tell the buried story openly that he will achieve what Putnam calls "a vision of the perfect self" ("On Defiling Eden," 115–16), I stress again that we must never underestimate the power of Hemingway's controlled rejection of the darker side of experience in his early work, the paradox

of a story such as "Big Two-Hearted River," whose tragic repression nevertheless, as Putnam has said, "dazzles" readers with richly multiple and conflicting meanings (ibid., 114).

### Chapter 2: Hemingway's *Sun*, Vonnegut's *Night*

1. Vonnegut, *Fates Worse than Death*, 62.

2. Ibid., 64. Vonnegut asserted that Hemingway's "anti-fascism, on paper, was of an unanalytical, rosy-cheeked-school-boy variety" (65). Vonnegut was of course right that the public figure of Hemingway is no longer "as imposing as General Motors or *The New York Times*," but his view of Hemingway as "not taught much anymore" because his subject matter—"bullfighting, nearly forgotten wars, and shooting big animals"—makes him "dated" (62), seems misinformed in light of the ongoing vitality of Hemingway studies.

3. Ibid., 146–47.

4. Ibid., 148.

5. Vonnegut, *Happy Birthday, Wanda June*, 174.

6. Vonnegut, *Fates Worse than Death*, 148. If Vonnegut's view of war is more grim and despairing than Hemingway's, I suggest this reflects Vonnegut's sense of horror over the World War II concentration camps and Hiroshima, which spoke to him of the world's fundamental insanity and self-destructive tendencies.

7. Ibid., 61.

8. Hemingway, *Selected Letters*, 293–40.

9. Hemingway, qtd. in Villard and Nagel, *Hemingway in Love and War*, 171–81. Scott Donaldson believes Hemingway wrote "A Very Short Story," about an unnamed soldier jilted by his nurse, to relieve himself of the emotional residue of being burned by Agnes. Comley and Scholes point to the age gap between the characters and in Hemingway's own relationship with Agnes and explain the story as Hemingway's rejection of the complex mother he both loathed and desired—"mother, nurse, and whore" (*Hemingway's Genders*, 34). In "In Another Country," "Now I Lay Me," and "A Way You'll Never Be," Jake Barnes's predecessor, a war-scarred Nick Adams, suffers sleepless nights like Jake, and Nick's fear of the dark mother in these stories anticipates Jake's impotence and further flight from women in *The Sun Also Rises*.

10. Vonnegut, *Mother Night*, vi, vii. Vonnegut's reference to "fried grasshoppers" invokes Hemingway's use of grasshoppers in "Big Two-Hearted River" and "Now I Lay Me" to portray nature's cruelty, especially in time of war.

11. Ibid., vii.

12. Qtd. in Allen and Smith, "An Interview with Kurt Vonnegut," 77.

13. Vonnegut, *Slaughterhouse-Five*, 21.

14. Vonnegut, *Fates Worse than Death*, 69.

15. Ibid.

16. Vonnegut, *Slaughterhouse-Five*, 21.

17. Nick's references to his mother are based on fact. The financing and construction of the spacious Hemingway house on North Kenilworth Avenue and Iowa Street in the fall of 1905 was, Lynn says, very much Grace's work (*Hemingway*, 18). Some years later, Clarence wrote to Grace, "Please don't burn any papers in my room or throw away anything that you don't like the looks of and I will do the same for you" (1917, Hemingway's personal letters, Kennedy Library).

18. Hemingway, "A Way You'll Never Be," 313.

19. Ibid., 312.

20. Ibid., 313.

21. Ibid.

22. Ibid., 310.

23. Ibid., 309, 314.

24. Vonnegut, *Slaughterhouse-Five*, 21.

25. Hemingway, "In Another Country," *CSS*, 208.

26. Tanner, *City of Words*, 157.

27. Vonnegut, *Mother Night*, 119.

28. Ibid., 53.

29. Ibid., 176.

30. Aldridge, *After the Lost Generation*, 123.

31. Warren, introduction to *A Farewell to Arms*, viii.

32. Baldwin, *Reading* The Sun Also Rises, 32, 99.

33. Ibid., 99.

34. Vonnegut, *Mother Night*, 52–53.

35. Hemingway, *Green Hills of Africa*, 27.

36. Ibid., 109.

37. Vonnegut, *Mother Night*, 169.

38. Ibid., 133.

39. Ibid., v.

40. Ibid., 120.

41. Ibid., 136.

42. Waldhorn, A *Reader's Guide to Ernest Hemingway*, 100–110.

43. Strychacz, *Hemingway's Theaters of Masculinity*, 185.

44. Hemingway, *The Sun Also Rises*, 136. Meyers supports my basic thesis that Jake's attraction to the bullfight represents the hero's ongoing oedipal struggle against the father for the possession of his mother. In Meyers's view the matador's triumphant domination of the bull at the moment of orgasmic death represents even a "virile defense against the threat of homosexuality" (*Hemingway*, 248).

45. Hemingway, *The Sun Also Rises*, 221.

46. Vonnegut, *Mother Night*, 113,

47. Ibid., 87.

48. Ibid., 181.

49. Jung, *Aspects of the Feminine*, 82, 83.

50. Ibid., 90–91.

51. Hemingway, *The Sun Also Rises*, 107.

52. Jung, *Aspects of the Feminine*, 166.

53. Davidson and Davidson, "Decoding the Hemingway Hero in *The Sun Also Rises*," 96.

54. Baldwin, *Reading* The Sun Also Rises, 105–7.

55. Hemingway, *The Sun Also Rises*, 148.

56. Baldwin, *Reading* The Sun Also Rises, 129.

57. Jung, *Aspects of the Feminine*, 166.

58. Ibid., 93.

59. Baldwin, *Reading* The Sun Also Rises, 137.

60. Vonnegut, *Mother Night*, 41.

61. Ibid., 40.

62. Strychacz, *Hemingway's Theaters of Masculinity*, 6.

63. Hemingway, letter to Pound, Burguete, Spain, July 19, 1924, in *Selected Letters*, 118, 119.

64. Qtd. in Strychacz, *Hemingway's Theaters of Masculinity*, 82.

65. Ibid., 127. Vonnegut's view of pure good pitted against pure evil as a dangerous form of "play-acting" (*Mother Night*, 186) suggests Hemingway's casting of Romero as Grail Knight and Barnes as the fated Fisher King. It is Resi Noth's belief in the pure young maidens and heroic knights of Campbell's romantic melodrama, "The Goblet"—which Campbell denounces as "moral pornography" (ibid., 148)—that leads to Resi's suicide.

66. Hemingway, *The Sun Also Rises*, 171.

67. Vonnegut, *Mother Night*, 131.

68. Ibid., 47.

69. Ibid., 150.

70. Ibid., 107.

71. Ibid., 66, 86.

72. Ibid., 43.

73. Waldhorn, *A Reader's Guide to Ernest Hemingway*, 111–12.

74. Rovit and Brenner, *Ernest Hemingway*, 141.

75. Svoboda, *Hemingway and* The Sun Also Rises, 32.

76. Spilka, *Hemingway's Quarrel with Androgyny*, 210. Spilka has explained that, as with Ernest and Marcelline, all their mother's children were raised to reflect their mother's androgynous makeup. Spilka concluded that Grace's remark to Marcelline, "Ernest is very much like me"—tender but strong, independent, and artistically gifted—was a "premise worth pondering" (ibid., 25).

77. Wagner-Martin, *New Essays on* The Sun Also Rises, 10. See Miller's "Brett Ashley" for the most penetrating and comprehensive discussion of Brett Ashley's richly complex nature.

78. Svoboda, *Hemingway and* The Sun Also Rises, 50.

79. As Cohn is to Jake, a reflection of Jake's own gender anxieties, Vonnegut argued Fitzgerald was to Hemingway: "I myself was asked one time why, in my opinion, Hemingway came to speak so contemptuously of F. Scott Fitzgerald. I made a guess that it was homosexual panic: that Fitzgerald was as beautiful and personable as Billy Budd, but Hemingway wanted to make clear that he himself was no pansy, that he had not fallen in love with him" (Vonnegut, letter to author, May 22, 2005).

80. Spilka, *Hemingway's Quarrel with Androgyny*, 204. As Spilka has pointed out, in a Freudian sense, Jake's physical wound suggests the female genitals. Like a woman, he cannot penetrate his beloved but can only rouse and be roused by her through her fervent kisses (ibid., 204). The important point is that Jake's "womanly identification" with Brett, as with Catherine Barkley in *A Farewell to Arms*, reflects his need, as Kraft says of Campbell, to reattach himself to the feminine if he is to begin writing well.

81. Jung, *Aspects of the Feminine*, 110. Jung wrote that, in association with the mythic mother's connection to "Stygian depths," the neurotic, traumatized male often imagines his mother as "a wild beast." Especially the children of "an overly anxious mother" regularly dream that she is a terrifying animal or witch, creating a split in the child's psyche that predisposes it to neurosis (ibid., 110–13).

82. Ibid., 5–24.

83. Ibid., 110–13.

84. Vonnegut, *Happy Birthday, Wanda June*, 189–96.

85. Vonnegut, *Mother Night*, 133.

86. Ibid., 132.

87. Svoboda, *Hemingway and* The Sun Also Rises, 133–34.

88. Vonnegut, *Mother Night*, xii.

### Chapter 3: Duty Dance with Death

1. Vonnegut, *Slaughterhouse-Five*, 21.

2. See above, page 190, note 33, for James Jones's comments to Vonnegut about Hemingway's lack of military training and for Vonnegut's comments about Hemingway's resentment of Irwin Shaw's *The Young Lions*.

3. Vonnegut, *Slaughterhouse-Five*, 20.

4. Ibid., 5.

5. Waldhorn, *A Reader's Guide to Ernest Hemingway*, 22.

6. Vonnegut, *Slaughterhouse-Five*, 77.

7. Hemingway, *A Farewell to Arms*, 191.

8. Hemingway, *CSS*, 337.

9. Qtd. in Spanier, "Hemingway's Unknown Soldier," 83. As seems clear from Hemingway's lampooning of religious belief in "Natural History of the Dead," Ernest, as Gregory insisted to Denis Brian, did not believe in an afterlife (*The True Gen*, 305). I think C. T. Lanham accurately summed up Hemingway's religious beliefs when he told Brian that Ernest "veered back and forth between believing in nothing and in being a half-assed Catholic" (*The True Gen*, 157).

10. Killinger's *Hemingway and the Dead Gods* explains how violence reveals the absurd for characters such as Henry and Pilgrim. The individual's awareness of the contrast between reality and ideal expectation produces Sartre's "nausea," a palpable spiritual disgust the hero experiences as early as the Indian camp episode of Nick Adams and the accidental murder of a pregnant housewife by Rudy Waltz.

11. Billy Pilgrim's life exists as a continuity of terror stretching all the way back to childhood, when his hairy father threw him in the pool at the YMCA and told him to sink or swim, and forward in time to the horrors of Dresden and his death when Paul Lazzaro makes good his promise to have Billy killed after the war.

12. In *Green Hills of Africa*, Hemingway argued that war was a vital part of his education as man and artist, and that no writer should be without it. He cited Tolstoy as someone war benefited inestimably and Thomas Wolfe as a writer who missed something irreplaceable (50).

13. Vonnegut, *Slaughterhouse-Five*, 178.

14. Spanier, "Hemingway's Unknown Soldier," 91–92.

15. Warren, introduction to *A Farewell to Arms*, xxxii.

16. Ibid., xii. According to Rackstraw, Vonnegut saw "staying alive with decency" as the primary function of literature: "inventing meaning and comfort for life's emptiness and absurdity, and to fill the gaps in human reason and intelligence" ("Dancing with the Muse," 133).

17. Tetlow, *Hemingway's* In Our Time, 70.

18. Bell, *"A Farewell to Arms,"* 116.

19. Vonnegut, *Slaughterhouse-Five*, 145.

20. Ibid., 99.

21. Tilton, *Cosmic Satire in the Contemporary Novel*, 46.

22. Bell, "*A Farewell to Arms*," 116.
23. Spilka, *Hemingway's Quarrel with Androgyny*, 212.
24. Vonnegut, *Mother Night*, 166.
25. Hemingway, *A Farewell to Arms*, 266.
26. Spilka, *Hemingway's Quarrel with Androgyny*, 216.
27. Strychacz, *Hemingway's Theaters of Masculinity*, 98.
28. Hemingway, *A Farewell to Arms*, 75.
29. Ibid., 242.
30. Ibid., 82.
31. Wagner-Martin, "The Romance of Desire in Hemingway's Fiction," 55.
32. Ibid., 61.
33. Ibid., 56.
34. Bell, "*A Farewell to Arms*," 118
35. Strychacz, *Hemingway's Theaters of Masculinity*, 98.
36. Wagner-Martin, "The Romance of Desire in Hemingway's Fiction," 62.
37. Hemingway, *A Farewell to Arms*, 57.
38. Ibid., 58.
39. Ibid., 59.
40. Ibid., 64.
41. Ibid., 232.
42. Strychacz, *Hemingway's Theaters of Masculinity*, 108.
43. Vonnegut, *Happy Birthday, Wanda June*, 176.
44. Warren, introduction to *A Farewell to Arms*, xvii.
45. Vonnegut, *Happy Birthday, Wanda June*, 110.
46. Ibid., 164–65.
47. Hemingway, *A Farewell to Arms*, 211.
48. Ibid., 146. Warren asserts that both Hemingway and Frederic Henry celebrate their wounds to certify their manliness and provide a source of masculine authority (introduction to *A Farewell to Arms*, xii).
49. Vonnegut, *Happy Birthday, Wanda June*, 176.
50. Vonnegut, *Slaughterhouse-Five*, 3.
51. Warren, introduction to *A Farewell to Arms*, xxxii.
52. Hemingway, *A Farewell to Arms*, 163.
53. Vonnegut, *Slaughterhouse-Five*, 65–67.
54. Ibid., 125.
55. Warren, introduction to *A Farewell to Arms*, xxiii.
56. Strychacz, *Hemingway's Theaters of Masculinity*, 100.
57. Warren, introduction to *A Farewell to Arms*, xi.
58. Hemingway, *A Farewell to Arms*, 173.
59. Vonnegut, *Mother Night*, 154.
60. Hemingway, *A Farewell to Arms*, 220, 221.
61. Ibid., 266.
62. Ibid., 240.
63. Ibid., 176.
64. Ibid., 175–78.
65. Vonnegut, *Happy Birthday, Wanda June*, 164–65.
66. Strychacz, *Hemingway's Theaters of Masculinity*, 100.

67. According to Killinger, Frederic Henry leaves the hospital after Catherine's death, "alone, tormented, but very much alive in the existential sense" (*Hemingway and the Dead Gods*, 48). Hemingway kills Catherine to free Henry from "the existential hell of a complicated life" (ibid., 47).

68. Spanier, "Hemingway's Unknown Soldier," 91.

69. Reynolds, *Hemingway's First War*, 263–74.

70. Bell, "*A Farewell to Arms*," 115.

71. Rovit and Brenner, *Ernest Hemingway*, 15.

72. Vonnegut, *Slaughterhouse-Five*, 84–85.

73. Jung explained that the loving or terrible mother of mythology, saint or whore, associated with both light and darkness, draws the male protagonist into life's "frightful paradoxes" (*Aspects of the Feminine*, 170).

74. Spilka, *Hemingway's Quarrel with Androgyny*, 212.

75. Bell, "*A Farewell to Arms*," 114. In *Strange Tribe* John Hemingway praises the work of scholars such as Carl Eby, Nancy Comley, Rose Marie Burwell, and Debra Moddelmog for bringing to light what his grandfather had been hinting about for years, the strongly resisted desire to be a woman. He documented the tragic effects on the entire Hemingway family of the failure of both Ernest and Gregory to understand and accept the feminine side of their natures.

76. Spilka, *Hemingway's Quarrel with Androgyny*, 219.

77. Bell, "*A Farewell to Arms*," 116.

78. Spilka, *Hemingway's Quarrel with Androgyny*, 215.

79. Vonnegut, *Breakfast of Champions*, 180.

80. Doris Lessing, qtd. in Broer, *Sanity Plea*, 351.

81. Kathryn Hume, qtd. in Broer, *Sanity Plea*, 199.

### Chapter 4: Spiritual Manifestos

1. Vonnegut, *Breakfast of Champions*, 4.

2. Ibid., 293.

3. Bloom, *The Anxiety of Influence*, 15.

4. José Luis Castillo-Puche, qtd. in Broer, *Hemingway's Spanish Tragedy*, 55. Michael Reynolds's *Hemingway: The Homecoming* reiterates my thesis in *Hemingway's Spanish Tragedy*: that the emerging Hemingway hero after *Death in the Afternoon*—rough, masculine, self-reliant—represents a radical break from figures in Hemingway's earlier work, whom Reynolds describes as "survivors" living precariously in a world in which they have little control. Stanton similarly repeats my view that Hemingway gave his American protagonists qualities acquired from Spanish matadors, though neither Reynolds nor Stanton acknowledged *Hemingway's Spanish Tragedy* as a source.

5. Salvador de Madariaga, qtd. in Broer, *Hemingway's Spanish Tragedy*, 54.

6. Hemingway, *Death in the Afternoon*, 45.

7. Ibid., 122.

8. Ibid., 8.

9. Ibid., 12.

10. Ibid., 5, 9.

11. Ibid., 233.

12. Angel Ganivet, qtd. in Broer, *Hemingway's Spanish Tragedy*, 61.

13. Ibid., 62. What Ortega called *pronunciamientos*—self-righteous proclamations of "truth"—show up in *Green Hills of Africa* in particularly unnerving ways.

14. Hemingway, *Death in the Afternoon*, 79.

15. Ibid., 81.

16. Ibid., 232.

17. Migel de Unamuno, qtd. in Broer, *Hemingway's Spanish Tragedy*, 66.

18. Hemingway, *Green Hills of Africa*, 23.

19. Ibid., 28.

20. If Spilka is right, Hemingway's betrayal of the female within himself crystallized with his marriage to Pauline Pfeiffer. Spilka calls *Death in the Afternoon*—the book Hemingway dedicated to Pauline—"a study in the ritual proving of manhood," arguing that Hemingway's life with Pauline was given over to such ritual provings—hunting in Africa, fishing off Key West and Bimini, boxing on shore with all contenders (*Hemingway's Quarrel with Androgyny*, 223). Reynolds sees Hemingway giving himself over to his "deadlier leanings"—the mask of machismo threatening to harden into permanent caricature of the more complex man beneath.

21. Spilka, *Hemingway's Quarrel with Androgyny*, 223.

22. Hemingway, *Green Hills of Africa*, 71.

23. Ibid., 148.

24. Hemingway, *Death in the Afternoon*, 81.

25. Hemingway, *Green Hills of Africa*, 115.

26. Ibid., 290.

27. Ibid., 148.

28. Ibid., 272.

29. Geismar, "Ernest Hemingway," 140.

30. Eastman, "Bull in the Afternoon," 95.

31. Strychacz, *Hemingway's Theaters of Masculinity*, 2. While on the one hand Strychacz demonstrates that *Death in the Afternoon* can be read in terms of Vonnegut's critique of Hemingway's machismo, he shows us that even in this seemingly most masculine of works, the author's richly contradictory art forces us to debate the work's moral issues within and among ourselves. We hazard interpretations that reflect our own values and interests. For such critic-aficionados as Allen Josephs and Edward Stanton, Hemingway's artful representation of the bullfight appears "sacramental," a high religious experience they believe offered Hemingway a cure for postwar angst. As a bona fide "animalarian," I, like Vonnegut, see in the *corrida* less that is spiritually transcendent than a reminder of mankind's capacity for brutality and violence.

32. Hemingway, *Green Hills of Africa*, 149.

33. Vonnegut, *Breakfast of Champions*, 116.

34. Hemingway, *Green Hills of Africa*, 148.

35. Ibid., 24.

36. See my essay "Images of the Shaman in the Works of Kurt Vonnegut." Vonnegut was drawn to the trauma theory of Freud's major disciple, Otto Rank, who emphasized the crisis of mother separation for the writer and making the unconscious conscious—proposing the assertion of will as the quintessence of psychological growth.

37. Vonnegut, *Breakfast of Champions*, 37, 293.

38. Ibid., 99.

39. Ibid., 84, 85. Relevant to Vonnegut's association of Hemingway with Trout, Bloom has noted that the strong writer transforms himself into a "fouled" version of himself that conflates with the figure of the precursor (*The Anxiety of Influence*, 62).

40. Dwayne's violence is both homophobic and racist, moral as well as physical.

41. Ibid., 210.

42. Ibid., 221.

43. Ibid., 5.

44. Ibid., 181.

45. Buck, "Vonnegut's World of Comic Futility," 190.

46. Vonnegut, *Breakfast of Champions*, 253.

47. Jung, *Aspects of the Feminine*, 95.

### Chapter 5: From Jailbird to Canary Bird

1. Wagner-Martin, "The Romance of Desire in Hemingway's Fiction," 54.

2. Comley and Scholes, *Hemingway's Genders*, 146.

3. Moddelmog, "Reconstructing Hemingway's Identity," 187. See the essays in Broer and Holland, eds., *Hemingway and Women*, for ways major female scholars have challenged traditional views of Hemingway and women, including the real women in Hemingway's life, who cared for him, competed with him, and ultimately helped to shape his art.

4. Spilka, *Hemingway's Androgyny*, 12, 13.

5. Stein, *The Autobiography of Alice B. Toklas*, 216–17.

6. Vonnegut, *Jailbird*, 238.

7. Ibid., xxxvii.

8. Hemingway, *To Have and Have Not*, 121.

9. Vonnegut, *Jailbird*, 3.

10. Hemingway, *To Have and Have Not*, 35.

11. Vonnegut, *Jailbird*, 118.

12. Ibid., 42. Starbuck's demoralized voice reflects Vonnegut's own troubled, divided soul, along with his ongoing quarrel with Hemingway's fatalism. Vonnegut's preface identifies the loss of that youthful socialist self who believed in employing unions to achieve economic justice. On the other hand, it says that resisting the pull of his defeatist self was necessary to life itself. If he were to go on living, Vonnegut wrote, he had better follow the lead of idealistic labor leaders such as Powers Hapgood (xiii). The industrialist Alexander McCone fragments Walter's identity by dividing him against his own father, McCone's driver, programming Walter to adopt the capitalistic power and money games of other white-collar criminals. In his father's RAMJAC limousine, Walter becomes fascinated by a pretend steering wheel the physical attributes of which are those of the Tralfamadorians as described in *Slaughterhouse-Five:* a green object protruding from a shaft attached to suction cups.

13. In *God Bless You, Mr. Rosewater*, the Buntline family maid, an intrinsically talented painter and musician, endures similar humiliation by her wealthy employers. In a slyly pejorative reference to Hemingway, the head of the orphanage who delivers Selena into the hands of the Buntlines fought in Spain during the Spanish civil war in the Abraham Lincoln Brigade and is addressed as "Daddy"—read "Papa." Selena appeals to him for relief, which never comes.

14. Hemingway, *To Have and Have Not*, 237–38.

15. Ibid., 97.

16. Ibid., 53.

17. Vonnegut, *Happy Birthday, Wanda June*, 74–75. *God Bless You, Mr. Rosewater* introduces us to Harry Pena, a fisherman like Morgan whose last name suggests cojones on display, a violent man who enjoys inflicting pain on people and animals alike. In a reference that recalls Mr. Sing flapping like a dolphin on a "gaff," Pena's boys "grabbed their gaffs" to jam them into the bellies of fish, which turn on the hooks in pure agony.

18. Ibid., 29.

19. Hume, "Kurt Vonnegut and the Myths and Symbols of Meaning," 442.

20. Walter's Dantesque descent into the catacombs—that is, his psychic underworld and Mary Kathleen's secret hiding place—teaches Walter more about Nixon's hatchet man, Evil Larkin (evil lurking in himself), primarily his capacity for moral escapism. See Rackstraw's "Dancing with the Muse" for further insight into Vonnegut's use of Dante's descent as the redemptive, metaphorical source of Walter's spiritual transformation. Exactly as I argue about Hemingway's hero, Rackstraw sees Vonnegut's protagonists growing in complexity and power in direct proportion to their achievement of "androgynous integrity," the integration of "a more balanced, androgynous soul" ("Dancing with the Muse," 126, 138).

21. Josef Benson, "The Two Harrys and the Two Hemingways," directed study, University of South Florida, Tampa, Spring 2008. Benson suggests that even Hemingway's inclusion of so many women's points of view in this novel counters Vonnegut's criticism that Hemingway values violence and machismo over intelligence and femininity.

22. Hemingway, *To Have and Have Not*, 261

23. Eliot, "What the Thunder Said," part 5 of *The Waste Land*.

24. Vonnegut, *Jailbird*, 128. The name "Mary" or derivations of it occur often enough in both writers' works to establish the importance of the Virgin Mother as their major mythic prototype for the feminine aspect of soul. While the eternal feminine generally represents a protective, nurturing force, a power of transformation and renewal, the contrast between Hemingway's Marie and Vonnegut's Mary makes Jung's point about the anima's contradictory nature, that she may represent both favorable and unfavorable meanings, and may even appear positive one moment and negative the next (*Aspects of the Feminine*, 90). Walter's wife, Ruth, helps him negotiate the "Dead Seas," but she is generally hopelessly pessimistic, a Trout-like harbinger of doom. Sounding like the fatalistic Marie Morgan, Ruth explains the mishaps of her life by declaring, "What else could I do" (Vonnegut, *Jailbird*, 16). Walter says that his wife believed all human beings were evil by nature, a "disease" that could only spread. By contrast to Ruth's belief that even the most intelligent human beings were so stupid that they could only make things worse by speaking their minds (Vonnegut, *Jailbird*, 155), the "saintly" Mary Kathleen counts intelligence and learning as the highest of human virtues, "daring" to be optimistic and humane.

25. Ibid., 63.

26. Hume, "The Heraclitean Cosmos of Kurt Vonnegut," 442.

27. Vonnegut, *Jailbird*, 9.

28. Ibid.

29. Ibid., 10.

30. Just as Vonnegut's autobiographical projections are always complex and ironically presented, Hemingway's portrayal of both men, Morgan and Gordon, suggest the author's personal contradictions. For instance, though Gordon's language is pretentious, his remark that he will not restrict his experience to bourgeois standards certainly speaks for Hemingway, a major theme in *The Garden of Eden*.

31. Hemingway, *To Have and Have Not*, 225.

32. Jung, *Aspects of the Feminine*, 87.

33. Hemingway, *To Have and Have Not*, 187. Among Reynolds's descriptions of Hemingway's psychic split—the mask and the man beneath the mask—examples of those by women, the first to feel Hemingway's abuse, yet the quickest to appreciate his contradictions, that he was far more vulnerable than he liked to pretend—stand out. As Jung wrote, "The wives of such men would have a pretty tale to tell" (*Aspects of the Feminine*, 83). Reynolds explains that, whereas Hadley and Pauline suffered Hemingway's insults, his neglect, and his need to dominate (a condition Jung describes as the wife's pretense of inferiority in order to provide her husband with proof that he is the masculine hero he projects publicly and not the inwardly more feminine self he is in private [*Aspects of the Feminine*, 85]), Martha and Mary were less willing to play limiting, self-effacing wifely roles, asserting their independence in ways that angered him and openly challenging him when he became abusive. When the adventurous and independent Martha told Ernest, "I have to live my own life as well as yours or there would not be any me to love you with," he called her "insane" (qtd. in Reynolds, *Hemingway: The Final Years*, 88, 90). Then there was Mary's declaration to Charles Scribner that the reason she planned to leave Ernest was his "program of being a tough guy," destroying what she used to think was an inexhaustible supply of devotion (qtd. in Burwell, *Hemingway*, 205). Reynolds reports that Martha Gellhorn's mother saw clearly that Hemingway was strangely divided, that there was something hidden beneath the surface that made her feel sorry for him. Gertrude Stein was perhaps the earliest of Hemingway's female admirers to sense the precarious "fictive mask" with which she said Hemingway was "about to enter the public arena" (*The Autobiography of Alice B. Toklas*, 220).

34. Hemingway, *To Have and Have Not*, 188.

35. Vonnegut, *Happy Birthday, Wanda June*, 176. Hemingway would certainly have included Vonnegut in the group of world savers.

36. Ibid., 168.

37. Ibid., 149.

38. Hemingway, *To Have and Have Not*, 211.

39. Ibid., 212, 213. The parody of Ginger Rogers is strikingly Vonnegut-like, invoking his concern with the power of fiction to influence reality.

40. Ibid., 117.

41. Ibid., 126.

42. Ibid., 115.

### Chapter 6: Anima and Animus in *For Whom the Bell Tolls* and *Slapstick*

1. De Falco, "Hemingway's Islands and Streams," 40.

2. Vonnegut, *Slapstick*, 1.

3. Ibid., 2.

4. Hemingway, *For Whom the Bell Tolls*, 43.

5. Ibid., 338.

6. Ibid., 335.

7. Ibid., 438.

8. Ibid., 406.

9. Ibid., 337.

10. Ibid., 67. Apropos of my view of the hero's developing feminized nature in *For Whom the Bell Tolls*, Jung called the masculine persona a "mask" between the individual consciousness

and society, designed to make "a definite impression upon others, and, on the other, to conceal the true nature of the individual" (*Aspects of the Feminine*, 81). In Jung's view this painfully familiar division of a consciousness between a public persona and a private, submerged identity into two figures, often preposterously different, constitutes an incisive psychological operation that is bound to have repercussions on the unconscious. The subject so identifies with his outer persona that he no longer knows himself, understanding neither demands from within nor from without (ibid., 81–82). In keeping with one's masculine ideals, it becomes easier to deplore what is perceived as feminine weakness, Jung's "shadow" or "darker self," than to shatter those ideals (ibid., 84). This provides particularly useful insight into David Bourne's rejection of his "devil" Catherine in *The Garden of Eden*, Jung's "jealous mistress" upon whom the subject projects his own darkness, forcing others into equally unconscious, dishonest roles that reinforce one's outward projected masculine identity (ibid., 89). In *Strange Tribe* John Hemingway's exposé of his father's "physical manifestation" of his grandfather's gender ambiguity documents the tragic effects on the entire Hemingway family of the failure of both men to understand and accept the feminine side of their nature.

11. Vonnegut, *Slapstick*, 3.

12. Hemingway, *For Whom the Bell Tolls*, 43.

13. Ibid., 162.

14. Josephs, *For Whom the Bell Tolls: Hemingway's Undiscovered Country*, 127.

15. As I did in *Hemingway's Spanish Tragedy*, Stanton in *Hemingway and Spain* questions the notion that Hemingway's "typically Spanish preoccupation with death" was positive, arguing that in the author's use of the Spanish matador for models of masculine conduct, one can see the "seeds of his own destruction" (95).

16. Vonnegut, *Happy Birthday, Wanda June*, 166.

17. Vonnegut, *Slapstick*, 3.

18. Ibid., 4.

19. Ibid., 18, 19.

20. Ibid., 60.

21. Ibid., 103, 104.

22. Ibid., 129–30.

23. Ibid., 138–39.

24. Ibid., 236.

25. Ibid., 96.

26. Waugh, *Metafiction*, 9.

27. Vonnegut, *Slapstick*, 230.

28. Ibid., 19.

29. Hemingway, *For Whom the Bell Tolls*, 165.

30. Ibid., 235.

31. Vonnegut, *Slapstick*, 192.

32. Hemingway, *For Whom the Bell Tolls*, 164.

33. Ibid., 333.

34. Strychacz, *Hemingway's Theaters of Masculinity*, 144.

35. Hemingway, *For Whom the Bell Tolls*, 166.

36. Ibid., 163.

37. Ibid., 237.

38. Ibid., 231.

39. In her discussion of the influence of Kierkegaard on Hemingway's work, J'aimé Sanders argues that facing the certainty of death through the bullfight "teaches the earnestness of life" (Kierkegaard), allows the individual to see life "whole," and promotes "lifeforce" ("The Art of Existentialism," 84–107).

40. Hemingway, *For Whom the Bell Tolls*, 287. This offers critical counterpoint to Hemingway's apparent sympathies with the enjoyment of killing in *Death in the Afternoon*. Whereas in *Death in the Afternoon*, Hemingway scorns people who identify with the pain of animals, he draws us here into a debate about the "brotherhood" of animals and humans that argues for moral advance. As Jordan and Anselmo inquire into the similarities of men and beasts in *For Whom the Bell Tolls*, they agree that distinctions between animals and humans are negligible.

41. Ibid., 113.

42. Ibid., 192.

43. Spilka, *Hemingway's Quarrel with Androgyny*, 213.

44. Lynn, *Hemingway*, 138.

45. Hemingway, *For Whom the Bell Tolls*, 346.

46. Ibid., 67.

47. Sinclair, "Revisiting the Code," 37.

48. Spilka, *Hemingway's Quarrel with Androgyny*, 247. Citing Freud, Bloom calls intra-artistic relationships between writers such as Hemingway and Vonnegut, his writer-son, a "family romance" (*The Anxiety of Influence*, 8).

49. Vonnegut, *Slapstick*, 160.

50. Hemingway, *For Whom the Bell Tolls*, 89.

51. Ibid., 139.

52. Vonnegut, *Bluebeard*, 2.

53. Moddelmog, "Queer Families," 174.

54. Josephs, *For Whom the Bell Tolls: Hemingway's Undiscovered Country*, 93.

55. Spilka, *Hemingway's Quarrel with Androgyny*, 251.

56. Josephs, *For Whom the Bell Tolls: Hemingway's Undiscovered Country*, 107.

57. Vonnegut, *Slapstick*, 116.

58. Jung, *Aspects of the Feminine*, 21.

59. Hemingway, *For Whom the Bell Tolls*, 341.

60. Ibid., 343.

61. Josephs, *For Whom the Bell Tolls: Hemingway's Undiscovered Country*, 98.

62. Hemingway, *For Whom the Bell Tolls*, 467.

63. Hemingway, *Islands in the Stream*, 283.

64. Strychacz, *Hemingway's Theaters of Masculinity*, 110. Though Strychacz wonders whether Hemingway through Jordan does not indulge fantasies of male power masquerading as historical necessity, Strychacz sees Jordan's "fascist" self as a construction capable of change (106–7).

65. Beegel, "Santiago and the Eternal Feminine," 143.

66. Hassan, *The Postmodern Turn*, 88.

67. Hemingway, *For Whom the Bell Tolls*, 289.

68. Ibid., 212.

69. Ibid., 437.

70. Ibid., 137–38.

71. Ibid., 420.
72. Ibid., 238.
73. Hassan, *The Postmodern Turn*, 91, 92.
74. Vonnegut, *Slapstick*, 96.

## Chapter 7: A Soldier's Confessions

1. Vonnegut, *Fates Worse than Death*, 60.
2. Ibid., 146.
3. Klinkowitz, *Rosenberg, Barthes, Hassan*, 109.
4. Wilde, *Horizons of Assent*, 131–32.
5. Waugh suggests that the cultural disintegration portrayed in Yeats's poem "The Second Coming" more aptly describes the postmodern vision of writers after World War II, fragments that resist such final structures of authority and meaning as exist in Eliot's *The Waste Land* and in Joyce's *Ulysses* (*Metafiction*, 24–25).
6. Hassan, *The Postmodern Turn*, 44, 45.
7. Clark, *The Modern Satiric Grotesque*, 29.
8. Vonnegut, *Fates Worse than Death*, 62.
9. Clark, *The Modern Satiric Grotesque*, 86.
10. Vonnegut, *Fates Worse than Death*, 184.
11. Reed, *Writers for the 70's*, 207.
12. Raeburn, *Fame Became of Him*, 43.
13. Hemingway, *Across the River and into the Trees*, 27.
14. Ibid., 114.
15. Vonnegut, *Hocus Pocus*, 254.
16. Ibid., 51,
17. Ibid., 59
18. Vonnegut, *Fates Worse than Death*, 67. John Hemingway remarked, "I keep thinking what a wonderful old man he [Ernest] would have made if he'd learned how" (Brian, *The True Gen*, 305).
19. Vonnegut, *Hocus Pocus*, 55.
20. Ibid., 155.
21. Ibid., 167.
22. Howe, "In Search of Moral Style," 229.
23. Waugh, *Metafiction*, 53.
24. In "The Strange Country," Roger Hancock and his youthful and beautiful traveling companion, Helena, travel in their used Buick convertible from Miami Beach to the Florida panhandle. As an extension of Hudson/Davis in *Islands in the Stream*, Roger repudiates the sins of his darker self, the "bad things" he says "were his own fault" (Hemingway, *CSS*, 630): the abuse of wives and children, the abuse to himself and his art in the form of heavy drinking, and the denial of the feminine aspect of his nature necessary to his completion as artist. While the omnipresent snakes and darkened swamps along Roger and Helena's allegorical road remind us of the hero's association of the feminine with loss and death, the ease with which the couple engage in mysteriously exploratory sex, the final "strange country," supports my view that the posthumous works represent Hemingway's efforts to understand his own complex sexuality, defying Oak Park prudishness by opening himself to a variety of sexual experiences. Roger reflects: "In the dark, he went into the strange country"—the compelling pleasures and risks of unconventional sex—"hard to enter" because "perilously

difficult" (ibid., 615), but promising a brighter happiness than he or Helena had ever known. Roger's vow to be a better person reminds us of Vonnegut's perpetual battle with pessimism and aggression. To be less selfish and cruel, Roger knows he must resist the undertow of hopelessness that tugs at him. Echoing Vonnegut's thought in *Bluebeard* that "Belief is nearly the whole of the universe," Roger tells himself that if he says words such as "belief," "possibility," and "love," perhaps he could *feel* them and believe them. Then perhaps they *would* be true (ibid., 610). Roger's awakened conscience, which nags him now in "boldfaced script" (ibid., 635), informs him that just as much as he welcomes Helena's sexual adventurism and assertions of equality in bed, he must accept her as his creative "partner," whose dreams of writing are as important as his.

    25. Burwell, *Hemingway*, 51, 52.

    26. Ibid., 49. Meredith observes that, just as the autobiographical connections between Hemingway and the soldier-narrator in "Black Ass at the Crossroads" are too close to ignore, so the figurative possibilities of "crossroads" in the title seem the first thing on his mind when he wrote the story ("Understanding Hemingway's Multiple Voices of War," 46–47). Explaining that the "Black Ass" in the title resonates with suggestions of regret and despair, Meredith suggests that this was probably not the first and last time Hemingway would be an assassin at crossroads (ibid., 50). In Meredith's words the author "sublimates" himself in this story into "disparate identities" (ibid., 50), coarsened war-weary guerrilla leader who narrates the story, and the persona "of his youth" represented conjointly by the young boy the narrator kills, who is approximately the age when Hemingway went to war, and his own repressed but now remorseful caring self. By no coincidence, the narrator observes of himself, "You split too easily. You want to watch that" (Hemingway, *CSS*, 583). Meredith underscores my central argument that Hemingway uses characters such as Maria, Renata, Manolin, Thomas Hudson's boys, and the later Nick Adams allegorically to represent his sense of betrayal of his own, more youthful self, the youthful female part of himself abandoned or killed off at those critical crossroads of the 1930s. When the narrator mortally wounds the boy, the death not only disconcerts him, it breaks his heart, remorse as profound as Santiago's destruction of his great fish, Thomas Hudson's regret of the death of the young German sailor in *Islands in the Stream*, or David Bourne's participation in the slaying of his elephant. Yet apropos of Meredith's observation that the story is about the hero's spiritual transformation ("Understanding Hemingway's Multiple Voices of War," 56)—the "exact moment" he changes from coarsened soldier to sympathetic youth, the narrator not only recognizes the terrible mistakes he has made, but attempts to rescue the vulnerable femme within him, like Orpheus descending to the rescue of Eurydice.

    27. Burwell, *Hemingway*, 49.

    28. Hemingway, *Across the River and into the Trees*, 271.

    29. Reynolds, *Hemingway: The Final Years*, 344.

    30. What matters most is not the idea that Hemingway or Fitzgerald finally resolved such dreadful contradictions through some sort of ultimate transcendence, but that their capacity for self-critical introspection produced moral amelioration and greater creative risk.

    31. Eby, *Hemingway's Fetishism*, 290.

    32. Kathleen Robinson, "Hemingway's *Across the River and into the Trees:* An Exploration of Trauma and Gender," seminar paper, Hemingway and Vonnegut Graduate Seminar. University of South Florida. Tampa, November 2008.

    33. Robinson, "Testimony of Trauma," 47.

34. The "big book" Hartke envisions corresponds to Cantwell's own self-trial and to the self-critical nature of Hemingway's posthumous works as a whole, especially the "Land, Sea, and Air" project. Hemingway said that Eugene Debs Hartke's socialist-pacifist namesake, was the only presidential candidate he ever voted for (Hemingway, *Selected Letters*, 648).

35. Vonnegut, *Hocus Pocus*, 150.

36. Hemingway, *Across the River and into the Trees*, 251.

37. Vonnegut, *Hocus Pocus*, 40.

38. Ibid., 34..

39. Ibid., 15.

40. Ibid., 142.

41. Ibid., 206.

42. Ibid., 148. Though I argue in *Sanity Plea* that Vonnegut made steady progress in his war with pessimism, he described this struggle more in terms of losing and regaining his "equilibrium"—what he called "Hunter Thompson's disease"—the affliction of "all those who feel that Americans can be as easily led to beauty as to ugliness, to truth as to public relations, to joy as to bitterness. . . . I don't have it this morning. It comes and goes" (*Wampeters, Foma & Granfalloons*, 235). Brian reiterated Vonnegut's view of himself and Hemingway as suffering from bipolar disorder or manic depression, "with probably self-image problems" (*The True Gen*, 310).

43. Vonnegut, *Hocus Pocus*, 36.

44. Vonnegut, *Fates Worse than Death*, 72.

45. Vonnegut, *Hocus Pocus*, 103.

46. Ibid., 290–91.

47. Ibid., 119.

48. Ibid., 192.

49. Ibid., 299.

50. Ibid., 180, 253.

51. Ibid., 102.

52. Ibid., 286.

53. Eby, *Hemingway's Fetishism*, 22.

54. Vonnegut, *Hocus Pocus*, 28.

55. Ibid., 163.

56. Eby, *Hemingway's Fetishism*, 221.

57. Moddelmog, *Reading Desire*, 126. According to Eby and Moddelmog, the hero's ambiguous sexuality assumes multiple forms, the desire to be androgynous, to be female, and to experience sex with another man (as suggested in Cantwell's attraction to Custer and to Dante). Renata may have Cantwell consciously or unconsciously in mind when she speaks of the homosexual boy who goes with many women "to hide what he is" (Hemingway, *Across the River and into the Trees*, 96). Cantwell appears conscious of such complex feelings when he answers Renata's question, "Could I be you?" with "that's awfully complicated" (ibid., 156). Truman Capote quipped that Hemingway was "a closet everything" (qtd. in Brian, *The True Gen*, 187). Consistent with my Jungian analysis, I like Spilka's explanation that the hero seeks to complete "the males' female incompleteness" (*Hemingway's Quarrel with Androgyny*, 144).

58. Vonnegut, *Bluebeard*, 118.

59. Eby, *Hemingway's Fetishism*, 229.

60. Stanton, *Hemingway and Spain*, 70.

61. Whitlow, "*Across the River and into the Trees:*—Hemingway and Psychotherapy," 41.

62. Qtd. in Meyers, *Hemingway,* 197.

63. Spilka, *Hemingway's Quarrel with Androgyny,* 259.

64. Qtd. in Brian, *The True Gen,* 225.

65. Knowles, "Hemingway's *Across the River and into the Trees,*" 199.

66. Baker, *Hemingway,* 477.

67. Hemingway, *Across the River and into the Trees,* 41.

68. Ibid., 242.

69. Ibid., 254.

70. Bakker, *Fiction as Survival Strategy,* 132.

71. Hemingway, *Across the River and into the Trees,* 223.

72. Ibid., 65.

73. Ibid.

74. Ibid., 83.

75. Ibid., 246.

76. Ibid., 42.

77. Ibid., 36.

78. Ibid., 27.

79. Ibid., 78.

80. Spilka, *Hemingway's Quarrel with Androgyny,* 248.

81. Ibid., 64. See Burwell, "West of Everything," which highlights the extent to which Hemingway's masculine "codes of conduct, standards of judgment, and habits of perception" (158) were shaped by his reading of Wild West fiction.

82. Spilka, *Hemingway's Quarrel with Androgyny,* 64.

83. Robinson, "Testimony of Trauma," 81.

84. Cantwell has many memories of Italy and Fossalta when he was eighteen and understood nothing of what was happening to him. He recalls the dust the troops raised as they passed the house Frederic Henry lived in, wondering if he ever got over his first war. He seeks the place where he had been hit and relieves himself in the same place where he was wounded thirty years before. Later he crosses the Tagliamento, which Henry had swum with his shattered knee. He concludes that no one of his other wounds had ever done to him what the first big one did.

85. Burwell, *Hemingway,* 50–52.

86. Ibid., 30, 31.

87. Hemingway, *Across the River and into the Trees,* 135.

88. Ibid., 237.

89. Ibid., 68, 273.

90. Ibid., 113.

91. Ibid., 227.

92. Ibid., 225.

93. Ibid., 134.

94. Ibid., 250.

95. Ibid., 257.

96. Ibid.

97. Ibid., 256.

98. Ibid., 257.

99. Ibid., 256.

100. Meredith, "The Rapido River and Hurtgen Forest in *Across the River and into the Trees*," 65.

101. Hemingway, *Across the River and into the Trees*, 242.

102. Vonnegut, *Hocus Pocus*, 234.

103. Hemingway, *Across the River and into the Trees*, 94.

104. Ibid., 95.

105. Ibid, 251.

106. Ibid.

107. Ibid., 273.

108. Ibid., 211.

109. Ibid., 173.

110. Hemingway, *For Whom the Bell Tolls*, 42.

111. Hemingway, *Across the River and into the Trees*, 98.

112. Ibid., 114.

113. Ibid., 154.

114. Ibid., 100. Cantwell's declaration that he wants Renata, but not to "own her," contrasts markedly with Frederic Henry's proclamation to Catherine, "I don't want any one else to touch you. . . . I get furious if they touch you" (Hemingway, *A Farewell to Arms*, 103).

115. Hemingway, *Across the River and into the Trees*, 48.

116. Ibid., 248.

117. Ibid., 271.

118. Ibid., 206.

119. Ibid., 207.

120. Ibid., 261.

121. Ibid., 232.

122. Jung, *Aspects of the Feminine*, 166, 67.

123. Hemingway, *Across the River and into the Trees*, 304.

124. Jung, *Aspects of the Feminine*, 167.

125. Hemingway, *Across the River and into the Trees*, 278.

126. Ibid., 225. Cantwell initially views animals and humans alike as military targets—"I barely have a squad," he says, about the "platoons" of ducks laid out before him (ibid., 299).

127. By extension, if Cantwell's remorse over the "murder" of the drake and the hen represents killing anger toward parents, offending wives, and difficult children, it is "treachery" he says he had always sought to understand (ibid., 288).

128. Ibid., 294.

129. Ibid., 298.

130. Ibid., 291.

## Chapter 8: Now It's Women's Turn

1. See my essay "Vonnegut's Goodbye." Vonnegut's satire of the ignorance and aggression of "fisher folk" in *Galapágos* offers direct rebuttal to what he views as Santiago's primitive simplemindedness. It is no doubt Santiago who Vonnegut had in mind in *Bluebeard* when Rabo Karabekian wonders what his hateful father would have made of a film about fishermen in the North Atlantic that starred Spencer Tracy.

2. Vonnegut, *Galapágos*, 252.

3. Ibid.

4. Ibid., 259.

5. Orpheus provides a meaningful analogue to Hemingway and Vonnegut in several respects. According to Kathryn Hume, as a quester, Orpheus embodies man's desperate wish to control time and outwit death, a failure whose experience nonetheless authenticates his prophetic/poetic vision ("Kurt Vonnegut and the Myths and Symbols of Meaning," 300). It is notably Orpheus's mother who gives him the gift of music and healing, which enables him to enchant the gods with his art and to dare making his fearsome journey to the underworld. Associated with both Apollo and Dionysus, Orpheus represents the ideal psychic balance these authors seek. Not only does Orpheus's descent into the underworld to rescue Eurydice represent the authors' efforts to resurrect the feminine—literally to expose submerged desires by returning to earth and the light of day—but, according to Ovid, Orpheus turned his sexual interest to men and thus introduced homosexuality to Greece. Brenner argues that as well as freeing Manolin from his father's tyranny, Santiago's heroic struggle against the sea includes understanding his erotic feelings for the boy (*The Old Man and the Sea: Story of a Common Man*, 31). If Brenner is right, Santiago's remark that he is "a strange old man" assumes an intriguing new psychosexual dimension, supported by John Hemingway's argument in *Strange Tribe* and Carl Eby's in *Hemingway's Fetishisms*.

6. Vonnegut, *Galápagos*, 44. Mary Hepburn questions the sanctity of male authority, facilitating the rise of a more spiritual era on Santa Rosalia by casting the mercenary and robotic computer Mandarax into the sea.

7. Ibid., 44.

8. Ibid., 265.

9. Ibid., 82.

10. Beegel, "Santiago and the Eternal Feminine," 131. Santiago may not, as he says, think any longer of women or his wife, but when he repeatedly denigrates his hands for cramping and being useless, he sounds much like a menstruating female. Burwell notes that, while there is no mention of Santiago's father, we may assume that his childhood—like that of Roger Davis, David Hudson, and David Bourne—included the entrapment of trying to please an adult and becoming implicit in adult cruelty (Burwell, *Hemingway*, 92). Burwell also notes that the old fisherman, whose lines "are as thick around as pencils," becomes another avatar of the writer (58).

11. Beegel, "Santiago and the Eternal Feminine," 131.

12. Hemingway, *The Old Man and the Sea*, 55, 58.

13. Beegel, "Santiago and the Eternal Feminine," 136, 137.

14. Brenner, *The Old Man and the Sea: Story of a Common Man*, 34.

15. Hemingway, *Selected Letters*, 780.

16. Hemingway, *The Old Man and the Sea*, 53. Observing that the sea-as-wife is not incompatible with Santiago's calling the marlin and other sea creatures his "brothers," Beegel explains that the word "brother" is never "gender-specific" in Hemingway's work, but rather reflects an Eden where male and female principles, as well as man and nature, come into harmony and balance ("Santiago and the Eternal Feminine," 139).

17. Hemingway, *The Old Man and the Sea*, 117.

18. Strychacz, *Hemingway's Theaters of Masculinity*, 235–58.

19. Hemingway, *The Old Man and the Sea*, 113.

20. Ibid., 116.

21. Beegel, "Santiago and the Eternal Feminine," 155.

22. Hemingway, *The Old Man and the Sea*, 13.

23. Spilka, *Hemingway's Androgyny*, 262.

24. Ibid, 189.

25. Beegel, "Santiago and the Eternal Feminine," 185.

26. Burwell, *Hemingway*, 132.

27. Qtd. in Meyers, *Ernest Hemingway: The Critical Heritage*, 428. When Vonnegut remarked how he sensed "intuitively" that *Bluebeard*, like *The Old Man and the Sea*, was the summation of its author's career, he made a point critical to this study: that even when he was not responding explicitly to Hemingway's work, he had his creative "secret sharer" in mind unconsciously (Allen and Smith, "An Interview with Kurt Vonnegut," 42). Whether Vonnegut understood Hemingway's posthumous works to be a continuation of that "summary" or not, *Bluebeard*, published shortly after the release of *The Garden of Eden* takes dead aim at *Islands in the Stream* and *The Garden of Eden*.

28. Eby, *Hemingway's Fetishism*, 272.

29. Vonnegut, *Bluebeard*, 73.

30. Ibid., 64.

31. Ibid., 147.

32. Ibid., 31.

33. Ibid., 18.

34. Ibid., 48.

35. Ibid., 243.

36. Ibid. 143.

37. Ibid., 166.

38. Ibid., 88.

39. Ibid., 84.

40. Ibid., 139.

41. Ibid., 147. Vonnegut probably had Hemingway in mind when he had Rabo remark how he once believed war was so horrible that nobody could ever be fooled by romantic pictures and fiction to march to war again (Vonnegut, *Bluebeard*, 156).

42. The reference to self-help books recalls Hemingway's admiration of Horatio Alger stories as a boy.

43. Rackstraw, *Love as Always*, 117.

44. Vonnegut, *Bluebeard*, 126.

45. Ibid., 44.

46. Ibid., 294.

47. Ibid., 298.

48. Ibid., 195.

49. Ibid., 35.

50. Ibid., 299.

51. Jung, *Aspects of the Feminine*, 91.

52. Vonnegut, *Bluebeard*, 22.

53. Ibid., 21.

54. Ibid., 118.

55. Jung, *Aspects of the Feminine*, 129.

56. Vonnegut, *Bluebeard*, 11.

57. Hemingway, *Islands in the Stream*, 6.

58. Jung, *Aspects of the Feminine*, 108.

59. Vonnegut, *Bluebeard*, 13.

60. Ibid., 54.

61. Ibid., 14.
62. Ibid.
63. La Capra offers a useful perspective, explaining working through traumatic experience not as a total redemption of the past or as absolute healing of traumatic wounds but as the articulation of experience that may provide openings to the future (*History in Transit*, 181).
64. Eby, *Hemingway's Fetishism*, 266.
65. Hemingway, *Islands in the Stream*, 175.
66. Jung, *Aspects of the Feminine*, 124.
67. Vonnegut, *Bluebeard*, 12.
68. Benvenuto and Kennedy, *The Works of Jacques Lacan*, 152–53.
69. Vonnegut, *Bluebeard*, 172.
70. Ibid., 170.
71. Ibid., 171.
72. Qtd. in Eby, *Hemingway's Fetishism*, 265–66.
73. Hemingway, *The Garden of Eden*, 15.
74. Ibid., 17.
75. Ibid.
76. Hemingway, file 124, Kennedy Library.
77. Vonnegut, *Bluebeard*, 99.
78. Ibid., 247.
79. Vonnegut, *Fates Worse than Death*, 188.
80. Jung, *Aspects of the Feminine*, 98.
81. Vonnegut, *Bluebeard*, 225.
82. Ibid., 300.
83. Ibid., 194.
84. Ibid., 285. Rabo's painting climaxes Vonnegut's ongoing discussion after *Breakfast of Champions* of the way women have been victimized by war and men in general. "Look closer. . . . Half the concentration camp people from the lunatic asylums are women. They just don't look much like women anymore." As to the healthy women in the cellar with the beets and potatoes, "they are putting off being raped as long as possible," but "they know that rape will surely come" (303).
85. Ibid., 279.
86. Ibid., 298.
87. Ibid. 297.
88. Ibid., 275.
89. Campbell, *The Hero with a Thousand Faces*, 259.
90. Hemingway, *Islands in the Stream*, 263.
91. Ibid., 272.
92. Burwell, *Hemingway*, 54.
93. Hemingway, *Islands in the Stream*, 19.
94. Campbell, *The Hero with a Thousand Faces*, 150.
95. Jung, *Aspects of the Feminine*, 165–67.
96. Ibid., 166.
97. Hemingway, *Islands in the Stream*, 52–53.
98. Ibid., 57.
99. Ibid., 39.
100. Ibid., 47.

101. Hinz and Teunissen, "*Islands in the Stream* as Hemingway's Laocoön," 26.

102. Hemingway, *Islands in the Stream*, 48.

103. Ibid.

104. Ibid., 78.

105. Nighttime is paradoxically terrible and wonderful for the Hemingway hero. It is when dreadful psychosexual desires and fears emerge, but also a time of discovery and release when strategies of denial cease to work. Just as Hudson and Davis experience a sense of oneness in the night, so the split in Vonnegut's ego represented by Paul Slazinger and Rabo Karabekian also heals "in the dead of night" (Vonnegut, *Bluebeard*, 195).

106. John Hemingway, *Strange Tribe*, 68. John Hemingway's argument that Gregory's transvestic tendencies reflected his father's own nighttime fantasies explains why their deepest connection, as with Andrew and Thomas Hudson, keeps them apart.

107. Burwell, *Hemingway*, 91, 92.

108. Hemingway, *Islands in the Stream*, 414. Whereas in *Green Hills of Africa* Hemingway rationalizes the killing of animals, Hudson appears remorseful about things he and Willie have shot together. Hudson's empathy for the wounded German soldier relates to the narrator's affection for the dying boy he shoots in "Black Ass at the Crossroads."

109. Hinz and Teunissen refer to Hudson as a "Priest of the Sea," like Laocoön, whose sons, like Hudson's, are tragically killed. In this instance Nancy Comley shares Vonnegut's view of Hemingway as being always in flight from fatherhood. She reminds us that when his sons were born, he looked for another woman. And when he turned to writing about them in *Islands in the Stream*, he killed them off (*Hemingway's Genders*, 17).

110. Eby, *Hemingway's Fetishism*, 274.

111. Hemingway, *Islands in the Stream*, 4, 5. The house provides a stable, nurturing environment that will allow the writer part of the Hudson-Davis split a writing rebirth. Hence Hudson encourages Davis to stay at the house indefinitely and write his next book there (ibid., 106).

112. Ibid., 17–19. This sounds remarkably like Vonnegut's oft-repeated response to pleasant experience, attributed to his Uncle Alex, "If this isn't nice, what is?"

113. Ibid., 11.

114. Ibid., 18.

115. Ibid., 340. Just as Karabekian rejects the purely cameralike representations of Dan Gregory, who paints the surface of reality, so Hudson improves on the limited surface art of Constable, his initial mentor. Thus, when Hudson promises to paint a picture of David's fish, he vows to paint it "truer than a photograph" (Hemingway, *Islands in the Stream*, 139).

116. Ibid., 17.

117. Ibid., 18–20.

118. Ibid., 20, 21.

119. The rising waters and tidal waves in Hudson's painting evoke Vonnegut's use of drowning imagery to represent the loss of moral identity, being engulfed or swallowed up by tidal waves or whirlpools. Like Karabekian's masterpiece, Hudson's painting includes as well fog and swamps.

120. Hemingway, *Islands in the Stream*, 20.

121. Qtd. in Eby, *Hemingway's Fetishism*, 123.

122. Hemingway, *Islands in the Stream*, 221–22.

123. Ibid., 237. It is no coincidence that Hemingway's characters share his own passionate fondness for life. Tinged with Hemingway magic such elemental experience as uncorking a

bottle of wine, writing in the good light of a café, or listening to rain on a tent takes on ceremonial importance. I think of Mary Hemingway's observation that Ernest's "enjoyment of life was so much greater than that of almost anyone" (qtd. in Brian, *The True Gen*, 292).

124. Hemingway, *Islands in the Stream*, 191.

125. Ibid., 325.

126. Baker, *Hemingway*, 408.

127. Hemingway, *Islands in the Stream*, 412.

128. Fleming, *The Face in the Mirror*, 122.

129. Hinz and Teunissen see the creative impulse still alive in Hudson, illustrated by Hudson's creative response to the living nudity of his crew. Watching his men soaping themselves in the strange light of a storm, he thinks they look "perversely beautiful" as in the bathers by Cézanne. As he imagines painting them, Hudson explains that it is not details he wants, but "the roseate mass on the gray brown flat" (qtd. in *"Islands in the Stream* as Hemingway's Laocoön," 43). If Hudson's self-critical knowledge comes tragically late, I stress again the circular aesthetic structure of the late works as one composition in which he joins Jordan, Cantwell, and Santiago as psychic projections of their author, determined to tell the truth about personal and artistic sins, a redemption of personal and artistic integrity that triumphs in David Bourne and the narrating Hemingway of *Under Kilimanjaro*.

130. Hemingway, *The Garden of Eden*, 194.

131. Ibid., 193.

132. Ibid., 70. The "wrenching" Catherine feels and the harshness of her criticism suggests the extraordinary honesty with which Hemingway faced his personal and artistic sins, in this case the guilt and anguish he felt about his unfinished work. David's courageous admissions of failure extend what Hemingway may have had in mind when Santiago says about the loss of his most beautiful and noble work, "They beat me, Manolin. They truly beat me" (124). Like Santiago, Hemingway's efforts to land the posthumous novels and stories—as beat up as he was—may constitute his greatest heroism.

133. Ibid., 30.

134. Ibid., 125.

135. Ibid., 148.

136. Ibid., 151.

137. In *A Moveable Feast* (1964) Hemingway made clear that David's anguish of being in love with two women at once, wanting them "alone and together" refers to his relationship with Hadley and Pauline. Describing the situation that existed in 1926, Hemingway wrote, "You live day by day as in a war. . . . The unbelievable wrenching, killing happiness, selfishness and treachery of everything we did gave me a terrible remorse" (65). Eby explains that Hemingway's infantile love triangle with his mother and sister served as the template for all the ménage à trois fantasies that occur in his fiction (*Hemingway's Fetishism*, 321).

138. Hemingway, *The Garden of Eden*, 132.

139. Ibid., 193.

140. Ibid., 203.

141. Hemingway, file 422, Kennedy Library.

142. Hemingway, *The Garden of Eden*, 195.

143. Ibid., 105.

144. Ibid., 30.

145. Ibid., 84.

146. Ibid., 84, 85.

147. Eby explains that in the earlier version of *Islands in the Stream*, Hudson states that he no longer cares what is or is not perversion. Jan had taught him to respect those things that were "old" in people or in their "blood" (Eby, *Hemingway's Fetishism*, 264). Eby and I agree that with whatever reservations one has about the published version of *The Garden of Eden*, its clarification of what Eby calls Hemingway's "perverse scenario" makes it a welcomed climax to Hemingway's life work, providing the clearest understanding of the author's inward struggle with the buried feminine. I find that differences in the full-length manuscript are too slight to change the meanings of Hemingway's published text. If, as Catherine says about Barbara Sheldon, "She's sort of the way I am except in a different way"—meaning more overtly lesbian—Barbara repeats Catherine's moral credo exactly: "Don't worry about anything that's fun and doesn't hurt other people" (file 422.5, Kennedy Library). We learn that Nick and Barbara Sheldon were already doing in Paris what David and Catherine contemplate in le Grau du Roi and that the "lovely pleasures" the Sheldons enjoy so guiltlessly simply stimulate and embolden their mirrored twins.

148. Several references in *The Garden of Eden* fuse the hero's war trauma with the sexual wounds from childhood, gender anxiety in the form of fears of emasculation or of turning into the opposite sex. At the prospect of sex with both women, Catherine and Marita, David grows "taut as a hawser" (97). In the Kennedy manuscript, David remarks that he was "trepanned in the war, which is like being circumcised, only it's the head" (file 422.5, Kennedy Library). The hero's longstanding head wound—phallic and cerebral surface in David's need to boast to Marita when she places her hand in his lap that he is always "very reliable that way" (Hemingway, *The Garden of Eden*, 99).

149. Hemingway, file 441, Kennedy Library.

150. Hemingway, *The Garden of Eden*, 167.

151. In the manner of Vonnegut's "timequakes," Hemingway returned in "The Last Good Country" to the summer of 1915, when Hemingway/Nick shoots a blue heron and subsequently hides from the law and from the same estranged parents we know from the earlier Nick Adams stories. As Nick flees with his sister Littless into the "virgin forest" of Hemingway's Michigan boyhood, Hemingway brings to its sharpest focus the drama of taboo sexual desire that causes Krebs and Nick to relate to their sisters as lovers, or protagonists such as Jordan, Cantwell, and David Bourne to relate to their lovers or wives as sisters or mothers, all women with whom the protagonist desires to merge both sexually and spiritually. Lynn explains that the further the fugitives retreat from civilization, the more incestuous they become. Thus the kisses they exchange at the outset of the story are merely "warm-ups" for the moment when Littless sits on Nick's lap and he gets an erection (*Hemingway*, 57). It could as well be Catherine as Littless who pleads with her seemingly reluctant companion to explore forbidden erotic feelings, telling him, "I've got to. . . . You don't know how it is" (*CSS*, 506). As with the erotic embraces of David and Catherine Bourne, or of Vonnegut's Eliza and Wilbur Swain, the release of repressed desire appears to unite the split off halves of the protagonist's fragmented psyche but also satisfies his need to experience all possible manifestations of human sexuality, no matter how forbidden or damning.

152. Hemingway, *The Garden of Eden*, 203.

153. Ibid., 190.

154. Ibid., 166.

155. Ibid., 148.

156. Ibid., 202.

157. Ibid., 182.

158. Ibid., 148.

159. Ibid., 200–201.

160. Ibid., 182.

161. Ibid., 169.

162. David's response echoes Vonnegut's repudiation of Harold Ryan's blood lust in *Happy Birthday, Wanda June*, that when his father "began to kill for the fun of it" he "became the chief source of agony of mankind" (Vonnegut, *Happy Birthday, Wanda June*, 194).

163. Hemingway, *The Garden of Eden*, 181.

164. Ibid., 201.

165. Ibid., 198.

166. Ibid., 203.

167. Lynn, *Hemingway*, 63. As with Thomas Hudson, no other Hemingway protagonist comes closer to his author or to understanding the world and himself than David Bourne. Valerie Hemingway, who traveled with Ernest while he was writing *The Garden of Eden*, tells us, "David Bourne was Ernest Hemingway," down to details of their similar writing habits and their view of writing as "an act of hope" (ibid., 108). Like David, Hemingway experimented with gender reversal in both appearance and sex with all his wives except Martha Gellhorn.

168. Hemingway, *The Garden of Eden*, 129.

169. Ibid., 154. In a moment that mirrors Karabekian's forgiveness of his father and offers further healing of the protagonist's psychic split, David concedes that the father he once hated enough to want to kill in fact possessed the necessary depth of understanding and feeling to have loved his elephant story.

170. Hemingway, file 124, Kennedy Library.

171. Hemingway, *The Garden of Eden*, 183.

172. Spilka, *Hemingway's Androgyny*, 261.

173. Lynn, *Hemingway*, 65.

174. Though in the manuscript for *The Garden of Eden* both David and Catherine have matured enough to understand that the dream of perfection can never be fulfilled, we leave them feeling more truly in love and caring more deeply about one another than ever before. Faithful to the definition of genuine love by the priest in *A Farewell to Arms*, Catherine tells David, "Let's love each other and do what we can for each other." "You are my dear beloved," David says, "I love you and you sleep well" (file 422.1, Kennedy Library).

175. Waugh, *Metafiction*, 19.

176. Like Hudson's and Karabekian's artistic masterpieces, David Bourne's narratives transcend the limited perspectives of the camera's eye by producing meanings that are circular and self-referential. Robinson believes Hemingway has this in mind when he likened his late work to the complexity of calculus ("Testimony of Trauma," 42). Klinkowitz describes the modernist ideal of structuring narrative as spatial form as "the almost routine practice" of writers such as Vonnegut, Barth, and Pynchon (*Structuring the Void*, 166). As with Vonnegut's metafictional art, David's narratives draw attention to themselves as constructions, dreamlike realities that depend on the intelligence and humanity of the dreamer for completion. David goes directly from dreaming to writing his African story, and Catherine worries about the dog in his story as if he were real. David knows that he can only be truthful to his father's complexity by examining the moral problematics of his father's own desires and fears.

177. Vonnegut, *Bluebeard*, 84

178. Ibid., 283.

179. Ibid., 152. Vonnegut's praise of Hemingway's "brush strokes" no doubt includes awareness of Hemingway's interest in subjectivity from the very start of his career—in terms of the spatial development of *In Our Time* (1925) and the subjective perceptions of Jake Barnes in *The Sun Also Rises*.

180. Putnam, "On Defiling Eden," 128.

181. Vonnegut, *Bluebeard*, 236.

182. Ibid., 295.

### Chapter 9: A Literary Farewell

1. As Klinkowitz says of *Timequake*, both texts "collapse the distinction between fictive narrator and composing author" (*The Vonnegut Effect*, 55). Some theorists maintain that there is no way to distinguish between autobiography and fiction, that the "self" is an ever-changing enterprise constructed and reconstructed in the mind.

2. Vonnegut, *Timequake*, 55. As Vonnegut pondered the loss of self-respect plaguing his mother and father, leading his mother to suicide, he thought of his mother first, followed by Hemingway, as if he were a family member. I suspect Vonnegut had his surrogate "Papa" in mind when he associated fears of impotence with depression and suicide, calling to mind Hemingway's famous remark, "It was undoubtedly better to die in the happy period of youth, going out in a blaze of light, rather than having one's body worn out and old, and illusions shattered" (qtd. in Leicester Hemingway, *My Brother*, 183). Observing that depression—"hating life while pretending to love it"—affects "more sensitive parts of the body, such as the ding-dong," Vonnegut declares, "Somebody shoot me while I'm happy!" (*Timequake*, 163).

3. Vonnegut, *Timequake*, 112.

4. Ibid., 93.

5. Ibid., 118.

6. Ibid., 163.

7. Ibid., 183.

8. As an example of the "celebratory" reviews of *Timequake*, Loree Rackstraw cites Jack Barrow's observations in the *Chicago Sun-Times* that, rather than rejecting the idea of free will, *Timequake* demonstrates "the robotizing effect of TV, computer technologies, meaningless work, and just plain human carelessness." Rackstraw suggests that, if Vonnegut believed there was something limiting humanity's potential for reform, it was simply human laziness (*Love as Always*, 197). Supporting my view that Vonnegut and Hemingway's fiction should be perceived in light of the creative evolution of one man seeking to overcome defeatism and to work out the psychologically damaging effects of childhood and war, Vonnegut referred to *Timequake* "as the last chapter in one long book" (qtd. in Rackstraw, *Love as Always*, 197).

9. Burwell observes that in the African manuscript, Hemingway wrote openly of things he rendered only symbolically in the other posthumous works, particularly sins against the feminine (*Hemingway*, 146).

10. Hemingway, *The Garden of Eden*, 183.

11. Ibid., 148. Bourne's remark reflects Hemingway's comment to Fitzgerald, "You see Bo, you're not a tragic character. Neither am I. All we are is writers and what we should do is write" (*Selected Letters*, 408). To the contrary, just as Hemingway experienced Fitzgerald's own homosexual anxieties, so Hemingway through David Bourne admitted that he "cheated" with his talents as he accused Fitzgerald of doing and suffered the same nervous and physical "crack-up" he attributed to Scott.

12. Leicester Hemingway, *My Brother*, 283.

13. Hemingway, *Under Kilimanjaro*, 359. Though Hemingway remarks that his actions are "a bit theatrical," he follows with "but so was Hamlet" (*Under Kilimanjaro*, 359), a character with whose oedipal longings he might well identify. Eby explains that in Hemingway's complex oedipal fantasy, the author reversed the normal positive Oedipus complex by developing hostile feelings for the mother and affection for the father, resulting in a "strongly bipolar and unresolved neurosis" (*Hemingway's Fetishism*, 308).

14. Vonnegut, *Timequake*, 211.

15. Ibid., 12.

16. Hemingway, *Under Kilimanjaro*, 116.

17. Ibid.

18. Ibid.

19. Ibid., 4.

20. Ibid., 380.

21. Ibid., 381.

22. Hemingway, *Under Kilimanjaro*, 329.

23. Ibid., 377.

24. Eby, *Hemingway's Fetishism*, 318.

25. Rose Marie Burwell, qtd. in Putnam, "On Defiling Eden," 128–29.

26. Spilka, *Hemingway's Quarrel with Androgyny*, 13.

27. Hemingway, *Under Kilimanjaro*, 23.

28. Ibid., 377.

29. Ibid., 266.

30. Ibid., 329.

31. Ibid., 178.

32. Ibid., 139.

33. Ibid.

34. Ibid., 85.

35. Ibid., 139.

36. Ibid. Countess Renata and Catherine Bourne scold their men for verbal or stylistic excess in exactly this way, an example of Hemingway's self-critiquing process in the late works and what I mean by the circularity of meaning from *For Whom the Bell Tolls* to *Under Kilimanjaro*. Burwell notes that Hemingway acknowledged the inadequacy of "male language" while writing *Under Kilimanjaro* (*Hemingway*, 139).

37. Hemingway, *Under Kilimanjaro*, 132.

38. Ibid., 312.

39. Ibid., 6.

40. Ibid., 259.

41. Ibid., 260.

42. Ibid., 259.

43. Ibid., 83.

44. Ibid., 126–27.

45. Ibid., 378.

46. Ibid., 339.

47. Ibid., 327.

48. Ibid., 416.

49. Ibid., 224–25.

50. Ibid., 130.

51. Ibid., 115.

52. The sympathy for Lawrence evokes Hemingway's striking female tenderness in the manuscript for *The Garden of Eden*. My student Joshua Cundiff suggests that Hemingway has not only become more comfortable with his femininity but with mortality itself ("Hemingway's Posthumous Protest," course paper, Hemingway and Vonnegut Graduate Seminar, University of South Florida, Tampa, Fall 2008). David Bourne confesses to personal "vulnerability," which he has tried to hide, and even to feelings of kinship with literary critics, whom he tells Catherine must feel and understand the same things they do (file 442, Kennedy Library).

53. Hemingway, *Under Kilimanjaro*, 309.

54. Ibid., 126.

55. Ibid., 433.

56. Ibid.

57. Ibid., 419. Hemingway waxes fervently Vonnegut-like when he insists that if you did not have the necessary dreams you must invent them. "Anyone to have any success in Africa must be able to invent dreams and then make them come true. This was elemental" (ibid., 282).

58. Ibid., 421.

59. Ibid., 439. I find *True at First Light*, Patrick Hemingway's edited version of *Under Kilimanjaro*, the superior text, one whose greater tension and thematic focus I believe would have pleased Patrick's father. Even more so than with the editing of *The Garden of Eden*, I see little excluded from Patrick's text that changes or harms the essential story.

60. Ibid., 439.

61. Ibid., 406.

62. Ibid., 407.

63. Ibid., 439.

64. Ibid., 440.

65. Vonnegut, *Timequake*, 19.

66. Ibid., 129. As Klinkowitz says of the birth and development of Rabo Karabekian's more open and personal work, art that is both "timely and timeless," Hemingway and Vonnegut made significant progress not only in healing the chief traumas of childhood and war, but in rediscovering their talents (*The Vonnegut Statement*, 70).

# Bibliography

Aldridge, John W. *After the Lost Generation.* New York: Noonday Press, 1963.

Allen, William Rodney, and Paul Smith. "An Interview with Kurt Vonnegut." In *Conversations with Kurt Vonnegut,* edited by William Rodney Allen, 265–301. Jackson: University Press of Mississippi, 1988.

Backman, Melvin. "Hemingway: The Matador and the Crucified." *Modern Fiction Studies* 1 (August 1955): 2–11.

Bair, Deirdre. *Beckett: A Biography.* New York: Harcourt Brace Jovanovich, 1978.

Baker, Carlos. *Hemingway: A Life Story.* New York: Scribners, 1969.

Bakhtin, M. M. *The Dialogic Imagination.* Translated by Michael Holquist. Austin: University of Texas Press, 1981.

Bakker, Jan. *Fiction as Survival Strategy: A Comparative Study of the Major Works of Ernest Hemingway and Saul Bellow.* Amsterdam: Rodopi, 1983.

Baldwin, Marc Decker, Jr. *Reading* The Sun Also Rises: *Hemingway's Political Unconscious.* New York: Peter Lang, 1997.

Beegel, Susan. *Hemingway's Craft of Omission: Four Manuscript Examples.* Ann Arbor: UMI Research Press, 1988.

———. "Santiago and the Eternal Feminine: Gendering la Mar in *The Old Man and the Sea.*" In *Hemingway and Women: Female Critics and the Female Voice,* edited by Lawrence Broer and Gloria Holland, 131–56. Tuscaloosa: University of Alabama Press, 2002.

———, ed. *Hemingway's Neglected Short Fiction: New Perspectives.* Ann Arbor: UMI Research Press, 1989.

Bell, Millicent. "*A Farewell to Arms:* Pseudoautobiography and Personal Metaphor." In *Ernest Hemingway: The Writer in Context,* edited by James A. Nagel, 107–28. Ann Arbor: University of Michigan Press, 1984.

Benson, Jackson J. *Hemingway: The Writer's Art of Self-Defense.* Minneapolis. University of Minnesota Press, 1969.

———, ed. *The Short Stories of Ernest Hemingway: Critical Essays.* Durham: Duke University Press, 1975.

Benvenuto, Bice, and Roger Kennedy. *The Works of Jacques Lacan: An Introduction.* New York: St. Martin's Press, 1986.

Bleikasten, André. "Fathers in Faulkner." In *The Fictional Father: Lacanian Readings of the Text,* edited by Robert Con Davis, 115–46. Amherst: University of Massachusetts Press, 1981.

Bloom, Harold. *The Anxiety of Influence: A Theory of Poetry.* New York: Oxford University Press, 1997.

Boon, Kevin, ed. *At Millennium's End: New Essays on the Work of Kurt Vonnegut.* Albany: State University of New York Press, 2001.

Bredhal, A. Carl, Jr., and Susan Lynn Drake. *Hemingway's* Green Hills of Africa *as Evolutionary Narrative: Helix and Scimitar.* Lewiston, N.Y.: Edwin Mellen Press, 1990.

Brenner, Gerry. *The Old Man and the Sea: Story of a Common Man.* New York: Twayne, 1991.

Brian, Denis. *The True Gen: An Intimate Portrait of Ernest Hemingway by Those Who Knew Him.* New York: Bantam, 1988.

Broer, Lawrence R. *Hemingway's Spanish Tragedy.* Tuscaloosa: University of Alabama Press, 1973.

———. "Hemingway's 'On Writing': A Portrait of the Artist as Nick Adams." In *Hemingway's Neglected Short Fiction: New Perspectives,* edited by Susan Beegel, 131–40. Ann Arbor: UMI Research Press, 1989.

———. *Sanity Plea: Schizophrenia in the Novels of Kurt Vonnegut.* Tuscaloosa: University of Alabama Press, 1989.

———. "Images of the Shaman in the Works of Kurt Vonnegut." In *Dionysus in Literature: Essays on Literary Madness,* edited by Branimir M. Riger, 197–208. Bowling Green, Ohio: Bowling Green University Popular Press, 1994.

———. "Vonnegut's Goodbye: Kurt Senior, Hemingway, and Kilgore Trout." In *At Millennium's End: New Essays on the Work of Kurt Vonnegut,* edited by Kevin Boon, 65–90. Albany: State University of New York Press, 2001.

Broer, Lawrence R., and Gloria Holland, eds. *Hemingway and Women: Female Critics and the Female Voice.* Tuscaloosa: University of Alabama Press, 2002.

Buck, Lynn. "Vonnegut's World of Comic Futility." *Studies in American Fiction* 3 (Autumn 1975): 182–98.

Burwell, Rose Marie. *Hemingway: The Postwar Years and the Posthumous Novels.* Cambridge: Cambridge University Press, 1996.

———. "West of Everything: The High Cost of Making Men in *Islands in the Stream.*" In *Hemingway and Women: Female Critics and the Female Voice,* edited by Lawrence R. Broer and Gloria Holland, 157–72. Tuscaloosa: University of Alabama Press, 2002.

Busch, Frederick. "Reading Hemingway without Guilt." *New York Times Book Review.* January 12, 1992, 3, 17–19.

Campbell, Joseph. *The Hero with a Thousand Faces.* Princeton: Princeton University Press, 1973.

———. *Transformation of Myth through Time.* New York: Harper & Row, 1990.

Castillo-Puche, José Luis. *Hemingway entre la vida y la muerte.* Barcelona: Ediciones Destino, 1968. Translated by Helen R. Lane as *Hemingway in Spain: A Personal Reminiscence of Hemingway's Years in Spain by His Friend.* Garden City, N.Y.: Doubleday, 1974.

Clark, John R. *The Modern Satiric Grotesque and Its Traditions.* Lexington: University of Kentucky Press, 1991.

Comley, Nancy R., and Robert Scholes. *Hemingway's Genders: Rereading the Hemingway Text.* New Haven: Yale University Press, 1994.

Cowley, Malcolm. "Nightmare and Ritual in Hemingway." In *Hemingway: A Collection of Critical Essays,* edited by Robert P. Weeks, 40–51. Englewood Cliffs, N.J.: Prentice-Hall, 1962.

D'Agonstino, Nemi. "The Later Hemingway." In *Hemingway: A Collection of Critical Essays,* edited by Robert P. Weeks, 152–60. Englewood Cliffs, N.J.: Prentice-Hall, 1962.

Davidson, Cathy, and Arnold Davidson. "Decoding the Hemingway Hero in *The Sun Also Rises.*" In *New Essays on "The Sun Also Rises,"* edited by Linda Wagner-Martin, 83–107. Cambridge: Cambridge University Press, 1987.

De Falco, Joseph. *The Hero in Hemingway's Short Stories.* Pittsburgh: University of Pittsburgh Press, 1963.

————. "Hemingway's Islands and Streams: Minor Tactics for Heavy Pressure." In *Hemingway in Our Time,* edited by Richard Astro and Jackson J. Benson, 34–51. Corvallis: Oregon State University Press, 1974.

Del Gizzo, Suzanne. "Going Home: Hemingway, Primitivism, and Identity." *Modern Fiction Studies* 49 (Fall 2003): 496–523.

Eastman, Max. "Bull in the Afternoon." *New Republic,* June 7, 1933: 94–97. Reprinted in *Ernest Hemingway: The Critical Reception,* edited by Robert O. Stephens, 130–32. New York: Burt Franklin, 1977.

Eby, Carl P. *Hemingway's Fetishism: Psychoanalysis and the Mirror of Manhood.* Albany: State University of New York Press, 1999.

Eliade, Mircea. *Shamanism: Archaic Techniques of Ecstasy.* Translated by Willard R. Trask. New York: Pantheon, 1951.

Eliot, T. S. "The Waste Land." 1922. In *Norton Anthology of English Literature,* edited by M. H. Abrams. 7th ed. Vol. 2C. New York: Norton, 2000.

Fleming, Robert E. *The Face in the Mirror.* Tuscaloosa: University of Alabama Press, 1994.

Flora, Joseph M. *Hemingway's Nick Adams.* Baton Rouge: Louisiana State University Press, 1982.

Foucault, Michel. *The Archaeology of Knowledge.* Translated by A. M. Sheridan Smith. New York: Harper, 1972.

Freud, Sigmund. *Civilization and Its Discontents.* Translated by James Strachey. New York: Norton, 1962.

Frost, Robert. "Mending Wall." In *Modern Poetry,* edited by Maynard Mack, Leonard Dean, and William Frost, 111. Englewood Cliffs, N.J.: Prentice-Hall, 1961.

Gajdusek, Robert E. "'Is He Building a Bridge or Blowing One?': The Repossession of Text by the Author in *For Whom the Bells Tolls.*" *Hemingway Review* 11 (Spring 1992): 45–51.

————. "Artists in Their Art: Hemingway and Valasquez—The Shared Worlds of *For Whom the Bells Tolls* and 'Los Meninas.'" In *Hemingway Repossessed,* edited by Kenneth Rosen, 17–27. Westport, Conn.: Greenwood Press, 1994.

Ganivet, Angel. *Idearium español.* Buenos Aires: Espasa-Calpe, 1945.

Geismar, Maxwell. "Ernest Hemingway: You Could Always Come Back." In *Ernest Hemingway: The Man and His Work,* edited by John McCaffery, 125–69. New York: World, 1950.

Gordon, David J. *Literary Art and the Unconscious.* Baton Rouge: Louisiana State University Press, 1976.

Griffin, Peter. *Along with Youth: Hemingway, the Early Years.* New York: Oxford University Press, 1985.

Gurko, Leo. *Ernest Hemingway and the Pursuit of Heroism.* New York: Crowell, 1968.

Halliday, E. M. "Hemingway's Ambiguity, Symbolism, and Irony." *American Literature* 28 (March 1956): 1–22.

Hassan, Ihab. *The Dismemberment of Orpheus: Toward A Postmodern Literature.* 2nd ed. Madison: University of Wisconsin Press, 1982.

————. *The Postmodern Turn: Essays in Postmodern Theory and Culture.* Columbus: Ohio State University Press, 1987.

Hemingway, Ernest. *The Sun Also Rises.* New York: Scribners, 1926.

————. *A Farewell to Arms.* New York: Scribners, 1929.

————. *Death in the Afternoon.* New York: Scribners, 1932.

———. *Green Hills of Africa.* New York: Scribners, 1935.

———. *To Have and Have Not.* New York: Scribners, 1937.

———. *For Whom the Bell Tolls.* New York: Scribners, 1940.

———. *Across the River and into the Trees.* New York: Scribners, 1950.

———. *The Old Man and the Sea.* New York: Scribners, 1952.

———. *Islands in the Stream.* New York: Scribners, 1970.

———. *Ernest Hemingway: Selected Letters 1917–1961.* Edited by Carlos Baker, New York: Scribners, 1981.

———. *The Garden of Eden.* New York: Scribners, 1986.

———. *The Complete Short Stories of Ernest Hemingway.* Finca Vigia Edition. New York: Scribners, 1987.

———. *Under Kilimanjaro.* Kent, Ohio: Kent State University Press, 1995.

Hemingway, Gregory. *Papa: A Personal Memoir.* Boston: Houghton Mifflin, 1976.

Hemingway, John. *Strange Tribe: A Family Memoir.* Guilford, Conn.: Lyons Press, 2007.

Hemingway, Leicester. *My Brother, Ernest Hemingway.* Sarasota, Fla.: Pineapple Press, 1996.

Hemingway, Marcelline. *At the Hemingways: A Family Portrait.* Boston: Little, Brown, 1961.

Hemingway, Mary Welsh. *How It Was.* New York: Knopf, 1976.

Hinz, Evelyn J., and John J. Teunissen. "*Islands in the Stream* as Hemingway's Laocoön." *Contemporary Literature* 29 (Spring 1988): 26–48.

Howe, Irving. "In Search of a Moral Style." *Literature and Liberalism: An Anthology of Sixty Years of the* New Republic, edited by Edward Zwick, 229–34. Washington, D.C.: New Republic, 1976.

Hotchner, A. E. *Papa Hemingway: A Personal Memoir.* New York: Carroll, 1999.

Hume, Kathryn. "Vonnegut's Self-Projections: Symbolic Characters and Symbolic Fiction." *Journal of Narrative Technique* 12 (Fall 1982): 177–90.

———. "Kurt Vonnegut and the Myths and Symbols of Meaning." *Texas Studies in Literature and Language* 24, no. 4 (1982): 429–47.

———. "The Heraclitean Cosmos of Kurt Vonnegut." In *Critical Essays on Kurt Vonnegut,* edited by Robert Merrill, 216–30. Boston: G. K. Hall, 1990.

Hutcheon, Linda. *A Poetics of Postmodernism: History, Theory, Fiction.* New York: Routledge, 1988.

Josephs, Allen. *For Whom the Bells Tolls: Ernest Hemingway's Undiscovered Country.* New York: Twayne, 1994.

———. "Hemingway's Spanish Sensibility." In *The Cambridge Companion to Hemingway,* edited by Scott Donaldson, 221–42. Cambridge: Cambridge University Press, 1996.

Jung, Carl G. *Aspects of the Feminine.* Translated by R. F. C. Hull. Princeton: Princeton University Press, 1982.

Justice, Hilary K. "Alias Grace: Music and the Feminine Aesthetic in Hemingway's Early Style." In *Hemingway and Women: Female Critics and the Female Voice,* edited by Lawrence R. Broer and Gloria Holland, 221–238. Tuscaloosa: University of Alabama Press, 2002.

Justus, James H. "The Later Fiction: Hemingway and the Aesthetics of Failure." In *Ernest Hemingway: New Critical Essays,* edited by A. Robert Lee, 103–21. London: Vision Press, 1983.

Keogh, J. G., and Edmund Kislaitis. "*Slaughterhouse-Five* and the Future of Science Fiction." *Media and Methods* 7 (January 1971): 38–40.

Kert, Bernice. *The Hemingway Women: Those Who Loved Him—the Wives and Others.* New York: Norton, 1983.

Killinger, John. *Hemingway and the Dead Gods: A Study in Existentialism*. Lexington: University Kentucky Press, 1960.

Klinkowitz, Jerome. *Literary Disruptions: The Making of a Post-Contemporary American Fiction*. 2nd ed. Urbana: University of Illinois Press, 1980.

———. *Kurt Vonnegut*. New York: Methuen, 1982.

———. *Literary Subversions: New American Fiction and the Practice of Criticism*. Carbondale: Southern Illinois University Press, 1985.

———. *Rosenberg, Barthes, Hassan: The Postmodern Habit of Thought*. Athens: University of Georgia Press, 1988.

———. *Structuring the Void: The Struggle for Subject in Contemporary American Fiction*. Durham: Duke University Press, 1992.

———. *The Vonnegut Effect*. Columbia: University of South Carolina Press, 2004.

Klinkowitz, Jerome, and John Somer. *The Vonnegut Statement*. New York: Delacorte / Seymour Lawrence, 1973.

Knowles, Sidney, Jr. "Hemingway's *Across the River and into the Trees:* Adversity and Art." *Essays in Literature* 5, no. 3 (1978): 195–208.

La Capra, Dominick. *History in Transit: Experience, Identity, Critical Theory*. Ithaca: Cornell University Press, 2004.

Lacan, Jacques. *Ecrits: A Selection*. Translated by Alan Sheridan. New York: Norton, 1977.

Laing, R. D. *The Divided Self*. New York: Pantheon, 1969.

Langer, Lawrence. *The Holocaust and the Literary Imagination*. New Haven: Yale University Press, 1975.

Larson, Kelli A. "Stepping Into the Labyrinth: Fifteen Years of Hemingway Scholarship." *Hemingway Review* 11 (Spring 1992): 19–24.

Lessing, Doris. "Vonnegut's Responsibility." *New York Times Book Review*, February 4, 1973, 35.

Lynn, Kenneth. *Hemingway*. New York: Fawcett, 1987.

Lyons, Donald. Review of *Hemingway: A Life Without Consequences*, by James R. Mellow. *American Spectator* 27 (October 1994): 72.

MacLeish, Archibald. *J.B.* Boston: Houghton Mifflin, 1956.

Madariaga, Salvador de. *Anarchy and Hierarchy*. New York: Macmillan, 1937.

Mandel, Miriam. "Ethics and 'Night Thoughts': Truer than Truth." *Hemingway Review* 25 (Spring 2006): 95–100.

McConnell, Frank. "Stalking Papa's Ghost: Hemingway's Presence in Contemporary American Writing." *Wilson Quarterly* 10, no. 1 (1986): 160–73.

Mellow, James R. *Charmed Circle: Gertrude Stein & Company*. New York: Praeger, 1974.

Meredith, Major James H. "The Rapido River and Hurtgen Forest in *Across the River and into the Trees*." *Hemingway Review* 14, no. 1 (1994): 60–66.

———. "Understanding Hemingway's Multiple Voices of War: A Rhetorical Study." In *War and Words: Horror and Heroism in the Literature of Warfare*, edited by Sara Munson Deats, Lagretta Tallent Lenker, and Merry G. Perry, 197–202. Lanham, Md.: Lexington Books, 2004.

Merrill, Robert. "Vonnegut's *Breakfast of Champions*: The Conversion of Heliogabalus." *Critique* 18, no. 3 (1977): 99–108.

———, ed. *Critical Essays on Kurt Vonnegut*. Boston: G. K. Hall, 1990.

Meyers, Jeffrey. *Hemingway: A Biography*. New York: Harper & Row, 1985.

———, ed. *Ernest Hemingway: The Critical Heritage*. London: Routledge, 1997.

Miller, Linda Patterson. "Brett Ashley: The Beauty of It All." In *Critical Essays on Ernest Hemingway's* The Sun Also Rises, edited by James Nagel, 170–84. New York: G. K. Hall, 1995.

Moddelmog, Debra. "Reconstructing Hemingway's Identity: Sexual Politics, the Author, and the Multicultural Classroom." *Narrative* 1, no. 3 (1993): 187–206.

———. *Reading Desire: In Pursuit of Ernest Hemingway.* Ithaca: Cornell University Press, 1999.

———. "Queer Families in Hemingway's Fiction." In *Hemingway and Women: Female Critics and the Female Voice*, edited by Lawrence Broer and Gloria Holland, 173–89. Tuscaloosa: University of Alabama Press, 2002.

Moreland, Kim. *The Medievalist Impulse in American Literature: Twain, Adams, Fitzgerald, and Hemingway.* Charlottesville: University Press of Virginia, 1996.

Mustazza, Leonard. *Forever Pursuing Genesis: The Myth of Eden in the Novels of Kurt Vonnegut.* Lewisburg, Pa.: Bucknell University Press, 1990.

Ortega y Gasset, José. *Obras.* Madrid: Espasa-Calpe, 1936.

Ozick, Cynthia. "The Muse, Postmodern and Homeless." In *Metaphor and Memory: Essays*, 136–39. New York: Knopf, 1989.

Putnam, Ann. "On Defiling Eden: The Search for Eve in the Garden of Sorrows." In *Hemingway and Women: Female Critics and the Female Voice*, edited by Lawrence R. Broer and Gloria Holland, 109–30. Tuscaloosa: University of Alabama Press, 2002.

———. "The Last Good Country." *Hemingway Review* 25 (Spring 2006): 132–35.

Rackstraw, Loree. "Dancing with the Muse in Vonnegut's Later Novels." In *The Vonnegut Chronicles: Interviews and Essays*, edited by Peter J. Reed and Marc Leeds, 123–45. Westport, Conn.: Greenwood Press, 1996.

———. *Love as Always: Kurt Vonnegut as I Knew Him.* Cambridge: Da Capo Press, 2009.

Raeburn, John. *Fame Became of Him: Hemingway as a Public Writer.* Bloomington: Indiana University Press, 1984.

Reed, Peter J. *Writers for the 70's: Kurt Vonnegut, Jr.* New York: Crowell, 1972.

Reynolds, Michael. *Hemingway's First War: The Making of* A Farewell to Arms. Princeton: Princeton University Press, 1976.

———. *The Young Hemingway.* New York: Blackwell, 1986.

———. *Hemingway: The Paris Years.* New York: Blackwell, 1989.

———. *Hemingway: The Homecoming.* New York: Norton, 1992.

———. *Hemingway: The 1930s.* New York: Norton, 1997.

———. *Hemingway: The Final Years.* New York: Norton, 1999.

Robinson, Kathleen K. "Testimony of Trauma: Ernest Hemingway's Narrative Progression in *Across the River and into the Trees.*" Ph.D. diss., University of South Florida, Tampa, 2010.

Rogers, Carl. *On Becoming a Person.* Boston: Houghton Mifflin, 1961.

Rovit, Earl. "On Psychic Retrenchment in Hemingway." In *Hemingway: Essays of Reassessment*, edited by Frank Scafella, 181–88. New York: Oxford University Press, 1991.

Rovit, Earl, and Gerry Brenner. *Ernest Hemingway.* Rev. ed. Boston: Twayne, 1986.

Sanders, J'aimé. "The Art of Existentialism: F. Scott Fitzgerald, Ernest Hemingway, Norman Mailer, and the American Existential Tradition." Ph.D. diss., University of South Florida, Tampa, 2007.

Sanderson, Rena, ed. *Blowing the Bridge: Essays on Hemingway and* For Whom the Bell Tolls. Westport, Conn.: Greenwood Press, 1992.

Schwartz, Nina. "Lovers' Discourse in *The Sun Also Rises:* A Cock and Bull Story." *Criticism* 26, no. 1 (1984): 57–60. Reprinted in *Dead Fathers: The Logic of Transference in Modern Narrative.* Ann Arbor: University of Michigan Press, 1994.

Seitz, Susan M. "The Posthumous Editing of Ernest Hemingway's Fiction." Ph.D. diss., University of Massachusetts, Amherst, 1993.

Shechner, Mark. *Joyce in Nighttown: A Psychoanalytic Inquiry into* Ulysses. Berkeley: University of California Press, 1974.

Sinclair, Gail. "Revisiting the Code: Female Foundations and the 'Undiscovered Country' in *For Whom the Bell Tolls.*" In *Hemingway and Women: Female Critics and the Female Voice,* edited by Lawrence R. Broer and Gloria Holland, 93–108. Tuscaloosa: University of Alabama Press, 2002.

Skipp, Francis E. "Metempsychosis in the Stream, or What Happens in 'Bimini'?" In *Fitzgerald/Hemingway Annual,* edited by Matthew J. Bruccoli, 137–43. Washington, D.C.: Washington Microcard Editions, 1974.

Spanier, Sandra Whipple. "Catherine Barkley and the Hemingway Code: Ritual and Survival in *A Farewell to Arms.*" In *Ernest Hemingway's* A Farewell to Arms, edited by Harold Bloom, 131–48. New York: Chelsea House, 1987.

———. "Hemingway's Unknown Soldier: Catherine Barkley, the Critics, and the Great War." In *New Essays on* A Farewell to Arms, edited by Scott Donaldson, 75–108. New York: Cambridge University Press, 1990.

Spilka, Mark. *Hemingway's Quarrel with Androgyny.* Lincoln & London: University of Nebraska Press, 1989.

Stanton, Edward F. *Hemingway and Spain: A Pursuit.* Seattle & London: University of Washington Press, 1989.

Stein, Gertrude. *The Autobiography of Alice B. Toklas.* New York: Vintage, 1990.

Strychacz, Thomas. *Hemingway's Theaters of Masculinity.* Baton Rouge: Louisiana State University Press, 2003.

Svoboda, Joseph F. *Hemingway and* The Sun Also Rises: *The Crafting of a Style.* Kansas: University Press of Kansas, 1983.

Sylvester, Bickford. "Hemingway's Extended Vision: *The Old Man and the Sea.*" In *Twentieth Century Interpretations of* The Old Man and the Sea, edited by Katherine Jobes, 81–96. Englewood Cliffs, N.J.: Prentice-Hall, 1968.

Tanner, Tony. *City of Words.* London: Cape, 1971.

Tetlow, Wendolyn E. *Hemingway's* In Our Time: *Lyrical Dimensions.* Lewisburg, Pa.: Bucknell University Press, 1992.

Teunissen, John J. "*For Whom the Bell Tolls* As Mythic Narrative." In *Ernest Hemingway: Six Decades of Criticism,* edited by Linda W. Wagner. Lansing: Michigan State University Press, 1987.

Tilton, John. *Cosmic Satire in the Contemporary Novel.* Lewisburg, Pa.: Bucknell University Press, 1977.

Unamuno, Miguel de. *Tragic Sense of Life.* Translated by J. E. C. Flitch. New York: Dover, 1954.

Villard, Henry S., and James Nagel. *Hemingway in Love and War: The Lost Diary of Agnes von Kurowsky.* Boston: Northeastern University Press, 1989.

Vince, Raymond. "War, Heroism, and Narrative: Hemingway, Tolkien, and Le Carre, Storytellers to the Modern World." Ph.D. diss., University of South Florida, Tampa. 2005.

Volpat, Carole Gottlieb. "The End of *The Sun Also Rises:* A New Beginning." In *Fitzgerald/Hemingway Annual,* edited by Matthew J. Bruccoli, 244–55. Washington, D.C.: Washington Microcard Editions, 1972.

Vonnegut, Kurt. *Player Piano.* New York: Dell, 1959. Reprint, 1971.

————. *The Sirens of Titan*. New York: Dell, 1959. Reprint, 1971.

————. *Mother Night*. New York: Dell, 1961.

————. *Cat's Cradle*. New York: Dell, 1963.

————. *God Bless You, Mr. Rosewater*. New York: Dell, 1965. Reprint, 1981.

————. *Wampeters, Foma & Granfalloons (Opinions)*. New York: Dell, 1965. Reprint, 1975.

————. *Happy Birthday, Wanda June*. New York: Dell, 1971.

————. *Slaughterhouse-Five*, 1969. New York: Dell, 1972.

————. *Breakfast of Champions*. New York: Dell, 1973.

————. *Slapstick, or Lonesome No More*. New York: Dell, 1976.

————. *Jailbird*. New York: Dell, 1979.

————. *Palm Sunday*. New York: Delacorte / Seymour Lawrence, 1979.

————. *Deadeye Dick*. New York: Delacorte / Seymour Lawrence, 1982.

————. *Galápagos*. New York: Delacorte / Seymour Lawrence, 1985.

————. *Bluebeard*. New York: Delacorte, 1987.

————. *Fates Worse than Death: An Autobiographical Collage*. New York: Berkley, 1992.

————. *Timequake*. New York: Putnam, 1997.

Wagner-Martin, Linda. "The Romance of Desire in Hemingway's Fiction." In *Hemingway and Women: Female Critics and the Female Voice*, edited by Lawrence Broer and Gloria Holland, 54–69. Tuscaloosa: University of Alabama Press, 2002.

————, ed. *New Essays on* The Sun Also Rises. Cambridge: Cambridge University Press, 1987.

Wain, John. Obituary for Ernest Hemingway. *Observer* (London), July 9, 1961, 21.

Waldhorn, Arthur. *A Reader's Guide to Ernest Hemingway*. New York: Octagon, 1981.

Warren, Robert Penn. Introduction to *A Farewell to Arms*. New York: Scribners, 1949.

Waugh, Patricia. *Metafiction: The Theory and Practice of Self-Conscious Fiction*. New York: Routledge, 1984.

Whitlow, Roger. "*Across the River and into the Trees*—Hemingway and Psychotherapy." *Illinois Quarterly* 40, no. 4 (1978): 39–47.

Wilde, Alan. *Horizons of Assent: Modernism, Postmodernism, and the Ironic Imagination*. Baltimore: Johns Hopkins University Press, 1981.

Williams, Wirt. *The Tragic Art of Ernest Hemingway*. Baton Rouge: Louisiana State University Press, 1984.

Wilson, G. R., Jr. "Saints and Sinners in the Caribbean: The Case for *Islands in the Stream*." *Studies in American Fiction* 18, no. 1 (1990): 27–41.

Young, Philip. *Ernest Hemingway: A Reconsideration*. University Park: Pennsylvania State University Press, 1966.

# Index